Fodor's EXPLORING
TURKEY

FODOR'S TRAVEL PUBLICATIONS, INC.

NEW YORK • TORONTO • LONDON • SYDNEY • AUCKLAND

WWW.FODORS.COM

Copyright © The Automobile Association 1999
Maps copyright © The Automobile Association 1999

Published in the United States by Fodor's Travel Publications, Inc.
Published in the United Kingdom by AA Publishing.

Fodor's is a registered trademark of Random House, Inc

ISBN 0-679-00279-0
Third Edition

Fodor's Exploring Turkey

Author: **Diana Darke**
Cartography: **The Automobile Association**
Cover Design: **Tigist Getachew, Fabrizio La Rocca**
Front Cover Silhouette: **Steve McCurry/Magnum Photos, Inc**

Printed and bound in Italy by Printer Trento srl
10 9 8 7 6 5 4 3 2 1

How to use this book

ORGANIZATION

Turkey Is
Discusses aspects of life in modern Turkey.

Turkey Was
Places the country in its historical context and explores those past events whose influences are felt to this day.

A–Z
An alphabetical listing of places to visit. The book begins with a chapter on Istanbul, and is subsequently broken down into regional chapters. Places of interest are listed alphabetically within each section. Suggested walks, drives and Focus On articles, which provide an insight into life in Turkey, are included in each section.

Travel Facts
Contains the strictly practical information that is vital for a successful trip.

Accommodations and Restaurants
Lists places to stay and places to eat alphabetically by region. Entries are graded budget, moderate or expensive.

ABOUT THE RATINGS
Most of the places described in this book have been given a separate rating. These are as follows:

▶▶▶   **Do not miss**

▶▶   **Highly recommended**

▶   **Worth seeing**

MAP REFERENCES
To make the location of a particular place easier to find, every main entry in this book is given its own map reference, such as 176B3. The first number (176) indicates the page on which the map can be found, the letter (B) and the second number (3) pinpoint the square in which the main entry is located. The maps on the inside front cover and inside back cover are referred to as IFC and IBC respectively.

Contents

How to use this book 4

Contents pages 5–7

My Turkey 8

TURKEY IS 9–26
  Image and reality 10–11
  Atatürk's legacy 12–13
  Secular and Muslim 14–15
  Istanbul versus the regions 16–17
  Diverse landscapes 18–19
  A growing economy 20–21
  Turkey's people 22–23
  Festivals 24–25
  Water 26

TURKEY WAS 27-45
  The Hittite Empire 28–29
  Greek and Roman rule 30–31
  Early Byzantium 32–33
  Late Byzantium 34–35
  The Seljuks 36–37
  The Ottoman Empire 38–39
  The Sick Man of Europe 40–41
  Atatürk's Revolution 42–43
  Recent times 44–45

A–Z 46–248

Istanbul 46–99
  Introduction 47–49
  Orientation 50–51
  Aya Sofya Müzesi 52–53
  Churches 58–59
  Mosques 62–63, 66–67

Museums 70–71
Palaces 72–73, 76–77
Parks and city walls 78–79
Istanbul environs 82–83, 86–87
Accommodations 88–89
Food and drink 90–91
Shopping 92–93
Nightlife 96–97
Practical points 98–99

Focus On
Islam 54–55
Turkish music 60
Turkish tiles 61
Ottoman architecture and art 64–65
The Turkish bath 74–75
Turkish carpets 94–95
Drives
Along the Asian Bosphorus and
Üsküdar 80–81
Belgrade Forest and the European
Bosphorus 84–85
Walks
The Grand Bazaar 56–57
Around the Aqueduct of Valens
68–69

The Aegean 100–133
Focus On
Turkish jokes and proverbs 106–107
Boat trips 110–111
Turkish movies 120–121
Drives
Kuşadası to Lake Bafa and
Heracleia 124–125
Marmaris to Knidos (Cnidos) 129
Walks
Alinda 116–117
Gerga 128

The Mediterranean 134–169
Focus On
Nomads 140–141
Alexander the Great 144–145
Inland lakes 148–149
Wildlife 154–155
Boat trip
Kekova 157
Walks
Mountain ridge from Kaş 160–161
The Chimera 164–165
Selge Canyon 168–169

Cappadocia 170–187
Focus On
Christian Turkey 178–179
Turkish desserts and pastries 185
Drive
Kayseri to Mount Erciyes 184
Walk
The Ihlara Gorge 182–183

Central Anatolia 188–211
Focus On
Atatürk 196–197
The Turkish language 200–201
Drive
Konya to Çatalhüyük, Karaman,
and Alahan 206–207
Walk
Ankara 194–195

Eastern Turkey 212–235
Focus On
Georgian valleys 218–219
The Kurds 222–223
Mountains 228–229
Drive
Circuit of Lake Van 234–235
Walk
Nemrut Dağı Volcano 217

The Black Sea 236–248
Focus On
The Laz 248
Drive
Amasra to Safranbolu 242
Walk
Trabzon Towers 243

TRAVEL FACTS 249–266
Arriving 250–251
Essential facts 252–253
Public transportation 254–255
Driving 256–257

Communications 258–259
Emergencies 260–261
Other information 262–265
Tourist offices 266

**ACCOMMODATIONS AND
RESTAURANTS** 267–281

Chronology 282–283

Index 284–288

Picture credits,
acknowledgments
and contributors 288

Maps
Turkey: regions and three-star
    sights IFC and IBC
The Ottoman Empire in 1676 38
Istanbul 46–47
Grand Bazaar walk 56
Aqueduct of Valens walk 68
Asian Bosphorus and Üsküdar
    drive and cruise 80
Istanbul environs 86
The Aegean 100
Efes (Ephesus) 114
Alinda walk 117
The Mediterranean 134–135
Kekova boat trip 157
Selge Canyon walk 168
Cappadocia 170
Ihlara Gorge walk 182
Central Anatolia 188–189
Ankara walk 194
Eastern Turkey 212
Georgian monasteries 218
Circuit of Lake Van drive 234
The Black Sea 236–237
Trabzon Towers walk 243

Diana Darke has lived, worked, and traveled extensively in Turkey and the Arab world for more than two decades, initially as an Arabic translator and interpreter for the British Foreign Office. She is also the author of guidebooks to Aegean and Mediterranean Turkey, Eastern Turkey and the Black Sea Coast, North Cyprus, Jordan and the Holy Land, the United Arab Emirates, and the Turkish Coast.

My Turkey

Unlike many Westerners who reach Turkey via Europe, I discovered the country from the east, while working for the British Foreign Office in Lebanon. It was 1979 and Lebanon was in the throes of its civil war. Forced to evacuate the country, I packed up my Citroën 2CV and headed west through Syria and into Turkey on my way home to London. At the time, much of Turkey was considered rough and barbaric, and I was ill-advised to linger. Compared to chaotic, war-torn Lebanon, however, Turkey seemed a haven of calm and politeness, even in its eastern provinces. Istanbul, cosmopolitan and sophisticated, I came to last of all. What for most visitors is the gateway to the Orient was for me the back door to Europe.

On that first trip, it was the scenery, so green and lush after the deserts of Syria, and the ruins, so extensive and unspoiled, that surprised me most. It was only on later visits that I grew to appreciate the Turks themselves. Unique among Mediterranean peoples in my experience, Turks are too dignified to stoop to hassling. They have a reserved friendliness, and are proud and nationalistic, with a keen sense of history and their past.

Stranded for 18 hours at Istanbul airport recently (government and service personnel be warned—you cannot buy a tourist visa on arrival, it must already have been purchased in advance at your local Turkish Embassy), might have been enough to alter my feelings. But the airport officials sympathized and advised me of the quietest place to sleep on the floor. Corruption is known to be rife in the upper echelons of government and business, but the average person is honest and decent. To me, this straightness is the most appealing of Turkish characteristics. Turks are not given to idle threats. If slighted or betrayed, they will act decisively, with little or no mercy—Turkish history reflects this.

Even seasoned observers of Turkey comment that the place is an enigma, defying conventional analysis on political, economic, and social fronts. This is for me its greatest attraction, and I know that after writing four books on the country I am still only scratching the surface.

Diana Darke

Turkey Is

Although it is variously classed as a struggling first-world economy and a developing nation, Turkey conforms to the conventional model of neither. The modern Turkish state is unique in that—rather than being the product of an imperialist power—against all the odds, it managed to create itself and evolve its own political identity.

IMAGE For centuries the Turks were seen through Western eyes as the scourge of Christendom and a threat to the European order. In the western countries of medieval Europe, the very word "Turk" came to symbolize everything that was savage or barbaric, and in the popular imagination of the time Turks took their place in the litany of plagues, floods, earthquakes, Tartars, and comets used by the Almighty as punishments for the wicked. In the 16th century, for example, Martin Luther prayed for deliverance from "the world, the flesh, the Turk, and the Devil."

From the Renaissance onward, the root of this prejudice lay partly in Europe's historic ties with Greece. As far as most Western thinkers were concerned, the Greek civilization stood at the dawn of their own. From

Fishing is a tradition that has kept its importance in modern Turkey

them they inherited so much, and all that was classical was considered noble and pure. As recently as the 19th century, poets such as Byron sang the praises of Greece, its great ideals and romantic traditions. With Turkey, on the other hand, the countries of northern and western Europe have fewer historical and religious ties. When the Greeks and Turks violently disputed Cyprus in the 1950s and 1960s, and when the island was partitioned in 1974, it was perhaps not surprising that many Westerners chose to side with the Greek Cypriots, simply because they seemed the more familiar faction. Thus the problem was assumed to be of Turkish Cypriot making, and world opinion apportioned more blame to Turkey than to Greece.

As far as the Ottoman Empire (which lasted from the 14th until the early 20th century) is concerned, in the minds of most Westerners it still conjures up images of decadence and harems, and it is left to a few historians to marvel at its extraordinary religious tolerance and at an astonishingly fair system of "promotion," under which a slave could (and frequently did) rise to be Grand Vizier, the equivalent of prime minister.

REALITY In 1949 Turkey became a member of the Council of Europe, and in 1952 it was admitted to NATO, largely because its strategic position controlling the Bosphorus Straits made it a vital ally against the Soviet Union during the Cold War. Military considerations and self-interest, therefore, lay behind these organizations' readiness to include Turkey among their members, rather

10

than any sense that Turkey truly belonged to the body of Europe.

Religion has, of course, played its part in the formation of these attitudes. The Hungarians, the Finns, and the Bulgarians all have their origins in the Eurasian steppelands over a thousand years ago, just like the Turks. Unlike the Turks, however, they converted to Christianity—and are now accepted as Europeans.

GEOGRAPHICAL POSITION It is hard to overemphasize the importance of Turkey's strategic position, lying at the geographical meeting point of different forces and ideologies, of Europe and Asia, of Christianity and Islam, and of Arabism, (vestigial) Communism, and Hellenism. If Turkey were to leave NATO and ally herself with ex-Soviet or Arab powers, the West would lose control of the vital Bosphorus, as well as relinquish its ability to carry out air strikes from Turkish NATO bases on Iraq (as it did in the Gulf War), Iran, or any ex-Soviet trouble spot. At present, Turkey represents the only

The natural harbor at Antalya, the main port on Turkey's southern coast for the past 2,000 years

area of relative stability in this most unstable and unpredictable part of the world.

❑ The Turks have a habit of doing the unexpected. In this century alone, after their official defeat in World War I, they fought back to oust the Allies, and went on to achieve recognition as an independent country. In 1945, President İnönü changed a dictatorship into a democracy overnight; and in 1961 the military, which had seized power in a coup 18 months earlier, handed it over in an orderly manner to a parliamentary regime. In each case, the Turks' actions ran contrary to the confident predictions of the experts. ❑

Modern Turkey is very largely the creation of one man, Mustafa Kemal, later known as Atatürk, Father of the Turks. Atatürk realized that his government could achieve his reforms only by securing the support of the mass of the Turkish people. In 1923, he formed the Republican People's Party, intending that its hundreds of thousands of members should constitute the local leadership in every town and village throughout the country.

KEMALISM According to Kemalist philosophy—that propounded by Atatürk—civilization assures freedom, and happiness lies in an independent life, that is, in life without political, social, or religious constraints. It especially abhors religious extremism, blaming it for creating many inequalities among people, for excluding women from playing an active role in society, and for provoking a large number of wars. It is opposed to the class system and scornful of the intellectual elite, believing passionately in the need to educate workers and peasants in order to deliver them from oppression and corruption. By popularizing language, literature, and music, it aims to bring civilization closer to the ordinary Turk. The final keystone is patriotism, considered essential for the defense of a people's independence. In its application, this remarkable philosophy demonstrated that, through disciplined education, it was possible to achieve in one generation what could easily have taken 10 or more.

A guard on duty at Atatürk's mausoleum in Ankara

WORLD WAR II By the time Atatürk died in 1938, his 15 years of decisive, if dictatorial, leadership had won Turkey a credible place in the international arena. That the regime he left behind him was able to withstand the stresses and strains of World War II so soon after his death is perhaps the best testimony to his achievement. Turkey managed to stay neutral during the war, despite pressure from the Western powers. The war years subjected the country to great economic strain, and the risky position of armed neutrality in a world at war gave rise to a more authoritarian government, which imposed martial law.

STRUGGLE FOR SECULARISM In the years since Atatürk's death, Turkey has been dominated by the struggle between secularism and religion, with the army officers, teachers, and

❑ The constitution laid down by Atatürk states that the Turkish army has a duty imposed by law "to defend and watch over the Republic of Turkey"—and to intervene when necessary. The army has three times invoked that duty—in 1960, 1971, and 1980. If the words of the constitution are interpreted literally, the only way future Turkish governments can safeguard against army intervention is to govern efficiently and in accordance with Atatürk's principles. ❑

bureaucrats who formed the backbone of the Republican People's Party supporting the former, and many rural people favoring the latter. After three coups in 20 years, the 1993 election of Tansu Çiller as the first woman prime minister seemed to make Turkey's break from its military past more secure. Çiller's True Path Party espoused many Kemalist principles, but she, an American-educated economist in her late 40s, has now been discredited, accused of fraud and embezzlement along with her husband, in a style reminiscent of Benazir Bhutto.

In late 1995 Atatürk's secular legacy was threatened as never before by the election of Turkey's first Islamist party, Welfare (Refah), with 20 percent of the overall vote making it the biggest single party. Its 70-year-old

Atatürk's mausoleum is a powerful symbol of the personality cult his memory has inspired

leader, Necmettin Erbakan, was forced to step down in summer 1997 after 18 months of intense pressure from the army, in favor of a secular government. Refah was banned in January 1998. Though the army remains the ultimate power in the country, it is unlikely that they could stage another coup in these post-Soviet times.

Election posters—a sign that military rule may be a thing of the past

> ❏ "Turkey is a bridge to peace, a bridge to the independent countries that have separated from Russia, a bridge for Western values in the Middle East."
> Tansu Çiller, Turkish Prime Minister, echoing the sentiments of Atatürk ❏

There is a distinction between Turkey as a state and the Turks as a people. The Turks are Muslim, but, since Atatürk's reforms, Turkey is not an Islamic state. Orthodox Muslims see Turkey's secularization as an apostasy from Islam, and Atatürk as a heretic.

TURKISH ISLAM Mosques in Turkey welcome foreigners, who, when correctly dressed (see page 62), are allowed to stroll around and spend some time. In the rest of the Islamic world, such tolerance of outsiders is rare, and many countries, including Morocco and Tunisia, do not permit non-Muslims to enter their mosques at all.

When you cross the border from Greece or Bulgaria into Turkey, it is

> ❏ The Islamic belief that all things are preordained is behind orthodox Islam's rejection of insurance. How can one insure against dying early or the collapse of a building, when such things are the will of God? Insurance is therefore seen as indicating a lack of trust in the supreme power of God. ❏

The skyline of much of urban Turkey is dominated by minarets—this is Fatih Camii in Istanbul

not the appearance of the people or their dress (almost everybody wears Western clothes) that makes the country visibly different, but its mosques and minarets. It is this obvious association with Islam that makes Turkey appear unlike any western European country. Although religion is not an explicit consideration, it is Islam that will probably always prevent Turkey from becoming a full member of the European Union.

Islam is a very visible religion: on hearing the call to prayer, people everywhere, but especially in rural areas, stop what they are doing and drop to their knees to perform the ritual bows laid down in the Koran. There is no embarrassment during these prayers, which last about 10 minutes, and nothing is allowed to intrude or distract.

"EUROPEANIZATION" Most of Atatürk's extraordinary reforms of the 1920s and 1930s were concerned with religion, recognizing that Turkey could not become part of Europe until Islam had been contained as much as possible. He therefore ended religious education in schools and replaced the Arabic alphabet with the Roman one; this

was a double blow for Islam, for Arabic is not only the script of the holy Koran, but also the sacred calligraphy that is used to decorate all mosques. The effect of the alphabet reform has therefore been to alienate the younger generation of Turks almost completely from their Islamic cultural background. Strict Muslims associate the very sight of the Roman alphabet with the infidel; while travelers arriving from Iran or Syria, on seeing signposts using the Roman alphabet, may think of Turkey as the gateway to Europe.

THE LAW No other Muslim country has abolished the Shariah (Koranic law): a remarkable reform, as in many ways the law is the most sacred part of Islam and the very essence of the religion. Atatürk replaced it with European codes of law—an action that was an extraordinary affront to the

The act of prayer five times a day is one of the Five Pillars of Islam, the basic tenets by which Muslims live

country's orthodox Muslims. All reference to Islam was erased from the new Turkish constitution, and by becoming a secular republic in 1923, Turkey effectively withdrew from the world of Islam.

After 50 years of Atatürk's secularism, many modern Turkish intellectuals occupying senior positions in government and business are more or less atheists, with manners and appearance that on first acquaintance frequently surprise many of their Western counterparts. Atatürk's aim was not to abolish religion, however, but to free the people from what he believed to be Islam's oppressive influence. He believed it was a necessary step if the country was to move toward the elusive goal of modernization.

Istanbul's intellectual elite would recoil in horror from the very idea of setting foot in an Anatolian village, and most have never done so. Cultural dualism is alive and flourishing in Turkey today, despite Atatürk's attempts to make the peasant "master of Turkey" and the blurring effect of contemporary peasant migration to the cities.

16

EAST–WEST DIVIDE The split between the residents of Istanbul and Ankara is illustrated by one of the nationalists' favorite epithets for Istanbul: *kozmopolit*, a word whose disparaging overtones are not conveyed by the English "cosmopolitan." A recent Turkish dictionary defines a person described thus as "having no national or local color, but assuming the outward form that suits his purpose." Atatürk himself deliberately did not set foot in the old imperial capital from 1919 to 1927.

The economic imbalance between the east and west of the country

The rural poor are flocking to Istanbul in search of prosperity

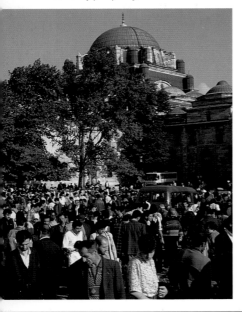

❏ "Ankara's one attraction," runs the wisdom of Istanbul, "is the road out." Another contemptuous Istanbuli description refers to Ankara as "a cloud of dust near the railroad track." ❏

constitutes one of Turkey's major long-term problems. Eastern cities such as Erzurum, Van, and Kars have almost no industries, and the cold, forbidding climate limits the possibilities for agriculture. Unemployment is endemic, resulting in a constant exodus of people to the big cities in search of a better life and more money. Braver people have even emigrated beyond Turkey, mostly to Germany or other parts of western Europe; many make the dramatic transition from their Anatolian villages to cities such as Düsseldorf, Munich, Vienna, and Paris without ever before having traveled farther than their nearest town.

DIFFERENT CUSTOMS A major area of difference between city and village life surrounds marriage and its customs. In the country, families encourage girls to marry at around 13 or 14 years old. The ceremony is religious, with no regard to Swiss-based civil law that states girls must be at least 15 years old and boys must be at least 17. In omitting the civil marriage ceremony altogether, these rural couples technically render their children illegitimate. Polygamy, banned under the civil code, still occurs in the villages (where, with family support, plus social disapproval, divorce is relatively

Resorts such as Alanya have boosted the economy of Mediterranean Turkey

rare), while in the cities, generally the civil law is obeyed and polygamy is unheard of. Traditionally, village husbands bought their brides with cash, a pre-Islamic custom that still continues in remoter central and eastern regions, though it is now much less common in the Aegean and Black Sea regions. As a girl's virginity greatly enhances her bride price, it is in her family's interests to marry her young.

Another tradition peculiar to the villages—especially in the eastern Kurdish and Black Sea areas—is the blood feud. In the Black Sea region, known as Turkey's Texas, it is estimated that blood feuds are responsible for about 500 murders each year. Sometimes continuing for generations and resulting in scores of deaths, blood feuds continue despite government's attempts to stamp them out.

ETHNIC MINORITIES Historically Turks have distanced themselves from the Jews, Armenians, and Greeks living in their country, viewing them as minorities that cannot be assimilated. Regarded as "crafty ones," the three ethnic groups are ranked in order by a Turkish proverb:

"One Greek can cheat two Jews. One Armenian can cheat two Greeks."

Turkey's 9 million or so Kurds, on the other hand, are seen as "mountain Turks" and their ethnic difference is not officially acknowledged (see pages 222–223).

Life remains hard in the vast, barren regions of eastern Turkey

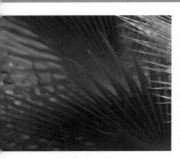

Turkey sits at the meeting point of three different climatic zones: the Euro-Siberian, the Mediterranean, and the Irano-Turanian. The result is a tremendous variety of topography and vegetation, on the scale of a continent rather than a country, with deserts, high mountains, coastal plains, forests, and pastures. In this diverse environment, a paradise for naturalists and botanists, 8,000–9,000 species of wildflower flourish.

CLIMATE Of Turkey's three climatic zones, by far the largest is the Irano-Turanian. This is the steppeland of the central Anatolian plateau. It is very dry in summer and cold in winter, with temperatures dropping as low as minus 105°F and snow lying for up to 120 days of the year. The Euro-Siberian zone includes the Istanbul region and the Black Sea coast. Here there are European-type deciduous forests, with ash, oak, and beech, and summer temperatures rarely exceed 82°F. On the Mediterranean coast lies a different world again; the fertile Cilician plain with its cotton fields, palm trees, and orange groves, has more of a Middle Eastern climate, with temperatures

A magnificent waterfall to the north of Lake Van

reaching as high as 115°F in the southeast. The seasonal variation in temperature here—sometimes as much as 100°F—is one of the most extreme anywhere in the world.

❑ In soil erosion and deforestation, the Anatolian plateau has undergone two catastrophes. The corn that has been grown on the plateau for centuries has exhausted the soil, and animal dung is burned as fuel instead of being used as fertilizer to replenish the soil nutrients. Deforestation is continuing despite attempts to stop it; the forestry service is understaffed and has little authority to enforce the laws. ❑

Gentle, rolling hills typify the hinterland of the Aegean coastline

GEOLOGY Turkey's geological structure is extremely complex, with rocks of almost all ages. The country consists largely of several old plateau blocks, against which masses of younger rock have been squeezed to form mountain ranges of varying sizes. These mountains run in many different directions with considerable irregularity, as one range unexpectedly gives way to another or turns abruptly to plain or plateau.

The highest mountains are in the east, forming a natural border with Georgia, Armenia, and Iran. Mount Ararat, an extinct volcano, is the highest peak in the country at 16,000 feet. Volcanoes have played an important part in the formation of landscapes in the central and eastern parts of Anatolia. In some places the lava sheets are so recent that soil has yet to form on top; in other areas, particularly Cappadocia, the volcanic tufa has created a wondrous landscape of spectacular rock formations (see pages 172–173).

In the north and west of the country there has been enormous cracking and disturbance of the rocks, with earthquakes occurring regularly.

Cappadocia's rock formations were caused by ancient volcanic activity

Cracks in two different directions, splitting the land so that the lower parts sank beneath the sea, are responsible for the long, indented Aegean coast with its numerous, oddly shaped islands and estuaries. Both the Bosphorus and the Dardanelles straits owe their origin to this faulting action, and the whole of the Black Sea coast is the result of subsidence along a series of such fissures.

The numerous saltwater and freshwater lakes— the result of a combination of topography and relatively high rainfall— are another remarkable feature of the Turkish landscape. The largest, Lake Van (see pages 234–235), covers almost 1,560 square miles, making it six times as big as Great Salt Lake, Salt Lake City.

Turkey is a potentially rich country: its mountains are full of minerals; its climate and land are perfect for a wide range of agricultural produce; the seas all around are full of fish. There is no shortage of manpower. But the country is burdened with huge foreign debts, and the struggle for growth has not been easy.

THE PROBLEMS The scale of Turkey's recent economic problems is the legacy of the dynamic but extravagant Menderes government (1950–1960; see pages 44–45), which incurred debts that will not be paid off until 2014. Another curious hangover from the past is the continuation of Atatürk's policy of exempting agriculture from taxation, a move he initiated in the 1920s to encourage expansion. At least half the population works in agriculture, which produces 35 percent of the gross national product (GNP) but less than five percent of total taxation. Although this is patently absurd, no government now dares to impose taxes on the big farmers and landowners, whose support is critical to them. Moreover, big landowners, known as *ağas*, seem to have no actual title to their lands, but seem to have simply acquired them, some-

Traditional farming methods survive in eastern regions

❑ Historically, the Turks have not been good businessmen. In Ottoman times, most commercial and technical matters were left to the talents of Greeks, Armenians, and Jews. With the expulsion of many members of these minorities at the end of the empire, the Turks had for the first time to run the economy of the country themselves, and their lack of experience and expertise showed. ❑

times by taking them over from peasants who have migrated to the cities. In much of central and eastern Anatolia, they "own" as many as 100 villages, and for thousands of peasants their word is law. At election time, the *ağas* are therefore in a position to deliver thousands of votes to whichever party they choose.

Population increase is another problem. The population has more

At least half the population of Turkey works on the land

than doubled in the last 25 years, and at three percent net increase per year, has one of the highest rates of growth in the world. Part of the reason for this is the fall in the death rate with the eradication of diseases such as malaria. Additionally, the birthrate is extremely high, and attempts to introduce birth control often encounter substantial opposition. Now there is enormous pressure on Turkey's resources, unemployment is rising, and the trade gap is widening as agricultural produce that could have been exported is needed to feed new mouths. Many children still receive no formal education, and in some rural areas a single teacher may face classes of up to 100.

THE SOLUTIONS Land reform, essential for any real economic recovery but never seriously attempted in the past, is now being implemented to a limited extent, together with reforms of the tax system.

Turkey's main raw materials of cotton, wool, mohair, beet sugar, olive oil, and tobacco tend to be produced by state-owned enterprises, and Tansu Çiller began a drive to privatize these and other state organizations, in an unsuccessful attempt to raise cash and to make

them more profitable. Market forces, it is believed, will increase the efficiency of the incompetent public sector, which currently sits on 40 percent of GNP.

CURRENT POSITION Inflation has run at around 80 percent, reaching as much as 125 percent in early 1994, so interest rates continue to discourage investment. Income from tourism has been adversely affected by the Kurdish terrorist campaign, and money has been pouring into the fight against the guerrillas. Yet, in spite of all this, shops are full, company profits are buoyant, and there are no shortages of commodities. Indeed, labor costs are low and confidence high; the economy grew by seven percent in 1998, with skilled bureaucrats and a productive unregistered economy helping to keep it afloat. Short-term visitors to the country, therefore, may well notice very few underlying problems.

❑ There is a long tradition of tax evasion in Turkey, aggravated by inefficient bookkeeping and incompetent collection methods. As a result, some of Turkey's richest citizens contribute little or nothing to the national treasury. ❑

As a people, the Turks are characterized by their dignity, nobility, honesty, great physical endurance, and courage, and in comparison to some of their neighbors, can be considered relatively silent. Instead of being volatile in a typically Mediterranean way, they are more like bottled-up volcanoes, erupting from time to time after long periods of quiescence.

22

WHO ARE THE TURKS? This is a vexed question that still puzzles historians. Just how was it that a relatively small number of Turkish invaders from the steppelands of Central Asia (between the Caspian Sea and Mongolia) succeeded, after a comparatively short period of time, in stamping their Turkish identity on Anatolia, rather than being absorbed by the ethnic mix that was already there? There were, after all, no massacres or mass deportations of the indigenous population. The pre-Turkish Anatolians were a thorough mixture of all the races that had gone before—Hittites, Phrygians, Lydians, Celts, Jews, Greeks, Romans, Armenians, Kurds, and Mongols. Yet when a mere handful of Turks

❏ "*Ne mutlu Türküm diyene*" ("How happy is he who can say he is a Turk") was one of Atatürk's great sayings, still to be seen all over Turkey on banners and carved into hillsides. "*Biz bize benzeriz*" ("We resemble ourselves") was another of his slogans designed to endow Turks with a sense of pride in their identity. ❏

arrived, they managed to transform a Greek- or Armenian-speaking Christian population into a mainly Turkish-speaking Muslim people, henceforth to be known as Turks.

THE TURKISH PERSPECTIVE The Turkish view of history, still taught in many schools today, is that the original Turkish homeland—from the Caspian to Mongolia—was the cradle of world civilization. One group of the people here migrated eastward in about 7000 BC and founded the Chinese civilization, another group went to India, and yet others headed to northern Europe (the Celts), south into the Middle East, and across to North Africa. As a result, some Turks regard the Greek and Roman civilizations as successors to earlier Turkic civilizations such as the Phrygians, Lydians, and Hittites.

PERSONALITY The Turkish character is one of extreme contradictions and contrasts. Turks are hardworking, yet realize the futility of hurry and worry;

A Turkish woman in the Aegean region

Young girls in traditional costume

serious, yet cherish a comic character as their favorite folklore hero (see pages 106–107). They respect the authority of the state, yet insist on democracy; they are ruthless, yet kind and hospitable. Many are poor, yet they disdain money. Trust and honor are paramount. Theft is regarded as the most shameful of all crimes and is rare outside the big cities. Murderers form the elite of the prison population, as most such crimes are the result of affairs of honor; thieves, on the other hand, are spat upon as the lowest of the low. Turks despise what they see as a lack of control: it does not pay to lose your temper with a Turk, for it achieves nothing and merely earns you contempt. Loyalty in male friendships is all-important, probably encouraged by the all-male military service. The military is extremely tough and compulsory for 18 months, and is regarded by most as an important educational experience, teaching the illiterate to read and write and instructing them

in a trade. Turkish officers, drawn from the middle and lower classes, regard themselves as the nation's elite and its social conscience: all reformist movements in modern Turkey have stemmed from the army.

A shepherd from the Kahta Cayi
mountains

The Turks love their festivals, which are not intended to impress tourists. All their folk culture is concentrated into these annual events, which usually last a week or more, each region having its own authentic specialties in terms of dance, music, and drama.

CITY FESTIVALS Most of the big cities throughout Turkey have an annual fair. The main one, not surprisingly, is in **Istanbul,** held from about June 20 to July 30 and featuring an extraordinary range of dance, art, and music at a number of venues. **Izmir** holds an International Fair from August 20 to September 20, which includes commercial exhibitions as well as cultural and folkloric events. **Samsun** holds a similar fair in July. **Bursa's** annual festival, from June 12 to July 12, is entirely cultural and attracts some international singers and musicians.

24

CULTURAL FESTIVALS IN ANCIENT SETTINGS Turkey is blessed with numerous magnificent venues for festivals, including Greco-Roman theaters, Byzantine churches, and medieval fortresses. In April and May each year **Ephesus** hosts an excellent **Culture and Art Festival,** with folk dancing in the Greco-Roman theater. The Asklepeion theater is the setting for the plays and dances during the entertaining **Pergamum Festival,** which takes place in May and June. In August, the **Çanakkale Troy Festival** uses the setting of ancient Troy for the mediocre folk dances and other musical performances, while the very professional **Antalya**

A dancer at Antalya

❑ Each region in Turkey has its own folk dance and its own costume. The men of the Black Sea region perform the Horon dance, dressed in black with silver trimmings. Bursa's Sword and Shield Dance, representing the Ottoman conquest of the city, is performed by men in early Ottoman battle dress. The celebrated Spoon Dance is performed from Konya to Silifke by both men and women, colorfully dressed and clicking a pair of wooden spoons like castanets in each hand. ❑

Film and Art Festival, held annually in October, makes creative use of the splendid Roman theater at **Aspendos**.

WRESTLING: MEN AND CAMELS
Grease-wrestling between two men is popular throughout Turkey; the major festival is held each year in the first week of July near **Edirne** on the little island of **Saray Içi**. Up to a thousand contestants take part, clad in leather loincloths and greased all over with olive oil. Gypsies arrive in force to provide entertainments, as well as the drum and single-reed oboe music that accompanies the wrestling warm-up exercises.

In the months of December and January throughout the province of **Aydın** in western Turkey, and more particularly in the small town of **Germencik**, you can see camel-wrestling. This involves two male camels pushing and shoving each other, and although it can turn out to be quite vicious, it is not usually a blood sport.

A performance in the Culture and Art Festival at Ephesus

MEVLANA FESTIVAL

This is probably Turkey's most famous festival, held each year in **Konya** from December 14 to 17 to commemorate the death of Mevlana, founder of the mystic Whirling Dervish order (see pages 204–205). Temperatures in Konya at this time are perishingly cold and hotel prices double, so many prefer to watch the famous dervish dance (known as *sema*) at the restored *semahane* (dance room) in **Galatasaray**, Istanbul.

Traditional dress is an important part of Turkish folk culture

❑ During the last week of June a remarkable festival, the Artvin Kafkasör Culture and Art Festival, takes place in Artvin, high in the Georgian mountains inland from the Black Sea coast. Bullfights are staged on the Kafkasör plateau, along with wrestling and folk dancing. ❑

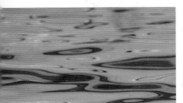

Turkey's mountainous topography and high rainfall combine to make it unusually rich in lakes and rivers—most notably the Tigris and the Euphrates, whose sources lie high on the Anatolian plateau. It has been predicted that water, the most essential of resources, will be the cause of the next war in the region.

THE SOUTHEAST ANATOLIA PROJECT

Known as G.A.P., this ambitious scheme envisions the transformation of the present wasteland around Şanlıurfa in southeast Turkey into fertile agricultural land, by means of a series of 22 dams on the Upper Euphrates, with the massive Atatürk Dam as the centerpiece. The Tigris, meanwhile, will be used mainly to provide hydroelectric power, and a planned total of 19 generating plants will then guarantee Turkey's self-sufficiency. The target year is 2005.

26

❑ When Turkey suspended the flow of water along the Euphrates in 1990 and 1992 to fill up the new Atatürk Lake behind the Atatürk Dam, it demonstrated its ability to turn off the faucets supplying both Iraq and Syria. Syria responded by giving support to the P.K.K., Turkey's Kurdish guerrilla movement. ❑

SOCIAL IMPLICATIONS Throughout the Middle East, more than 80 percent of water is consumed by agriculture. Such water consumption is almost always heavily subsidized by governments, not only because they want to ensure food supplies, but also because by supporting the rural economy they hope to stem the drift to the cities. The Turkish government's hope is that any dissident Kurds engaged in sheep-rearing in the Urfa area will be tempted by the hundreds of thousands of new jobs in the cotton and cereal fields, and that social unrest will thus be calmed by economic prosperity.

Water is one of Turkey's most precious natural resources

Turkey was

The most ancient relics found so far in Asia Minor date to the 7th millennium BC. Remains from the early 2nd millennium BC reveal the existence of Assyrian trading colonies in Cappadocia and an important Copper Age culture in Central Anatolia. Later in the 2nd millennium, most of Asia Minor fell under the rule of the Hittites, whose empire flourished from about 1750 to 1200 BC, peaking in the 14th and 13th centuries BC.

MYSTERY OF THE HITTITES Three thousand years ago, the ancient Hittites rivaled the Egyptians as the greatest power on earth. Yet until a century ago they remained a mystery race, with the only documentary evidence of their existence appearing in the Old Testament, where they were mentioned as a tribe living in Palestine. When Egyptian hieroglyphs were first deciphered, an

Powerful carvings such as this are among the most evocative relics of the Hittite civilization

inscription was found relating to a defense treaty between Rameses II and Hattusilis, king of the Hittites. To cement the treaty, Rameses married the Hittite king's daughter.

No further clue as to the mystery of the lost Hittite Empire was found until in 1834 a Frenchman, Charles Texier, discovered the ruins of the Hittite capital, Hattusas, at Boğazkale. In 1906, German excavations on the site uncovered thousands of cuneiform tablets. When these were finally deciphered in the 1940s, the full history of the Hittites was at last revealed, an achievement heralded as one of the greatest archeological triumphs of the 20th century. As most of the research and decipherment was carried out by German and Czech scholars, Hittite culture remains less well known in the English-speaking world than perhaps it should be.

❏ The bronze "sun disks" found in the graves at Alacahöyük are unique to Hittite art. They were thought to be endowed with mystical properties, and their unusual crisscross pattern was possibly meant to symbolize the sun and its rays. Sometimes an antlered stag appears at the center of the design, indicating that the piece is the work of a mountain people. A sun disk has been chosen as the emblem of the Turkish Ministry of Culture and Tourism. ❏

❏ The most memorable relics left by the Hittites are the rock-cut sculptures, found on all their sites, depicting their gods and ceremonies. The simple, powerful figures—broad and squat, with none of the grace and subtlety associated with Egyptian or Babylonian art—indicate a tough, warlike mountain people, used to a harsh climate and conditions. Hittite culture stands in sharp contrast to the cultures of Mesopotamia and the Nile, where the inhabitants were able to pasture their flocks peacefully beside the great rivers, and where there was no need for defenses or fortifications. ❏

MOUNTAIN CULTURE The Hittites were the only ancient civilization to exist and develop in inhospitable, mountainous country. While their military strength, necessary to their survival, was awesome, they were humane in the treatment of conquered enemies (unlike the Assyrians), and in peacetime were governed by statesmen with sound and well-developed policies. A practical and intellectually unpretentious

Many of the finest Hittite sculptures are displayed in the Museum of Anatolian Civilizations in Ankara

people, they lacked the sophistication and graces of their Near Eastern neighbors.

TUTANKHAMUN LINK One of the cuneiform tablets found at Boğazkale indicates a curious link between the Egyptian boy-king Tutankhamun and the Hittites. According to the inscription, the Hittite king Shubbililiuma was encamped by the Euphrates when a messenger arrived from the Egyptian queen, begging him to send her one of his many sons to marry, for her own husband Tutankhamun had died. Shubbililiuma eventually sent one of his sons, who was put to death on his arrival in Egypt on the orders of an ambitious official who went on to marry the queen himself. Scholars, intrigued by the fact that the fall of Troy coincided roughly with the disintegration of the Hittite Empire, have also found evidence recently to suggest a link between ancient Troy and the Hittite kingdom.

Storage amphorae excavated on the site of the Hittite capital

29

After the breakup of the Hittite Empire, Asia Minor disintegrated into a number of dynasties and peoples—Phrygians, Cimmerians, Lydians, and others—which remain largely obscure. At this time the Greeks began to invade the Aegean coast, entering upon a long struggle that included the Trojan War.

ALEXANDER AND HELLENIZATION

When, in the spring of 334 BC, this 21-year-old Macedonian crossed the Hellespont into Asia Minor at the head of some 35,000 soldiers, he was heralding the dawn of an era that was to last a thousand years, to be eclipsed only by the rise of Islam. The Greeks and the Persians had battled for decades over the cities of Asia Minor, and Alexander resolved now to drive them out once and for all. Having swept triumphantly through western and southern Anatolia, by 333 BC he stood poised at Issus, in the easternmost corner of the Mediterranean, where his army routed a Persian force three times its size. The cultural consequences of these great military exploits were immeasurable, since by opening up a corridor for cultural interaction and fusion between East and West, Alexander was initiating the process that was later to become known as Hellenization (see pages 144–145).

The Hellenistic age was characterized by independent city-states such as Antioch, with fine public buildings erected at the ruler's expense. Although these states were constantly at war with one another, a solid administrative foundation was nevertheless created by the various Hellenistic kings of Asia Minor, which was later to prove very useful to the Roman Empire.

One of the remarkably preserved streets of the Greco-Roman city of Ephesus

❏ Alexander's avowed ambition on marching into Asia was to liberate the Greek cities from their Persian rulers under Darius the Great. Alexander had been brought up on the works of Homer, and throughout his campaign against the Persians he kept a copy of the epic poems beside him to remind himself of that earlier Greek war against the east. ❏

Ankara retains many vestiges of its Roman past

The atmospheric ruins of the sanctuary of Zeus at Labranda, near Milas

❏ The Romans were altogether less refined than their Greek predecessors; their theaters were generally used not for sophisticated perfomances of plays and music, but for bloody fights, with savage beasts tearing each other—or early Christians—limb from limb. ❏

THE ROMAN AGE The Romans were at first drawn with reluctance into Asia Minor, crossing the Hellespont in 190 BC to crush the ambitious Seleucid king. When in 133 BC the king of Pergamum bequeathed his entire kingdom to Rome, the Romans were obligated to organize western Asia Minor into the Roman province of Asia. Problems with troublesome Cilician pirates and the Pontic kingdom of Mithridates in the 1st century BC later drew the Romans eastward to take over the whole of Anatolia, which enjoyed 200 years of comparative peace and prosperity under Roman rule.

The Romans recognized the cultural achievements of the Greeks who were now subject to them: Roman artists, writers, and architects gradually began to imitate all forms of Greek art. Throughout the eastern reaches of the empire there sprang up cities inspired by Greek models, with a distinctive Roman provincial city architecture—often including magnificent theaters such as that at **Aspendos**. While landowners and the ruling elite enjoyed lives of opulence in these cities, the peasants were tied to the land.

This period of stability lasted until the late 2nd century AD, when a succession of barbarian invasions caused havoc and weakened the economic structure of the empire.

Even during times of prosperity, Christianity had been troublesome to the Roman emperors, and the Christians were brutally persecuted for their refusal to comply with the cult of the emperor. Gradually opposition to the new religion waned, however, and in 312 the Roman Emperor Constantine was himself converted. The following year he proclaimed Christianity the official religion of the Roman Empire.

A gracefully carved column at Perge, near Antalya

The name Byzantium is derived from Byzantion, a former trading colony of ancient Greece said to have been founded in 657 BC by a Greek named Byzas. In AD 330 the Roman Emperor Constantine moved the capital of his new eastern Roman Empire here and changed the name to Constantinople.

START OF THE EMPIRE After the collapse of the rival western empire, the eastern Roman Empire, known henceforth as the Byzantine Empire, acquired great political strength, untold wealth, and a dynamic cultural life. Clear evidence of this last can be seen in the mosaics and miniatures created in its monasteries, and in the impressive architecture of its churches, of which **Aya Sofya** is the most important. The Byzantine civilization, centered on Constantinople, became by far the most influential of all the eastern Christian cultures, and the Byzantine emperors considered themselves to be the representatives of God's will on earth.

A detail from the Obelisk of Theodosius in the Hippodrome

❑ Justinian the Great's rule (AD 527–565) is considered the zenith of the Byzantine Empire. His wife Theodora, a former actress and a notorious sexual libertine, was his most influential councillor, and her courage during riots at Nica saved the throne. ❑

Within Constantinople the three key buildings were Aya Sofya, the center of religious life; the palace (on the site of the later **Topkapı**), the center of political and administrative life; and the **Hippodrome** (**At Meydanı**), which was the focus of public and social life. On the site of the gardens that now lie between the **Blue Mosque** and Aya Sofya was the Forum of Augustus, the public meeting place.

DOCTRINAL DIVISIONS The early years of the Byzantine Empire were racked with divisions over doctrine, and many church councils were convened to resolve questions of heresy. The earliest, at Nicaea (Iznik) in AD 325, was held to discuss what became known as the Arian heresy,

❑ Pondering on the contrast between Turks and Byzantines, the English novelist Rose Macaulay observed that it was "difficult to discuss theology with Turks, as one had been used to with Byzantines, who had reasoned themselves in and out of all the heresies in the world." ❑

32

Aya Sofya contains some of the finest of all Byzantine mosaics

promoted by Arius of Alexandria, according to which Jesus Christ was not the Son of God. The rejection of this new teaching resulted in the Nicene Creed, still an important part of Christian worship. The Council of Nicaea also declared the emperor head of the church as well as of the state, with five bishops—of Rome, Constantinople, Alexandria, Antioch, and Jerusalem—preeminent under his rule.

BYZANTINE ART Although it was heir to the cultures of ancient Greece and Rome, Byzantine art rejected the balanced proportions that had been so central to Greek aesthetics. The figures in Byzantine art, which was always essentially religious in subject matter, were deliberately depicted as flat and two-dimensional, using techniques that were apparently less skilled than those to be seen in the murals of ancient Rome and Greece.

The intention, however, was to create the illusion that all the religious figures depicted were, in fact, observing the spectator, rather than the other way around.

JUSTINIAN THE GREAT In the 6th century, under Justinian, the arts flourished; some of the finest achievements were in architecture, with the construction of Aya Sofya, Aya Irena, and many other churches.

Military matters were also in the ascendant as North Africa, Italy, and southern Spain were regained by the empire. Such success was not to continue after Justinian's death, however, when the empire suffered a series of setbacks. Persian aggression under the Sassanians was followed by the rise of the Arabs with their new religion, Islam. Arab incursions all along Turkey's south coast during the 7th and 8th centuries were to have a gradual weakening effect on the empire.

The Battle of Manzikert in 1071 signaled the beginning of the end of the Byzantine Empire. The Byzantines were defeated by fierce horsemen from Central Asia, known as Turks or Seljuks, who then cut a swath through the country as far as the Sea of Marmara.

BREAKUP OF THE EMPIRE Civil war followed, and the empire began to disintegrate. The Seljuk Turks rapidly seized control of most of Asia Minor, leaving only the Aegean regions and the capital under Byzantine rule. Although the beginning of their rule was marked by massacres, enslavements, and forcible conversions to Islam, the Seljuk Turks soon established a secure state administered from their new capital Nicaea (Iznik).

ARMENIA One of the most successful states to break away from the Byzantine Empire was the Cilician

A 19th-century representation of the fall of Constantinople in 1453

❏ Despite its economic weakness, the Byzantine Empire saw a last tremendous flowering of art and scholarship in the early 14th century. The mosaics and frescoes in Istanbul's Kariye Museum date from this time. ❏

kingdom of Armenia, which established itself in 1080 and continued until 1375. In its heyday, under Levon the Magnificent (1187–1219), the kingdom introduced advanced systems of justice and taxation as well as many social improvements, and the arts flourished. Many of Armenia's castles, such as **Anamur** and **Silifke,** date from this time.

34

THE CRUSADES The growing tension between the Byzantine Empire and the Crusader nations led to the greatest blow that Constantinople had yet suffered. At the time of the First Crusade, the Byzantines were willing to support any movement that might help them reestablish their own political control in Asia Minor, whatever its stated aims. In the event, although they did actually regain a number of cities, their lands suffered considerably from the undisciplined passage of the motley Crusader army. One of the Norman Crusader princes even founded a principality in Antioch, which then renounced its allegiance to the empire.

By the time of the Second Crusade, in 1147–1149, the Byzantines were much more reluctant to allow the Crusaders free passage, and once again the armies left a trail of rape and pillage in their wake. The German emperor Frederick Barbarossa, impatient with the Byzantines, this time encouraged the Seljuks to march on Constantinople. The armies met near Lake Eğridir in 1176, and the Byzantines were defeated almost as decisively as at Manzikert a century earlier.

The Third Crusade, again led by Barbarossa, began in 1189 with the storming of Adrianople (Edessa), but petered out when Barbarossa drowned in a river near Silifke. The fateful Fourth Crusade gathered at Venice in 1202 with the express aim—prompted by the trading ambitions of the Doge—of taking Constantinople en route to the Holy Land. After the Crusaders sacked Constantinople,

The Crusaders' capture of Constantinople in 1204 was one of the most violent episodes in its history

their lust for conquest was finally sated, enough so that they abandoned their march on the Holy Land and crowned a Flemish prince the first Latin Emperor of Constantinople. Afterward a handful of small successor states sprang up, and one of these, based at Nicaea, recaptured Constantinople in 1261, retaining it until the Ottoman conquest in 1453. The real death blow to the Byzantine Empire had been dealt in 1204, however, when the Crusaders captured the city.

The city besieged from the sea by Mehmet II in 1453

❏ The historian Steven Runciman noted that "There was never a greater crime against humanity than the Fourth Crusade. Not only did it cause the destruction or dispersal of all the treasures of the past that Byzantium had devoutly stored, and the mortal wounding of a civilization that was still active and great; but it was also an act of gigantic folly... It upset the whole defense of Christendom." ❏

The Seljuk Turks formed the first wave of the Turkic peoples who were eventually to make themselves masters of the Byzantine Empire. With their arrival, the culture of Anatolia saw a dramatic change: many of its Greeks fled westward, but others remained and their descendants adopted the Turkish language. By the 15th century, almost all of Asia Minor was Turkish-speaking.

ORIGINS The Seljuks, originally nomads from the region of Samarkand and Bukhara, trace their ancestry back to the Tu-Kin people of the Mongolian steppes (hence the modern name "Turk"). In the 11th century, a wave of Seljuks surged out from their homeland and into Persia, Iraq, Syria, and Palestine, where they were converted to Islam. When they pushed up from Antioch (modern Antakya) into Anatolia and Konya, under the leadership of Alp Arslan in

Ishak Paşa Sarayı, at Doğubayazıt, combines elements of the Seljuk, Persian, Georgian, Armenian, and Ottoman styles of architecture

1067, they brought their new religion with them.

Although the Seljuks were effective fighters renowned for their physical prowess, once the fighting was over, their greatest sultans—notably Alp Arslan, Malik Shah, Keykavus I, and Keykubad I (Alaeddin)—were enlightened rulers who laid the foundations for commercial prosperity and the development of education and the arts. Over the two centuries of their rule, the Seljuks evolved a remarkable form of welfare state, in which medical schools were linked with hospitals, orphanages, poorhouses, mental homes, baths, and religious schools, all offering free services to the needy.

ART AND ARCHITECTURE The 13th century was the high point of Seljuk civilization in Asia Minor, with a flowering of military and artistic

> ❏ The network of caravansaries established along trade routes was a great encouragement to commerce. The services they offered to traveling merchants were remarkable: around the central mosque and ablution fountain were arranged sleeping quarters, baths, cafés, blacksmiths' and leatherworkers' workshops, and areas for listening to music. The most remarkable aspect of all was that these services were offered free by the state, which funded the system through taxation. ❏

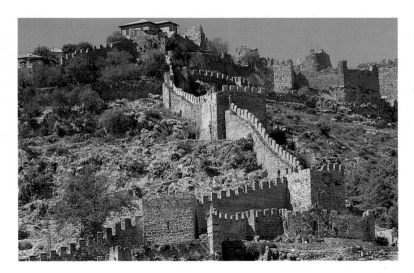

talent. The elaborately decorated tiles and carvings of Seljuk architecture distantly reflect Persian influence, and the massive power of their castles and minarets displays traces of Syrian Arab influence. But whereas the later Ottomans often converted churches into mosques, Seljuk mosques were without exception built on new foundations. They also developed their own distinctive forms of architecture, such as the cylindrical mausoleum (*türbe*) on a square base with a conical roof (the most famous example being the **Mevlana Tomb** in Konya), whose shape recalls the pointed tents of the Seljuks' nomadic origins. The double-headed eagle, symbol of the Seljuk state, can be seen on many of their buildings, which were usually plainly constructed in red brick, in contrast with the very elaborate decorations and carving in niches and doorways. The main entrance was always intricately decorated with honeycomb (or stalactite) carving, as can be seen in the surviving caravansaries (inns) and *madrasas*. *Madrasas* were generally charitable foundations that were similar to the gymnasiums of the ancient world, teaching theology, the arts, and sciences alongside sports. Their layout was similar to the classical model, too, with buildings arranged around a courtyard.

The impressive Seljuk fortifications at Alanya

The Seljuks were also prolific and skilled builders of bridges, many of which, solidly built in stone with a single pointed arch, remain in use today. The Seljuk pointed arch, used to great effect in windows and doorways, was possibly taken back to Europe by the Crusaders as the inspiration for the later Gothic arch.

The Seljuks brought the exquisite art of tilework (unknown to the Greeks and Romans; see page 61) with them from Persia, developing the Persian style into their own form of tile mosaics in plain colors and geometric designs, so often seen on their mosques, tombs, and *madrasas*. The other great Seljuk art, recalling their nomadic background, was carpet-weaving (see pages 94–95).

❏ The Seljuks' single most significant contribution to religion was the foundation in the 13th-century of the Mevlana order of Whirling Dervishes at Konya, the Seljuk capital. This form of Islamic mysticism continues today, despite Atatürk's dissolution of the order in 1925 as part of his drive to secularize modern Turkey. ❏

In the 13th century the Seljuk sultanate of Konya fell into decline. It was succeeded by a number of smaller principalities, among them one ruled by Osman Gazi (1288–1326), who gave his name to a small tribe known as the Ottomans or Osmani Turks.

EXPANSION Under Osman, the Ottomans embarked on a great movement of expansion, and by 1400 ruled most of the Balkan peninsula

38

and Anatolia. In 1453, after a siege led by Mehmet II, they took Constantinople and established their capital there. Renamed Istanbul by the Turks, the city remained the capital of the Ottoman Empire until 1923.

While maintaining many aspects of the Byzantine administrative system, the Ottomans also made innovations, introducing institutions such as the corps of Janissaries and *vakifs*. The latter were religious trusts, set up on captured land to provide revenues with which baths, hotels, and other public amenities were established.

SÜLEYMAN THE MAGNIFICENT The reign of Süleyman the Magnificent (1520–1566) was unquestionably the climax of the Ottoman age. A contemporary of Henry VIII of England, the Hapsburg emperor

Left: Süleyman the Magnificent
Below: The Ottoman Empire in 1676

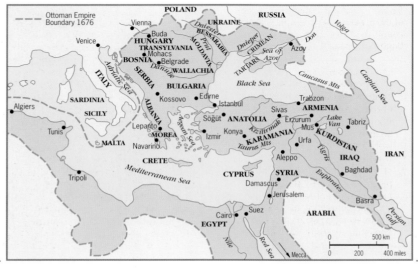

Charles V, François I of France, and Ivan the Terrible, Süleyman was an outstanding leader, legislator, and patron of the arts. Under his rule the Ottoman Empire doubled in size. His armies took Belgrade in 1521, Buda in 1526, and almost captured Vienna in 1529. His navy evicted the Knights of Saint John from Rhodes in 1522, ravaged the French, Spanish, and Italian coasts, and in 1538 defeated the navies of Europe. These victories were made possible not only by the quality of his troops and generals, but also by their superior weapons, the superb financial organization of his armies, and above all by their discipline, the envy of European rulers. Süleyman's architects, notably Sinan (see page 65), court architect from 1538, transformed the skylines of the great cities of the empire: Istanbul, Edirne, Damascus, Baghdad, Jerusalem, and Mecca.

Ottoman soldiers (1825), before the abolition of the Janissaries

❏ On the death of their father Murat I, Beyazit I had his brother Yakoub murdered, thereby initiating the Ottoman sultans' practice (or frequently their wives') of having all their male relatives killed on the day of their accession, in order to avoid any quarrels over legitimacy. The Koranic verse claiming that "rebellion is worse than execution" was cited in their justification. ❏

Early 19th-century Ottoman dress

❏ Founded by Murat I (1362–1389), the Janissaries for centuries formed the backbone of the Ottoman army. Chosen from Christian families on the basis of physical prowess, they were converted to Islam and trained to exceptionally high standards of discipline in the palace schools. By the 18th century the Janissaries had become something of a law unto themselves, and they were finally abolished in 1826. ❏

Süleyman's successors, incapable of emulating his great powers of leadership, found themselves increasingly unable to control his vast and disparate empire. Only five years after his death, in 1571, the once invincible Ottoman navy was destroyed by Venice and her allies at Lepanto, off the Greek coast.

HAREM POLITICS Süleyman's marriage to Hürrem Sultan, known as Roxelana in the West—the first time in two centuries that a sultan had committed himself to a single wife—helped to forge the first link in the chain of events that eventually brought about the downfall of the Ottoman Empire. Also of crucial importance was the fact that the administration of the empire had never been in Turkish hands, but was always entrusted to a huge, mainly Christian slave community, trained in the palace schools.

40

❏ In her book *Beyond the Sublime Porte* (1931), Professor Miller wrote of Süleyman: "Between him and his immediate successors, who ceased with surprising suddenness to be either soldiers or statesmen, there was no graduation whatever. Enervated and enfeebled by seclusion and idleness, filled with ennui, they sought pleasure and diversion in every conceivable form of extravagance, self-indulgence, and vice." ❏

The seeds of the empire's demise were thus already sown, but it was hastened by the ineffectual rules of a long string of sultans—starting with Roxelana's son Selim "the Sot"—who were feeble, incompetent, or worse. Selim's disastrous rule ended when, in an alcoholic daze on the way to his bath, he fell and cracked his skull. His wife, Nur Bana, shared Roxelana's obsessive ambition for power, and from then on politics and policies were decided from the harem and implemented through murder and intrigue. Thus the empire was left to decay gradually from within.

THE YOUNG TURKS AND WORLD WAR I The first stirrings of a new spirit among the Turks (prompted by political developments in western Europe) came during the reign of Selim III (1789– 1807), and for much of

Le Petit Parisien
Supplément Littéraire Illustré

LA RÉVOLUTION EN TURQUIE
Sanglant combat autour d'Yildiz-Kiosk. ∴ Victoire des Jeunes-Turcs

In 1909 Le Petit Parisien reported victory for the Young Turks at Yıldız-Kiosk

the 19th century reforming sultans and ministers worked on a program of modernization. This process came to an abrupt end in 1876 with the accession of Abdul Hamid II, who ruthlessly repressed every liberal thought and reform. In 1908 the Young Turks, a liberal opposition group, led a revolution that temporarily overthrew Abdul Hamid in the name of freedom but soon degenerated into a dictatorship, rent by internal dissension and foreign wars.

In 1914 Turkey entered World War I on the side of Germany, an alliance that was of immense military value to the Central Powers but disastrous for the Turks. Having held out against Allied attacks on the Dardanelles (Gallipoli) and Mesopotamia, they were finally isolated by British attacks from Egypt and India, and signed an armistice in 1919.

After the debacle of World War I, the victorious Allies drew up their arrangements for the dissolution of the Ottoman Empire, "the Sick Man of Europe." Under the terms of the Treaty of Sèvres, described by historians as "the death warrant of the Ottoman Empire," the empire lost all its lands except Istanbul and part of Anatolia. So harsh were these conditions—harsher by far than those imposed on Germany— that they were to inspire a popular nationalist uprising among the Turks, under their new leader Atatürk.

❑ German influence, which had grown under Sultan Abdul Hamid II (1876–1909), increased yet further under the Young Turks. German officers reorganized the Turkish army; German businessmen and technicians extended their hold on the country's economy; and German engineers and financiers began construction of the famous Baghdad Railway, which was to provide a direct rail link between Germany and the Middle East. ❑

LE CONCERT EUROPÉEN

A French view of the war between Turkey and Greece in 1897

Sultan Abdul Hamid, overthrown by the Young Turks

41

The excessively harsh terms of the Treaty of Sèvres were in fact never implemented in full, for while the Allies were busy imposing their conditions on the sultan and his government in Istanbul, in the depths of Anatolia a new Turkish state was rising up, based on a total rejection of the treaty.

42

WAR OF INDEPENDENCE So complete was Turkey's defeat at the end of World War I, and so abject its humiliation under the Treaty of Sèvres, that the spirit of its people might well have been crushed. The Allied division of Ottoman lands might have continued unhindered had it not been for the exaggerated territorial ambition of Greece, which set its sights on occupying the whole of the Aegean coast. Opposed by all the Allies except Britain, Greece landed an invasion force at Izmir in May 1919. Pushing deep into the interior, it was routed by forces under the command of Atatürk. This was the catalyst needed by the budding Turkish nationalist movement. The Turkish campaign against the Greek forces (1919–1922) became known as the War of Independence, and during these years the nationalist movement, which had started among a small class of intellectuals,

Atatürk remembered—throughout Turkey buildings are named after him

❑ Atatürk's words, "In life the only real guide is science," are inscribed on the faculty buildings of Ankara University, which was founded by him. ❑

mushroomed into a countrywide uprising bent on creating a Turkish state based in Anatolia. Atatürk's efforts were crowned by the terms of the Treaty of Lausanne in 1923, under which Turkish sovereignty was recognized within approximately its present-day borders.

WESTERNIZING REFORMS During the remaining 15 years of his life, Atatürk effectively ruled Turkey as a dictator at the head of a single-party state. The Republican People's Party implemented his far-reaching reforms, which sought to westernize Turkey and integrate it into the modern world.

The Turkish war memorial at Gelibolu (Gallipoli), where Allied troops were routed by Turkish forces commanded by Lt. Col. Kemal, later known as Atatürk

Having exiled the sultan, Atatürk issued a series of edicts abolishing the Ministry of Religious Affairs, religious orders and religious schools, and sequestering religious land. He abolished Koranic law, replacing it wholesale with European legal codes, and in 1928 disestablished Islam itself and amended the constitution to make Turkey a secular state. Atatürk was not opposed to religion in itself, and upheld everyone's right to be a devout Muslim in private, but he was convinced that religious concerns should not impinge on public or political life. He abolished the Arabic alphabet, in which the Koran was written, giving a body of academics just six months (they had asked for six years) to devise a new Roman alphabet for Turkish. Once ready, this alphabet was introduced virtually overnight, resulting in total chaos in the printing world: only one book was published in the whole of 1929.

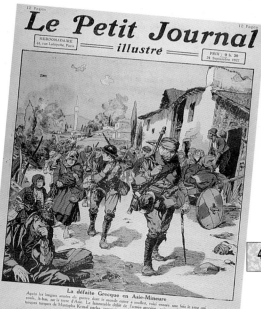

Le Petit Journal illustré

La défaite Grecque en Asie-Mineure

In 1922 the Greek army was finally vanquished in what came to be known as the Turkish War of Independence

Concerned to improve the position of women, whom he wanted to see accepted as equals, he encouraged the casting off of the veil, which he called an oppressive device used by men to hold women back; and in 1934 he gave women the vote and the right to run for parliament. He himself married a woman as modern and emancipated and independent in spirit as he declared all Turkish women should be, but the marriage was soon dissolved.

Although undoubtedly an autocrat, Atatürk was not only an outstanding leader but also a man with a great appetite for life, renowned for his sense of humor, charm, and sheer stamina. His early death—at the age of 57, from cirrhosis of the liver—was a tragedy for Turkey (see pages 12–13 and 196–197).

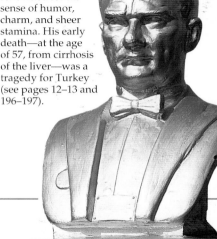

❏ "Civilization" is referred to again and again in Atatürk's speeches: "We shall live as a progressive, civilized nation. We shall follow the road to civilization and get there. We must prove that we are capable of becoming active members of the society of civilized peoples." By "civilization" he meant the secular civilization of the West, as opposed to the religious civilization of Islam. ❏

A bust of Atatürk at Gallipoli

43

Turkey was the only defeated power in World War I that went on to achieve a negotiated settlement with the Allies. As an independent republic, it sought to increase its GNP through industrialization and more efficient agriculture and to play a part in world affairs.

THE REACTION When in 1945 President İnönü turned Turkey into a democracy, there was a popular movement away from Kemalism, or the secular ideology of Atatürk (see pages 12–13), which had been widely misunderstood and opposed as an assault on Islam. This movement back toward religion, known in Turkey as the Reaction, became extremely influential, and ruling parties have ever since felt compelled to make concessions to it for the sake of gaining votes. In an unpopular move, for example, Atatürk had changed the call to prayer from Arabic to Turkish; in 1950 Adnan Menderes' Democrat Party changed it back to Arabic in order to gain popular support. Most political parties since then have exploited the power of Islam for the sake of political advantage, with leaders having themselves photographed at prayer,

Süleyman Demirel led the Justice Party to victory in the 1965 election

❏ Atatürk's belief in the new Turkey never translated itself into a desire to take over other nations' territory. He wished only to keep Turkey for the Turks, and his foreign policy slogan was "Peace at home, peace in the world." ❏

promising to build more mosques, and so on. Since 1949, religious education, abolished under Atatürk, has also crept back by popular demand and continues to expand. Increasing numbers of Turks now make the pilgrimage to Mecca and observe the fasting of Ramadan.

THE 1960 COUP After 10 years of controversial rule by Adnan Menderes, this near-bloodless coup was the army's attempt to return Turkey to Kemalist principles. Menderes' mishandling of the economy had resulted in massive inflation, huge foreign debts, budget deficits, and falling exports. His response to criticism was to muzzle the press and imprison journalists, and he also managed to antagonize the army and alienate Kemalist intellectuals and writers. Tried and hanged by the army, he became

❏ President İnönü, a man of brilliant intellect and a contemporary of Atatürk, inspired the observation that "40 foxes go around in his head, and the muzzle of one fox never touches the tail of the next." Active in politics over 60 years, he knew every move in the game. ❏

44

something of a popular legend. General elections in 1965 returned the Justice Party, under Süleyman Demirel. By the end of Demirel's term of office, in 1971, Turkey was slipping into chaos.

THE 1980 COUP In September 1980 the armed forces, led by General Evren, seized power in a bloodless coup, prompted by the government's failure to deal with economic and political chaos, the ineffectiveness of the police force, and the sudden resurgence of Islamic fundamentalism. They detained thousands of "extremists," establishing law and order at the expense of human rights. The West responded by banning Turkey from the Council of Europe and suspending EEC aid. Elections were reintroduced in 1983. Türgüt Özal and Demirel served as prime minister before Tansu Çiller's election in 1993 as the first woman prime minister, followed by

Istanbul today: capital of a struggling democracy or of a regime of political oppression and abuse?

Necmettin Erbakan as the first Islamic prime minister.

Mrs. Çiller's now discredited government had one notable success— Turkey's entry into the European Customs Union. Under Erbakan Turkey was rejected for full EU membership because of its Islamic culture, and a significant military cooperation accord was reached with the Israelis.

Turkey today again has a fragile secular coalition government, while its frustrated people remain hungry for reforms.

Istanbul

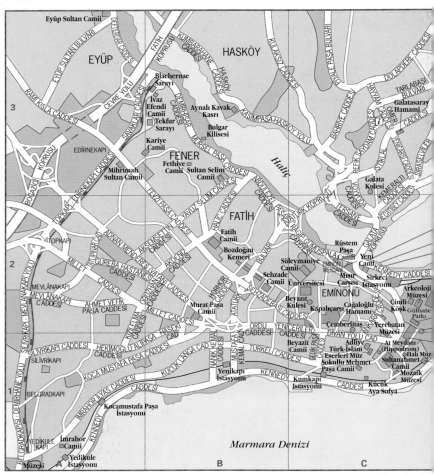

▶▶▶ REGION HIGHLIGHTS

Aya Sofya Müzesi
pages 52–53

Bosphorus Cruise
page 81

City Walls *page 78*

Dolmabahçe Sarayı
page 72

Kariye Camii *page 59*

Süleymaniye Camii
pages 66–67

Sultanahmet Camii
page 67

The Grand Bazaar
pages 56–57

Topkapı Sarayı
pages 76–77

Yerebatan Müzesi
pages 71

46

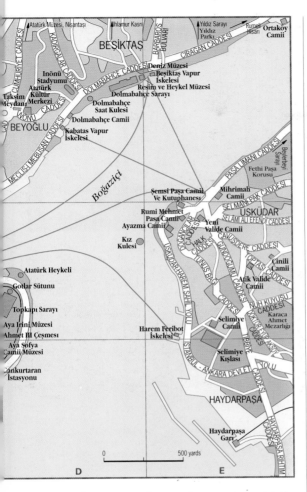

Map labels (as shown):

Atatürk Müzesi, Nişantaşı · Ihlamur Kasrı · Yıldız Sarayı · Rumeli Hisarı · Ortaköy Camii
Yıldız Parkı
BEŞİKTAŞ · BARBAROS BULVARI · ÇIRAĞAN CADDESİ
İnönü Stadyumu · Deniz Müzesi · Beşiktaş Vapur İskelesi · Resim ve Heykel Müzesi
Atatürk Kültür Merkezi · DOLMABAHÇE CADDESİ · Dolmabahçe Sarayı
Taksim Meydanı · Dolmabahçe Saat Kulesi
CUMHURİYET CADDESİ · KADIRGALAR CADDESİ
BEYOĞLU · Dolmabahçe Camii
Kabataş Vapur İskelesi
MECLİSİ MEBUSAN CADDESİ
Boğaziçi
PAŞA LİMANI CADDESİ · Fethi Paşa Korusu · Beylerbeyi Sarayı
Şemsi Paşa Camii Ve Kutuphanesi · Mihrimah Camii
SELMAN AĞA CADDESİ · ÜSKÜDAR
Rumi Mehmet Paşa Camii · SELAMİ ALİ EFFENDİ CADDESİ
Ayazma Camii · Yeni Valide Camii
Kız Kulesi · DOĞANCILAR CADDESİ · HALK CADDESİ · ÇAVUŞDERE CADDESİ
TOPTAŞI CADDESİ · Çinili Camii
ÜSKÜDAR HAREM SAHİL YOLU · GÜNDOĞUMU CADDESİ · Atik Valide Camii
Atatürk Heykeli · TUNUSBAĞ CADDESİ · NUH KUYUSU CADDESİ · Karaca Ahmet Mezarlığı
Gotlar Sütunu
Topkapı Sarayı · Selimiye Camii
Aya İrini Müzesi · Harem Feribot İskelesi · TIBBİYE CADDESİ
Ahmet III Çeşmesi · Selimiye Kışlası
Aya Sofya Camii Müzesi · İSTANBUL - ANKARA DEVLET YOLU
Cankurtaran İstasyonu
HAYDARPAŞA · HAYDARPAŞA RIHTIM CADDESİ
Haydarpaşa Garı

0   500 yards

D   E

ISTANBUL If you want to do more than merely scratch the surface of Istanbul, you need a full two weeks, though few of us ever have this luxury. One week with a carefully planned itinerary (see panel, page 49) will enable you to visit the essentials; if you have less time you may find it helpful to choose days from the suggested itinerary rather than attempting to rush around and see everything in too short a time.

Any first-time visitor to Istanbul immediately becomes aware of the sense of ancient culture, a legacy of the city's distinguished history as capital to three empires, the Roman, the Byzantine, and the Ottoman. For nearly a thousand years this was one of the dominant cities of the Western and Near Eastern worlds.

THE SETTING More than 2,000 years before Christ, the city's position made it a vital link on the trade route from eastern Europe to Asia Minor. Covering the hills on both sides of the estuary of the Bosphorus with the Sea of Marmara, it was the halfway point between the cultures

Previous page: Yeni Cami. Above: barbecued fish on sale at Galata landing stage

Outside Istanbul University

of Europe and the Orient. Its natural harbor, the inlet of the Golden Horn, provided a safe base for both naval and commercial shipping. During the Byzantine period, wealth poured into the city from all corners of the world: silk, ivory, and spices from China and India; wheat and dried fruits from Anatolia and Egypt; and skins and furs from Russia, transported by river and across the Black Sea. All routes then led to Constantinople (modern Istanbul), and the city's colossal waterways were busy with the shipping necessary to serve the capital of a vast empire.

LIFE AND VIBRANCY Besides the staggering wealth of its historical monuments, contemporary Istanbul is also memorable for its vibrant atmosphere, alive with movement and bustle. More magic is added by the city's setting astride the Bosphorus Straits, so that its humming activity is transferred from land to water and back again, as vehicles cross bridges reflected in the Golden Horn and ferries ply their way to virtually every quarter.

"...it must look more splendid than any other city one comes to by sea. Even Father Chantry-Pigg, who did not think that Constantine's city and the Byzantine capital ought to have had all those mosque-domes and minarets built onto its old Byzantine shape... even he thought the famous outline climbing above the Bosphorus and the Sea of Marmara, with all its domes and minarets poised against the evening sky, was very stupendous."
Rose Macaulay, 1956

A tea vendor on Eminönü Square, considered the hub of the city by Istanbulis

CURRENT STATUS When Atatürk moved political power to Ankara and made it the new capital of Turkey in 1923, Istanbul was deprived of its status as a capital city for the first time in 16 centuries. Yet, in the minds of most of the city's inhabitants, it remains Turkey's most important center, the place where almost all cultured and educated Turks would choose to live. It continues to generate around 40 percent of the country's gross national product (GNP) through its commercial and cultural activities, and its population is expected to exceed 12 million by the year 2000 (compared with Ankara's projected population figures of 4 million).

Population growth has been especially high in recent decades, with the number of inhabitants doubling every 15 years since 1950 as country dwellers have flocked to the city in search of a better lifestyle. Their unsightly shantytowns sprawl out from the suburbs of Istanbul, especially on the Asian side, unseen by most visitors. Even so, the consequences are clearly evident in the over-crowding on roads and public transportation and the pressure on the city's struggling infrastructure. If the dreaded century-long earthquake cycle continues (the last major ones were in 1766 and 1894), these shantytowns will most likely be hardest hit.

For now, however, in defiance of all its problems, Istanbul is a positive, active, energetic place, with the confidence of a city assured of its dominant role. Yet so much of its rich past remains for the visitor to discover in its astonishing legacy of historic buildings and monuments: James Wilde, correspondent for *The Times* in London, called the city "the best-kept secret in the world."

ONE-WEEK ITINERARIES
Day 1 AM Topkapı Sarayı.
Day 1 PM Archaeological Museums, Aya Irena, Aya Sofya, Yerebatan Sarayı.
Day 2 AM Sultanahmet Mosque, Hippodrome, Ibrahim Paşa Sarayı.
Day 2 PM Grand Bazaar, Turkish Bath.
Day 3 AM Dolmabahçe Sarayı, ferry from Kabataş to Üsküdar.
Day 3 PM Karaca Ahmet cemetery, Selimiye Barracks, ferry back to Galata Bridge.
Day 4 AM Süleymaniye Mosque, Rüstem Paşa Mosque, Spice Bazaar.
Day 4 PM Along the Golden Horn, Kariye Museum, Tekfur Sarayı, Pierre Loti Café for sunset.
Day 5 AM and PM Bosphorus cruise up to Anadolu Kavağı and back.
Day 6 AM Princes' Islands cruise.
Day 6 PM Yedikule and walk along the Land Walls. Sunset view from Galata Tower.

STAMBOUL
This is the Western name for the oldest quarter of the city, the original Constantinople. Aya Sofya, Sultanahmet Camii (the Blue Mosque), the Grand Bazaar, the Topkapı Palace, and the Süleymaniye Mosque are all found in this area.

Orientation

Istanbul is divided into its European and Asian sides by the Bosphorus. The famous monuments lie almost exclusively on the European side, as do the wealthier suburbs. The Asian side, traditionally a place of quiet retreat, has become home to large numbers of migrants seeking a better life in the city. Overcrowding has contributed to a deterioration of its utilities and rising levels of pollution.

BEYOĞLU This huge quarter full of grand 19th-century Italianate buildings lies on the European side, known in Ottoman times as Pera. Before the capital moved to Ankara in the 1920s, it was home to all the European embassies. After the move it went into decline, but then experienced a revival and now bustles with jazz bars, late-night tavernas, movie theaters, and shops such as furniture restorers and antiquarian bookstores. A tramway was reinstalled in 1990, and pedestrians-only zones have been created, notably in the main street, **Istiklal Caddesi**. At the upper end of this is **Taksim Square**, the commercial hub of the city, busy with traffic and studded with modern hotels and fast-food restaurants. Famous landmarks in Beyoğlu include the conical **Galata Tower**, built by the Genoese in 1348 (it now houses a restaurant and nightclub), and the elegant but faded **Pera Palas**, built to accommodate travelers on the Orient Express and still functioning as a hotel.

BOĞAZI (BOSPHORUS) The 20-mile-long straits between the Black Sea and the Mediterranean have largely created Istanbul's character. Two bridges link the European and Asian sides. The first, known as the old **Bosphorus Bridge** (**Boğazi Köprü**), was built in 1973. The second, **Fatih Sultan Mehmet Köprüsü**, was completed in 1988 and spans the narrowest point, between the famous fortresses of **Rumeli Hisarı** and **Anadolu Hisarı**, where the Persian King Darius built his bridge of boats in 512 BC.

The Bosphorus Bridge, linking the Asian and European sides of the straits

HALİÇ (GOLDEN HORN) This inlet of the Bosphorus, which separates old Stamboul from Beyoğlu, originally formed Constantinople's safe natural harbor. Now it is crossed by three bridges: to the north the Haliç expressway bridge, linking the Bosphorus Bridge to the international airport; in the center the Atatürk Bridge, running up under the **Aqueduct of Valens**; and to the south the new Galata Bridge, which recently replaced the old Galata Bridge after an explosion in one of its colorful floating restaurants blew a hole in it. The Stamboul shoreline of the Golden Horn makes a very pleasant quiet stroll.

NİŞANTAŞI North of Beyoğlu, farther away from the old heart of Istanbul, Nişantaşı is the most fashionable part of Istanbul, with chic hotels and restaurants and sophisticated shopping. The main shopping street is **Teşvikiye Caddesi**, turning into **Rumeli Caddesi**.

EMİNÖNÜ SQUARE
Considered the hub of the city by its inhabitants, this perpetually bustling square lies below the Topkapı on the western shore of the Golden Horn. All the boat stations are to be found here, as well as the European train station, Sirkeci.

In a crowded city, every space is valuable: here a flat roof serves as play area and workshop

51

MINARET COUNTING
Aya Sofya has four minarets and the Blue Mosque has six, so you can always tell them apart in the Istanbul skyline. The norm for other mosques throughout the city is just a single minaret.

SULTANAHMET This district takes its name from **Sultanahmet Camii**, the **Blue Mosque** (see page 67), and is the heart of the old city. The city's major sights are concentrated here, within easy walking distance of each other. The main entrance of the Blue Mosque faces the long, thin **At Meydanı** (**Hippodrome**), recognizable by the Egyptian obelisk in its center. The side entrance, the one open to tourists, takes you out onto **Aya Sofya Meydanı**, the pedestrians-only, landscaped gardens that lie between the Blue Mosque and **Aya Sofya** (see pages 52–53), the domed 6th-century Byzantine basilica that was the largest building in the world for the first thousand years of its existence. It is now a museum. Behind it lie Istanbul's main **archaeological museums** (see pages 70–71), and just behind these is the entrance to the **Topkapı Sarayı**, former pleasure palace of the Ottoman sultans and now also a museum (see pages 76–77).

ÜSKÜDAR This sprawling suburb on the Asian side of the Bosphorus, directly opposite the Sultanahmet district, offers superb views over the Istanbul skyline. It also contains the wild and picturesque **Karaca Ahmet Mezarlığı**, the largest Muslim cemetery in the world.

A jewelry seller in the courtyard of the Blue Mosque

INGENIOUS DESIGN
The original architects—
the Greeks Anthemius of
Tralles and Isidorus of
Miletus—designed a vast
platform over 20 feet
deep to form the founda-
tions. Their plans were
carried out by 10,000
workmen supervised by
100 master masons.
Special bricks made at
Rhodes were used in the
dome, so light that 12 of
them weighed the same
as a single ordinary brick.

▶▶▶ Aya Sofya Müzesi
(Haghia Sophia Basilica)   *46C1*

Aya Sofya Meydanı, Sultanahmet
Open: Tue–Sun 9:30–5. Admission charge
This extraordinary building, a masterpiece of Byzantine
architecture, embodies the different phases of the city's
history more than any other structure in Istanbul.

Many incarnations The first church on this site was conse-
crated by Emperor Constantine in AD 360 to Divine
Wisdom (Haghia Sophia in Greek) in the 4th century, and
was enlarged by his son Constantius to become the epis-
copal church of the capital. In 404 and 532 this building
and the church that succeeded it were burned down
during revolts, and it was in February 532 that Emperor
Justinian ordered work to begin on the current structure,
then the largest church in Christendom. In 1453, on
the very day that Constantinople fell to the Turks,
Mehmet the Conqueror entered the basilica and
ordered it to be converted to a mosque named Aya
Sofya. The building remained a mosque until the
early 1930s when, in recognition of its unique
and pivotal role in Byzantine and Ottoman
history, Atatürk turned it into a museum. It was
at this time that the American Byzantine
Institute embarked on excavation work and
on the restoration of the mosaics, which was
to continue for some 30 years.

Earthquakes have taken their toll on the overambitious
dome, which has caved in several times over the centuries, to be shored up again each time by increasingly
larger buttresses. These massive structures make it difficult to work out the shape of the original ground plan of
the basilica from the outside, and the minarets, added by
various sultans along with yet more buttresses, help to
further disguise the original. The outlines of the building
today seem to suggest an enormous crab, tensely poised.

*The distinctive outlines
of Aya Sofya, a master-
piece of Byzantine
architecture*

The interior The internal architecture of Aya Sofya remains as stupendous today as it must have been in the early days. You enter the precinct through an attractive courtyard garden, in which are scattered various tombs of Ottoman sultans to your right, and the old kitchens and ablutions fountain to your left.

As you enter the vestibule, look for the 9th-century bronze-covered doors into the narthex, and for the lovely 10th-century mosaic showing the Virgin Mary holding the baby Jesus, with Constantine I offering her the city on one side and Justinian giving her a model of the basilica on the other. There is another notable mosaic just above the main door to the basilica itself. Dating from the late 9th century, it depicts Christ enthroned and holding out his right hand in blessing, while an inscription on his left hand bears the message: "Peace be unto you. I am the light of the world."

Inside, the stonework of the nave is truly awe-inspiring; the gigantic green and purple columns supporting the dome, the walls sheathed in marbles of all colors, and above all the sheer scale of the interior space combine to produce a spectacular sight.

The huge alabaster urns on either side of the entrance were donated by Sultan Murat III, and were once used as ablutions fountains, while Süleyman the Magnificent gave the two candelabra on either side of the *mihrab* (the prayer niche facing toward Mecca). The great chandelier hanging from the center of the dome was given by Sultan Ahmet III. The tops of the columns are dominated by huge disks bearing the names—in Arabic script—of Allah and Muhammad, along with those of Abu Bakr, Hussein, Hassan, Ali, and Umar, the key figures of early Islamic history.

On the left-hand side of the nave as you enter is the stairway to a cobbled ramp that zigzags up to the galleries just below the dome (*Open* daily 9:30–11:30, and 1–4). The south gallery contains the celebrated Gates of Heaven and Hell, false doors of marble decorated with elaborate reliefs from which they take their name. The basilica's most magnificent mosaics are concentrated in the galleries, where the Ottomans inadvertently preserved them in the 18th century by covering them with a thick layer of whitewash. The most famous of all is the 13th-century *Deësis*, or *Prayer*, mosaic, considered to be one of the finest of the late Byzantine period. Against a gold background, the figure of Christ is flanked by an expressive Virgin and an agonized John the Baptist.

The greatest internal damage the basilica has sustained throughout its long history was in 1204, when the Catholic armies of the Fourth Crusade stormed it, stripping it bare and hacking the altar to pieces.

ANCIENT PILFERING
To make the new basilica the most magnificent in existence, precious materials, fine marbles, and sculptures were plundered from the most celebrated temples of the ancient world. The eight green breccia columns were taken from the Temple of Artemis at Ephesus, and further columns were pillaged from temples in Baalbek (Lebanon), Athens, and Delos.

53

The 13th-century Deësis *mosaic, considered the finest of Aya Sofya's mosaics*

THE SWEATING COLUMN
Near the entrance to the gallery stairway stands a porous column known as the Sweating Column of Saint Gregory; for centuries the moisture exuded by this column has been said to cure eye diseases and infertility.

Islam originated in the early 7th century in Mecca on the Arabian peninsula with the charismatic figure of Muhammad. It spread to Turkey in the 11th century with the arrival of the Seljuks from Persia, and remained the state religion until 1923, when Atatürk officially secularized the Turkish republic.

CLEANLINESS NEXT TO GODLINESS
"He who performs the ablution thoroughly will extract all sin from his body, even though it may be lurking under his fingernails."
The Prophet Muhammad

54

Muslim prayer beads

A selection of editions of the Koran on a stall in Istanbul's book market

ALLAH IS ONE
"'The great stumbling block to Moslems,' said Father Chantry-Pigg, 'is the Blessed Trinity. To a people who hear the One God proclaimed so many times a day, and so loudly, the Triune God raises all kinds of difficulties in the mind.'"
Rose Macaulay, 1956

Later called the Prophet, Muhammad proclaimed himself the mouthpiece of Allah: in no way divine himself, he was simply the medium through which Allah had chosen to reveal his word. Muhammad was illiterate, but the Koran (literally "Recitation") was revealed to him in bursts over a period of 22 years ending in 632, the year of his death at the age of 62. The entire text of the Koran consists of God speaking to man, offering divine instruction and guidance in the Arabic language. Because of this, Muslims all over the world, whatever their own nationality or language, pray and recite the Koran in Arabic, having learned it by heart even though they may not understand its meaning. One consequence of this phenomenon is that classical Arabic has altered less over the last 1,300 years than any other language.

Islam, meaning "submission to the will of God," spread rapidly from the Arabian peninsula as a result of the exhortation to *jihad* (holy war), imposing an obligation on all believers to spread the word to unbelievers. Within 10 years, Arab armies had conquered Syria, Egypt, Mesopotamia, and the Persian Sassanid Empire. The tolerance shown by Muslims to Christians and Jews was frequently in stark contrast to the persecution these groups had suffered previously, and many converted to Islam voluntarily.

Relationship with Christianity and Judaism Christians and Jews are referred to in the Koran as "People of the Book" (that is, of the Bible), a separate category from straightforward unbelievers. This is because Islam regards Allah as being the same God as the one worshipped by Christians and Jews. Its main point of

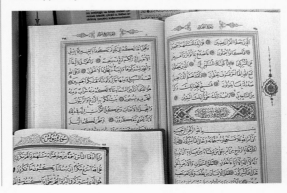

conflict with Christianity lies with the Christian doctrine of the Trinity and the belief that Jesus was the Son of God, rather than merely a prophet like Muhammad. The Koran affirms the righteousness of previous prophets and revelations: "Surely, We sent down the Torah full of guidance and light," and "We caused Jesus son of Mary to follow in their footsteps...and We gave him the Gospel." Muhammad is claimed to be the "seal" of the prophets, however, the last one with the final word.

The Five Pillars The five basic tenets of faith as laid down by the Koran are known as the Five Pillars. The first is the declaration of faith that "there is no God but God, and Muhammad is the Messenger of God" (proclaimed in the calls to prayer from mosque minarets). The second is the act of prayer, made five times a day—at dawn, noon, mid-afternoon, sunset, and before bed. Ritual ablution of hands, feet, and face is compulsory before prayer. The third is *zakat*, or alms tax, a yearly charitable donation. The fourth is fasting during Ramadan, the month in which the first revelation of the Koran was given. The 30-day fast during daylight hours applies to food, drink, and smoking; the old, the sick, and children of up to about eight are exempt. The fifth is the pilgrimage (*hajj*) to the Kaaba, the House of Allah at Mecca, to be undertaken at least once in a lifetime by any Muslim who can afford it.

Islamic culture When it was at its peak, between the 7th and 13th centuries, Islamic culture was responsible for many great intellectual and scientific discoveries, some of which were later borrowed by the Western world. Arabic numerals, geometry, and algebra all came to western Europe via the Islamic traders of Spain and North Africa. In the field of medicine, meanwhile, many important advances were made by philosopher-scientists such as the 11th-century physician Avicenna.

Midday prayers: every Muslim should stop work for prayers five times a day

WOMEN AND ISLAM
Muslim men are allowed to take up to four wives, but it is now rare for them to do so, especially in Turkey, and most have only one. Traditionally a man may divorce a woman, but not vice versa, though the law has now been reformed in many countries, including Turkey. The Koran exhorts women to cover all parts of the body that might be a temptation to men, but again this is loosely interpreted: most educated Turkish women, especially in the cities, now wear Western-style clothes.

The map shows the Grand Bazaar area of Istanbul with streets and landmarks including:

Beyazıt Kulesi, MERCAN CADDESI, FUAT PAŞA CADDESI, SURURI, CAKMAKCILAR YOKUŞU, CARICILAR SOKAGI, MAHMUT PAŞA YOKUŞU, TARAKCI CAFER SOKAGI, TARAKCILAR CADDESI, İstanbul Universitesi Merkez, TAYA HATUN, Yolgeçen Han, Pastırmacı Han, Mahmut Paşa Hamamı, SULTAN MEKTEBI SOKAGI, BEZCILER SOKAGI, BAKIRCILAR CADDESI, CADIRCILAR CADDESI, Astarcı Han, İç Cebeci Han, Çukur Han, İmameli Han, Kalcılar Han, Sarnıçlı Han, Zincirli Han, AYNACILAR SOKAGI, Çuhacılar Hanı, MAHMUT PAŞA SOKAGI, BEYAZIT MEYDANI, Havuzlu, HALICILAR CARSISI CADDESI, İç Bedesten, KUYUMCULAR CADDESI, Nuru Osmaniye Camii, YORGANCILAR CADDESI, Ali Paşa Ham, PTT, FERACECILER SOKAGI, Sandal Bedesteni, NURU OSMANIYE SOKAGI, VEZIRHANI CADDESI, Beyazıt Camii, Sahaflar Çarşısı, Bodrum Han, KESECILER CADDESI, Rabia Hanı, Yağcı Hanı, Nuru Osmaniye, BEYAZIT, FESCILER SOKAGI, KALPAKCILAR CADDESI, OKCULARBAŞI CADDESI, BALMUMCULAR SOKAGI, CARSIKAPI SOKAGI, BILEYCILER SOKAGI, TAVUK PAZARI SOKAGI, YENICERILER CADDESI, TIYATRO CADDESI, Çemberlitaş, Vezir Hanı, Atik Ali Paşa Camii, Çemberlitaş Hamamı

0 — 100 yards

56

Walk

The Grand Bazaar

Beginning at Istanbul University, this walk wanders through the Grand Bazaar—the world's largest bazaar and an essential expedition for all

Colorful traditional slippers

visitors to Istanbul—and ends with a well-deserved Turkish bath. The walk described takes about two hours; the Bazaar is open 8:30–7, except Sundays. Admission free.

Start by taking a taxi to Beyazıt Meydanı. At the back of this busy square, up a few steps, is a large gateway in Moorish style that opens onto the grounds of Istanbul University, on the site of the palace of Mehmet the Conqueror. The only building of any age is now the **Beyazıt Tower** (1823), straight ahead. From the upper gallery there are fine views.

Return to the Beyazıt Meydanı and walk through the attractive marble-paved courtyard of the **Beyazıt Camii**. Descend the steps at the back to reach some sidewalk cafés. From here an alleyway leads to the right into the **Sahaflar Çarşısı**, Istanbul's premier book market.

Leave by the far end and cross the busy **Çadırcılar Caddesi**, Street of the Tentmakers, to enter the Grand Bazaar at the **Fesçiler Caddesi** (Fez Makers Street), which, with the demise of the fez, now sells denim and canvas bags.

A glittering array of brassware

In accordance with Asian tradition, all merchants in the Bazaar are grouped together by trade in order to ensure the keenest competition between them. The Grand Bazaar (Turkish Kapalı Çarşısı, meaning "Covered Market") has occupied the same site since the 15th century in many incarnations, burning down at regular intervals—most recently in 1954. As you walk through, look up at the tilework high on the walls and pillars. The streets are estimated to total 5 miles in length, with 4,000 shops.

Bear left for refreshment at **Havuzlu Restaurant**, considered the best in the Bazaar. From here head right into **Halıcılar Çarşısı Caddesi** (Carpet sellers Street) until you reach the little fork right into the **İç Bedestan**, the heart of the Bazaar and the oldest part.

Leave by the opposite exit and walk in a straight line (never easy here) to reach **Kalpakçılar Caddesi** (Fur Cap Makers Street), the main thoroughfare. Turn left and, after a short detour into **Sandal Bedestan**, a 16th-century hall where carpet auctions used to be held, leave the Bazaar by the attractive Nuruosmaniye Gate. Turn right along

Tavukpazarı Sokağı to reach the Column of Constantine (AD 330), its dark porphyry drums reinforced with metal bands. Beside this is **Vezir Hanı**, once Istanbul's principal slave market, next door to which stands the **Çemberlitaş Bath**.

Bargaining is expected

Part of the painted deco-
ration in Mehmet the
Conqueror's Fatih Camii

58

NEW ROLES
Most churches in
Istanbul were converted
into mosques in the 15th
century by the conquer-
ing Ottomans, who added
minarets externally and
mihrabs (prayer niches)
and *minbars* (pulpits)
internally. Others served
as warehouses, arsenals,
or grainstores.

*A detail of one of the
superb 14th-century
mosaics in Kariye Camii,
which mark a turning
point in Byzantine art*

Churches

▶ Aya Irini Müzesi (Haghia Eirene Museum) 46C2

Between Aya Sofya and the Topkapı Palace, Sultanahmet
The basilica of Haghia Eirene (Divine Peace), tucked away
in a corner of the Court of the Janissaries as you approach
the Topkapı Palace, was one of the first Christian sanctuaries of Byzantium. The present building is virtually
contemporary with Haghia Sophia. In Ottoman times it
served as the Janissaries' arsenal, and now it is used as a
venue for concerts during the Istanbul Festival.

▶ Bulgar Kilisesi (Saint Stephen of the Bulgars) 46B3

Mürsel Paşa Caddesi, Fener
This extraordinary church, made entirely of cast iron, was
prefabricated in Vienna in 1871 and shipped down the
Danube and across the Black Sea to be assembled here on
the shoreline of the Golden Horn. It is usually locked, but
a caretaker who is often found in the garden can be per-
suaded to open it for a small donation. Istanbul's tiny
Bulgarian community still worships here regularly.

▶▶ Fethiye Camii (Church of the Theotokos Pammakaristos) 46B3

Fethiyekapası Sokak
Open: Tue–Sun 9:30–5. Admission free
This large red and white stone church was the seat of the
Greek Orthodox patriarchate until 1568, when it was con-
verted into a mosque.

Following restoration work by the Byzantine Institute,
the mosque area has been divided off, allowing part of the
church to be turned into a museum exhibiting the 14th-
century mosaics that survive in the dome and the side
chapel. It is open only with special permission from the
authorities at Aya Sofya.

▶▶ Imrahor Camii (Saint John the Baptist of Studius) 46A1

Imam Asır Sokak, off Imrahor Ilyas Bey Caddesi, near Yedikule
There is no entry fee to see this impressive ruined church
built in AD 463 and for years the focus of the Byzantine
monastic movement. An important center of intellectual
life, it became home to the University of Constantinople
in the early 15th century. Later that century it was turned
into a mosque by Beyazit II. In 1894 it was abandoned

after a severe earthquake, which brought down part of the minaret. Among the remains are some fine columns and a lovely mosaic pavement.

The breathtakingly colorful mosaics of Kariye Camii

►►► Kariye Camii
(Saint Saviour in Chora) 46A3
Kariye Meydanı, near Edirnekapı
Museum open: Wed–Mon 9–4:30. Admission charge
The magnificent early 14th-century frescoes and mosaics in this church reveal a new style of Byzantine art, anticipating the Renaissance in its spirituality and vitality, with a striking use of color and a tremendous sense of passion. The American Byzantine Institute restored them between 1948 and 1958, and today they cover the walls in images of astonishing variety, including scenes from the lives of Christ and the Virgin Mary, Christ's miracles, portraits of the saints, and the Last Judgment. Perhaps the most celebrated of all is the fresco of the Harrowing of Hell, between the apse and the dome, in which Christ is shown forcibly wresting Adam and Eve from their tombs.

The Byzantine name Saint Saviour in Chora means "in the country," as the church stood outside the original city walls. Now a museum, it is set in a pretty cobbled courtyard, away from the traffic of central Istanbul.

► Küçük Aya Sofya
(Saints Sergius and Bacchus) 46C1
Küçük Aya Sofya Caddesi, Sultanahmet
One of the most beautiful Byzantine churches surviving in Istanbul, Küçük Aya Sofya was built by Justinian in AD 527, before the great basilica of the same name, which it is said to resemble in miniature. The interior has an original carved marble frieze above the red and green marble columns. The garden courtyard, heavily overgrown, has an almost rural feel. The church was converted to a mosque in about 1500 and is used as such today. The entrance is through a picturesque quarter of old wooden Ottoman houses with characteristic overhanging balconies. Leave a tip for the caretaker.

WOOD ONLY
After the Ottoman conquest, Christians in Istanbul were not allowed to build churches with domes or masonry roofs, lest their silhouettes should detract from the new mosques. From the 15th century, all Christian churches in the city were therefore built as small basilicas with timbered roofs; a good example is the Greek Orthodox patriarchate church of Saint George (1720).

MOSAIC MASTERPIECES
The 14th-century mosaics and frescoes of the Kariye Camii are held to be the finest examples of Byzantine mosaic art in the world, splendidly preserved thanks to the whitewash with which the Ottomans painted the walls during the centuries when the building was used as a mosque.

Turks love music, and in Istanbul you will be struck by the number of tape cassette stores offering a variety of styles. "Arab-esque" or taverna music can frequently be heard in shops, teahouses, and even on buses, while live music is frequently played in restaurants, especially in the evenings.

JAZZ RENAISSANCE
Istanbul has recently become a flourishing jazz center, featuring performers of international stature as well as local talent. The best venues are Kerem Görsev Jazz Bar in Tesvikiye and Café Gramafon in Tünel.

60

Folk music in an Istanbul restaurant

TURKISH POP MUSIC
American travel writer Bill Bryson could not bear the sound of it blaring from every radio. He described is as "a man having a vasectomy without anaesthetic, to a background accompaniment of frantic sitar-playing."

A traditional reed flute, or ney

Turkish folk music Apart from the special folkloric evenings held for tourists in cities, Turkish folk music is also still performed in its natural setting, at village weddings and festivals, as an accompaniment to dancing by segregated groups of men and women. More specialized is *ozan*, the music of the folk poets or *aşıks* ("those in love") of Anatolia, who accompany themselves on the *saz*, a kind of lute with three sets of strings. *Aşıks* still wander the towns and villages of central Anatolia, and many of them—notably the blind Aşık Veysel, who died in 1973—have recorded their music on cassette.

Kurdish folk music differs markedly from Turkish folk music: its *dengbeis* (bards), the best-known of whom are Sivan, Perwer, and Temo, sing of Kurdish myths and legends and the Kurdish struggle for freedom, to the accompaniment of haunting wind instruments. In the cities you may hear the style called *özgün*, the protest music of Turkey. The most famous of *özgün* musicians is Livaneli, whose cassettes—some of them recorded with the famous Greek musician Theodorakis—are widely available. Ahmet Kaya köy is another well-known singer with a style similar to Livaneli.

Turkish Ottoman and religious music The classical music of the Ottoman court can be heard on the radio or in concert. Ensembles of more than 30 play traditional instruments such as the *ney* (a reed flute), the *tambur* (a long-necked lute), and the *kemençe* (a three-stringed fiddle, held vertically). The dominant religious music is that composed by the Mevlevi order of dervishes. You can hear it performed on the *ney* and the *kudum* (small kettledrums) live in Istanbul or at the annual Mevlana Festival in Konya (see pages 24–25 and 204–205).

The development of tile and ceramic art began in Turkey in the 11th century, when the Seljuks moved westward from their newly established capital in Persia. When in 1097 they made Konya their western capital, the town soon became one of their leading tile and ceramic production centers.

Konya ware The Seljuk polychrome technique, known as *minai* (from *mina*, meaning "enamel" in Persian), was brought from Persia. The ceramic slabs were first painted in pale blues, greens, or turquoise, covered in a transparent glaze, and fired. Then they were decorated in black and vitrifiable colors such as red, yellow, blue, and brown and fired again. The tiles were usually star-shaped and used a blend of Persian-style motifs and images of hunting dogs and horses, inspired by the steppelands of central Asia. There are some good examples in early Seljuk palaces such as that of Alaeddin Keykubad I (1220–1235) beside Lake Beyşehir.

Iznik ware In the 15th century the center of production moved to Iznik—a traditional center of Byzantine earthenware—in response to a sudden and unprecedented need for fine tiles and ceramics to decorate the palaces and mosques springing up in the new Ottoman capital, Istanbul. During the 16th century styles gradually became more refined, with delicate "blue and white" decoration used to imitate Chinese motifs such as wave scrolls and lotus flowers. Turquoise, green, and red (produced from a thick clay rich in iron found only near Erzurum in eastern Turkey, and especially characteristic of the period 1560–1600) extended the range of colors; flower motifs became popular; and the Iznik production remained highly successful until the 17th century.

Kütahya ware From the early 17th to the mid-18th century, tiles of a lower quality were produced in great numbers in Kütahya. In the 20th century, the industry has undergone a revival, producing many good-quality tiles.

THE BEST DISPLAY
The best place to see a full range of ceramics and tiles is the Çinili Köşk, the Tile Museum in Istanbul. It shares the courtyard, entrance fee, and opening hours with the Archaeological Museum (see page 70).

61

A section of Iznik tiles from the Eyüp mosque complex, showing the exceptional beauty attained in both their colors and their motifs

Panels of Iznik tiles decorate the walls of the shrine to Eyüp, one of the holiest places in the Muslim world

MOSQUE ETIQUETTE
Shoes must always be removed before entering a mosque, and women should cover their head and shoulders. You will be struck by the lack of furniture (to allow room for prostrations during prayer) and also by the relaxed atmosphere, far removed from that of the average church. Working mosques are open daily and can be visited at any time except during prayers. There are no entry fees, though the shoe attendant generally expects a small tip.

Ablutions fountains at the Eyüp mosque complex, which houses the sacred tomb of the Prophet Muhammad's friend and standard-bearer

The baroque türbe (tomb) of Mehmet the Conqueror, rebuilt after an earthquake in 1766

Mosques

►► Atik Valide Camii   47E2
Kartal Baba Caddesi, Üsküdar
Built in 1583 by the famous architect Sinan (see page 65), this mosque complex dominates the Üsküdar skyline. It is considered to be his finest building in Istanbul after the Süleymaniye (see pages 66–67) and one of the city's best examples of Ottoman architecture. Its refined decorative features now stand in contrast to the poverty—even squalor—of its present-day surroundings.

►►► Aya Sofya Camii   46C1
See pages 52–53.

► Çinili Camii (Tiled Mosque)   47E2
Çavus Dere Caddesi, Üsküdar
This small sanctuary built in 1640 is an excellent example of a highly decorated Ottoman mosque, covered with magnificent Iznik tiles, predominantly blue in color. From here there are superb views over Istanbul and its skyline.

►► Eyüp Sultan Camii   46A3
Cami Kebir Caddesi, Eyüp
The most sacred shrine in Istanbul is built around the tomb of Eyüp, friend and standard-bearer of the Prophet Muhammad, who is reputed to have been killed here in AD 670 during the Arab siege of Constantinople. The current mosque complex was built in 1800, earlier structures

having been destroyed by earthquakes. The tomb lies off the courtyard in a curiously shaped room whose walls are covered with Iznik tiles of exceptional beauty.

▶ Fatih Camii
(Mosque of the Conqueror)   46B2
Tophane Sokağı Fatih
This vast complex, built for Mehmet the Conqueror from 1463 to 1470, was the largest and most elaborate in the entire Ottoman Empire at that time. Mehmet's express intention was to outdo Aya Sofya, the symbol of Christian Byzantium, and according to tradition he cut off the architect's hands in rage on discovering that the dome of his mosque was slightly smaller than that of its rival. The "Külliye" or theological college also included eight *madrasas* (schools), a hospital, a caravansary, public baths, a hospice, a soup kitchen, and a graveyard.

An earthquake destroyed most of the complex in 1766, and it was immediately rebuilt to a different plan. The mosque's exterior features are of most interest. The attractive courtyard has cypress trees surrounding the central *şadırvan* (ablutions fountain) and contains fragments of marble columns that are thought to be the remains of the earlier Church of the Holy Apostles, the ruins of which served as a convenient quarry for the new mosque.

A Muslim at prayer

▶▶ Fethiye Camii   46B3
See page 58.

▶▶ Imrahor Camii   46A1
See page 58.

▶▶▶ Kariye Camii   46A3
See page 59.

▶ Küçük Aya Sofya   46C1
See page 59.

▶ Mihrimah Sultan Camii   46A3
Edirnekapısı
One of the most prominent landmarks on the Istanbul skyline, this mosque stands on a raised terrace just inside the Edirne Gate, on the summit of the sixth of Istanbul's seven hills and the highest point in the old city. Built by Sinan for Princess Mihrimah, favorite daughter of Süleyman the Magnificent, the mosque has a delicate, almost feminine feel. Notice especially the marble and granite porch columns as you enter and the exquisite white carved marble of the *minbar* (pulpit).

▶▶ Rüstem Paşa Camii   46C2
Kutucular Caddesi, Eminönü
Built in 1561, this is one of Sinan's most beautiful and unusual mosques, hidden away in a narrow street inland from the Spice Bazaar and Eminönü Square. It stands above a row of vaulted shops and has internal steps that lead to an open courtyard among the rooftops. Supposedly, it's the only one of its kind in the city. The most famous feature, however, is its extensive and beautiful tilework, all from the most distinguished Iznik period (1555–1620).

63

TERRACE WITH A VIEW
From the Eyüp mosque complex, take the path up through the famous Ottoman cemetery for 10 minutes to reach the Pierre Loti Café, a simple place with a wonderful rustic terrace with fine sunset views over the Golden Horn.

MINARET TECHNOLOGY
Mosques are always recognizable by their minarets—the tall, thin towers from which the call to prayer is made. The *muezzin* used to climb the stairs to the top to summon the faithful, but nowadays his voice is usually broadcast by tape recorder and loudspeaker.

After the Turkish conquest of Constantinople in 1453, there developed the distinctive style of art and architecture that we now think of as typically Ottoman. It reached its peak in the reign of Süleyman the Magnificent (1520–1566), and the buildings now considered to be most typical of the Ottoman style are the grand imperial mosques such as the Fatih (see page 63), the Süleymaniye, and the Sultanahmet (Blue Mosque; see pages 66–67).

EXOTIC DRINKING WATER

The fountain house of Ahmet III, built in 1728 at the entrance to the Topkapı Palace, is Istanbul's most magnificent, a perfect example of Turkish rococo architecture, with every surface elaborately decorated in rich golds, greens, and reds.

64

Public fountains were a precious source of free, pure water in Ottoman times

Ottoman institutions These mosques lay at the center of huge religious, educational, and philanthropic foundations called *külliyes*, which consisted of *madrasas* (theological schools), *mekteps* (elementary schools), a *darüşşifa* (hospital), a *han* (inn), and *imaret* (public kitchen). Travelers would visit the *külliyes* and get free food and lodging for three days after their arrival at the city, and the district's poor people would also get food here. The *hans*, built around a courtyard like most Ottoman buildings, provided all the services necessary to traveling merchants, even blacksmiths; these inns became the key to Istanbul's thriving commerce during Ottoman times. Recently, some of these remarkably advanced Ottoman institutions have been restored to serve as libraries, student dormitories, and clinics.

Two other notable Ottoman foundations were the *hamam*, or public baths, over 100 of which still function today; and the *çeşme*, or public fountains, more than 700 of which are still standing. In Ottoman times, attendants would stand at these fountains handing out cups of clean drinking water free of charge to passersby.

The typical Ottoman mosque has a large central dome with cascades of smaller domes clustered around it, off-set by the tall, thin minarets. The basilica of **Aya Sofya** (see pages 52–53) is thought to have provided the inspiration for the dome, but the other elements are original to the Ottoman style.

Süleyman's patronage The arts flourished under Süleyman the Magnificent, and the hallmark of this period was its scrupulous attention to and delight in detail. This is clearly evident in superbly illustrated and decorated copies of the Koran, as well as in ceramics, textiles, and paintings. Ottoman rulers such as Süleyman were not only connoisseurs and patrons of book-binding, calligraphy, and illumination, but were also themselves prolific authors, especially of poetry. The art of calligraphy was highly esteemed, and its techniques were applied both to books and to the design of monumental inscriptions for mosques in Istanbul. Calligraphy even appeared on garments, such as the talismanic shirts worn for

THE GREAT SINAN
Sinan, the greatest and most prolific of all Ottoman architects, built an astonishing 81 large mosques, 50 smaller ones, 55 *madrasas*, 19 mausoleums, 15 public kitchens, 3 hospitals, 6 aqueducts, 32 palaces, 22 public baths, and 2 bridges. No fewer than 84 of his buildings remain standing in Istanbul. His achievement is all the more remarkable in view of the fact that he did not build his first mosque until he was 50; he completed his masterpiece, the Selimiye Mosque at Edirne, at the age of 85.

65

Sultanahmet Camii, or the Blue Mosque, built in the early 17th century for Sultan Ahmet I and one of the most beautiful of Istanbul's imperial mosques

protection on the battlefield, decorated with victorious verses from the Koran. All court costumes were elaborately decorated with leaf and flower patterns, with such lavish use of gold and silver thread and costly materials and jewels (Süleyman's parade helmet and mace were encrusted with turquoises, rubies, and gold) that the Hapsburg ambassador to the sultan's court was spellbound: "...everywhere the brilliance of gold, silver, purple, and satin... No mere words could give an adequate idea of the novelty of the sight."

Sinan The name of a single architect, Sinan, is virtually synonymous with the architecture of the Ottoman era. The protégé of Süleyman was born to Christian parents in Kayseri, Cappadocia, and was recruited into the sultan's service at the age of 20. Having served in the Janissaries as a military engineer, he was promoted in his late 40s to the position of Chief of the Imperial Architects. By the time of his death in 1588, at the age of 100, he had changed the skyline of Istanbul forever. This contemporary of Michelangelo and Leonardo da Vinci remains little-known in the West, perhaps because nonfigurative art is not widely appreciated there.

The courtyard at Sokullu Mehmet Paşa Camii, built by Sinan for one of the greatest grand viziers

*The sumptuous
Süleymaniye Camii,
built by the great archi-
tect Sinan as a tribute to
his patron Süleyman the
Magnificent*

Mosques

▶▶ Sokullu Mehmet Paşa Camii   *46C1*

Sehit Mehmet Paşa Yokusu, Sultanahmet
This lovely mosque lies down a steep hill below the Blue
Mosque, on the way to Küçük Aya Sofya. A minor
masterpiece, it was built by Sinan for Sokullu Mehmet,
one of the greatest grand viziers of the Ottoman Empire.
The exterior courtyard, with its little domed roofs around
the sides, is particularly charming and it still houses a
Koranic school. Inside, there are some splendid tile
panels, especially around the prayer niche. The square
of black stone set above the entrance is from the Kaaba
in Mecca.

▶▶▶ Süleymaniye Camii   *46C2*

Hesapçeşme Caddesi, Beyazit
Universally considered the finest and most sumptuous of
Istanbul's imperial mosques, the Süleymaniye was built
by the great architect Sinan (see page 65) as a tribute to his
patron master, Sultan Süleyman the Magnificent.

Second in size only to the Fatih complex (see page 63),
the Süleymaniye is the largest of the many mosques that
Sinan built in Istanbul. It was begun in 1550 and surprisingly took only seven years to complete. One of the
distinctive aspects of the exterior is Sinan's method of dis-
guising the enormous buttresses needed to support the
four central piers of the dome: incorporating them into
the walls as far as possible, he camouflaged the remaining
projections by building double galleries with arcades of
columns between them.

As you enter the vast walled outer courtyard, the
mosque's sheer scale and power become apparent. The
terrace to the north has a fine view over the rooftops to
the Golden Horn. The inner courtyard is ringed by a

OTTOMAN CLIMAX
The Süleymaniye is the
most important building
in Istanbul. Tucked into
the walled garden behind
the Süleymaniye are the
impressive octagonal
türbes (tombs) of
Süleyman and his wife
Roxelana ("the
Russian"), decorated
inside with extremely fine
Iznik tiles in far greater
numbers than in the
whole vast space of the
mosque itself. Sinan's
own *türbe* stands a short
distance to the northeast
of the complex, just past
the inn.

porticoed colonnade with columns of porphyry, marble, and granite, and a minaret stands at each of the corners.

There are no galleries or aisles, but the powerful austerity of the vast space is relieved by splashes of color from the stained-glass windows. There are a few panels of Iznik tiles patterned with leaf and flower motifs in turquoise, dark blue, and red, the earliest known examples of their type (see page 61).

▶▶ Sultanahmet Camii (Blue Mosque)   46C1
Mimar Mehmet Ağa Caddesi, Sultanahmet
Popularly known as the Blue Mosque from the predominant color of its interior decoration, Istanbul's chief mosque competes with the Süleymaniye for the title of the city's most beautiful imperial mosque. Built for Sultan Ahmet I by the architect Mehmet Ağa between 1609 and 1616, it is the only mosque in Istanbul to have six minarets. Its position close to the Topkapı Palace ensured that it was used by sultans for the following 250 years, with imperial processions from the palace to the mosque.

Tourists enter through the side door facing Aya Sofya and are restricted to the back half of the mosque. The finest feature of the interior is the tilework on the lower walls and galleries: over 20,000 tiles in all, of the best Iznik workmanship, decorated with a variety of rose, tulip, lily, and carnation motifs, mainly in blues and greens. Light floods in through the 260 windows with their reproduction stained glass.

▶ Yeni Cami (New Mosque)   46C2
Eminönü Meydanı
Dubbed "new" because it is a mere 300 years old, this Ottoman mosque is notable mainly for its prominent setting looking out over the Golden Horn. The courtyard has a lovely şadirvan (ablutions fountain). The interior walls are decorated with 17th-century tiles in shades of blue, but the overall effect is rather somber, not least because of the accumulated filth on the windows from exhaust fumes and smoke.

67

The tranquil interior of Sokullu Mehmet Paşa Camii, one of Sinan's minor masterpieces

Walk

Around the Aqueduct of Valens

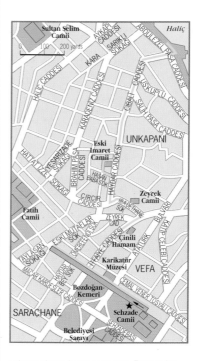

Starting at the imposing Aqueduct of Valens, this walk leads through narrow streets with ramshackle wooden Ottoman houses and early churches-turned-mosques, to end with a stroll along the shoreline of the Golden Horn (see Central Istanbul map on pages 46–47). Covering a total distance of 1½ miles, the basic walk will take at least two hours. It can easily be extended by an hour or more by continuing northward along the shore-line of the Golden Horn, past the church of Saint Stephen of the Bulgars to the Eyüp mosque complex. If you still have the energy you can continue through the Eyüp cemetery to reach Pierre Loti's Café, with its views back over the Golden Horn and the Istanbul skyline. This will make a 5-mile walk, ending with a steep 20-minute ascent through the graveyard.

Take a taxi to the **Aqueduct of Valens** (Turkish Bozdoğan-Kemeri), the colossal, two-tier structure linking Istanbul's third and fourth hills, which still runs for nearly two-thirds of its original $^1/_2$-mile length. Its highest point today straddles **Atatürk Bulvarı**.
Stairs at either end climb to the top,

The colossal arches of the Roman aqueduct dwarf modern traffic

where there is no parapet. Begun by Constantine the Great and completed by Emperor Valens in AD 378, the aqueduct channeled water to the Byzantine palace. Restored by both the Byzantines and the Ottomans, it remained in use until the late

19th century, when it was replaced by the present water system.

At the foot of the aqueduct, housed in a 16th-century *madrasa* (theological college) with a pretty courtyard garden, is the **Karikatur Müzesi** (*Open daily 9–6. Admission free*) with a display of cartoons that changes weekly and gives an intriguing insight into the Turkish sense of humor.

Now walk along the foot of the aqueduct to **Itfaiye Caddesi.** Turn down this street to investigate the **Çinili Hamam** (Tiled Baths), built by Sinan in 1545 and probably the prettiest and most intimate of the Turkish baths that welcome foreigners.

Continuing downhill, turn left to **Zeyrek Camii,** originally the 12th-century Byzantine Church of the Pantocrator, which is locked except at prayer times. Two of the last three Byzantine emperors are buried here.

Carry on through the steep cobbled streets of **Zeyrek,** a little-explored district of Istanbul whose charm lies principally in its dilapidated wooden houses, which give an idea of what the city may have looked like in Ottoman times.

Head now toward **Haydar Caddesi,** forking left on **Hasan Baba Sokağı,** then right on **Küçük Mektep Sokağı,** at the end of which stands **Eski Imaret Camii,** its 12-sided dome belying its origins as a 12th-century church. It has one of the most important and interesting exteriors of any Byzantine church in the city, with ornate brick-work designs including rose medallions, Greek keys, and other symbols.

From the little square in front of the church there is a fine view across to the Golden Horn. Head down to the harbour shoreline, turning left into the landscaped parkland that now runs the whole length of this western side of the Golden Horn.

Masonry built to last

Museums

▶▶ Arkeoloji Müzesi (Archaeological Museum)   *46C2*

Open: Tue–Sun 9:30–4:30. Admission charge

The entrance to this complex of museums—it also houses the **Eski Şark Eserleri Müzesi** (Museum of the Ancient Orient; *Open* daily 9:30–12)—lies just past Aya Irini. A pair of Hittite lions flank the portal of the Museum of the Ancient Orient. Inside are fascinating ancient Egyptian, Sumerian, Babylonian, Hittite, Urartian, and Assyrian exhibits. Among the most memorable are a series of Babylonian blue and yellow tile panels of lions and a number of colossal Hittite sculptures in black basalt.

In the courtyard in front of the Archaeological Museum are the purple porphyry sarcophagi of various Byzantine emperors. Inside, the museum is huge, and a full visit would take many hours. If pressed for time, concentrate on the main floor, where there's a vast collection of Roman and Greek sculpture, including the head of Alexander the Great and the Alexander Sarcophagus.

▶▶▶ Aya Sofya Müzesi   *46C1*

See pages 52–53.

▶ Halı Müzesi (Vakiflar Carpet Museum)   *46C1*

Sultanahmet
Open: Tue–Sat 9–4. Admission free

The museum is housed in huge vaulted rooms that once served as storerooms and elephant stables, in the northeast corner of the Blue Mosque.

▶▶▶ Kariye Müzesi   *46A3*

See page 59.

▶ Mosaik Müzesi (Mosaic Museum)   *46C1*

Sultanahmet
Open: Wed–Mon 9:30–5. Admission charge

Tucked between the Blue Mosque and the new Arasta Bazaar, this small museum shelters the remains of the Great Palace of the Byzantine emperors, consisting largely of 6th-century mosaics of great vivacity.

▶ Sadberk Hanım Müzesi   *80B5*

Piyasa Caddesi, Büyükdere
Open: Thu–Tue 10–5. Admission charge

This fine collection of Turkish and foreign antiquities is housed in a late 19th-century *yalı* (summer house) on the European shore between Büyükdere and Sarıyer.

▶▶▶ Topkapı Müzesi   *47D2*

See pages 76–77.

▶▶ Türk-Islam Eserleri Müzesi (Museum of Turkish and Islamic Art)   *46C1*

At Meydanı, Sultanahmet
Open: Tue–Sun 10–5. Admission charge

Formerly housed in the Süleymaniye, this museum has

A statue from the Arkeoloji Müzesi

FISHY RESERVOIR
In the century that followed the Ottoman conquest, the whereabouts of the city's largest underground water cistern, built in the mid-6th century and now known as Yerebetan Müzesi, were unaccountably forgotten. It was the detective work of an enterprising 16th-century French archaeologist— who discovered that people in the neighbor-hood were drawing water from holes in their basement floors, and sometimes even catching fish—that brought it to light again.

A traditional rug displayed in the Türk-Islam Eserleri Müzesi

moved to the 16th-century palace of Ibrahim Paşa, the splendid building that occupies most of the Hippodrome frontage directly opposite the Blue Mosque. This magnificent palace, the largest private residence ever built in the Ottoman Empire, makes an excellent setting for the fine collection of carpets, illuminated copies of the Koran, woodcarvings, ceramics, and glassware. There is also an impressive display of the tents and furniture used by the Yürük people, who are Anatolian nomads.

►► Yerebatan Müzesi (Underground Museum)   46C1

Yerebatan Caddesi, Sultanahmet
Open: daily 9–5. Admission charge
This remarkable underground cistern is the largest of all those left by the Byzantines. Built by Emperor Justinian in the mid-6th century and known as the Basilica Cistern, it was used throughout the Byzantine period to supply water to the palace, its gardens, and all surrounding buildings. The insignificant entrance at street level gives no clue to the splendor that lies below. Steps lead down to slippery walkways, and operatic music complements the dramatic setting. There are 336 columns, which make the cistern the same width as Aya Sofya.

A reclining figure from the Arkeoloji Müzesi

FAMOUS RESIDENTS
Beylerbey Palace was used as a summer lodge for successive generations of visiting royalty, including Empress Eugénie of France, Emperor Franz Joseph of Austria, Edward VIII of England and Mrs. Simpson, and Shah Nasreddin of Persia. Abdul Hamid II, the last Ottoman sultan, lived the last years of his exile here and died in the palace in 1918.

ATATÜRK'S DEATHBED
Atatürk used the Dolmabahçe as his residence on visits to Istanbul from his new capital at Ankara. It was here that he died in 1938, in a modest upstairs room, still furnished as it was then, with the Turkish flag draped over his bed.

The sumptuous interior of Beylerbeyi Sarayı

Palaces

▶ Aynalı Kavak Kasrı (Pavilion of the Mirroring Poplars)   *46B3*

Kasımpaşa-Hasköy Yolu, Hasköy
Open: Fri–Sun and Tue–Wed 9:30–4. Admission charge
This mid 19th-century palace is a lovely example of late Ottoman architecture. It is noted in particular for its stained-glass windows.

▶▶ Beylerbeyi Sarayı (Beylerbey Palace)   *80B2*

Asian Bosphorus
Open: Fri–Sun and Tue–Wed 9:30–5. Admission charge
Set in beautiful gardens next to the old Bosphorus Bridge, Beylerbey is the biggest and most impressive palace on the Asian Bosphorus. The present 19th-century building is divided into the *selamlık* (male reception areas) and the harem, the former being magnificently decorated with treasures from all over the world. The best way to reach it is to take a ferry to Üsküdar, then a taxi.

▶▶▶ Dolmabahçe Sarayı   *47D3*

Dolmabahçe Caddesi, Beşiktaş
Open: Fri–Sun and Tue–Wed 9–12 and 1:30–4:30 .
Admission charge
This beautiful building, with its 600-yard-long white marble façade overlooking the Bosphorus near the Beşiktaş landing stage, became the residence of the sultans on its completion in 1853, replacing the hilltop Topkapı Palace.

Visits are by guided tour only, and there is a daily limit of 1,500 visitors, after which the palace closes. Some two-thirds of the enormous interior is taken up by the harem; the lavish furnishings, the most fabulous of any palace in Turkey, are reminiscent of Versailles. In the attractive gardens are a café, souvenir shop, and bird pavilion, and

nearby stands a matching white marble waterfront mosque for the private use of the palace.

▶▶ Ibrahim Paşa Sarayı   46C1
See Türk-Islam Eserleri Müzesi pages 70–71.

▶ Ihlamur Kasrı (Linden Pavilion)   80A2
Ihlamur Teşvikiye Yolu, Teşvikiye
Open: Fri–Sun and Tue–Wed 9–4. Admission free
This attractive excellently restored 19th-century palace in the hills above Beşiktaş consists of two pavilions, the **Maiyet Köşkü** (for the sultan's harem) and the **Merasim Köşkü** (for his guests).

▶ Küçüksü Kasrı (Little Waters Pavilion)   80C3
Küçüksü Caddesi, Göksu
Open: Fri–Sun and Tue–Wed 9:30–5. Admission free
This tiny but exquisite 19th-century rococo palace was once a retreat for the Ottoman sultans. It stands on the Asian Bosphorus at the estuary of two rivers known as the **Sweet Waters of Asia**.

▶ Tekfur Sarayı
(Palace of the Porphyrogenitus)   46A3
Şişhane Caddesi, Avçi Bey
The three-story façade with red brick arches and multi-colored marble is virtually all that remains of this 10th-century palace. There is no ticket booth, but the owner of the nearby hut will expect a small tip.

▶▶▶ Topkapı Sarayı   47D2
See pages 76–77.

▶ Yıldız Sarayı   80B2
Yıldız Caddesi, Yıldız
Open: Tue–Sun 9:30–4. Admission charge
Set in Istanbul's loveliest park, the pavilions and mosque of **Yıldız Palace** enjoy superb views over the Bosphorus. The lavishly decorated main pavilion, the **Şale Köşk**, has some 50 rooms and was used by visiting royalty.

The white marble façade of Dolmabahçe Sarayı, residence of the sultans from the mid-19th century, viewed from the waters of the Bosphorus

73

The Şale Köşk is the largest and grandest of the pavilions of Yıldız Sarayı, with some 50 magnificently decorated rooms

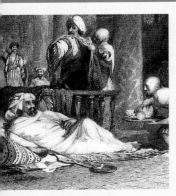

No trip to Turkey is complete without a visit to a Turkish bath. Set aside any prudishness and take the plunge, as it is likely that you will remember this as one of the high points of your visit, savoring that feeling of supreme cleanliness and relaxation that is so different from the experience of a Western bath or shower. In fact, Western-style baths are regarded as unhygienic by Muslims, who cannot understand why anyone would want to sit and wash in their own dirt—hence the absence of plugs in sinks; it is always considered best to wash under running water.

EVER POPULAR
There are still over 100 functioning *hamams* in Istanbul. The Ottomans founded these baths as a public utility and used the revenues to support other foundations, such as schools and hospitals. Today, the *hamams* are still as popular among Istanbul's poor as they were in Ottoman times, mainly due to the city's water shortages.

Sybaritic pleasures in the hot steam room

74

The best time to visit a Turkish bath is at the end of a long and dusty day's sightseeing, and the best place to visit one is Istanbul. Here there are several baths geared to the requirements of foreigners (see side panel), where English is spoken and where you will probably see quite a few other non-native bathers.

The layout The interior design of a Turkish bath is roughly the same as an ancient Roman bath, with three distinct areas: the *camekan* (Roman *apoditarium*) is the reception and changing room, where you undress and leave your clothes and sip tea afterward; the *soğukluk* (Roman *tepidarium*) is like a passageway between the *camekan* and the steam room, and where you'll most likely find the lavatories; and the *hararet* (Roman *calidarium*) is the hot steam room, where you actually

bathe and get massaged. The *hararet* is usually the most elaborate and beautiful chamber of all, with marble-clad walls and marble sinks with brass faucets around the sides. In the center is a large marble slab, heated by a wood fire below in the furnace room. This is the so-called belly-stone, where you lie to sweat, relax, and be massaged, all the while gazing up at the shafts of patterned light that pour through the domed ceiling.

Prices for a *kese* massage (during which a masseuse rubs you with a camel-hair glove), face massage, and foot massage are displayed in the *camekan*. If you are only going to make one visit, try them all, as the total cost still amounts to very little.

The ritual Mixed bathing is not permitted except in the *hamams* of tourist hotels; indeed, the penalty for a man discovered entering the women's baths used to be death. On undressing, both sexes are given wooden clogs to wear into the *hararet* and a towel for drying off later. In men's baths, where modesty is strictly observed, a cotton sarong called a *peştamal* is issued for wrapping tightly around the waist, an impediment that makes thorough washing a little tricky.

Women's baths are more relaxed and you can either wear underpants or go naked. It's common for children to run around the women's baths. The masseuses are friendly, full of songs and gossip, arms flying wildly as they scrape off the layers of grime and lather you all over into a soapy, bubbling heap. You will emerge feeling you have shed 10 years' worth of ingrained dirt. Allow at least an hour for the whole process.

The Turkish bath: the perfect marriage of the need for cleanliness (required by Koranic law) and the desire for sensual indulgence

BEST FOR FOREIGNERS
The best *hamams* for foreign visitors to try in Istanbul are the Cağaloğlu and the Çemberlitaş, both near the Grand Bazaar, or the smaller Çinili Hamam, near the Aqueduct of Valens. They offer separate facilities for men and women, and function between 8 AM and 8 PM daily. The interiors of all three are architecturally interesting, and they still have their original marble basins. Their prices, though very low by Western standards, are too high for most Turks.

HAREM ETIQUETTE

The harem system originated when soldiers who were to be away from home locked up their women and had eunuchs guard them. From this beginning, a complex hierarchy evolved in the harem of the sultan's palace, governed by strict rules. Each night, for example, the sultan selected the "lucky" lady to be his companion in the imperial bedchamber. He expected her to kiss the imperial bedclothes at the foot of the bed before wriggling her way under them until she encountered the waiting sultan. No Turkish woman is ever thought to have been thus favored—only thousands of foreigners.

The Baghdad Köşk in the Fourth Court, built by Murat IV in 1638 in honor of his capture of that city

ACROPOLIS SETTING

In about 1460 Mehmet the Conqueror built the Topkapı on the site of the acropolis, or citadel, of ancient Byzantium. It was laid out on the highest ground and surrounded by gardens stretching down to the seashore. Despite the ravages of fires and earthquakes, the three inner courtyards remain largely as they were in the 15th and 16th centuries.

►►► Topkapı Sarayı (Topkapı Palace)   47D2

Sultanahmet
Open: Wed–Mon 9:30–5. Admission charge

If you have time to see only one thing in Istanbul, it should be the Topkapı. Ideally you should spend the whole day here, breaking for lunch at the excellent restaurant in the farthest court, with its stunning views over the Bosphorus towards Üsküdar. The Topkapı has an amazing capacity to absorb swarms of people, and its setting on the headland of old Stamboul, in the city's center but away from all the noise and traffic, makes it a relaxing place to visit.

The buildings This vast palace was the residence of the Ottoman sultans from the 15th to the 19th centuries; it has been a museum since 1924, displaying a breathtaking collection of porcelain, jewels, calligraphy, weapons, and other valuables belonging to the Ottoman Court. The Topkapı was also the seat of government, housing institutions such as the judicial council, known as the *divan*, in its different courtyards. The First Court (sometimes called the Court of the Janissaries) was the palace service area, containing dormitories for guards and servants, storage areas, the state mint, an arsenal, a bakery, and a hospital. It now contains the ticket booth. The Second Court housed the *divan*, flanked by kitchens and stables. The Third Court was devoted to the palace school, where young men (often Christians) from all over the empire were trained for the civil service and for the Janissaries. Finally, the

Fourth Court, with its gardens and pavilions, was reserved for members of the sultan's household. The main residential quarters, including the harem, occupied the whole of one side of the first three courts.

The harem The harem was officially disbanded in 1909, and some of its rooms were opened to visitors in 1960. It has a separate ticket booth in the Second Court and may only be visited in guided tours (daily 10–12 and 1–4) of up to 60 people, on a first-come, first-served basis. Lines can be long at peak season. Only some 20 rooms out of the total labyrinth of about 300 are open to the public, and many of these are surprisingly small. The Valide Sultan, the sultan's mother, presided over life in the harem. Her apartments lay in the center, well placed for her customary domination and manipulation. Black Eunuchs, who had their quarters alongside, guarded the harem. The White Eunuchs, mainly Caucasians, were not allowed in the harem but served in the men's reception area, while a third group of special servants, the Halberdiers-with-Tresses, acted as guards and porters. Once a month they were permitted to enter the harem carrying firewood, their gaze restricted by their extraordinarily high collars flanked by wool tresses.

The exhibits The museum proper begins in the Second Court, which contains collections of porcelain—including a rich collection of Chinese porcelain—clocks, and arms and armor. In the Third Court is the world-famous Treasury, which along with the harem is the most popular—and most crowded—part of the palace. Here, celebrated exhibits are the Topkapı Dagger, with three colossal emeralds, the Spoonmaker's Diamond, the fifth largest in the world, and jewel-encrusted thrones. At the entrance to the Fourth Court, do not miss the ever-changing collection of Turkish and Persian miniatures.

A fine example of the calligrapher's art

77

The gardens are a haven of peace, with panoramic views

Parks and city walls

▶▶ City walls
46A1–B3

Emperor Theodosius built these imposing walls in the 5th century, when they were held to be the strongest in Christendom. They run from the Sea of Marmara over the hills to the Golden Horn, enclosing the city of Byzantium. For added protection there was a deep moat, 65 feet wide, which was flooded at times of attack. The original structure comprised an inner and outer wall; what remains today is mostly the inner wall and its towers.

The walls begin at the Sea of Marmara with the 40-foot-high Marble Tower—once a prison—standing on a little promontory. Farther inland, some half a mile distant, stands Yedikule, the Castle of Seven Towers.

Yedikule▶▶ (*Open Tue–Sun 9:30–4:30. Admission free*) This curious structure, built onto the inside of the wall by the **Golden Gate**, is a hodgepodge of Byzantine and Turkish styles, with four of its towers set in the Theodosian wall itself, and three extra towers built inside by Mehmet the Conqueror. It is open today as a museum. In Ottoman times it served as a prison, and instruments of torture feature large among the exhibits. The Golden Gate itself was originally a free-standing Roman triumphal arch, later bricked up when the arch was incorporated into the walls.

It is possible to walk along the top of the walls from Yedikule to **Belgrad Kapısı**, passing 11 towers, and on to **Silivri Kapısı**, past another 13 towers. After this the walls deteriorate until you reach **Edirnekapısı**, the highest point in the old city, just beside the **Mihrimah Sultan Camii** (see page 63). From here you can walk inside the walls to the impressive façade of the **Tekfur Sarayı** (see page 73) and on down the hill past the **Ivaz Effendi Mosque** into the area that was once the **Palace of Blachernae**. Now largely reconstructed, this final section

78

A bizarre part-Byzantine and part-Turkish construction, Yedikule has seven towers, four of which are built into the 5th-century walls

The gardens of the imperial Dolmabahçe Palace offer restful views over the Bosphorus

before the Golden Horn has no moat but is much thicker, and shelters clusters of picturesque, though slightly squalid, houses.

Relaxing in Gülhane Parkı

▶ Emirgan Parkı   80B4

8 miles north of the city center on the European side

Famous for its tulip gardens, this lovely park overlooking the Bosphorus has three delightful café pavilions, all restored by the Turkish Automobile and Touring Club. The gardens are at their best during the annual Tulip Festival, which is held in April.

▶ Gülhane Parkı   46C2

Sultanahmet

This is a welcome place to stroll after a visit to the Topkapı and the Archaeological Museum complex, with fine views over the headland of Saray Burnu. Istanbul's modest zoo is based here; the aquarium is worth visiting for its setting in a Roman cistern.

▶ Haliç (Golden Horn)   46B3

An Istanbul mayor transformed the European shoreline of the Golden Horn into pleasant parkland with children's playgrounds. It makes an enjoyable stroll away from the busy streets of central Istanbul, especially at sunset.

▶▶ Yıldız Parkı   47E3

Set on the European shoreline of the Bosphorus just north of the Çirağan Kempinski Hotel, this park is regarded by most connoisseurs as the most beautiful in Istanbul. Within it lie the imperial pavilions—in the old Ottoman style—and gardens of the **Yıldız Palace** (see page 73).

UNESCO PROTECTION

There were 10 gates in the original 5th-century walls, and although parts of the walls have been knocked down to make way for railways and new highways, nearly all the ancient gates are still in use. UNESCO has designated the land walls and the area they enclose as one of the cultural heritage sites of the world.

RAMPART WALKS

The Byzantine walls that protected the city for over a thousand years make an interesting walk. As they are over 4 miles long, the walk takes three to four hours in all. If you are short of time, concentrate on the stretches around Yedikule and the Tekfur Sarayı.

Drive and Cruise

Along the Asian Bosphorus and Üsküdar

This five- to six-hour, 40-mile excursion follows the Asian shore of the Bosphorus, visiting the splendid waterfront palaces on the way to the northernmost point at Anadolu Kavağı. The journey back is by ferry, stopping to explore the Asian district of Üsküdar. Organized Bosphorus cruise boats are so fast that you should only take them if your sightseeing time is limited. Either way, be sure to take a pair of binoculars, the better to appreciate the magnificent buildings lining the shore.

Take a taxi out through Beyoğlu on the Ankara road, then across the elegant old Bosphorus suspension bridge. The first stop is the **Beylerbey Palace** (*Open* Fri–Sun and Tue–Wed 9:30–5, guided ours only. *Admission charge*), just beside the Bosphorus Bridge, built in 1865 by Sultan Abdulaziz (see page 72). You can have tea in the gardens.
   Continuing north through Cengelköy, the next stop is at **Kırmızı Yalı**, the best preserved of all the seaside mansions, built of wood and painted the traditional oxblood color. The interior cannot be visited.
   Continue north to **Küçüksü Kasrı** (*Open* Fri–Sun and Tue–Wed 9–5. *Admission charge*), another charming imperial pleasure palace (see page 73). A short walk above it is the ruined castle of **Anadolu Hisarı**. From here you can rent boats (with owner) to explore the Bosphorus at your leisure.
   The drive north leads on through **Kanlıca**, famous for its yogurt, before reaching **Anadolu Kavağı**, a n attractive town with typical wooden balconied houses lining the shore and a huge selection of fish restaurants. To work up an appetite, climb up to the Genoese castle for views of the

Clashing Rocks that Jason and the Argonauts had to navigate in their quest for the Golden Fleece.
   After lunch, catch a ferry down the length of the Bosphorus,

Boats crowd the shore at Anadolu Kavağı

81

disembarking at **Üsküdar** (formerly Scutari). Stroll around the harbor to visit the little **Mihrimah Camii** built by Sinan in 1547 (see page 65), then take a taxi to the **Selimiye Barracks**, housing the colossal building that was Florence Nightingale's hospital, now a school. Continue by taxi to the **Karaca Ahmet Mezarlığı**, the largest Muslim cemetery in the world and a wonderfully wild, overgrown place. From here, you could take the taxi up to the pleasant café and teahouse on **Büyük Çamlıca**, the highest point in the area, from where there are unforgettable views over the Stamboul skyline. Finally, catch the ferry back from Üsküdar to Eminönü, passing close to **Kız Kulesi**, the Maiden's Tower, a 12th-century customs house overlooking the harbor.

Traditional houses line the Bosphorus seafront

Capital of the Ottoman Empire in the 14th century, Bursa has much of historic interest to offer, as well as its famous spa waters

OLD-FASHIONED TRANSPORTATION
One of the principal charms of Büyükada and Heybeliada lies in the absence of cars. Aside from a few bicycles, the chief mode of transportation is the phaeton, a horse-drawn carriage. Large numbers of colorful phaetons wait in a special parking area close to the ferry terminal, with set rates for long and short tours of the islands. Equipped with roofs that fold back during fine weather, they also boast large cellophane side flaps that flop down during showers. Tinkling bells and clip-clopping hooves make a welcome change from the blare of horns and revving of engines.

Istanbul environs

▶▶ Bursa   86C1

Much of this ancient spa's prestige derives from the fact that it became the first Ottoman capital in 1326. Bursa has since developed as a significant center for the manufacture of silk and cotton. The three-hour trip from Istanbul takes you through dusty modern developments and includes the car-ferry crossing to Yalova. If you want to enjoy the spa waters, you should spend a night here, as the better hotels all have private thermal baths. Tour agencies offer organized tours of the main sights, which are scattered over quite a long distance.

Bedesten▶ This maze of little streets right in the city center, beside the squat brick minarets of the **Ulu Cami** (Great Mosque), is Bursa's covered market, where you can find local cotton goods. Keep an eye out, too, for **Koza Hanı**, the silk cocoon caravansary (market), with shops selling beautiful silks and brocades.

Çekirge▶ The spas and best hotels are concentrated in this pleasant suburb, which still has two public baths (14th-century and 16th-century) open to male visitors.

Muradiye complex▶ This complex, built in the reign of Murat II (1421–1451), includes a mosque, *madrasa* (theological school), *imaret* (soup kitchen), and a very attractive cemetery and lies west of the center of town.

Tophane Park▶ The citadel area above Ulu Cami still has fragments of the Byzantine and Ottoman city walls, as well as the tombs of Osman Ghazi, founder of the Ottoman dynasty, and his son. There are good views from the café at the summit.

Uludağ▶ The ancient Mount Olympos of Mysia, Uludağ rises 7,883 feet above Bursa, 28 miles away, and is Turkey's premier ski resort. It can be reached by car (one hour) or cable car (30 minutes). Snow covers the summit from December to May; in summer it is a popular spot for picnics and walks.

Yeşil Cami and Yeşil Türbe▶▶ Bursa's two principal monuments face each other across a square on a hillside to the east of the city. The mosque, Yeşil Cami, is considered one of the finest examples of early Ottoman architecture. Opposite it is Yeşil Türbe, the tomb of Sultan Mehmet I (died 1421) and Bursa's most beautiful building. Its interior is covered with spectacular tilework.

▶ Büyükadalar (Princes' Islands)   86C1

These nine islands, of which only the main five are now inhabited, are popular retreats from the noise and bustle of Istanbul. From Byzantine times onward, the islands' convents and monasteries also served as places of exile for out-of-favor royalty.

Büyükada, the largest and most developed island, is hilly, with pine forests. A monastery still stands on each of its two principal hills. Its old-fashioned charm is emphasized by the variety of its vacation homes—each more imaginative than the last—built over the years by Istanbul's wealthy. The older ones are really delightful, with elaborately carved balconies and ornate façades.

Heybeliada, the second largest island, is equally charming, but with a more intimate feel. In summer its beaches are crowded with tourists.

Yassiada, one of the smallest islands, was bought by the British ambassador in 1857. The castle he built later became a prison for political detainees. Turkish Prime Minister Adnan Menderes was hanged here in 1961.

The islands are about 16 miles or one hour's ferry ride from Istanbul. Ferries leave regularly from Sirkeci near the Galata Bridge and from Kadikoy or Bostanci on the Asian side. In summer, air-conditioned hovercrafts run, taking just 30 minutes. There are also ferries between the four main islands—always be sure to check times at the terminal on the day.

▶ Çanakkale (Dardanelles)   86A1

A frequent car ferry crosses these straits separating Europe from Asia. The town has a very pretty seafront, with busy hotels and fish restaurants. The Archaeological Museum (*Open* Tue–Sun 8:30–12:30 and 1:30–5. *Admission charge*) has fine displays, including exquisite gold and jewelry from tumuli (grave mounds) in the area.

A display of coffeepots in Bursa

83

A phaeton on car-free Büyükada

Waterfront houses at Sarıyer

Drive

Belgrade Forest and the European Bosphorus

See map on page 80.

Sarıyer's delightful quayside

This five-hour, 45-mile drive starts by heading straight out to the Belgrade Forest, 13 miles north of the city, before returning along the European shore of the Bosphorus, taking in the fortress of Rumeli Hisarı, to finish up with tea at Yıldız Park.

Take the road from Beşiktaş north to **Büyükdere**, then across to **Bahçeköy** on the eastern edge of the forest. Originally the hunting ground of the Ottomans, this is the largest woodland near Istanbul and is very popular, especially on weekends. Its name derives from the Belgrade people settled here by Süleyman after his conquest of the city in 1521. Their job was to look after the reservoirs that supplied the city, and the remains of dams, water towers, and aqueducts can still be seen here. The finest surviving aqueduct, past Pirgöz on the way to Kısırmandıra, is the **Uzun** or **Long Aqueduct** (2,219 feet), built by Sinan in 1564.

Now head for **Sarıyer**, a pretty town with a charming waterfront, a lively fish market, and a few fish restaurants. A little farther south is the **Sadberk Hanım Müzesi** (*Open* Thu–Tue 10–5), a 19th-century *yalı* on the Bosphorus with exceptional archeological and ethnographic displays (see page 70).

Follow the coast road south through **Tarabya**, a wealthy district famous for its fish restaurants and the Büyük Tarabya, one of the best hotels on the Bosphorus. Many of the mansions that line the shore here are summer residences for foreign embassies.

The next stop, **Rumeli Hisarı** (*Open* Tue–Sun 9:30–5), is the highlight of the European shoreline. The fortress was built by Mehmet II in 1452 in preparation for the siege of Constantinople. It was completed within an astonishing four months. From here there is a good view of the **Fatih Sultan Mehmet** suspension bridge, built in 1988.

Continuing south, the road enters the sweeping bay of **Bebek**, a wealthy

The Rumeli Hisarı fortifications

suburb with many magnificent mansions on the shore. On a hilltop above is the **Bosphorus University**, the most prestigious school in Turkey. The road continues through **Arnavutköy** and **Ortaköy**, suburbs on either side of the old Bosphorus Bridge (1973), with lively street markets that have now become fashionable.

A fitting climax to this tour of the European shore is a stroll around **Yıldız Park** (*Open* daily 8:30–sunset), Istanbul's largest and prettiest park, and tea at one of its beautifully restored pavilions or conservatories.

Exceptionally pretty Sarıyer

This rather flat, non-descript area comprises the three percent of Turkey that lies geographically within Europe, having borders with Greece and Bulgaria. Much of it was a military area until the late 1960s, but access is now freely permitted. The only major point of interest for visitors is the town of Edirne.

Istanbul environs

Istanbul environs

▶ Edirne (Adrianople) 86A2

If you're approaching Turkey by car, make an overnight stop in Edirne, a typical Turkish town with a lively bazaar quarter and some superb mosques.

Selimiye Camii▶▶▶ The architect Sinan (see page 65) was already 80 years old when he started work here, but still he was able to bring together his vast experience in Ottoman architecture to construct this colossal yet surprisingly graceful mosque, which he completed in 1575. He regarded it as his masterpiece. Its four minarets are the tallest in the world after those in Mecca, and the dome is bigger even than that of Aya Sofya in Istanbul (see pages 52–53). The *mihrab* (prayer niche) and *minbar* (pulpit) have very elaborate geometric stonework, and the imperial lodge in the southwest corner is the finest in Turkey.

Other mosques worth visiting are the **Muradiye Camii** (1435) and the **Üç Şerefeli Cami** (1447).

▶ Gelibolu (Gallipoli) 86A1

This slim peninsula on the northern side of the Dardanelles has now been designated a national park. In 1915, Allied warships tried to force their way through the straits with a view to opening a supply line to Russia via the Black Sea. They were ill-prepared, however, for the strength and skill of the Turkish resistance, led by Lt. Colonel Mustafa Kemal, later to become known as Atatürk. They were also exceptionally badly led by their own commanders. Half a million soldiers are estimated to have lost their lives in the Gallipoli campaign; ANZAC (Australia and New Zealand Army Corps) casualties were especially high. The various war memorials sit rather incongruously in this attractive landscape of green

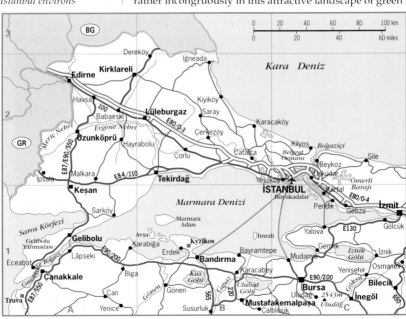

hills, pine forests, and pretty beaches. Unless you have your own transportation, it is best to take an organized tour. Most last about four hours, starting from either Gelibolu or Çanakkale, on the other side of the straits.

► **Iznik (Nicaea)** 86C1

Once a great city, Iznik is a mere shadow of its former self, shrunk within the mighty Byzantine double walls that defended it against many invading armies, and which are still remarkably well preserved. Iznik became the tile and ceramics center of Turkey in the 16th century, when Selim the Grim sent 500 Persian potters and their families to settle here. The **Aya Sofya Museum** (*Open* Tue–Sun 9–12 and 1–5. *Admission charge*) in the center is all that remains of the famous Byzantine church where two important general councils took place, whose deliberations were central to the development of early Christianity.

► **Kilyos** 86C2

Ten miles north of Sarıyer, a Bosphorus suburb of Istanbul, Kilyos is the best and closest beach to Istanbul on the European shore of the Black Sea, with a good selection of hotels and restaurants.

► **Marmara Denizi (Sea of Marmara)** 86B1

This is a region of pleasant if unexciting scenery; on the northern shore the only resort to consider is **Sarköy**, while on the southern shore the most attractive section is from the Erdek peninsula westward. From **Erdek** itself, with its pretty cobbled esplanade, you can visit a small group of islands. **Avşa** is the most rewarding, with good beaches and clear water. The largest, **Marmara**, has very few beaches and is a little bleak. East of Erdek the coastal developments are unsightly and the water polluted.

► **Şile** 86C2

Şile is a pretty beach resort on the Black Sea, only hours from Üsküdar. Though it gets crowded on weekends and holidays, it is a delightful place, with cliffs and white sandy beaches, a tiny island with a ruined Genoese castle, a striped lighthouse, and good hotels and restaurants.

The ruined Genoese castle at Şile

ANZAC MEMORIAL
"Those heroes that shed their blood
And lost their lives...
You are now lying in the soil of a friendly country,
Therefore rest in peace.
There is no difference between the Johnnies
And the Mehmets to us where they lie side by side,
Here in this country of ours.
You, the mothers,
Who sent your sons from faraway countries,
Wipe away your tears.
Your sons are now lying in our bosom
And are in peace.
After having lost their lives on this land, they have become our sons as well."
Kemal Atatürk, 1934

The Victory Beach Memorial, Gallipoli

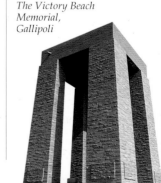

HEIGHT OF LUXURY

The Çırağan-Palace Hotel: Kempinski is probably Istanbul's most luxurious, with prices to match. Gutted by fire in 1910, it remained a ruin until its conversion by the Forte hotel chain. The restored palace now houses a conference center and restaurants, while accommodations are in a new building. The location— on the Bosphorus between Beşiktaş and Ortaköy and below Yıldız Park—is hard to match.

Like other special license and Touring Club hotels, the Yeşil Ev offers rooms furnished in Ottoman style

Accommodations

The majority of Istanbul's comfortable hotels used to be in the Beyoğlu district. Staying here always involved a taxi ride across the Galata Bridge to the old city of Stamboul to go sightseeing. Now that many old Ottoman houses have been converted into hotels, you have the attractive option of staying in Stamboul. If you want to stay in a particular hotel, always make reservations, as popular ones fill up quickly. Prices are displayed by law in the reception area, often in U.S. dollars.

Expensive hotels These uniformly large hotels (260–500 rooms), mostly operated by chains such as **Hilton** and **Sheraton**, tend to be located in the business and commercial parts of Istanbul. Many have panoramic rooftop restaurants, beauty salons, health clubs, shopping arcades, swimming pools, and bars. Prices range from $180 to $360 for a double.

Special license and Touring Club hotels These smaller hotels (14–58 rooms) are housed in historic buildings, almost invariably restored by the Turkish Automobile and Touring Club. They offer comfortable if rather small rooms furnished in Ottoman style. Some, such as the **Kariye** and the **Yeşil Ev**, also have a good reputation for traditional yet imaginative Turkish cuisine. A few have Turkish baths, and most have a mini-bar and TV in the rooms. Prices range from about $80 per double in simpler *pansiyons*, such as the **Turkoman Hotel** and the **Sümengen**, to $125 per double room at the top of the range (for instance Yeşil Ev).

Moderate hotels Mid-range hotels tend to be in rather unprepossessing modern buildings in the less exciting parts of the city. The best known are the **Pullman Etap Istanbul**, the **President**, and the **Kalyon**, which enjoys an unusually good location on the Sea of Marmara waterfront, below Sultanahmet. The **Pierre Loti Hotel** is attractive and centrally located on Divan Yolu, within

FAMOUS PERA PALAS

The Pera Palas was built in the 19th century as the terminus hotel for passengers on the Orient Express. The rooms are expensive, at around $220 for a double, but are large and stylish with 19th-century furnishings. If you just want a peek, the bar and café are open to the public.

easy walking distance of the Grand Bazaar and Aya Sofya. Prices here range from around $100 to $165 per double room.

The Atatürk Room in the Pera Palas Hotel, built to accommodate passengers on the Orient Express

Inexpensive hotels Most of the nicest modestly priced hotels and *pansiyons* are located in Sultanahmet, the tourist heart of Istanbul, in particular around the Hippodrome. Other reasonable hotels are found in the Taksim commercial area, which provides a good base both for nightlife and for access to the Bosphorus. The **Büyük Londra**, a 19th-century Italianate building close to the Pera Palas with a good restaurant and well-furnished rooms, is probably the best of the bunch at around $85 per double room.

Campgrounds Istanbul's campgrounds—serviceable but rather noisy because of the proximity of the highway and airport—are all along the Sea of Marmara, beside the main thoroughfare that runs from Atatürk International Airport to the city's center. All have restaurants, and most have swimming pools.

The Yeşil Ev serves imaginative Turkish cuisine in traditional surroundings

ÇİÇEK PASAJI
Beyoğlu's colorful "Flower Passage," lined with many small restaurants burned down; devotees insist, however, that its special atmosphere has not suffered from the renovation. Food here is now a bit overpriced.

Stopping for coffee and cakes—Turkish pastries are gooey concoctions that betray a sweet tooth

Food and drink

Istanbul is the culinary highpoint of any visit to Turkey. Residents take their food very seriously, as the colossal variety of restaurants attests. Turkish cuisine typically uses the freshest and highest quality ingredients, all of which are traditionally home-grown.

Turkish specialties For many people, the most novel aspect of Turkish meals is the *meze*, an apparently endless succession of delicious appetizers. Some are cold, such as eggplant purée or yogurt and cucumber; others, such as vine leaves stuffed with meat, and *börek* (tiny fine pastries filled with cheese, spinach, or meat), are hot. By the time the main meat or fish course arrives—usually served grilled with rice and a salad—the uninitiated have often filled up on *mezes*. The key is to learn how to pace yourself. In places where the food is displayed, always choose from the display rather than the menu; in the simpler *lokanta* (see below), where there may not be a menu, it is customary to go to the kitchen and choose.

Turkish cooking makes generous use of olive oil: an excellent accompaniment to the cuisine is the Turkish national drink, *rakı*, an aniseed-flavored liquor drunk with ice and water. Turkish wine is very good and always cheap, the best reds being Yakut and Buzbağ, the best whites being Çankaya and Kavak. The nonalcoholic national drink is *ayran*, a thin, slightly sour yogurt drink served chilled, and therefore very refreshing. Turkish desserts are described in detail on page 185.

Hot tea is the universal drink in Turkey

Types of eating place These range from the *kahve*, serving only Turkish coffee and tea, to the *restoran*, a formal restaurant serving Turkish and international food with alcoholic drinks. In between are the *lokanta*, informal restaurants with home-cooked Turkish meals and no alcohol; the *içkili lokanta*, similar to the *lokanta* but serving alcohol; the *gazino*, the same as the last, plus entertainment; the *kebapçı*, serving grilled meats and kabobs (with meat either cubed and skewered, or thinly sliced and served in a pita pocket); and the *pideci*, a Turkish pizza parlor.

DİVAN
TURKISH DELIGHT
PISTACHIO

Made in Turkey

Which district? For the best and cheapest fish, available in abundance and variety, head for the **Kumkapı** district, just inland from the Sea of Marmara, where scores of fish restaurants compete with each other in lively, narrow streets. The more expensive fish restaurants are on the Bosphorus shores, and include the **Ali Baba** in Kireçburnu and **Abdullah Effendi** at Emirgan.

In the main Sultanahmet area you can eat interesting, if expensive, Turkish dishes of all kinds at the **Sarnıç**, a converted Roman underground cistern, and at the **Yeşil Ev**, in a pretty courtyard between the Blue Mosque and the Aya Sofya. For a good, reasonably priced meal, go to **Sultanahmet Köftecisi**, on a corner close to the Yerebatan Müzesi; invariably it's full of locals eating tasty *köfte* meatballs, which can also be packed to go. In the Grand Bazaar, the best *lokanta* is the **Havuzlu**; and if you find yourself at the Egyptian Spice Bazaar, climb the stairs to **Pandeli**, an excellent place to stop for lunch. In the north of the city, **Aşitane**, the restaurant of the Kariye Hotel, serves good traditional Ottoman cuisine in a very pleasant courtyard garden beside the Kariye Müzesi. When visiting the Süleymaniye mosque, look for the **Darüzzyafe**, housed within the mosque complex, serving authentic Ottoman cuisine.

Traditional Turkish meals start with a selection of mezes

TURKISH FAST FOOD
Istiklal Caddesi, the main street in Beyoğlu, is the fast-food paradise of Istanbul, with office workers and shoppers stopping at its many stalls to savor such delights as meatballs stuffed with walnuts (*içli köfte*), kabobs and salad in pita bread, and sausage sandwiches (*zümküfül*). The best places to try these and other dishes are Şampiyon Kökoreç, Expres, and Konak.

Sizzling kabobs are available in a variety of mouthwatering forms

VEGETARIAN'S DELIGHT
Since many Turkish dishes are based on eggplant, tomatoes, onions, rice, and pine nuts, vegetarians have many options, including such favorites as a cold eggplant starter known as *imam bayıldı*—literally, "the imam fainted" with delight, naturally)—and stewed okra.

A shop in the book market beside the Grand Bazaar

FLEA MARKETS
Istanbul is rich in flea markets (*bit pazarları*), which are really more like streets full of junk shops. The Sunday arts and crafts market in the trendy suburb of Ortaköy is an enjoyable place to browse.

Chic clothes shops line Istiklal Caddesi

Shopping

In Istanbul you can find almost anything you want, as long as you know where to look. Prices vary enormously: except in clothes boutiques and bookstores, bargaining is the norm, and you should aim to get at least a third off the initial asking price. Normal shopping hours are 9–1 and 2–7 except Sundays, and the Grand Bazaar is open 8:30–7 except Sundays.

Carpets, kilims, and souvenirs Carpet shops abound all over the city, but the biggest concentrations can be found on **Takkeciler Caddesi** in the Grand Bazaar and in the secondhand shops off **Istiklal Caddesi** around Altıpatler Sokak.

There is a good selection of carpets and souvenirs at the **Arasta Bazaar**, the renovated Ottoman street market behind the Blue Mosque, and beside the Mosaic Museum. Prices here are a little more expensive than in the Grand Bazaar, but the quality is good and the pace gentler.

The best place for antiques is the **İç Bedestan** in the center of the Grand Bazaar, which also sells old silver jewelry and copperware. Gold jewelry is sold all over the Bazaar, but especially on **Kalpakçılar Caddesi**.

Turkish ceramics, brassware, onyx ware, and intricately handpainted meerschaum and camel-bone boxes are less expensive and make good gifts or souvenirs. Look in the **Sandal Bedestan** for these crafts. Other good gifts are the multicolored thick wool socks and gloves knitted by nomads from Erzurum—found at **Yağlıkçılar Caddesi** in the Bazaar—and excellent Russian and Turkish wool hats, too, found on the same street.

Clothes and leather Since designer Rifat Özbek rose to fame, Turkish fashion has been taken more seriously. Clothing manufacturers also have the advantage of

TURKISH FASHION
The exclusive VAKKO clothing shop held its first fashion show in the 1950s, and opened its store on Istiklal Caddesi in 1962. Famous for shoes and accessories as well as clothing, the store also contains an art gallery and elegant tearoom.

AMAZING FISH
The Balık Pazarı (fish market) just off Istiklal Caddesi in Beyoğlu is a good place to stroll without buying, to acquaint yourself with the sheer range of fish available in Istanbul.

The Grand Bazaar is a good hunting ground for reasonably priced gifts and souvenirs

home-produced materials such as Bursa silk, angora (Ankara) wool, and fine leather. Apart from the casual leather clothing and jeans available in the **Grand Bazaar**, most of Istanbul's classier boutiques are located in **Nişantaşı, Şişli,** and **Istiklal Caddesi** in Beyoğlu. The easiest clothes shopping is probably at the **Galleria**, a shopping center at Ataköy, near the airport, where shops are grouped by type in Turkish bazaar style. The complex also contains fast-food cafés and even an ice-skating rink. Bursa towels, considered among the best in the world, can be bought here at the **Özdilek** shop.

Food Turkish delight (a gelatin-based confection), candies, and fresh spices all make good gifts. The easiest place to buy them is the **Egyptian Spice Market**, just beside Yeni Cami in Eminönü Square. This crowded covered pedestrian street is lined with shops bursting with Turkish candies, which shopkeepers will package in any combination or quantity. It is easy to get carried away, so remember that sweets are very heavy and will weigh your suitcase down unmercifully. Spices, on the other hand, may aromatically penetrate everything in your case, but at least they weigh almost nothing.

Books The **Sahaflar Çarşısı**, beside the Grand Bazaar at the Beyazıt Cami end, is an excellent place to browse for new and old books in both English and Turkish. Also to be found here are a few places selling Turkish miniatures and old prints at fairly reasonable prices. Otherwise, the best bookstore for English guides and art books is **Haşet Kitabevi** on Istiklal Caddesi.

Street vendors are everywhere in Istanbul, selling tempting snacks

Turkish carpets are world famous, and their patterns and designs are so complex that it takes many years to build up sufficient knowledge to enable you to identify their origin at a glance.

BARGAINING TECHNIQUE
The best way to get a real bargain is to convince the dealer that you really do not like the rug in question. If there are two of you, pretend that one likes it and the other does not. Ask lots of questions about several rugs, so that the dealer cannot tell which is your favorite.

94

Nowhere will you find carpets in greater variety than at the Grand Bazaar

Colors can be a useful clue to a carpet's age: the pinks and oranges in this design indicate that the rug was made after about 1850

Kilims Most Turkish carpets are of the kilim variety; *kilim* means "flat-woven," and these carpets are characterized by their almost total lack of pile. Kilims were traditionally made by women for use in their own homes; the patterns and colors were therefore never dictated by commercial motives, but instead reflected the weaver's character and origins. The craft of weaving these intricately patterned carpets was introduced to Turkey in the 11th century by the nomadic Seljuk people, for whom carpets were an essential piece of tent furniture. The material used is normally sheep's wool, but they are sometimes also made of cotton and goat hair. In the Hakkâri and Malatya regions of eastern Turkey, silver and even gold Lurex thread are sometimes incorporated, as they are thought to ward off the devil or the evil eye. Useful not only as floor coverings, the ubiquitous kilims also served as wall hangings, door curtains, tent dividers, and prayer rugs. They were even made into large bags to be used as cushions or saddlebags, or smaller bags to hold salt, bread, grain, or clothes.

Natural and chemical dyes Traditionally, natural dyes were used to color the wool, cotton, or silk. These were derived—often by lengthy and laborious processes—from roots, bark, berries, vegetables, and minerals. In the

A traditional carpet-making workshop in Anatolia

second half of the 19th century aniline chemical dyes became available, and these have gradually replaced most of the old vegetable dyes. Watch out for pink and orange in rugs claiming to be older than this, as these are colors that could never be produced from natural dyes. The quality of chemical dyes has now improved considerably, and they can be very deceptive: if you want to be convinced that colors are natural, look for mid-weave color changes, because with natural dyes there are always slight variations of color between batches.

Buying a carpet Always be prepared to spend time talking with carpet dealers, asking about the symbols used and their meanings. This will not only give you a feel for the dealer's expertise, but will also make you more knowledgeable about your carpet, if you decide to buy it and take it home.

As older kilims have become rarer and therefore more valuable, dealers have begun to develop techniques for fading newly woven rugs. Leaving them out in sunlight is the commonest method—this can often produce quite effective and pleasing results with mellower colors, but it adds nothing to the rug's value. To detect a sun-faded rug, part the surface and compare the colors at the very bottom of the weave with those at the top. Also, comparing the colors on the underside with those on the top can give an indication of the rug's true age. Some rugs are artificially aged by washing them in bleach, a process that rots the fibers and reduces the life of the kilim. A quick sniff usually reveals whether bleach has or has not been used. Dirt and deliberate scorch marks are other common aging tricks.

Smaller kilims sell more quickly than larger ones, so sometimes larger ones are cut into pieces and sold as originals. Watch out for the newer ends added to make them complete. To find out if colors have been touched up to hide repairs or fading, rub a damp handkerchief or your hand over the surface. In doing so, you'll see if felt-tip coloring or shoe polish has been used. Look, too, at the closeness of the weave: the closer the weave and the smaller the knots, the better the quality and durability of the carpet.

PRAYER RUGS
All prayer rugs have a solid, arch-shaped block of color to represent the *mihrab*, or prayer niche, of a mosque wall. These rugs were used exclusively for prayer, and the symbols commonly found on them include the hands of prayer, the mosque lamp, the tree of life, the water jug, the jewel of Muhammad, and the star of Abraham.

WHERE TO BUY
Istanbul's Grand Bazaar offers the greatest selection anywhere, as its dealers scour the country in search of rugs to bring back and sell. The other noted centers for carpets are Konya and Kayseri, both in Central Anatolia, where the prices are a little cheaper. Coastal resorts such as Bodrum and Kuşadası also have a reasonable selection, though prices are generally higher than in Istanbul.

Traditional dancing in stylish setting

OASIS ON THE BOSPHORUS

For an evening of sophisticated disco music, good food, and dancing, do not miss the sybaritic Club 29 (*Open* 9 PM–1 AM), in its beautiful setting right on the Asian Bosphorus. The decor was inspired by Hadrian's villa in Rome. It is reached by a 10-minute boat ride from Istinye, on the European side.

Folk dancing is an important part of most cabaret shows

ILLUMINATIONS

Many of Istanbul's most prominent monuments are illuminated at night. Don't miss the chance to see them—especially the Aya Sofya and the Blue Mosque—in this new and spectacular light.

Nightlife

For most Istanbulis, nightlife means an evening spent in a bar listening to live music or a jazz pianist. Belly dancers are out—except in expensive cabaret nightclubs visited almost exclusively by tourists. The Atatürk Cultural Center stages concerts, ballets, and exhibitions, especially during the annual Istanbul Art and Culture Festival (see page 97).

Bars, cafés, and discos Although these are scattered all over the city, they are concentrated especially in the Taksim/Harbiye district and are popular with the after-work crowd. Try **Taksim Sanat Evi** (with jazz music; open until 2 AM) in Taksim. The suburbs of the European Bosphorus also offer lively bars and clubs, such as the **Ziya Bar** (open until 1 AM) in Ortaköy, with its attractive garden and outdoor bar.

If you want loud music and dancing, **Club 29** (see panel) is easily the most exciting venue in Istanbul, frequented

by the Turkish and foreign jet set. In winter it moves from the waterfront at Çubuklu to Nispetiye Caddesi, Etiler, where the food is excellent and the kitsch but fun decor includes leopard-skin seats. Istanbul's other famous disco is **Andromeda**, with a young clientele arriving around midnight and dancing into the early hours; the evening often ends with patrons jumping into the pool fully clothed. Its futuristic laser show and "video wall" make it one of the leading discos in the world as far as technical equipment is concerned. In summer months the disco has a capacity to hold more than 2,000 people.

Opera and ballet The **Istanbul State Opera and Ballet** starts its season in October and presents a range of performances, from classics such as Mozart's *Don Giovanni* to experimental modern ballet. Telephone the ticket office (02511 1023-5600) for programs.

Art and Culture Festival The **International Art and Culture Festival** is held each year in June and July, with internationally famous visiting performers. Most performances are given in the Atatürk Cultural Center, though the Open Air Theater, the Haghia Eirene basilica, and the Rumeli Hisarı, as well as several newly opened cultural centers and foreign cultural institutes, are also used as venues for movies and exhibitions. See pages 120–121 for more details on Turkish movies.

Nightclubs and cabarets The nightclubs frequented by tour groups are the expensive **Kervansaray** and **Orient House**, where the shows begin around 8 PM. You are not likely to spot a Turk here, and both the food and the show are distinctly mediocre. Besides belly dancing, there is usually some folk dancing in traditional costumes. It is all over by midnight. The Orient House also goes in for audience participation, soliciting female spectators to come up on stage and attempt belly dancing.

For a different style of cabaret you could try **Eski Yeşil** in Taksim, where you will find a Turkish clientele, often from the media and film worlds, and where the floor show offers such delights as cabaret scripts from the 1920s or spoofs of Ottoman life, with all parts performed by men. The action starts at midnight.

Belly dancing is usually found in tourist spots

97

The men's folk dances can be as spectacular as the women's

GALATA TOWER
The nightclub on the top floor of this 14th-century Genoese tower enjoys fabulous views over Istanbul. The after-dinner floor show begins with belly dancing. (*Open* daily, 10–6 and 8 PM onward).

RENOVATED TRAMS

The tramway along Beyoğlu's Istiklal Caddesi was reestablished in 1990; the old trams have been renovated and brought back into use, and the road is now closed to traffic. The very first horse-drawn trams came to Istanbul in 1868, to be replaced by electrified trams in 1914. The last of these stopped running in 1961, until this new revival. There is also a new underground tramway, but its route is designed for commuters from the suburbs rather than for tourists.

Shared taxis or dolmuş, can be stylish as well as practical

Old-fashioned trams serve the shopping street of Istiklal Caddesi

Practical points

If you drive in Istanbul you face the constant headache of navigation and parking problems. Walking is by far the best way to get around the city; for longer distances, take taxis or ferries. Buses are cheaper but slower, less flexible, and impossibly crowded.

From the airport Between 7 AM and 9 PM Turkish Airlines (THY) runs a half-hourly bus service from Atatürk International Airport to the THY office at Şişhane, near the top of the Tünel. If your hotel is central, use this bus and then catch a taxi. Otherwise, most people take a taxi

straight from the airport for the sake of speed and convenience: the journey to the center takes about 30–40 minutes.

Taxis The conspicuous yellow cars with black taxi signs on the roof are prolific and very reasonably priced by Western standards. They all have meters, and it is always worth checking that you are being charged at the appropriate rate: the nighttime rate (after midnight and before 6 AM) is double the daytime rate. You don't have to tip, but you should round up the fare to the nearest TL1000. Taxi drivers usually speak a little English and are glad to chat.

Dolmuş (literally "stuffed") are shared taxis, taking up to eight people and running along set routes. The main *dolmuş*

stations are at Eminönü, Taksim, Sirkeci, Beşiktaş, Aksaray, Üsküdar, and Kadiköy. Though most are mundane minibuses, *dolmuş* are occasionally 1950s Cadillacs, Chevrolets, and Plymouths shipped over from the U.S. after World War II.

Buses Slow, erratic, and always packed, Istanbul buses are recommended for only the most masochistic of visitors. Tickets are bought in advance at designated areas at the *otogar* (bus station) or newspaper and cigarette booths. On the European side, the main bus stations are at Taksim Square, Eminönü, and Beyazıt near the Grand Bazaar. On the Asian side they are at Üsküdar and Kadiköy.

Ferries These passenger-only boats run constantly up and down the Golden Horn and across the Bosphorus. The three main landing stages (*iskeles*) are at Eminönü near the Galata Bridge, and the ferries are clearly labeled with the relevant destination. To board, you need a brass token bought at the appropriate *iskele*. The boats are very crowded with commuters from 8 until 9 AM and from 5:30 until 8 PM, so aim to use them off peak. The boats are shabby and dilapidated, but have their own faded charm. Wear clothes you do not mind getting a bit grubby. A vendor brings tea around on a tray.

Trains Only use trains if you're traveling long distances outside of the city. On the European side the station is at Sirkeci (near the Galata Bridge), and trains run out to the suburbs of Ataköy and Florya (the campground); on the Asian side the terminal is at Haydarpaşa, serving Ankara and all routes east.

Opening hours Banks are open 9–12 or 12:30 and 1 or 1:30–5 Monday to Friday, except at the airport, where they are open 24 hours. Better rates are offered by the ubiquitous money changers at the Grand Bazaar and at the numerous exchange offices, open evenings and weekends, but you should always first check the official daily rate.

Typical restaurant hours are 12–3 for lunch and 6:30–10 for dinner, though most smaller, informal restaurants are open all day. Stores open 9–1 and 2–7 and shut on Sundays, and the Grand Bazaar is open 8:30–7 daily except Sundays. Note that most museums are closed on Mondays, and palaces on Mondays and Thursdays. The notable exception is Topkapı, which closes on Tuesdays.

Ferries are frequent and full of character, if rather dilapidated

TIME-SAVING FUNICULAR
The Tünel is the world's shortest funicular railway, running from Karaköy (the other side of the Galata Bridge from Eminönü Square) up to the start of Istiklal Caddesi. It takes just two minutes, instead of an exhausting half-hour climb by foot.

The Aegean

GR

Kara Deniz

Çorlu — E80/0-3

İSTANBUL

E80/0-4

İpsala

Tekirdağ

Boğaziçi

İzmit

Keşan

E84/110

Sarköy

E87/550

Marmara
Adası

*Marmara
Denizi*

Büyükadalar

130

Samothráki

Gelibolu

Erdek

Mudanya

Yalova

575

İznik

İznik
Gölü

Eceabat

Lâpseki

Bandırma

Karacabey

Gemlik

Bursa

Bilecik

Gökçeada

E90/200

Biga

Kuşçenneti
Milliparkı

İnegöl

Límnos

*Çanakkale
Boğazı*

Çanakkale

Gönen

Kuş
Gölü

*Uluabat
Gölü*

2543m
Uludağ ▲

E90/200

Bozcaada

Truva
(Troja)

Yenice

Mustafakemalpaşa

Susurluk

Ayvacık

Altınoluk

Edremit

Balıkesir

Dursunbey

Tavşanlı

Behramkale

Küçükkuyu

Ören

230

Alaçam Dağları

Kütahya

Baba Burun

Assos

E87/550

240

Aezanı

Ayvalık

Akrapol

Sındırgı

Simav

Gediz

Lésvos

**Pergamum
Asklepiyon**

Bergama

Demirci

Dikili

Akhisar

*Demirköprü
Barajı*

Çandarlı

Uşak

Ege

Foça

Yenifoça

565

*Marmara
Gölü*

İzmir Körfezi

Gediz

Manisa

Turgutlu

E96/300

Kula

Karaburun

Psará

Ildır

Erythrai İncıraltı

Urla

İzmir

Sart

Salihli

*Adıgüzel
Barajı*

Khíos

Ilıca

0-32

Boz Dağları

Alaşehir

Denizi

Çeşme

Siğacık

Teos

Ödemiş

Buldan

**Hierapolis
Pamukkale**

Gümüldur

Tire

Nazilli

Büyük Menderes

Ak Han

Sámos

Selçuk

0-31

Aydın

Denizli

Laodikeiá

Acıgöl

Efes

Kuşadası

Karacasu

Afrodisias

İkaría

Söke

E87/320

Meryemana

Solda
Gölü

**Dilek
Milliparkı**

Güzelçamlı

Priene

*Bafa
Gölü*

Alinda

Çine

Gerga

Kemer
Barajı

Kale

Acıpayam

Mikonos

Pátmos

Milet

Didim

Altınkum

Heraklcia

Labranda

Yatağan

Akçay

Gölgeli Dağları

E87/585

Euromos

Güllük

Milas

550

Muğla

Dalaman

Léros

Ortakent

Torba

Náxos

Kálimnos

Turgutreis

Bodrum

Gökova Körfezi

400

Köyceğiz

Dbodbekánisos

Kos

Marmaris

Caunus

Dalyan

Dalaman

Amorgós

Knidos

Datça

İçmeler

Fethiye Körfezi

Fethiye

Oınoanda

Anáfi

Astipálaia

Sími

Ölüdeniz

Telmessos

Thíra

Tilos

Xanthos

Patara

400

Ródhos

Kaş

Kekova
Adası

Ak Deniz

| 0 | 50 | 100 km |
| 0 | 20 | 40 | 60 miles |

A **B** **C**

Kuşadası, or Bird Island

*Wicker drying in
bunches near Usak*

The Aegean

THE AEGEAN SEA The Çanakkale Boğazi (the Dardanelles Strait) marks the northern edge of the Turkish Aegean (Ege Denizi), a region that runs southward through Troy and Pergamum to İzmir, then continues through the heavily developed tourist centers of Kuşadası, Bodrum, and Marmaris, as far as the airport of Dalaman at the southern extremity.

LANDSCAPES The countryside is for the most part one of gently rolling hills and fertile valleys covered in olive groves, vineyards, cypresses, and pine trees. Farming and fishing provide livelihoods for the bulk of the population.

▶▶▶REGION HIGHLIGHTS

Afrodisias *page 104*
Bodrum *page 108*
Dalyan *page 112*
Ephesus (Efes) *page 113*
İzmir *page 118*
Kuşadası *page 122*
Lake Bafa (Bafa Gölü) *page 124*
Marmaris *page 126*
Pamukkale *page 130*
Pergamum *page 132*
Troy (Truva) *page 133*

The Aegean

The impressive Greek ruins at Didim

ITINERARIES
One week, northern Aegean:
Day 1 Izmir
Day 2 Pergamum
Day 3 Ayvalık (good base)
Days 4–5 Behramkale (best base)
Day 6 Truva (Troy)
Day 7 Behramkale
Day 8 Izmir

One week, southern Aegean:
Day 1 Dalaman
Day 2 Dalyan, Bodrum
Day 3 Milas, Lake Bafa, Altınkum (good base)
Day 4 Didim, Miletos, Priene, Kuşadası (good base)
Day 5 Efes (Ephesus), Kuşadası
Day 6 Afrodisias, Pamukkale
Day 7 Muğla, Dalaman

Two weeks from Izmir:
Day 1 Izmir
Day 2 Kuşadası, Efes (Ephesus)
Day 3 Kuşadası, Didim, Miletos, Priene
Days 4–5 Bodrum
Day 6 Afrodisias
Day 7–8 Pamukkale
Day 9 Sardis, Izmir, Foça
Day 10 Pergamum
Day 11 Ayvalık
Day 12 Behramkale
Day 13 Truva (Troy)
Day 14 Ayvalık
Day 15 Izmir

The region falls into two distinct sections, of which the northern part, from the town of Çanakkale to Izmir, is the less visited. The sea temperature there is lower (average 69°F in summer), and many of the beaches are rocky. The most beautiful stretch of coastline, and also the most developed, lies to the south of Izmir. In ancient times a great flowering of culture took place here, well in advance of that on the Greek mainland, and the ancient cities of Ephesus and Miletos produced a string of remarkable scientists, historians, and poets. In addition to these great cities, the area is dotted with the remains of literally hundreds of others, the legacy of the waves of Greek settlers who arrived here after the fall of Troy in about 1200 BC. Some of these ancient ruins have been excavated, while many others still lie overgrown with scrub and wilderness. Unfortunately, only a handful can be mentioned in a book this size.

Basket weavers on their way to market near Türgütlü

RESORTS The largest Aegean resort north of Izmir is Ayvalık, on an indented coastline covered in pine forests. Scattered to the north are the 23 islands of the Edremit Körfezi (Gulf of Edremit), and opposite is the island of Lésvos, or Lesbos (Turkish Midilli). Sometimes known as the Olive Riviera because of its extensive olive groves, the Edremit area also has some smaller resorts, such as Çanlık and Sarmişaklı, with its golden sandy beaches, as well as the vacation towns of Őren, Akçay, Altınoluk, and Küçükkuyu. The small resort of Behramkale, just north of Lesbos, is probably the best base for a tour of the northern Aegean, as it is within easy reach of both Troy and Pergamum. If you have the chance, stop off at Çandarlı to see one of the best-preserved Genoese forts in Turkey.

South of Izmir and directly opposite the island of Khíos, or Chios (Turkish Sakız) is the headland of Çeşme, popular with Turks for its fine sandy beaches. Farther south are the small resorts of Sığacık and Gümüldür. Then comes Kuşadası, the major resort of the Aegean, opposite the island of Sámos (Turkish Sisam), with the great showpiece site of Ephesus just inland. The pretty resort of Altınkum has grown up south of Kuşadası near the sites of Didim and Miletos, and is a quieter, yet accessible base. Farther south are the two charming peninsula resorts of Bodrum and Marmaris, with clusters of smaller offshoot resorts around them; neither of these makes a good touring base because of the long drive up the peninsula. At the southernmost point, very close to the airport of Dalaman, is the attractive resort of Dalyan in its unusual estuary setting.

The three airports serving Turkey's Aegean coast are the International Airport at Izmir (for the north and Kuşadası), the Bodrum/Milas Airport (for the center), and the Dalaman International Airport (for the south, Bodrum, and Marmaris).

ENDLESS INDENTATIONS
Turkey's Aegean shore is endlessly indented with bays and inlets, the result of earth movements over the millennia. This makes the coastline tremendously long and means that, although a few pockets are now heavily developed, you need never go very far to find empty beaches and unspoiled fishing villages.

103

TIMING
If you are touring in this area, using either Izmir or Kuşadası as a base, a circuit of the places described would take roughly two weeks.

The Yalı Mosque, Izmir

IONIAN CLIMATE
Herodotus, the famous historian and native of Asia Minor, claimed that the region known as ancient Ionia (from Izmir to Altınkum) had the best climate in the world, with a constant gentle breeze in summer to temper the heat.

The Greco-Roman stadium at Afrodisias, seating 30,000, is one of the best preserved in the world

RESIDENTS OF ASSOS
Aristotle lived at Assos from 347 to 344 BC, studying zoology, botany, and biology under the patronage of the eunuch ruler, Hermeias. Saint Paul also stayed here, in AD 56, during his third apostolic voyage.

The Greco-Roman style attained a peak of perfection in the city of Aphrodite

▶▶▶ Afrodisias (Aphrodisias)   *100C2*

The relatively isolated ruined city of Aphrodite lies some two and a half hours' drive inland from Kuşadası, on flat, fertile ground surrounded by distant mountains. It owes its outstanding reputation today to Professor Kenan Erim, a Turkish national attached to New York University, who in 1961 began excavations on the site—abandoned since the 14th century—and devoted the remaining 30 years of his life to the site. He is now buried here.

Entry tickets are sold at the site museum (*Open* daily 9–5 winter, 9–6:30 summer), which should be left until last. The path leads first out toward the perfectly preserved theater, originally Greek, then converted by the Romans for gladiatorial spectacles. Nearby are an *agora* (marketplace) and the theater baths. Beyond the manmade hill into which the theater is set lie the impressive Baths of Hadrian, with a handsome exercise ground in black and white marble. From here the path leads to the little *odeon* (theater) with nine rows of perfectly preserved seats, the most charming of the remains at Aphrodisias. Next to it is the so-called Bishop's Palace, with its lovely blue marble columns from local quarries. Beyond there looms the gigantic Temple of Aphrodite itself, with 14 of its columns re-erected from the confusing jumble left by the earthquakes and by the building's conversion into a basilica (law court) in the 5th century. To the north is the extraordinary stadium, one of the best preserved in the Greco-Roman world, with seating for 30,000. The path then loops back toward the museum, passing the recently excavated *sebasteion*: two grandiose porticoes enclosing a processional where many statues were found.

▶ Ayvalık
100A3

The major resort of the north Aegean, Ayvalık boasts a picturesque marina, an attractive traditional town center, and good sandy beaches. Three miles from the center is the island/peninsula of **Alibey**, famous for its fish restaurants and Aegean white wines. The frescoes in the Church of St. Nicholas are also worth a visit. Ayvalık's Greek Orthodox churches, notably **Taksiyarhis Kilesi**, now serve as mosques. The little islands in **Edremit Körfezi** (the Gulf of Edremit) also bear the remains of monasteries. In summer there are daily departures to the Greek island of **Lesbos** (two hours by car ferry). The best beaches are found 4 miles south of Ayvalık at **Sarmısaklı** (Garlic Beach), where the tourist hotels are clustered. The site of **Pergamum** is less than an hour's drive away.

▶▶ Behramkale (Assos)
100A3

Considered by many to be the prettiest small harbor in the northern Aegean, Behramkale offers the unusual combination of the ruins of a Greek city set on the clifftop above, and an attractive little fishing port below, lined with busy small hotels, restaurants, and cafés.

As you approach the ruins of Assos from Ayvalik, passing a 14th-century Ottoman bridge on the way, there are fine views of the headland site with the village clinging to the ridge beside it. The Hellenistic and Byzantine fortifications are still impressive, and at the summit stands the Temple of Athena (530 BC), the oldest Doric temple to have survived in Asia Minor. The view from here toward Lesbos and the Gulf of Edremit is spectacular.

EXPRESSIVE SCULPTURE
One of the ancient world's most famous schools of sculpture was housed at Afrodisias, and it is the quality and quantity of these sculptures, carved from the local marble and displayed in the on-site museum, that make a visit here memorable. Notice especially the expressive faces of the gods and goddesses—and of the Roman officials.

105

Ayvalık is both a busy, little working port and the major resort of the north Aegean

The importance of humor to the Turk is easily overlooked by outsiders, who may see only a dour exterior. Humor, and especially satire, form a key part of the Turkish character. Turks display a keen taste for political mockery and a finely developed sense of the absurd.

WEEPING FOR UGLINESS
Many stories involve the folk hero Nasreddin and the Mongol conqueror Tamerlane. In one, Tamerlane weeps for two hours because he has glimpsed his face in a mirror and is appalled by its ugliness. Nasreddin continues weeping, and when Tamerlane asks why, he replies: "If His Majesty weeps for two hours after only catching a glimpse of his face, then surely I, who see him all the time, should weep much longer."

A sense of humor helps when bartering

Nasreddin Hoca Innumerable tales covering most aspects of life are attributed to this great legendary sage, said to have lived in Akşehir in the 13th century. Here are a few of them.

A neighbor comes to borrow Hoca's rope. "I'm sorry," says Nasreddin, "I can't lend you my rope, my wife's spreading flour on it." "What do you mean?" asks the baffled neighbor. "That doesn't make sense." "I'm perfectly serious," says Hoca. "If I don't want to lend somebody my rope, flour can very easily be spread on it." Spreading flour on a rope has passed into idiomatic Turkish as a metaphor for avoiding something you don't want to do.

A young man comes to Hoca in despair, having lost all his money. "What will become of me," he wails, "without my money and my friends?" "Don't worry," says Hoca, "you'll soon be all right." The young man perks up. "You mean I'll get rich again and get back my friends?" "No," says Hoca, "but you'll get used to being poor and friendless."

Hoca had lost his donkey. While looking for it, he prayed and thanked God. "Why are you so grateful, when you have lost your precious donkey?" he was asked. "I'm happy because I was not riding the animal at the time. Otherwise I would have been lost, too!"

Arriving at a banquet in scruffy clothes, Hoca was ignored and not shown to a table. He went home, changed into his fur coat and came back again. This time he was shown to the best table. On sitting down he deliberately dipped his fur coat into the soup, saying, "Eat, eat, my fur coat, for it is you to whom this meal was proffered, not me."

Proverbs Here is a selection of authentically Turkish proverbs (as opposed to Arabic or Persian), highly revealing of the national character:
The thicker the veil, the less it is worth lifting.
The only worry-free head is a scarecrow's.
Hard work means a long life but short days.
Even if a woman's candlestick is cast in gold, it is the man who must supply the candle.
On a winter's day, the fireside is a bed of tulips.
Distant drums, sweet music.
Where the Turk rides, grass will not grow.
Success depends on a man's reputation, not on his soul.
If you dig a grave for your neighbor, measure it for yourself.

Political jokes Akbulut, prime minister from 1989 to 1993 under Türgüt Özal, and notorious for his stupidity, was the butt of many jokes. In a typical example a taxi driver asks his passenger: "Have you heard the latest Akbulut joke?" "I am Akbulut!" cries the outraged passenger. "Don't worry," replies the taxi driver, "I'll tell it very slowly."

Turkey also has a long tradition of satirical newspapers, with cartoons playing a very prominent role. Some examples can be seen in changing displays at the **Karikatur Müzesi** (Cartoon Museum) in Istanbul (see page 69).

Karagöz shadow plays For centuries these were a popular form of humor, but superseded by press, radio, and movies, they are now almost extinct. The two main characters were Karagöz, the "common man," and Hadjivat, the pompous intellectual, and many of the skits ended with Hadjivat being kicked off stage. Toward the decadent end of the Ottoman Empire, these shadow plays developed a strong tendency toward political satire. A young man would ask Karagöz, for example: "What should I do to further myself in my job?" And Karagöz would reply: "As you are completely ignorant, I advise you to become Chief Admiral." At this time the Sultan's son-in-law was Chief Admiral and a known incompetent.

TYPICAL INVECTIVE
"A horse, an ox, and a donkey lived up in the hills. One day the Devil whispered to them: 'Why not go to town and see what the humans are like?' So they did. A few years later they met to compare stories.

The horse and the ox both related how they were caught and forced to carry heavy loads and pull carts. The donkey laughed and told how he had arrived in town at election time and joined in the hullabaloo, shouting louder than everyone else, until he was elected to rule. 'But didn't they notice you were a donkey?' asked the incredulous horse and ox. 'They did in the end, but by that time four years had gone by and it was time for the next election.'"
From a left-wing satirical paper

107

The Aegean

▶▶ Bodrum (Halicarnassus)   *100B1*

Known as the most upscale and bohemian of Turkish resorts, Bodrum, with its pretty, whitewashed houses and abundant flowers, has always attracted a sophisticated crowd. Despite the invasion of mass tourism in recent years, it has managed to retain its special atmosphere, bustling with people and colorful activity. With its wonderful harbor and marina, full of expensive international yachts and elegant wooden Turkish *caiques* (light skiffs), available for charter or daily rental, it is also the yachting center of the Aegean. If you are touring, two nights are enough to sample the nightlife and restaurants and visit the castle. The Bodrum/Milas Airport, opened in 1998, is a 40-minute drive north, and flies international and domestic flights.

The Castle▶▶▶ (*Open* Tue–Sun 8–12 and 1–5. *Admission charge*) This Crusader castle, built to dominate the harbor by the Knights Hospitaller of Saint John in 1402, is one of the last and finest examples of Crusader architecture in the east. The knights occupied the castle until 1523, when Süleyman the Magnificent's conquest of

The superb Crusader castle at Bodrum

their base on the Greek island of Rhodes (Ródhos) forced them to withdraw to Malta. A leisurely tour takes between two and three hours.

As you enter the castle through an impressive series of seven gates plus a moat, look for the fragments of reliefs from the Mausoleum set into the walls and over the gates. Inside are several museums (*Open* daily 10–12 and 2–4) and open-air cafés. An imaginative **Museum of Underwater Archaeology** charts the techniques used by an American team to excavate the wreck of a ship that sank 32 centuries ago and was found sitting in water 90 feet deep.

From the fine towers and sentry walkway along the escarpment walls there are dramatic views over the bay and harbor.

Shopping in Bodrum

DIVING OUTINGS
Diving has recently become a popular way of exploring the nearby shores, with their caves and unusual rock formations. One-day trips with transportation and a picnic lunch can be arranged through many tour operators on the harbor front. A popular spot is the "Akvaryum" in the Ada Boğazı (Island Strait), with unusually clear water and plentiful fish.

109

Shopping and nightlife Strolling around Bodrum at any time of day or night is always a great pleasure. The main bazaar area lies in the pedestrian precinct at the foot of the castle, but little shops of all sorts abound in all the narrow streets. Local specialties include natural sponges, soft cotton clothes, and lapis lazuli beads to ward off the evil eye, along with the usual endless selection of carpets, jewelry, copper, ceramics, leather, and embroidery.

Bodrum is justly renowned for its nightlife, with scores of bars, restaurants, and nightclubs, as well as some of the best discos in Europe—notably the **Halicarnassus**, with a laser show focused on the castle. Another form of evening entertainment is the promenade along the waterfront, where you can enjoy the spectacle of locals, beach bums, and jet-setters all watching each other.

An herb and spice stall in the bazaar

Beaches Swimming at the town's small beach can be crowded and noisy, so boats and *dolmuş* (shared taxis) run regularly to nearby beaches on the peninsula. On the southern side there are good sandy beaches at **Bardakçı**, **Gümbet**, **Bitez**, **Ortakent Yalısı**, **Karaincir**, **Bağla**, and **Akyarlar**, which has fine, powdery sand. Ortakent has the longest stretch of undeveloped sand, while Karaincir, with its small village, is one of the most beautiful on the whole peninsula. On the western tip are **Turgutreis**, **Gümüşlük**, and **Yalıkavak**, ideal for swimming and water sports, all with friendly villages. On the northern side of the peninsula are the tiny fishing villages of **Gölköy** and **Türkbükü**, with their handful of *lokantas* (informal restaurants), and the modern resort of **Torba**, with its marina and popular vacation village.

One of the greatest pleasures of vacationing in Turkey is the ease and speed with which you can hop on a boat to visit one of many offshore islands with the minimum of formalities—even when that island is actually part of Greece, not Turkey.

TO THE GREEK ISLANDS

Many Greek islands—Lesbos, Chios, Sámos, Cos, and Rhodes being the major ones—lie just off the Turkish coast and can be reached by regular ferries. No visas are required, and tickets can simply be bought on the Turkish port waterfront. Take your passport along.

A gület under construction at Kemer

Aegean outings Most boat trips are concentrated in the southern Aegean region, mainly from **Marmaris** and **Bodrum**. The only northern excursion of note is from **Ayvalık marina** to the **Ayvalık islands**, all uninhabited and with beautiful beaches and ruined monasteries. There is also a car ferry service (daily in summer, weekly in winter) from Ayvalık to **Midilli**, the Greek island of Lesbos (Lésvos), taking two hours each way.

Chios (Khíos, or Turkish Sakız) is an easy hop from the Turkish resort of **Çeşme**, and in season boats run twice daily from **Kuşadası** to **Sámos** (Turkish Sisam). From **Bodrum** you can take a boat trip to **Karaada** (Black Island), 30 minutes away, where you can improve your skin by bathing in a grotto filled with warm mineral springs. You can also rent a boat or take a yacht tour lasting two, three, or seven days around the **Gulf of Gökova** (Gökova Körfezi), with its thickly wooded coastline and clear turquoise waters. Most boats are rented from the western harbor. Ferries also run to **Cos** (Kos, or Turkish Istanköy).

From **Marmaris**, ferries run daily except on Sundays to **Rhodes** (Ródhos). As the trip takes two and a half hours, most people spend at least one night there, exploring the walled Crusader town. If possible, avoid going in July and August when the narrow streets on the island can become excessively crowded.

***Gület* cruising** Vacations on *gülets*, traditional motor yachts built from the red pine that grows in profusion all along Turkey's southern shore, are becoming increasingly popular. These extremely attractive boats, with pointed bow and stern, come complete with cook and crew, who ensure your total relaxation.

Marmaris, **Bodrum**, **Fethiye**, **Kalkan**, and **Kaş** are the main *gület* centers, and in a 14-day cruise it is possible to explore the coastline all the way from Bodrum to Fethiye. Boats sleep eight to 12, and most of the cabins are equipped with shower and toilet. Hot water is provided by an on-board generator, and most boats also have a cassette player for you to play your own tapes. A windsurfing board or two is usually provided. As on all boats, space is at a premium, so pack sparingly. There is always a shaded area on deck, and the captain consults with the passengers to see whether they would like to drop anchor for a swim or explore an ancient Greek ruined city. The cook also consults about menu preferences for breakfast and lunch. Passengers usually eat dinner at a restaurant at that night's mooring. Children under 12 are accepted only if the whole boat has been booked by a single party: most *gület* cruises are booked by couples without children.

Specialized tour operators book vacations of this type (your local Turkish Tourist Office can give you a list). Out of season (April, May, and October) you can arrange them on the spot, though bear in mind that hefty deposits are required. In peak season (June to September) prices jump considerably.

A boat trip from Dalyan, where boats are moored along the riverbanks ready to take tourists to local beaches, spas, and Greek ruins

SORTIE TO TURKISH CYPRUS
If you have the time you could catch a boat at Alanya or Taşucu and find yourself in Kyrenia (Turkish Girne), on the northern coast of Cyprus (five or two hours, respectively). Fares are cheap, no visa is required for E.U. or U.S. citizens, and no advance booking is necessary. The currency here is the Turkish lira, and the cost of living is even lower than in Turkey: with rental car rates at only a third of those in Turkey, this is an ideal way to explore the Crusader castles, classical sites, and Greek monasteries in the area.

The Aegean

►► Dalyan (Caunus) 100C1

A 20-minute drive from Dalaman Airport, Dalyan makes an excellent base for vacations in the lower Aegean: it is an easy hop from here to the **Marmaris** and **Bodrum peninsulas**, and it is also on the doorstep of **Lycia**, the beautiful mountainous coastline that begins at Fethiye and runs eastward to Antalya.

Set on the riverbank at the mouth of the freshwater **Lake Köyceğiz**, Dalyan has been spared the worst excesses of tourist development and boasts a growing selection of tasteful hotels and restaurants. The local specialty is the fish—mainly mullet and bass—bred in the estuary.

In the town, boats are moored along the riverbank ready to take you to **Istuzu beach**, or 10 minutes upriver to the hot thermal baths at **Ilıca**, where you can wallow in mud that reaches approximately 110°F. The third destination is **Caunus**, the ruined Greek city that lies downriver in the marshes. Among its attractions are the astonishing rock tombs that are set in the cliffs opposite Dalyan.

A remarkable series of ancient tombs is hewn out of the living rock opposite Dalyan

The boat ride from Dalyan to Caunus takes approximately 15 minutes, and there is a further 10-minute walk to reach the site. The first buildings you see are a Byzantine basilica and a huge Roman bath to your left. The well-preserved theater is set into the acropolis hill, which is crowned by a 4th-century BC fort. Notice, as well, the impressive city walls. These were built by King Mausolus and also date from the 4th century BC. Excavations began on the site in 1967 and are still continuing, using labor from the prison in Dalaman.

Originally on the sea, Caunus now lies 2 miles inland, owing to the silting up of the river over the centuries. If you look down on the site from the top seats of the theater, it is possible to make out the location of the original port.

TURTLE SANCTUARY
Since the wildlife campaign led by British conservationist David Bellamy, Dalyan has been famous for its loggerhead turtles (*Caretta caretta*), which hatch on the local Istuzu beach between May and October. The beach is now protected by wardens, though it remains open to the public for swimming and sunbathing, and all building projects have been banned. Mosquitoes also thrive in this marshy environment, so go armed with repellent.

113

▶▶▶ Efes (Ephesus) *100B2*

Famous throughout history for its Temple of Artemis, one of the Seven Wonders of the Ancient World, this great and sacred city lay in ruins until the early 20th century. Now it is one of the most extensive archaeological sites in the world. It falls into three distinct areas: the **Artemision** (site of the Temple of Artemis); the area around the town of **Selçuk**, with the **site museum** and the **Basilica of Saint John**; and, finally, the Roman city of **Ephesus** itself, which is some 2 miles west of Selçuk along the road to Kuşadası. If you are short on time, concentrate on Ephesus.

The Artemision▶ (*Open 8:30–5:30. Admission free*) Signs direct you from the town of Selçuk to the site, set in a hollow and encircled by trees. All that remains is a single column rising out of a muddy pool, and you need to muster all your imaginative powers to visualize the original 127 columns, each one nearly 60 feet high and altogether covering an area four times greater than that of the Parthenon. Throughout Asia Minor, Ionic temples usually were sited on low ground, the better to show off their tall, slender columns; broader, squatter Doric columns, on the other hand, needed a higher position (as with the Parthenon) to be visually effective.

Artemis of the Ephesians was a Greek adaptation of Cybele, the Anatolian earth-mother goddess whose outstanding quality was her fertility. On her annual feast day, great orgies took place here. When the Romans arrived they identified her with Diana, their own fertility goddess, and the cult continued for more than a thousand years, conferring great wealth on the city as devotees flocked to it from all over the world. The downfall of the goddess came with the advent of Christianity.

A small part of the remains at Ephesus— much of the site is yet to be excavated

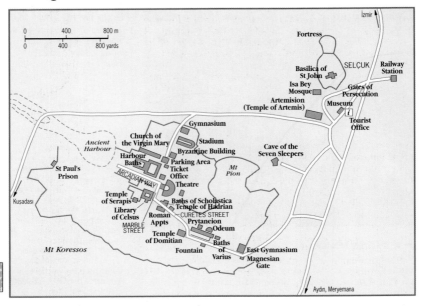

İzmir

| 0 | 400 | 800 m |
| 0 | 400 | 800 yards |

Fortress

Basilica of
St John

SELÇUK   Railway
Station

Isa Bey
Mosque

Gates of
Persecution

Artemision
(Temple of Artemis)

Museum

Tourist
Office

Gymnasium

Church of
the Virgin Mary

Stadium
Byzantine Building

Cave of the
Seven Sleepers

Ancient
Harbour

Harbour
Baths

Parking Area

St Paul's
Prison

ARCADIAN WAY

Ticket
Office

Mt
Pion

Theatre

Kuşadası

Temple
of Serapis

Baths of Scholastica
Temple of Hadrian

Library
of Celsus

Roman
Appts

CURETES STREET

Prytaneion

MARBLE
STREET

Odeum

Temple
of Domitian

Baths
of
Varius

East Gymnasium

Mt Koressos

Fountain

Magnesian
Gate

Aydın, Meryemana

114

Ephesus

LINKS WITH EGYPT
The colossal Temple of
Serapis at Ephesus illus-
trates the popularity of
the bull cult in the eastern provinces. Serapis
was an invention of the
Ptolemies, who superim-
posed the features of a
Greek god on its original
Egyptian features.

*The Library of Celsus at
Ephesus, built in* AD 110

Selçuk and the Museum►► Many of the beautiful marble blocks of the Artemision can today be seen in the
Basilica of Saint John (*Open* 8–6. *Admission charge*) and the
Isa Bey Mosque (*Admission charge*), less than half a mile
away. The 14th-century mosque, built at the foot of the
acropolis hill by the Seljuks who gave the town its present
name, is a picturesque ruin.

A short climb up the road leads to the precinct of the
crenellated fortress, originally Byzantine but rebuilt by
the Seljuks, within which lies the Basilica of Saint John, a
vast early 6th-century building in which a few floor
mosaics and frescoes remain.

By the tourist office is the **Efes Museum** (*Open* Tue–Sun
8:30–12:30 and 1:30–5:30), visited primarily for its two
marble statues of Artemis Ephesia.

The Ephesus Site►►► The Artemision originally
stood on a natural sheltered harbor, but the river mouth
silted up, and soon after Alexander's death in 323 BC the
city was moved to this new site farther west. The silting
process continued even so, despite the efforts of Nero and
Hadrian, and the ancient port of Ephesus is now over 3
miles from the sea.

The approach road today takes you past the ruins of a
vast **Roman gymnasium** and **stadium** (*Open* daily 8 until
sunset. *Admission charge*).

Head straight to the intersection of the marble road and
the Arcadian Way, where you can climb the steps of the
theater for good views of the site. The grandiose ruins
date almost exclusively to the Roman imperial age, and
their sheer extent and completeness (thanks to the efforts
of the Austrian excavators) help to give a feel of what life
in an ancient Greco-Roman city must have been like. The
Hellenistic **theater**, with Roman additions, has been renovated to make it safe for audiences during the Seljuk
Ephesus Festival of Culture and Art, held each May. The

white marble **Arcadian Way** used to lead straight down to the harbor and was lined with shops and porticoes; it even had street lighting as early as 400 BC. It was here that Cleopatra made her triumphal entry into Ephesus to visit Mark Antony.

Next, explore the enormous **Harbor Baths** and the curiously long and thin **Church of the Virgin Mary**, the setting for the violent Third Ecumenical Council in AD 431, at which Nestorius denied the doctrines of the virgin birth and the divinity of Jesus.

Walk along **Marble Street**, noting the ruts made by chariot wheels, to reach the imposing two-story façade of the **Library of Celsus**, the best-preserved structure of its kind in the world. Behind the library stands the massive **Temple of Serapis**, still with traces of the original blue and red paint on its columns.

From the library, the impressive **Curetes Street** snakes up the hill to the **Magnesian Gate**. To the right are expensive villas and to the left are various public buildings. Among these, do not miss the **Baths of Scholastica**, with their communal latrines in white marble, and the adjacent brothel. The 1st- to 6th-century villas, some with well-preserved murals and mosaic floors, give a vivid picture of the luxurious lifestyle of their rich owners.

Outside the site you can take a horsedrawn carriage (phaeton) to the **Cave of the Seven Sleepers**, site of a Byzantine necropolis at the foot of Mount Pion.

115

One of the two marble statues of Artemis Ephesia

The beautifully decorated façade of the Temple of Hadrian

HOUSE OF THE VIRGIN MARY
In the forested hills 5 miles from Ephesus lies the house/chapel known as Meryemana (*Open daily 8–7. Admission charge*), where the Virgin Mary is said to have lived her last days. The house was "discovered" in the 19th century after an invalid German lady, for years confined to her bed, and who had never set foot in Turkey, described its exact location as revealed to her in a vision. A priest from Izmir read her description and in 1891 set out to find the house. It is now a destination for pilgrims from all over the world.

Walk

Alinda

The impressive hilltop ruins of Alinda, an ancient Greek city where Alexander the Great once stayed, are an easy day trip from Bodrum, Marmaris, Kuşadası, or even Izmir, with a chance to see some beautiful inland scenery.

The modern town at the foot of the ruins is Karpuzlu, 16 miles off the main Aydın- to- Muğla highway. The total distance from Bodrum or Kuşadası is about 70 miles (taking about an hour and a half). The walk up to the ruins is pretty steep, and also takes about 90 minutes, but you can drive to the summit if you prefer.

The ruins of Alinda, unquestionably among the finest in the area, are only rarely visited as they lie somewhat off the beaten track. In Karpuzlu, follow the market street lined with booths and stalls; at the end, a small blue sign marked "Alinda" points up

The neglected but beautiful Greek theater at Alinda

a winding track to the right. Follow this and park at the side of the road on the edge of the town, looking for the small path on the right that zig-zags past the final group of houses.

This brings you after a few minutes to an open *agora* (marketplace), at the end of which is a vast and impressive building. The best-preserved of its kind in all Asia Minor, a three-story **market hall** still stands over 50 feet high, evoking the experience of ancient Greek shopping more vividly than any other surviving structure.

From here a steep and slippery path climbs for about 15 minutes to a hollow in the hillside where the heavily overgrown **Greek theater** looks out over the town below. Characteristic vaulted passages added by the Romans have survived intact, as has much of the stage building. From all around there are excellent views of the superb defensive walls with their towers and battlements.

After an energetic half-hour scramble you'll reach the **Hellenistic tower** on the summit. Alternatively, you can

ALİNDA, AYDIN-TÜRKIYE

T.C.
VALILIĞI

D

RENYERI
BİLETİ

90663

TL.

116

return to your car and drive up the road until you reach the well-preserved arches of an **aqueduct**, which makes a good picnic spot with fine views. Beyond, a small path climbs to the main acropolis of Alinda. Here are the foundations of what were probably the royal apartments of Queen Ada, exiled to Alinda in a power struggle with her own family. When Alexander the Great swept through Asia Minor in 333 BC, she offered to help him plot the siege of Halicarnassus (modern Bodrum), where her younger brother was ruler. Alexander accepted and together, probably on this very hilltop, they prepared for the attack. After the success of their campaign, Alexander brought Ada out of exile and proclaimed her Queen of all Caria.

On your return drive, explore the derelict houses on the outskirts of town, some whitewashed with blue shutters, others with wooden overhanging balconies. Many have court-

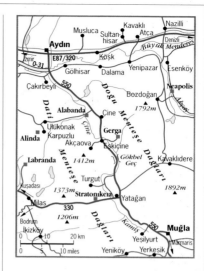

yards littered with carved blocks from the ancient ruins.

Alinda's ruins, redolent of antiquity

117

CULTURAL CAPITAL

Izmir has built a reputation for itself as Turkey's second cultural capital, after Istanbul. The Cultural Center hosts opera, theater, ballet, and concert performances, with the additional high points of the International Arts Festival in June and July and the International Fair in August and September. Many of these events are staged in the huge and beautiful Kültür Park.

Its strategic position at the end of the peninsula leading to Izmir means that the attractive town of Çeşme has always been an important naval base; now, thanks to its spa and beaches, it is a busy resort as well

▶▶ Izmir (Smyrna) — 100B3

Izmir is the modern successor to Miletos and Efes (Ephesus) as the major port on the Aegean; it is also Turkey's third city, after Istanbul and Ankara. Attractively set on the hillsides that line the sweep of its bay, Izmir is a typically Levantine city, densely populated, lively, dusty, and colorful; this is especially true of its old quarters, where little houses painted in shades of green, yellow, blue, and ocher crowd together beneath red-tiled roofs. If you want to get away from the bustle of the city, stay in Foça to the north or Siğacık to the south.

Earthquakes and the disastrous fire that took place in 1922, during the War of Independence, have destroyed most of Izmir's buildings of historic interest, leaving only the Roman marketplace (*Open* 8:30–5:30 daily. *Admission charge*), the **bazaars** inland from the elaborate **Ottoman clock tower** on the seafront, and the flat-topped **Kadifekale**, the ancient acropolis. From here there is a superb view over the town and harbor, especially at sunset. If you are just passing through, try to stop for lunch at one of the excellent seafront **fish restaurants**, which serve specialties such as lobster and sea bass.

ENVIRONS OF IZMIR Çeşme▶ The biggest and most famous of the beach resorts around Izmir, Çeşme is an essentially Turkish resort and thermal spa (Çeşme means "spring"), dominated by its 14th-century Genoese fortress with a labyrinth of twisting back streets behind. The attractive promenade is lined with restaurants. The long, sandy beaches where most of the hotels are concentrated lie a little outside the town.

Foça▶ Very well placed for access to Izmir Airport, this pretty fishing village has a bustling harborfront with excellent seafood restaurants. Club Med has a village nearby, but otherwise there are just a few hotels. With its whitewashed houses and cobbled streets, it has a very Turkish feel about it.

Yalı Mosque, Izmir

RICH AS CROESUS
Croesus, last and greatest of the Lydian kings, became phenomenally wealthy as a result of the gold deposits discovered in the River Paktolos. The Lydians are believed to have been the earliest people to mint coins, using gold taken from the small stream that flowed through Sardis. The gold was collected by laying sheepskins in the water to catch the particles: the origin of the Golden Fleece.

Sart (Sardis)▶▶ Rarely visited (because its location 56 miles east of Izmir makes it difficult to incorporate into an itinerary), **Sardis**, wealthy capital of the ancient Lydian Empire, is one of the most impressive sites in Turkey. The unusual rock formations in the nearby hills lend it a uniquely strange atmosphere, and this curious pointed landscape shelters hundreds of Lydian tombs, some dating back to the 7th century BC. It is the **Roman ruins** of Sardis, excavated by American teams since 1958, that are particularly impressive now, consisting of a road lined with shops, a gymnasium, and a synagogue (originally a basilica). There is lovely marble throughout, as well as mosaic flooring.

The other part of the site lies half a mile or so away, around the most striking monument in Sardis, the **Temple of Artemis**. Of the original 82 columns only two remain intact, with parts of 13 others still standing. The Ionic capitals on these columns are among the most beautiful known. Sacrifices to the goddess were made on the altar located at the top of the flight of steps.

Sığacık▶, a little resort 75 minutes' drive south of Izmir, has a headland on either side of which lie two small sheltered bays with camping facilities and hotels. Nearby lies the ancient site of **Teos**, picturesquely lost among the olive groves. The village of Sığacık has a fine Genoese fortress which rises high above its little fishing harbor and its yachting marina.

REVOLTING ANCIENT WINE
The famous Pramnian wine, described by Homer as the drink of heroes, is said to have come from Smyrna. Mixed with seawater or honey, chalk, and powdered marble (thought to make it sweet), it must have been pretty revolting in its original, undiluted state in order to have warranted such adulteration.

Carnival time in Izmir

In movie theaters throughout Turkey, mass audiences enjoy films featuring good guys against bad guys with lots of fights, or cloyingly romantic tales of rural teenagers whose love is thwarted by their families and the world in general, but who triumph in the end and live happily ever after. Since the 1960s, however, bolder directors have been exploring more realistic subjects, such as the consequences of the drift of the rural population to the cities and the breakdown of traditional lifestyles.

HEART OF TURKISH MOVIES

Beyoğlu is where movies began in Istanbul. The first showings were in 1897, and the Luxembourg Cinema, the first in Turkey, opened a few years later. A series of extravagantly decorated theaters then followed: Pathé (1908), Cine Palace (1914), Electra (1920), and Elhamra (1922). Turkish movie theaters are now concentrated on Istiklal Caddesi and Yeşilçam Sokağı.

Istanbul's annual film festival is a showcase for new work

Yılmaz Güney By far the best known Turkish director—and possibly the only one to have established an international reputation—is Yılmaz Güney. He produced his first major film in 1970; called *Umut (Hope)*, it is the tale of a desperate and gullible taxi driver who loses his house, his horse, and finally his mind. The final scene is unforgettable: the blindfolded hero circles a hole in the ground to the accompaniment of haunting music played on the reed flute.

In 1971 Güney made two more movies—*Ağıt (The Elegy)*, about a man driven to smuggling by abject poverty, and *Acık (Sorrow)*, on the subject of lost love and revenge. After the 1971 coup Güney was put in prison and not released till 1974, only to be imprisoned again on the charge of murdering a judge.

It was during this spell in prison that Güney produced his best work, writing the scripts in his cell and passing them out secretly to friends, along with exact instructions on how to film each scene. These scripts usually revolved around Güney's abiding interest, the problems of the rural poor, a theme which he developed further in each film.

In 1979 *Sürü (The Herd)* was released. Güney wrote it in prison and Zeki Ükten directed it in Güney's absence. The movie follows a Kurdish family taking their sheep to market in Ankara, and shows their bewilderment at the world in which they find themselves. Güney's most famous movie, *Yol (The Road)*, also written from prison and directed this time by Şerif Gören, was finally released in 1982. It follows the fortunes of five prisoners allowed out on parole for a week, each of whom encounters a changed and alien world and finally meets with tragedy. Having escaped from jail, Güney was able to edit the film himself while in exile in France. Aged 46, he died of cancer.

New developments Political turbulence and censorship imposed severe restrictions on Turkish movies in the late 1970s and 1980s, but a few notable works did nevertheless emerge. One of these was

ULUSLARARASI İSTANBUL FİLM FESTİVALİ

İSTANBUL KÜLTÜR VE SANAT VAKFI

FİLM

ULUSLARARASI / INTERNATIONAL İSTANBUL FİLM FESTİVALİ

13

AP RI L 2 - 17 Nİ SA N 1994

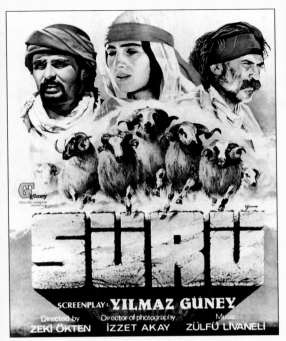

SCREENPLAY: YILMAZ GÜNEY

Directed by	Director of photography	Music
ZEKİ ÖKTEN	İZZET AKAY	ZÜLFÜ LİVANELİ

MUCH ALLEGORY

Fairly strict censorship is applied to movies in Turkey, and many Western ones are banned for being too sexually or politically explicit. Turkish filmmakers face the same constraints, with the result that they often deal with their subjects obliquely, using allegorical characters and plots.

Released in 1979, Sürü (The Herd), *which follows the fortunes of a Kurdish family taking their sheep to market in Ankara, was written by Yilmaz Güney from his prison cell*

A Season in Hakkâri by Erdan Kırel, a West German co-production, which follows the experiences of a young schoolteacher sent to work in a remote Kurdish village.

Other subjects treated for the first time include the position of women in Turkish society, social hypocrisy, and the problems faced by migrant workers in Germany. Of these, one of the best is *Forty Square Meters of Germany*, directed by Tevfik Başer and released in 1987.

There were indications in the 1990s that government censorship may be easing up. The 1995 movie, *Blackout Nights* by Yusuf Kürçenli, discusses the short-sightedness of censorship and political oppression: a hopeful sign for the future of Turkish film-making.

Güney himself (left) starred in his first major film, Umut (Hope), *as well as writing and directing it*

The Aegean

The island that gave Kuşadası its name, now linked to the mainland by a concrete causeway

The great Medusa's head is an indication of the grand scale of Didim's ruins

▶ **Kuşadası (Bird Island)**　　　　　*100B2*

This is the most overdeveloped resort in the Aegean, for one simple reason—its proximity to **Ephesus**. Buses flood in from Izmir Airport, 60 minutes away, and cruise ships disgorge their passengers at the harbor. The result, predictably enough, is a resort that has lost most of its original charm, and in which the local people have lost their souls to tourism and hard selling. Even other Turks express their dislike of it. That said, its location still makes it a good base for excursions inland, and there is a wide selection of nightlife, entertainment, restaurants, and shops. There is also a new and well-equipped yachting marina.

In summer, boats run daily across to the Greek island of **Sámos**. The public beach on the main Kuşadası bay is rather overcrowded, and most prefer the sandy **Kadınlar Plajı** (Ladies' Beach) 2 miles away, where hotels such as the Imbat are found. Kuşadası gets its name from the former island now linked to the mainland by a concrete causeway. The Genoese castle on the island has been converted into discos and cafés.

ENVIRONS OF KUŞADASI Priene▶▶ This modest Greek city dating from the 4th century BC, in a setting that is unquestionably the most spectacular of all the ancient Ionian cities, makes a telling contrast with the grandiose Roman monuments of nearby Ephesus. Once a flourishing port, it now languishes nearly 10 miles away from the Aegean, owing to the silting up of the Maeander river. A steepish 10-minute climb leads from the ticket booth (*Open* daily 8:30–sunset. *Admission charge*) to the ancient city center, where the Temple of Athena once stood. A thorough exploration takes two hours or more and involves a fair amount of climbing.

Milet (Miletos)▶▶ Like Ephesus and Priene, the ancient port of Miletos was marooned by the retreating sea and ruined by the consequent loss of its trading role.

The ticket booth (*Open* daily 8:30–sunset) stands in front of the magnificent **theater**. Note the well-preserved vaulted passages leading to the seats at either side. From the crumbling **Byzantine fortress** on the acropolis above the theater, you can make out the contours of the **old harbor** to the east. Much of this area is marshy or even under water today, and a raised dirt track has been constructed to give easier access to the ruins in the former city center. The major monuments here are an *agora* (marketplace) with **baths** and a **gymnasium**, a *buleterion* (council chamber), and a *nymphaeum* (monumental fountain). Also impressive are the **Roman Baths of Faustina**, a complex of rooms with walls still standing nearly 50 feet high.

A powerful sculpture of a lion from Didim

Didim▶▶ Site of the great **oracle temple of Apollo**, Didim is at its most impressive at sunset, striking in its sheer scale. Seven high steps lead up to the main platform; this originally had 120 colossal columns, 103 of which still stand today. Many have decorated bases and capitals, though the most memorable carving by far is the huge, cracked head of Medusa (1st century BC) lying on the ground, having fallen long ago from the frieze.

Before issuing a prophecy, the oracle priestesses were said to fast for three days, then inhale the sulfur fumes from the spring until they swooned in a state of divine inspiration. Their utterances were then translated into hexameter verse by the oracle priests.

ANCIENT THEATERS
Turkey has more than 200 ancient Greek and Roman theaters. The finest Greek example is at Priene; the best Roman one is at Aspendos (see page 146). The most outstanding Greco-Roman example, holding no fewer than 15,000 spectators, is at Miletos.

123

SAGE OF MILETOS
The most famous citizen of Miletos was Thales, one of the Seven Sages of Antiquity, who was born in the 6th century BC. He thanked the gods for three things: that he was human and not an animal; a man and not a woman; and a Greek and not a barbarian. His most famous dictum, "Know thyself," is inscribed on the temple at Delphi.

The ruins of the oracle temple of Apollo at Didim still inspire awe through their sheer size and grace

Drive

Kuşadası to Lake Bafa and Herakleia

This drive makes an exhilarating day trip from either Kuşadası or Bodrum, offering the chance to enjoy the setting of Lake Bafa (Bafa Gölü), sample its fish, swim in its waters, and explore the romantic ruined city of Herakleia ad Latmos on its shores.

The distance from Bodrum is 66 miles, an 80-minute drive, and from Kuşadası 52 miles, taking just an hour. The main road from Efes (Ephesus) and Kuşadası to Bodrum and Marmaris passes along the southern lakeshore, where you come to a clutch of simple restaurants and a motel/camp-grounds. You can lunch here or at a restaurant on the opposite shore,

below Herakleia ad Latmos. Choose the excellent Bafa fish.

Continuing toward Bodrum and Marmaris, you will reach the village of Çamiçi, where a yellow sign points left to Herakleia (6 miles). The narrow track winds back to the eastern lakeshore, where the ancient ruins lie in their dramatic setting beneath **Mount Latmos** (4,700 feet). The mystery and charm of the lake's atmosphere are enhanced by the remains of a **Byzantine church** and **convent** on its little islands. Over the centuries a number of religious communities sought refuge from persecution here, but all their buildings fell into ruin after the Turkish conquest.

In antiquity Herakleia stood on the coast, and what is now a freshwater lake was then an inlet of the Aegean, afterward cut off by the silting up of the Maeander river. By the restaurant at the foot of the site you can swim through the reeds to the islet. The

Looking over Lake Bafa from Herakleia

A rural scene on one of the quiet roads near Herakleia

ancient city's fortifications are its most remarkable feature: for from 300 BC it was enclosed by extensive **defense walls**, which still climb to a ridge some 1,500 feet up the slopes of Mount Latmos and cover a total distance of 4 miles. Many of the towers, windows, gates, and stairways up to the parapets are still in excellent condition.

According to legend, this is the spot where the handsome demigod Endymion was sleeping when the moon goddess Selene saw him and fell in love with him. Zeus, jealous of a rumored liaison between Endymion and Hera, had decreed that Endymion should sleep forever on Mount Latmos, and in his dreams Selene slept with him and bore him 50 daughters. In Christian times Endymion was adopted as a local mystic saint, and Christian anchorites pronounced an ancient tomb discovered here to be Endymion's and made it a sanctuary.

This **sanctuary** can still be seen to the right of the road as you approach. Walk beyond it to the headland where the ruins of a fortified **Byzantine monastery** stand.

Continuing toward the mountain, you come to the most prominent building of ancient Herakleia: the **Temple of Athena**, a simple edifice with beautifully crafted masonry walls perched on a promontory.

Inland from this lies the *agora* (marketplace), where the school of the adjacent village of Kapıkırı now stands. On the south side of the agora is a well-preserved **market building** divided into shops. A little farther inland is the charming *buleterion* or council chamber, poorly preserved but in a fine setting among the trees on the edge of the village. There is also a **theater** about 300 yards away to the right up the mountain, again poorly preserved, as are the unidentified temples above it.

The glow of sunset adds to Lake Bafa's peaceful charm

100B1

▶▶ Marmaris

The resort of Marmaris boasts Turkey's largest yachting center and is the embarkation point for many *gület* cruises. Despite the damage caused by an earthquake in 1958, it remains a pleasant town, with a more Turkish feel than Bodrum.

The attractive harbor is lined with palm trees and crammed with cruise boats, and a walk along the length of the promenade makes an enjoyable hour's stroll. The older part of town is now pedestrians-only, and parking along the main promenade has been prohibited in order to reduce noise and congestion (this sometimes means the nearest parking for seafront hotels is a 15-minute walk away). Colorful restaurants and cafés line the front, and the market and shops sell an excellent selection of Turkish crafts, including jewelry, leather, and carpets. Be on the lookout, too, for the delicious local honey. The town's only relic of any great age is its crumbling **Ottoman castle**, built in 1522 by Süleyman the Magnificent, which squats heavily on a hillock jutting out into the bay in the old quarter.

The town beaches are crowded and noisy: by far your best bet is to take a day trip by boat to sandy beaches nearby, such as **Sedir Adası** (Cedar Island) and **Ingilizlimanı**.

Boats run daily to Rhodes (Ródhos), which lies directly opposite, a journey of two to three hours. The transfer time from Dalaman airport is one-and-a-half hours.

▶ Milas (Mylasa)   100B2

A busy market town set at a natural crossroads, Milas offers a few unusual and surprising monuments that are worth seeking out. The first, which stands on the western outskirts of the town, is a relic of ancient Mylasa: a large Roman mausoleum known in Turkish as **Gümüşkesen**. It is all the more interesting for being a replica in miniature of the Mausoleum in Halicarnassus, a famous Wonder of the Ancient World of which nothing now remains. The second is the **Firuz Bey mosque**, built in 1394 from pinkish marble blocks taken from ancient Greek temples. Most impressive of all, however, is the splendid castle, **Beçin Kale** (*Open* daily 8–sunset. *Admission charge*), originally Byzantine but adapted by the 14th-century Menteşe emirs, and set 3 miles south of Milas on an unmistakable flat-topped rock. Within this small walled citadel are houses, a little *madrasa* (theological school), and a mosque. The castle can be reached by a dirt road.

ENVIRONS OF MILAS Euromos▶▶
The elegant columns of this temple to Zeus stand by the road some 10 miles north of Milas. It is one of the best-preserved temples in Asia Minor today, still with much of its structure intact, possibly as a result of its sheltered position in the lee of three

Among the many attractions of the Marmaris area is its delicious honey

FJORD SETTING
Marmaris sits in a huge, almost landlocked bay with pine forests reaching down to the sea in a fjord-like setting. In 1798 the British national hero Admiral Horatio Nelson had his fleet shelter in this anchorage before sailing to Egypt, where it destroyed the French fleet in the Battle of the Nile.

Men playing dominoes at a bar in Muğla

wooded slopes. The temple was originally part of an ancient city, the ruins of which lie over the hill, still unexcavated and lost among the trees and scrub.

Labranda▶▶ The atmospheric ruins of Labranda make an unusual excursion from Milas, 11 miles to the north. Site of a hilltop sanctuary of Zeus, Labranda belonged to Mylasa, and used to be linked to it by a paved sacred way, used for religious processions. Festivals including sporting contests used to be held here, and the ruins of a stadium have recently been located by the site's Swedish excavators. The ruins of the sanctuary area are impressive, with gateways, monumental tombs and baths, as well as the temple itself.

127

▶ Muğla   *100B2*

This large town, capital of Muğla province, merits a brief stop to visit the picturesque winding streets and bazaar area of its old Ottoman quarter.

The characteristic red-tiled roofs of Muğla's 19th-century Ottoman houses

Walk

Gerga

See map on page 117.

A rarely visited hilltop settlement set in a rugged landscape that is in sharp contrast to the coast, Gerga makes an unusual excursion from Kuşadası or Bodrum. The ruins here are the only known surviving example of an early indigenous town, untouched by Greek or Roman influences, and quite different from the sophisticated cities of the Aegean coast. The modern Turkish name for Gerga, Gavurdamları, means "infidel-roofed sheds," a reference to the strange rural architecture here. The drive from Kuşadası or Bodrum takes about 90 minutes, and the walk about three hours. Pack a picnic lunch, as there are few local facilities.

After passing the **Seljuk mosque** in Eskicine, look for a drivable road to the right leading to the village of Ovacık (2½ miles), then go another 4 miles until you reach the village of Kırksakallar (Forty Beards). Park beside the school and follow the walled path out into the fields. When the path stops, continue in the same direction for about a half hour, until you come upon a large toadstool-like rock bearing the inscription GERGA in huge Greek letters. For the next 20 minutes of your walk, you will encounter a number of such ancient signposts.

A descent down a ridge brings you in sight of the first of Gerga's remains, a stone-roofed hut with two lion's heads projecting beneath the roof. Farther along the shady man-made terrace, shored up by impressive buttresses, stands Gerga's most famous building, an extraordinary little **temple** with a stone-slabbed gabled roof, and the name "Gerga" carved on its pediment. Scattered nearby are various fallen statues, olive presses, and some weird obelisks (pillars).

The monolithic temple at Gerga

Drive

Marmaris to Knidos (Cnidos)

The beautiful theater at Knidos

This pretty and scenic drive leads from Marmaris to the tip of the peninsula, where you can walk around the extensive and evocative ruins of Knidos, lunch at one of the simple fish restaurants, and swim in the still waters of the sheltered headland bay.

The total drive of just over 50 miles takes about two hours, climbing up through wooded hills, with some spectacular hairpin bends and perpendicular precipices, before descending to lush fertile meadows. At the fork to Datça, follow the yellow sign to Knidos; after Reşadiye the paved road gives way to a track, which continues to the tip of the peninsula. This track is not always straight, so be careful driving. There are two confusing intersections and there is no yellow sign: take the left fork in both cases.

Just over a mile from the tip of the peninsula the drive takes you past an extensive **necropolis** on the hillside. Around a bend after this you catch your first sight of the twin harbors

and lighthouse of Knidos, with restaurants along the bay. The road now leads through the middle of the ruins of this important city founded in 400 BC, and you can clamber up the original steps to reach the **Sanctuary of Demeter.** Lower down is a relatively well-preserved **theater**, from the 3rd century BC.

The most interesting remains now lie to the right, up on the hillside above where the road ends. Here are the foundations of temples, including the circular marble base stones of the **Temple of Aphrodite**, discovered in 1969 by the aptly named American archaeologist Dr. Iris Love. Fragments believed to be of the famous statue of Aphrodite by Praxiteles, declared by Pliny to be the finest statue in the world, were found nearby.

A walk out over the lighthouse headland will be rewarded with the discovery of the **Lion Tomb**, whose lion now resides in the British Museum in London.

Pamukkale's bizarre calcified waterfalls

FESTIVE MOOD
The very strangeness of the landscape and thermal spa at Pamukkale (admission charge and parking fee), so unlike any other place, seems to put most visitors in a festive mood.

The detailed theater of Hierapolis

►►► Pamukkale (Cotton Castle) 100C2

One of the natural wonders of Turkey, the thermal spa of Pamukkale has abundant supplies of remarkable hot spring waters laden with calcareous salts; as the waters have spilled over the plateau edge down the centuries, they have deposited their salts to create an extraordinary network of fantastical rock formations, gleaming white stalactites, cataracts, and basins.

The spot is now highly commercialized, with seedy souvenir stands and vendors abounding even in the area below the plateau. The big hotels used to surround the main rock pools, but UNESCO, the World Bank, and the Turkish government have joined forces to ban this practice because it was damaging the delicate rock formations. Now, hotel pools are man-made, but are at least heated by the warm spa water.

Historically the water's chief virtue seems to have lain in its ability to make dyed sheep's wool colorfast. Nowadays it is also claimed to benefit heart and circulation complaints, as well as digestive disorders and rheumatic and kidney diseases. Certainly nobody can dispute its excellent stress-relieving properties: a half-hour wallow will certainly relax you.

Ancient Hierapolis►► Many visitors are so focused on the amazing rock formations, they barely notice that the high plateau is also the site of the ancient spa of Hierapolis, built by the Romans to dominate the spring-water and harness its reputed religious and mystical qualities. Most of the ancient ruins are set back from the plateau edge; the first group you come to as you walk "inland" are the original **Roman baths**, consisting of two tall, vaulted rooms now housing a small museum. Beside this is a *palaestra* or open courtyard for exercise, and behind that lie the remains of a vast **basilica** with three naves, thought from its size to have been the cathedral erected in the 6th century, when Hierapolis became a bishopric.

Farther up the plateau stands the restored *nymphaeum* (monumental fountain), and close by is the **Temple of Apollo**, recognizable by its wide flight of steps. The modern road follows the course of the original main street for a mile until it reaches the **monumental gate** to the north, passing on the right the colossal **theater**, still well preserved and with some magnificent carvings and reliefs. Outside the city, the road leads up to a vast building on the hillside; Italian excavators have discovered that this housed the tomb of the Apostle Philip, who was martyred here in AD 80.

Do not miss the tombs that line the old road out to Ephesus from this northern gateway. Over 1,200 have been counted, making this one of the most extensive ancient cemeteries in Asia Minor.

ENVIRONS OF PAMUKKALE Ak Han▶ Standing by the main road to Dinar is this impressive 13th-century Seljuk inn with a courtyard, faced in pinkish marble. The door is finely carved, as always, and you can still walk up onto the roof.

Laodiceia▶ This ancient city, which lies some 9 miles from Pamukkale, is the site of one of the seven churches mentioned in the Revelation to Saint John. Known in ancient times as the "City of Compromise," Laodiceia was rebuked by Saint John for its people's indecisiveness: "I know your works; you are neither hot nor cold... So because you are lukewarm and neither hot nor cold, I will spew you out of my mouth." The main surviving monuments are the stadium, a large gymnasium, an *odeon* (originally a roofed theater used more for music than drama), a *nymphaeum*, and two theaters, both poorly preserved.

NOXIOUS GROTTO

In a chamber below the Temple of Apollo lies the infamous Plutonium Grotto, the noxious fumes of which were described as deadly by ancient historians such as Strabo. The exhalations were said to kill anyone who breathed them; eunuchs, however, were able to enter the grotto unscathed, according to the Greek historian Dio Cassius, as they were particularly good at holding their breath. When the grotto was discovered by Italian archaeologists in 1957, the foul fumes seriously impeded their excavations, though no deaths were reported.

131

FURY OF THE DEAD

Many of the tombs in the necropolis at Hierapolis bear inscriptions in the form of curses of various kinds, including this particularly all-embracing example: "May he who commits transgression, and he who incites thereto, have no joy of life or children; may he find no land to tread nor sea to sail, but childless and destitute, crippled by every form of affliction, let him perish, and after death may he meet the wrath and vengeance of the gods below. And the same curses on those who fail to prosecute him."

Pamukkale's colorfully striated rock

ORIGIN OF BOOKS
Jealous of Pergamum's challenge to his cultural supremacy, Ptolemy, creator of the mighty Library at Alexandria, banned the export of papyrus from Egypt. In response, the king of Pergamum ordered that animal skins should be used instead. The results came to be known as "Pergamum books," from which the English word parchment is derived. As the skins were too thick and heavy to be scrolled like papyrus, they were cut into pages which were laid on top of each other.

▶▶▶ Pergamum
100B3

So extensive are the remains of this impressively sited ancient Greek city that just to walk between the three main areas takes all day, and even with a rental car a visit takes a good three hours. One of the most pleasurable ways to see Pergamum is to arrive in time to see the sunset from the acropolis, then to stay overnight and explore the rest of the site in the morning.

After Athens lost its political importance in the 2nd century BC, Pergamum and Alexandria became the two main—and competing—centers of ancient civilization. Pergamum's famous **library** and the **Temple of Zeus** were constructed at this time, along with the vast **artificial terraces** on the hillside, which allowed the city to spread downward. All its rulers were devoted patrons of the arts and sciences, with the exception of the last, Attalus III, who in an act of extraordinary eccentricity bequeathed his entire kingdom to Rome. Pergamum thenceforth became the capital of the Roman province of Asia, which stretched as far south as Caunus.

German excavators have reconstructed enough of the acropolis area today to give an impression of how the upper city would have looked during the Roman period. The most spectacular structure is certainly the **theater**, a remarkable piece of engineering built into an exceptionally steep hillside.

The lower terraces are best explored from the parking lot at the foot of the acropolis. Here are a vast **gymnasium**, the **Temple of Demeter**, and Hellenistic houses and shops on streets rutted by chariot wheels. The lowest part of the city is now largely covered by the town of **Bergama**, with an attractive old quarter. Above rises the colossal Roman **Red Basilica**, originally a temple to Serapis and later converted to a church by the Byzantines.

132

The vast ruins of the city of Pergamum

The massive Red Basilica built by the Romans at Pergamum

EXCAVATING A DREAM
The discovery of the site of ancient Troy became an obsession for a 19th-century German business-man named Heinrich Schliemann. In 1870 he obtained permission to excavate here, using money he had amassed in the California gold rush. Schliemann devoted the next 20 years to the excavations, and discov-ered of no fewer than four Troys, one on top of the other. He also found the fabulous "jewels of Helen," which he kept for his wife's use for 20 years before bequeathing them to the Berlin Museum (they disappeared after the Russians entered the city in 1945). Despite his success, Schliemann never gained the accep-tance he craved from the academic world, which scorned him as an ama-teur who had destroyed much valuable evidence.

133

Finally comes the **Asklepieion** (*Open* daily 9–dusk. *Admission charge*), the foremost medical center of the ancient world, founded primarily on the fame and reputa-tion of Galen, the greatest physician and medical writer of late antiquity, who was born here in Pergamum in AD 29.

▶ Truva (Troy)   100A4
Open: daily 8:30–sunset. Admission charge
Those who come to Troy cherishing visions of Homer's great fortified city are frequently disappointed by the series of mounds and ditches that are Troy today. For others it is enough that a city so powerfully linked with legend should exist at all. But there can be few for whom the name of Troy does not conjure up images of ancient romance and heroism, and a visit here takes on the quality of a pilgrimage to the place where Western literature had its begin-nings, with Homer's *Iliad* and *Odyssey*.

Excavations have now uncov-ered nine major layers of habi-tation on the site, the favored contenders for Homer's Troy being Troy VI (1800–1275 BC) and Troy VIIa (1275–40 BC). The layers are clearly labeled and the recom-mended circuit is signed, but by its nature the site remains confusing.

At the site entrance stands a huge wooden horse, a gesture toward the legendary climax of the siege of Troy, when the Greeks tricked their way inside the city walls concealed in a colossal wooden horse.

The wooden horse guards the entry to Troy

The Mediterranean

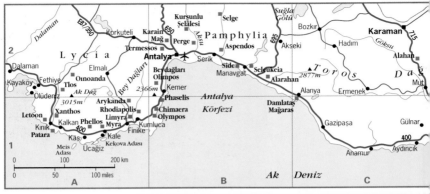

▶ ▶ ▶ REGION HIGHLIGHTS

Alanya *page 142*
Anamur *pages 142–143*
Aspendos *page 146*
Kalkan *page 156*
Lake Eğrider *page 149*
Ölüdeniz *pages 150–151*
Olympos *page 162*
Selge *pages 168–169*
Side *pages 166–167*
Termessos *page 147*
Xanthos *page 156*

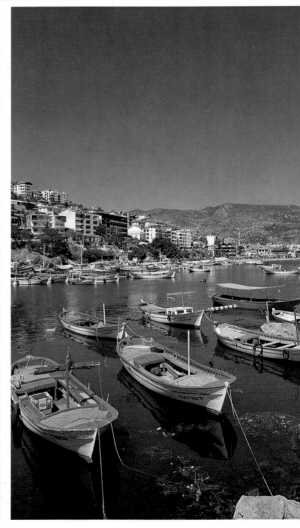

*Right: popular with
Turkish families and
foreign visitors alike,
Alanya is one of the
liveliest resorts on the
Turkish Riviera*

*Far right: the scenery of
Selge Canyon, in the
Köprülü Kanyon
National Park inland
from Antalya and Side,
makes for one of the most
exciting excursions in the
Mediterranean area*

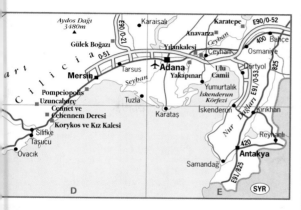

THE MEDITERRANEAN Served by the airports of Dalaman, Antalya, and Adana, Turkey's southern coastline, known as the Turquoise Coast or the Turkish Riviera, extends for nearly 400 miles, starting from Fethiye in the west and continuing to Antakya and Iskenderun, near the Syrian border, in the east. This region is one of the loveliest areas of coastline anywhere in the Mediterranean, with many fascinating excursions to be made inland as well.

LANDSCAPE The coastline falls into several very distinct regions. The first of these, known as **Lycia**, stretches from Fethiye to Kemer and is Turkey's wildest and most beautiful section of coastline, with dramatic mountains tumbling down into the sea. The beaches, including the

The Mediterranean

ITINERARIES
From Dalaman, two weeks:
Day 1 Dalyan (Caunus)
Day 2 Fethiye
Day 3 Ölüdeniz
Day 4 Patara (Letoon, Xanthos)
Day 5 Kalkan
Day 6 Kaş
Day 7 Finike
Days 8–9 Antalya (Termessos)
Days 10–11 Eğridir
Days 12–13 Pamukkale (Afrodisias)
Day 14 Muğla
Day 15 Antalya

From Antalya, two weeks:
Days 1–2 Antalya (Termessos)
Day 3 Kaş (Phaselis, Myra)
Days 4–6 Side (Perge, Aspendos, Sillyon, Manavgat, Selge)
Day 7 Anamur (Alanya)
Days 8–9 Taşucu (Kız Kalesi, Diocaesarea)
Days 10–11 Konya (Mut, Alahan)
Days 12–13 Eğridir
Day 14 Antalya

From Antalya, three weeks:
Days 1–2 Antalya (Termessos)
Day 3 Kaş (Phaselis, Olympos)
Days 4–7 Side (Perge, Aspendos, Sillyon, Manavgat, Selge)
Day 8 Anamur (Alanya)
Days 9–10 Taşucu (Kız Kalesi, Diocaesarea)
Days 11–12 Adana (Karatepe, Yılankalesi)
Days 13–15 Nevşehir (Göreme, Ürgüp)
Days 16–18 Konya
Days 19–20 Eğridir
Day 21 Antalya

famous **Ölüdeniz** (Dead Lagoon), are the most glorious in Turkey, and inland there are spectacular ancient Lycian ruins to visit.

From Antalya eastward lies the region known as **Pamphylia**, a flat and fertile coastal plain that runs as far as Manavgat, with mountains rising farther inland. In antiquity this plain supported the five great cities of **Attaleia** (Antalya), **Perge**, **Aspendos**, **Sillyon**, and **Side**.

Farther to the east, from Alanya to the Syrian border, is **Cilicia**. The first section, around the headland to Silifke, is rugged and sparsely populated; the second part is the Cilician Plain, a monotonous but fertile flatland devoted to rice and cotton crops. The scenery along the coast between Alanya and Silifke is magnificent, with cliffs dropping away into the sea, but the coastal road—winding endlessly over wooded headlands and around deep bays—makes for tiring driving. The vegetation is subtropical, and lush orange groves and banana plantations line the road.

RESORTS Within Lycia the main resorts are **Fethiye**, **Kalkan**, **Kaş**, and **Kemer**, though tourist development is still relatively small in scale here in comparison with the giant resorts of Kuşadası, Bodrum, and Marmaris. The

Ölüdeniz is one of the most popular destinations on the Mediterranean coast of Turkey

PERFECT FOR PIRATES
The rugged coastline of Cilicia was notorious for the piracy and brigandage that plagued it in ancient times; its numerous tiny inlets and coves made perfect hiding places from which to launch attacks, and the heavily wooded terrain inland protected the robbers from pursuit. Assaults on ships plying the important trade route from Syria to the Aegean were so relentless that they seriously weakened the economy of Syria's mighty Seleucid Empire.

137

paved road linking the towns and villages of Lycia's coastline was not completed until 1981, so the region has been generally accessible only for the last 20 years. Kemer is the only resort with hotels of 200 rooms or more, many of them run by and for Germans; in the other resorts the emphasis is on smaller, family-run *pansiyons* (inns). All the resorts now have yachting marinas.

Antalya has put a lot of money into its development as the premier resort of the south coast, completely renovating its old harbor to turn it into a chic new yachting marina with classy hotels. The main beaches are 3 miles out of town at **Lara**, where large hotels stand on the water's edge. In **Cilicia**, both **Side** and **Alanya** are lively traditional resorts, very popular with Turkish and German families. The beaches are long and sandy, lined with hotels, large and small, though Side retains more of a village feel, with its narrow winding streets in the old center. East of Alanya the only place that could qualify as a resort is **Silifke**, with a few beach hotels. From Mersin eastward the coastline is largely agricultural or industrial.

A 20-minute drive inland from Side brings you to the waterfalls at Manavgat, with an unusual restaurant nearby—a refreshing change from the tourist beaches

NO ESCAPE FROM FATE

According to the local legend, Kız Kalesi (Maiden's Castle) was built out to sea by a king who wished to protect his only daughter after a prediction that she would die of a snakebite. One of her admirers, however, unwittingly sent her a basket of fruit in which a snake was lurking and so she was indeed bitten and died.

The imposing black and white marble minaret of the 16th-century Ulu Cami, or Great Mosque, in Adana

▶ Adana   135E2

Turkey's fourth largest city, with a population that is growing fast, is the center of the prosperous cotton industry, set in the heart of a rich agricultural plain. The River Seyhan runs through the middle of the city, whose only ancient monument worth mentioning is the **Taş Köprü** (Stone Bridge) built by Hadrian. Nearby is the only notable Turkish monument, the **Ulu Cami** (Great Mosque), built in 1507 of black and white marble, with surprisingly fine tiles inside. Adana has many good hotels, and the city would make a comfortable base from which to visit the places described below.

ENVIRONS OF ADANA Anavarza (Dilekkaya)▶ This pleasant detour, 45 miles northeast of Adana, takes you to a **Roman-Byzantine** city in a lovely setting at the foot of a mountain. The remains consist of a Roman triumphal arch and theater, from which a stairway cut out of the rock leads to the upper town. The well-preserved fortress at the summit encloses a funerary church of the Cilician Armenian kings, still with traces of frescoes inside.

The remote and unusually beautiful neo-Hittite site of **Karatepe▶▶** (*Open daily 8–5. Admission charge*) was discovered in 1945. The well-signposted detour takes a good three hours from the main Adana–Maraş road, but is well worth it. In a wooded setting overlooking the Ceyhan lake are the neo-Hittite stone reliefs (see pages 28–29) in situ, in a quantity and state of preservation unique in Turkey—or, for that matter, in the world. On the way you will pass to the left the site of **Hieropolis Castabala** (1st century BC), with its fine castle on the hilltop and rows of columns marching across the fields.

Kız Kalesi (Maiden's Castle)▶ This much-photographed castle consists of two buildings: the first, built in the 12th century by Armenian kings, stands on the sandy beach, while the other rises from its own island in the sea (see panel) and was originally reached by a causeway. The beaches here are popular for camping.

The largest town as you drive east along the coast from Anamur, **Silifke▶** has a pleasant open feel, on the banks of the wide Göksu river. A Roman bridge crosses the river, but apart from this the only monument is the large Crusader castle on the hill. Built originally by the Byzantines in the 7th century as a defense against Arab raiders, it was rebuilt by the Crusader knights of Rhodes, complete with 23 towers and bastions. Now it is wild and overgrown: be careful if you decide to walk on the crumbling battlements. On the hill to the west of Silifke stands the Byzantine church of **Haghia Thekla**, dedicated to Saint Paul's first convert, who was also the first female Christian martyr.

LOCAL DELICACY
The Castle of the Snakes (Yılankalesi) earned its name from the snakes that still abound in the region. They are eaten with relish by the local pigs, whose flabby snouts protect them from bites.

One of the two castles at Kız Kalesi, isolated on its island

Uzuncaburç (Diocaesarea)▶▶ This is a worthwhile detour, for the drive itself—19 miles north of Silifke along a winding road—is attractive, and the ancient site is one of the most impressive along this coast. After parking in the center of the small village that lies among the ruins, you walk through a monumental Roman arch to reach the Temple of Zeus Olbius (*Open* daily 8–6. *Admission charge*), built by Seleucus I in the 3rd century BC and the oldest-known temple of the Corinthian order. Most of its columns still stand, and it was converted to a church in the Byzantine era. Other monuments are a theater, the Temple of Tyche, and a Hellenistic tower about 80 feet high.

Yakapınar (Misis)▶ (*Admission charge*) A sign 15 miles east of Adana points to these early mosaics, housed in a makeshift "museum." The main mosaic is said to represent Noah's Ark and the animals, though its poor condition makes this very hard to tell.

Yılankalesi (Castle of the Snakes)▶▶ (*Admission free*) Some 25 miles east of Adana, look for this magnificent 12th-century Armenian castle set up on a hill to the right. Inside, the dungeons and living rooms are well preserved.

139

CENNET AND CEHENNEM (HEAVEN AND HELL)
The names of these two caves give a clue to their contrasting characters. Fortunately only Heaven can be visited, a huge natural chasm on the edge of a field of Roman and Byzantine ruins. Descent is via an easy path to the chasm bottom; from here a trickier, slippery path continues to a cave where a pretty church dedicated to the Virgin Mary has stood since the 5th century. Inside, you will hear the roar of an underground river, said to be the Stream of Paradise. Hell, by contrast, is a frightening narrow pit that is accessible only to experienced cavers. Superstitious locals tie rags to nearby trees and bushes in order to ward off any evil spirits who might escape from below.

Street vendors in front of the great Stone Bridge built by Hadrian across the River Seyhan in Adana

From their origins on the steppes of Asia, the Turks arrived in Asia Minor in the 10th century, having adopted the religion of the Arabs en route. These nomadic tribesmen were fierce fighters and horsemen who were descended from the Tu-Kin tribes of Mongolia—hence the modern name "Turk."

DIFFERENT VALUES
"The life of insecurity is the nomad's achievement. He does not try, like our building world, to believe in a stability which is non-existent; and in his constant movement with the seasons, in the lightness of his hold, he puts something right, about which we are constantly wrong..."
Freya Stark, 1956

140

Nomad women and children near Antalya

The Seljuks The first nomads settled with apparent ease, founding what became known as the Seljuk Empire of Rum with its capital at Konya. Their stable and enlightened rule over the following two centuries led to the first flowering of a Turkish civilization.

The Seljuks encouraged large numbers of nomads to settle in areas as far west as **Lycia**, where they remained in effect seminomadic, migrating with their flocks and herds from their *yaylas* (summer pastures) in the mountains down to the coastal towns in the winter. Travelers who visited these parts in the 19th century wrote colorful descriptions of the caravans setting off for the mountains in about May, the men riding horses or camels in front, the women generally on foot and herding the flocks of sheep and goats, the donkeys laden with pots and pans, and the children playing with the dogs and chickens and bringing up the rear.

To this day there are still a surprising number of villages up in the Lycian mountains that are empty in winter, the houses left just as they are, with no thought of theft. But increasingly, the villages also remain empty in summer: as tourism in towns like Kaş and Kalkan brings in a more lucrative income, the seminomadic tradition of centuries is breaking down.

Eastern nomads Most nomads remaining in Turkey today live much farther to the east; many are Kurds

(known officially as "mountain Turks"), especially in the regions south and southeast of **Diyarbakır**. The authorities persist with resettlement programs, trying to persuade nomadic Kurds to give up their age-old practice of growing only what they need to survive, and gaining a small income by selling their livestock from time to time in order to purchase the other essentials of life. Instead they are being encouraged to do some farming, and so to help supply food for the big cities.

   The distinctive black goat-hair tents of the *yürük* ("walkers") are today seen most often in the foothills of **Ararat** and the valleys of the Zap river in **Hakkâri**. The women remain unveiled, and they and the children still dress in colorful clothes, often with much gold jewelry. The sheepdogs, wearing spiked collars, are savage in the extreme and should be avoided at all costs.

Nomadic traits of the modern Turk Turks remain extremely proud of their nomadic heritage, and their attachment to the tenets of this way of life shows itself in many ways, including their special love of woven carpets, once the most important piece of tent furniture and now given pride of place in many Turkish houses. Those houses themselves also often appear flimsy, less solid and less lavishly furnished than those of purely sedentary peoples. All over Turkey you will be struck, too, by the number of museums with ethnographic displays, showing the costumes worn by the nomads, the layout of their tents, and their chattels. Far from being for the benefit of tourists, these exhibitions are intended for the Turks themselves, anxious not to forget their nomadic origins.

A Kurdish nomad woman in front of a traditional goat-hair tent, or yürük

TAX EVASION
The Turkish authorities used to experience great difficulty in collecting taxes from the nomadic Kurds. Whenever they expected a visit from the tax collector, they would pack up their chattels and migrate to the mountains, returning to the plains only when they learned that the coast was clear.

PROBLEMS OF SETTLING DOWN
The nomadic life can be viewed by those who lead it as a relatively free one. The prospect of settling down to an agricultural life can therefore seem like a prison sentence, an endless drudge of exhausting manual labor, with no escape through movement and change.

LICENTIOUS ANTIOCH

In Roman times the city of Antioch was a great cultural, artistic, and commercial center, which became notorious for its depravity and its indulgence in life's pleasures. For this reason it was chosen by Saint Peter for his first mission to the Gentiles, and his converts here were the first to be called Christians. Out of town on the Aleppo road is a grotto with a secret escape tunnel where Saint Peter is said to have founded the first Christian community. The church here was built by Crusaders in the 13th century.

The mighty Seljuk fortifications and harbor at Alanya, dominated by the great octagonal Red Tower

▶▶ Alanya   134C2

The approach to the town of Alanya is unmistakable, its great rock crowned by the crenellated red fortress that dominates the coast from afar. By virtue of its impressive site and good beaches, Alanya has in recent years become the most developed resort along this southern coast after Antalya. Hotels have mushroomed, and there is a clear divide between the old town, perched in the fortress up on the rock, and the modern sprawl of development on the two beaches beneath it. In the 13th century, under the Seljuks, the fortress was used by the sultan as his winter quarters, and the town was a naval base protected by the prominent **Red Tower** (Kızıl Kule). A remarkable and unique structure, octagonal in shape and with five internal stories, this is the major monument of the lower town, along with the old **Seljuk dockyard** beside it, still in use today. You can drive all the way up to the old fortified town (*Open daily 8–5. Admission charge*), still partially inhabited, to reach the citadel at the top and the remains of the sultan's palace. A platform at the very edge of the cliff gives a magnificent view. This was the spot from which condemned prisoners and women convicted of adultery used to be hurled onto the rocks below.

At the foot of the rock promontory, approached from the beach to the west, is the stalactite grotto of **Damlataş**, whose very high levels of humidity are thought to be beneficial to sufferers of asthma and bronchial disorders. From here boats can be rented to explore the many caves that honeycomb the foot of the rock.

▶▶ Anamur   134C1

Open: Tue–Sun 8–5. Admission charge
This medieval castle is the largest on Turkey's southern coast, with all its walls and 36 towers still intact. Mamure Kalesi (Marble Castle), as it is known locally, stands on the water's edge, with the waves lapping at its outer walls.

The castle was the last foothold of the Cypriot Lusignan kings, this being the southernmost point of the coast

and directly opposite Cyprus, which is only 40 miles away. The Ottomans expanded the castle and continued to use it until the last days of the empire in 1921. The custodian sells tickets, and there are a handful of simple restaurants and motels nearby; the unexceptional modern town of Anamur is a couple of miles away inland.

On a hillside a mile to the west of the castle are the interesting ruins of ancient **Anamurium**, a Byzantine city deserted in the 7th century when the wave of Arab incursions began from Damascus. So complete are the remains, including many private houses, with traces of mosaic and painting, that it gives the impression of being a ghost town deserted just a few years ago.

▶ Antakya (Antioch)   135E1

This city close to the Syrian border is the site of ancient Antioch; though only a shadow of its former self, it is still picturesque enough, with its narrow lanes leading down to the Orontes river and its segregated districts inhabited by different religious communities in Ottoman times. The outline of the ancient city walls, 18 miles long in total, give an indication of the extent of the city in its heyday.

In Antakya today the only ancient monuments are the **Roman bridge** and the **Mosque of Habib Haccar**, originally a church. Don't miss the **Archaeological Museum** (*Open* Tue–Sun 8:30–12 and 1:30–5. *Admission charge*), which has a collection of Roman floor mosaics, the finest in the world, from the villas of ancient Antioch and nearby **Daphne**, home to many wealthy Romans.

The fine Crusader castle at Anamur

143

Handpainted dolls from Alanya

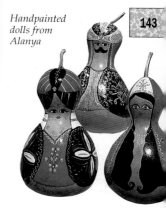

The Friday market at Alanya: a fascinating opportunity to observe local life and sample the produce of the region

A RED GIBRALTAR
The mighty red fortified town of Alanya, a splendid example of Seljuk military architecture with its 146 towers, is unlike anything along this coast. The rock on which it sits is said to resemble Gibraltar.

Alexander the Great's extraordinarily swift conquest of Asia Minor and the whole of the Persian Empire brought an enormous region under Greek control, creating conditions in which ideas and cultures could cross-fertilize, resulting in a flowering of thought and art that was to transform the civilized world.

144

MARCHING ON ITS STOMACH

Just 22 years old when he entered Asia Minor, Alexander possessed political vision and military genius combined with a youthful energy and enthusiasm for adventure. The master tactician always made sure his army was well provided with food and drink. Later, when he had amassed the wealth to pay for them, he made considerable use of mercenaries.

Above right: a tetradrachm (a coin worth four drachmas) showing the head of Alexander the Great

Below: a mosaic from Pompeii depicts Alexander (left) defeating Darius at Issus in 333 BC

The man Born in 356 BC, Alexander the Great was the eldest son of Philip II, King of Macedon (359–336 BC); the philosopher Aristotle was one of the young Alexander's tutors. When Philip was assassinated, Alexander first consolidated his position in Europe, then set out to liberate the Greek cities to the east and overthrow the Persian Empire of Darius the Great. In 334 BC he crossed the Hellespont into Asia Minor, with an army of 32,000 infantry and 5,000 cavalry.

In some cities, such as Ephesus and Phaselis, Alexander was greeted as a liberator; in others, notably Halicarnassus (modern Bodrum), Miletos, and Aspendos, he was resisted as a conqueror. After campaigning in Asia Minor for just one year, Alexander won his first major battle, defeating Darius at Issus in 333 BC; he then pressed on into Egypt, where he was accepted by the priests as the land's new ruler. Next he swept eastward, across the Persian Empire to the edge of the Himalayas, beginning—as he moved ever farther from Greece—to enlist Persian soldiers and to appoint Persian nobles to positions of authority. After a mutiny by his exhausted

Macedonian soldiers in 324 BC he turned back. He died of a fever in Babylon the following year, at the age of just 32. In 10 years he had built up the largest empire the world had ever known (see also pages 116–117).

The problem of succession On his sudden death Alexander left no clear successor. His wife Roxana was pregnant when he died, and a regent was therefore appointed, but both mother and child were murdered in the disputes among Alexander's generals that followed his death. After 20 years of squabbling, three main kingdoms emerged under three generals: Ptolemy in Egypt, Seleucus in Syria, and Antigonus in Greece. The Seleucids and the Ptolemies, supposedly descended from Apollo and Dionysus, were worshipped as gods, and throughout all three kingdoms Alexander himself was honored as a god, from whom all the kings claimed descent. In spreading Greek culture and ideas throughout his empire, Alexander founded many cities, endowing a number of them with his name. Some, such as Alexandria in Egypt, survive to this day. Throughout all three kingdoms these cities became centers of wealth and power, often free to administer their own affairs with an unusual degree of independence.

The Hellenistic legacy The period from Alexander's death until the gradual extinction of his successor kingdoms—largely absorbed by the Roman Empire in the 2nd and 1st centuries BC—is known as the Hellenistic Age (from the Greek *hellenistes*, meaning "imitator of the Greeks"). It was an era marked by an extremely competitive spirit on all levels. Cities rivaled each other for power and trade, while their citizens competed to amass great fortunes, flaunting their wealth by financing the construction of civic monuments. It was also a period of great cultural activity, stimulated by the cross-fertilization of Asian and Western cultures and marked by great scholastic innovation. The two out-standing centers of learning were Alexandria in Egypt and Pergamum (see pages 132–133); both left a legacy of learning, the influence of which cannot be overstated.

The dizzying terraced seats of Pergamum's theater, one of the many remarkable surviving buildings of this ancient center of learning

THE GORDIAN KNOT
According to a prophecy in the Central Anatolian town of Gordion, whoever could untie the Gordian knot would be master of Asia. The knot had been tied by the Phrygian king, who was of peasant stock, to fix the yoke of his oxcart to the pole. Alexander, hearing of the prophecy, could not resist the challenge. Stopping off at Gordion, he simply sliced through the knot with his sword. The significance of the knot remains in dispute: some say it represented the importance of the peasantry to the kingdom; others say it symbolized Gordion's strategic value as the key to the ancient road network.

146

The new marina at Antalya, converted from the old harbor

T.C. KÜLTÜR BAKANLIĞI

ANTALYA MÜZESİ GİRİŞ BİLETİ   № 195649

WATERFALLS AND CAVES
Near Antalya are two sets of waterfalls: the Düden Şelâlesi on the road to Lara, where the river hurtles over the cliff edge into the sea; and the Kurşunlu Şelâlesi, inland on the Isparta road, a spectacular sight set in mountainous scenery.

There are also two sets of caves: the Karain cave, inhabited in neolithic times, on the Burdur road; and, on the same road farther north, the Insuyu caves, a series of interlinked chambers with underwater lakes, stalactites, and stalagmites.

▶ **Antalya**   *134B2*

Antalya is the main port on the southern coast of Turkey, as it has been for the last 2,000 years. The town is set on a natural harbor with its industrial port area lying to the west, with large U.S. Navy ships often seen in the bay. The tourist hotels are clustered around the pretty, newly restored yachting marina in the old Kaleiçi quarter and out on the beaches of **Lara** to the east. Half a day is enough to see Antalya's sights: these consist of the 13th-century **Yivli Minare** (Fluted Minaret), in typical Seljuk red brick; the **Karaalı Park** up on the clifftop, with some remains of fortifications; and the modern **museum** (*Open* Tue–Sun 9–5. *Admission charge*) on the western outskirts, noteworthy for its impressive sarcophagi from Perge.

The sites around Antalya merit far more time: a stay of three nights would be needed to visit the places described below.

ENVIRONS OF ANTALYA Aspendos▶▶ (*Open* daily 8–6. *Admission charge*) boasts the finest example of a Roman theater—indeed of any ancient theater—in the world. Under the Roman Empire Aspendos prospered: it produced salt from the nearby lake, which dries up in summer, cultivated vines and corn, and produced coarse Pamphylian wool from the local sheep. The ancient city lies 30 minutes' drive east of Antalya on the banks of the Eurymedon river, which is crossed on the approach to the site by a pretty 13th-century Seljuk bridge, still in use and perfectly sound. Before arriving at Aspendos proper, fork left to reach an extraordinary aqueduct, with a tall water tower that provided enough pressure to force water to flow up to the main city on the acropolis.

The main road leads to the parking area directly in front of the stupendous theater, built in the 2nd century AD and still nearly intact. A scramble up the hill above the theater reveals the ruins of a market hall, a *nymphaeum* (monumental fountain), an *agora* (marketplace), and a council chamber, all of them invisible from the theater below.

Perge▶ (*Open* daily 8–6. *Admission charge*) Set on the flat plain 3 miles west of Antalya, the ruined city of ancient Perge has some striking features, notably its tall, round Hellenistic gates and its evocative main street complete with chariot ruts. It also has a fine stadium, the best preserved in Asia Minor after that of Afrodisias (see page 104).

Sillyon▶ Lying between Perge and Aspendos, the acropolis of Sillyon, jutting up from the coastal plain, is visible from a long way off. Following a severe landslip in 1969, half its monuments toppled over the cliff, leaving the other half on the edge; these are still extensive, however, so allow about three hours for a visit. Notice in particular the impressive southern and northern ramps leading up into the city, remarkably well preserved and with handsome paving.

Termessos▶▶▶ (*Open* daily 8–6. *Admission charge* to national park and site 5½ miles farther up) A visit to the ancient ruin of Termessos is one of the most exciting excursions in the whole of Turkey. Known as the Eagle's Nest, it is set high in the mountains behind Antalya. The journey takes a full day, so come prepared with a picnic lunch. Exploring the site involves some steep climbing, and good, comfortable footwear is a necessity.

A well-signposted path leads through the defenses of the lower and upper city walls to reach the first main monument, the gymnasium, built in the impressive dark gray stone that is characteristic of Termessos. Higher up, the theater has the most impressive setting of any in Turkey, with splendid views across the mountains. A complex of temples lies a little higher up near the marketplace, and beyond this on the hillside lies the extraordinary necropolis, littered with hundreds of sarcophagi from the first three centuries AD, presenting an apocalyptic vision.

MISSING GODDESS
Despite extensive excavations, the whereabouts of the cult temple of Artemis Pergeia, the dominant goddess here, remain a mystery. Although it was known to be rich with the offerings of her worshippers, thorough searches of the hilltops and hillsides of the area have revealed no trace as yet of the famous temple.

147

The ancient theater at Aspendos: the finest example in the world

FORMIDABLE FEROCITY
Inhabited in ancient times by people of legendary ferocity—known as Solymians after Mount Solymus, under which the city lies—Termessos also has some of the most formidable natural defenses of any ancient city in Turkey. Alexander the Great took one look and decided to waste no more time, moving on to easier prey. Homer tells us that one of the trio of seemingly impossible tasks allotted to the young mythological hero Bellerophon was the slaying of the Solymi.

The ruined city of Perge

In peak season and on public holidays, when the beach resorts of the Aegean and Mediterranean are crowded, it is worth remembering the fresh-water lakes of Beyşehir, Eğridir, and Burdur, which lie just two hours' drive inland from Antalya. Set in magnificent scenery surrounded by greenery and mountains, they offer excellent swimming in a peaceful environment, along with a few simple but surprisingly pleasant hotels and restaurants. The lakes may be approached on a circuit from Konya as well as from Antalya, and they make a delightful change in atmosphere from the tourist resorts of the coast.

148

KOVADA NATIONAL PARK

This wild forest centered on Kovada Lake, just over 15 miles south of Eğridir, is rarely visited. The lake is rich in carp and bass, and the forests are said to shelter bears, wolves, and wild boar. The roads are almost empty, and the only signs of habitation are the black goat-hair tents of the nomads who graze their flocks here in summer. Camping is permitted at the lakeside, and the area is excellent for hiking.

Eğridir's unrivaled lakeshore setting

Beyşehir The easternmost of the three lakes, 56 miles from Konya, this is a shallow, freshwater lake rich in carp. The main town of the lakeshore, also called Beyşehir, is at first sight a grubby, sprawling place, but deserves a closer look. Overnight accommodations here are not good, but at least aim to have lunch either by the lake or at the pretty Beyaz Park in town, and then visit the 13th-century **Eşrefoğlu mosque** and **türbe** (tomb), an unusual pair, the mosque with a forest of columns and some stunning carpets. You can rent a boat to explore the 20 or so islands in the lake and, if you have time, the unique 13th-century Seljuk **Kubadabad Palace**, on the western shore and accessible only by boat. On the beautiful **Kızkalesi Island**, opposite, is another Seljuk palace.

Another excursion, this time by car, takes in the enigmatic Hittite sanctuary of **Elfatun Pınarı**, 13 miles from Beyşehir on the Isparta road. The approach road to the site is bad, but drivable; you are rewarded by the

sight of these deserted and atmospheric ruins, with huge carved blocks covered in Hittite reliefs showing monsters and sun disks, symbols of the divine force.

Eğridir The most beautiful of the lakes and the best for swimming, Eğridir should be first choice for a base from which to explore the other inland lakes, as it offers the best hotels in the area. Cars can also be rented via the tourist information office. The water is cold except in the height of summer (the altitude is 3,000 feet), but is exceptionally clear and blue. The mountain setting is ravishing, the trees and vegetation making a welcome contrast to the bleak Anatolian plateau.

The town itself is set on a little promontory forming a peninsula on the lake. Here the remains of a Seljuk castle with a minaret enclose an amazing series of old Turkish houses, perched in precarious positions on the edge. A pebble-built causeway now links the promontory with two little islands, also covered with houses. A Greek basilica stands on the far island, its roof still intact. To find deserted beaches from which to swim, drive north along the lakeshore toward Barla.

Burdur and Salda On Lake Burdur is Cendik Beach, a mile from Burdur town, 3 miles long and good for swimming, though the water here is very saline. Salda, the westernmost of the lakes, is better for swimming: the water is crystal green, and the shore is lined with campgrounds, picnic areas, and restaurants.

The most interesting excursion in the area is to the ruins of **Sagalassos**, near Ağlasun, south of Isparta. The well-preserved remains are impressive for their remarkable setting high on a plateau and for their good condition, especially the theater. You'll need about a day for a visit, as the city can only be reached on foot, a one-and-a-half-hour signposted walk from Ağlasun.

Lake Eğridir

LOCAL DELICACIES
As might be expected, the local fish, a staple in all the restaurants, is a culinary highlight. Carp (*sazan*) and bass (*levrek*) are abundant, and Eğridir also specializes in baby crayfish. The food in the lakes area is generally of a very high standard, and is also much cheaper than in the coastal resorts.

The timeworn entrance to the old bazaar in Eğridir

The Mediterranean

WHO WERE THE LYCIANS?

The origins of the Lycians remain a mystery. Most scholars now agree that they were not an indigenous people, but that they came from Crete in about 1400 BC under the leadership of Sarpedon, brother of King Minos. They always remained distinct from their neighbors, and Lycia was the last region in Asia Minor to be incorporated into the Roman Empire. They had their own language, even now not fully understood, which somewhat resembled Hittite. According to one theory, the Lycians are the Lukka referred to in Hittite records.

▶ Fethiye

134A2

The bustling town of Fethiye, set on a large, sheltered bay backed by mountains, was always the principal port of Lycia. In the last 10 years it has developed considerably as a resort, with a new yacht marina and hotels lining the bay known as Çalış Beach on the western approach to the town. The seafront is crowded with caïques (light skiffs) offering day trips to other nearby beaches, and the wide promenade has a string of cafés. The cobbled streets inland are full of shops and restaurants, and the daily open-air food market hums with life.

There are three main sights: the rock tombs cut in the cliffs above the town, involving a steep climb, but worthwhile, especially at sunset; the medieval castle attributed to the Knights of Saint John, now crumbling, set on the old acropolis; and the superb sarcophagus set in the middle of the road in front of the town hall, left there by the earthquakes of 1856 and 1957. One of the finest in Lycia, it represents a two-story Lycian house and has a curved, arch-shaped lid decorated inside and out with splendid reliefs of warriors.

ENVIRONS OF FETHIYE Kayaköy▶ Until the exchange of populations in 1923 (see page 283), Fethiye was largely

The lagoon at Ölüdeniz: Turkey's most beautiful beach and now a conservation area

Greek. Extraordinary evidence of this can be seen in Kayaköy, the largest Greek ghost town in Turkey, once home to 3,500 Greeks; it is a couple of miles inland, about 20 minutes' drive en route to Ölüdeniz. A walk around the deserted houses and churches is an eerie experience.

Ölüdeniz▶▶ This is Turkey's most beautiful beach, adorning the front of numerous brochures, and the serene splendor of the lagoon (the Turkish name means "Dead Sea") lives up to all expectations. The beach area was at risk of being overdeveloped, but mercifully has been designated a conservation area, so most of the new hotels and buildings are about 2½ miles inland, at Hisaronu and Ölü Ata. Cheap *dolmuş* taxis run constantly between these villages and Ölüdeniz. An advantage of staying inland in midsummer is that it's cooler than being on the beach.

*Do not expect to find
uncrowded beaches at
Ölüdeniz*

LYCIAN MAGIC

Fethiye is the western
gateway to the region
known as Lycia, the
bulge in Turkey's south-
ern coastline between
Fethiye and Antalya. An
isolated and mountainous
region, Lycia has distin-
guished itself from its
neighbors. Until 1981,
the paved road stopped
at Fethiye, leaving the
region beyond inacces-
sible except to four-
wheel-drive vehicles and
horses. Trailblazing
English traveler Freya
Stark explored the coast-
line by boat (*The Lycian
Shore*, 1956), and George
Bean, the illustrious
explorer, classicist, and
academic, visited most of
the area on foot. Despite
the development now
affecting some parts, the
landscapes of Lycia have
kept their savage beauty;
the mountains, the
remote and ancient hill-
top ruins, and the lovely
Xanthos valley all exert a
magic unequaled
elsewhere in Turkey, and
are possessed by its
bewitching quality.

An entry fee is charged to the lagoon beach itself, but
there is another long, pebbly stretch to which access is
unrestricted. The resort appeals to a young crowd, and
nightlife is a real feature. A 20-minute walk along the
coast road brings you to **Kudrak**, Paradise Beach, still relatively empty even in peak season.

Tlos▶ (*Open daily 8–5. Admission charge*). The five-hour
round trip from Fethiye to Tlos makes an exciting day
trip, and a good place to picnic. Set on a rocky outcrop
dominating the valley of the Xanthos river, this ancient
Lycian fortress on its summit is visible from many miles
away, with characteristic tombs cut into the rock face
below. The castle was used as a winter palace by the local
feudal ruler in the 19th century, and Tlos was one of the
very few Lycian cities to remain inhabited right through
to the 19th century.

Of the rock tombs, do not miss the tomb of Bellerophon,
with carvings of Bellerophon mounted on the winged
horse Pegasus, his right arm raised to slay the mythical
Chimera (see pages 164–165).

Lying in the flat lee of the acropolis is the charmingly
overgrown theater, with many carved blocks depicting
actors' masks still to be found among the ruins; beyond
stands the memorable baths building, with its seven-
arched windows overlooking
the Xanthos valley.

151

*Lycian rock tombs
at Tlos*

LYCIAN RUINS

The ruins of some 40 ancient Lycian cities have now been identified. Many are remote, perched up on rocky outcrops and accessible only by arduous walks from the nearest road or village. The sites mentioned here (pages 150–165) are accessible by car, and sometimes a short walk—never more than half an hour—and worth the effort.

Part of the ruins of Arycanda in their impressive hillside setting

▶ Finike

134A1

Now a thriving agricultural town with an active harbor, Finike is set at the western edge of a fertile plain. A handful of small hotels and *pansiyons* (inns) make it a good base for exploring the Lycian sites.

ENVIRONS OF FINIKE Half an hour's drive inland from Finike on the Elmalı road is the splendid hillside site of **Arif (Arycanda)**▶▶ (*Open daily 8–5. Admission charge*). A 15-minute walk leads to the lowest building, thought to be the ancient citadel. Walk on to Roman temple tombs, some with carvings. Above them tower the colossal baths, and beside these stands the gymnasium, with an open-air exercise courtyard in front. The path now crosses the stream bed, dry in summer, to reach a large, sunken, oblong *agora* (marketplace), connected by archways to a small *odeon* (theater). The magnificent theater looks out over the valley, with the cliff as its natural backdrop, and above it a crumbling stairway leads to the stadium, which is the highest building in Arycanda.

A couple of miles inland from Finike, **Limyra**▶ has a remarkable necropolis, the most extensive in Lycia. On the plain below, a road leads to the small theater, opposite which is a pleasant stream with the picturesque ruins of a Byzantine nunnery on its banks. On the hillside behind the theater stands the famous 4th-century BC tomb of Catabura, an elaborate sarcophagus and plinth covered in reliefs of the judgement of the dead and a funeral banquet. Farther up, and the most dramatic of all, is the tomb of Pericles, also from the 4th century BC, set on a natural rock platform with fabulous views some 800 feet above the plain. Its unique reliefs and caryatids display both Greek and Persian influences. The 20-minute approach is from a village to the west: local children will undoubtedly show you the way.

153

The Lycian rock tombs—many of them house tombs—at Myra

▶ Kale

134A1

A dusty, sprawling town, Kale (formerly known as Demre) is not somewhere you would linger were it not for the surprisingly beautiful and unusual sights that lie close by.

ENVIRONS OF KALE The little harbor of Kale lies 2 miles from the town center; in ancient times, when it was known as **Andriake** (now **Cayağzı**)▶, this was the port to the Lycian city of Myra (see below). The ruins now stand in the swampy estuary. Do not miss the vast, gray stone building known as **Hadrian's Granary** (*Open* daily 8–5. *Admission charge*), a 10-minute walk from where the drivable road ends. Busts of Hadrian and his empress Faustina rest over the central doorway. The road ends by a pretty beach along an icy estuary, and a footbridge over the river leads to some fish restaurants.

The necropolis and Roman theater of the ancient Lycian city of **Myra**▶▶ (*Open* 8:30–sunset. *Admission charge*) are truly spectacular and not to be missed. The ruins nestle at the foot of the cliff behind Kale. .

The theater still has its vaulted entrance, below the seats, used by audiences so many centuries ago. A path leads up to the cluster of tombs cut in the cliff face, most of which are of the house type. The main tomb has beautiful reliefs showing a funeral banquet.

Delicate carvings on one of the rock tombs at Myra

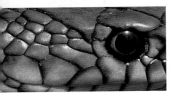

Turkey is blessed with massive tracts of virgin landscape, which have been preserved by turning them into national parks. Most of the parks are in heavily forested areas, often with lakes and rivers, and all have an abundance of flora and fauna.

154

HUNTING

Hunting has long been a popular pastime in Turkey, as in most Mediterranean countries, with the result that many species—such as the brown bear—have been hunted to the brink of extinction. Popular game birds include wild duck, wild goose, quail, partridge, and pheasant. Foreigners may hunt only in parties organized by Turkish travel agencies; these agencies will provide all relevant information on seasons, authorized zones, permits, and weapons. In nonprohibited regions, tourists can fish for sport without obtaining permits.

Cistus albidus, a native Turkish rock rose

National parks The Aegean region the **Dilek Milliparkı**, on Dilek Burnu south of Efes (Ephesus) and close to Priene (see page 122), combines a spectacular area of 3,700-foot-high jagged mountains with flat marshland rich in birdlife. The mountains are home to many birds of prey, as well as to jackals, striped hyenas, wild boar, and even the very occasional leopard.

Abundant wildlife is also found in the **Olympos Milliparkı** on the Lycian coast near Antalya (see page 162), with its 6,000-foot-high mountains covered in Calabrian pines. On this coast you may see shearwaters flying in long formations, and Cory's shearwaters are also common. April and May are the best months to visit, when flowering shrubs such as lavender and rock roses attract hosts of butterflies.

In inland parks, such as the **Kovada Milliparkı** between Lake Eğridir and Antalya, the forests provide shelter for red and roe deer, wild boar, wolves, and even a small number of brown bears. In the **Yedigöller Milliparkı** (the name means "Seven Lakes"), 30 miles inland from Zonguldak on the Black Sea (see page 247), the deciduous and coniferous woodland of the national park is home to a similar range of wildlife.

Turtles The beach at **Dalyan**, near Dalaman Airport on the Aegean coast (see page 112), is the biggest nesting beach for loggerhead turtles (*Caretta caretta*) in Turkey, and the second most important, after the Greek island of Zakynthos, in the Mediterranean. The turtles are threatened because the sandy beaches where they lay their eggs are increasingly being developed for tourism. During their two-month incubation period, the eggs are vulnerable to disturbance from digging and trampling. When they hatch, at nighttime, the baby turtles scurry down to the sea, attracted by the natural luminescence of the surface and the reflected light of the moon; bright lights from hotels confuse them, and as they hesitate they are easily picked off by scavengers, while many others simply die of exhaustion before ever reaching the sea.

Bird-watching Bird-watching in Turkey can usually be combined with sightseeing or even lazing on the beach: armed with a pair of binoculars and a field guide, you can add a whole new

dimension to your vacation. Because of its geographical position on the edge of Europe, Asia, and Africa, Turkey has a tremendous range of bird-life. Spring and autumn are the most exciting times because of the great north-south migrations of colossal numbers of birds—from sparrowhawks and eagles to black and white storks—visible even from Istanbul itself, especially from the Çamlıca hills on the Asiatic side.

May is probably the best month for bird-watching, when even the inexperienced may spot well over 100 species on a typical touring vacation. No one can fail to notice the tall storks, which build enormous nests on minarets, rooftops, and telegraph poles, or the vultures and birds of prey that hover overhead. On the road, you'll likely notice the crested lark, which runs under the wheels of the car, while on the telegraph wires you can usually spot yellow black-headed buntings, colorful bee-eaters, and bright blue rollers.

Turkey also has several bird sanctuaries, notably **Kuş Cenneti** (Bird Paradise) by the Sea of Marmara, and **Birecik** near the Syrian border. Here you can see, among other species, the ugly and near-extinct bald ibis, the subject of a Worldwide Fund for Nature rescue operation.

Loggerhead turtles are threatened by tourist developments, which disrupt their nesting beaches

155

DANGERS TO THE EXPLORER
In summer, the most aggravating form of wildlife you will encounter in the Aegean and Mediterranean regions is the mosquito, so take repellent, especially if you intend to eat outdoors. Scorpions and snakes are not abundant, but be careful when walking off the beaten track in sandals and shorts.

The short-toed eagle (Circaetus gallicus) is one of the many species that can be spotted in Turkey's bird sanctuaries

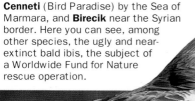

One of Kalkan's picturesque narrow streets

MASS SUICIDES
So fiercely independent were the people of Xanthos, the principal city of Lycia, that on two occasions they fought to the death rather than submit to the yoke of foreign rule. The first occasion was in the 6th century BC when the Persians threatened to conquer them: on realizing that they could not win, the men of Xanthos set fire to their city with the women and children inside, then marched out to fight to the last man. The second occasion was during the Roman civil wars in the 1st century BC, when Brutus laid siege to Xanthos. Rather than submit, the men slaughtered their women and children and then burned themselves alive. Even the cold-hearted Brutus is said to have wept at the sight.

A Lycian house tomb at Xanthos

▶▶ Kalkan   *134A1*

A good base for exploring Lycian sites inland, Kalkan is an attractive town climbing up the hillsides that encircle its fishing harbor. There is an ever-growing number of small, family-run hotels in renovated village houses, many of which have characteristic roof terraces, and the narrow cobbled streets have relatively sophisticated souvenir shops and restaurants. The beaches are man-made.

ENVIRONS OF KALKAN Xanthos▶▶ (*Open* daily 8–5. *Admission charge*) Reached from unsavory Kınık, 11 miles inland from Kalkan, Xanthos is a magnificent site, as befits the remains of Lycia's greatest city. It is very extensive: a thorough visit takes a good three hours, with a fair bit of walking and scrambling. In the 19th century, the British plundered its sculptures filling 70 huge crates; most of them are now in the British Museum in London.

Any tour of Xanthos should begin with the theater and its extraordinary pair of pillar tombs, 25 feet high. The reliefs (plaster casts, as the originals are now in London) depict amazing creatures, half-bird, half-woman, carrying children in their arms, thought to represent either the Harpies or spirits carrying off the souls of the dead. On the acropolis stand the remains of a Lycian **royal palace**, overlooking the river valley. On the other side of the parking lot is an extensive Byzantine basilica with mosaic flooring, and farther uphill is the necropolis, with a cluster of house tombs dominated by another pillar tomb. At the top of the hill are the remains of a Byzantine monastery and large Roman temple.

Boat Trip

Kekova

An enjoyable day trip combines a swim with lunch at a village restaurant and a stop at several partly submerged ancient Lycian settlements.

Buy your tickets at Kaş harborfront. The boat generally leaves at 9 AM and returns by 6 PM. Boats also run from the little harbor of Demre, called Çayağzı. Private boats have more flexible hours, but are more expensive. Bring a mask and flippers, so you can snorkel around the underwater ruins. Scuba diving is forbidden.

After setting off from Kaş and passing the Greek island of Kastellorizo, 90 minutes' cruising brings you to the ruins of **Aperlae**, a Lycian town of the 4th century BC. In the shallow waters of the bay you can discern the outlines of streets and buildings submerged as a result of earthquakes.

After another 45 minutes you reach a pretty cove on Kekova Island, where the ruined apse of a Byzantine church stands on the beach. This is a good swimming spot; look for the foundations of houses at the far end of the

Kekova's ruins: Byzantine above and Lycian beneath the waters

157

bay. Keep a lookout, too, for occasional sea urchins.

The boat now hugs the shoreline of Kekova Island, where you will see more ruins beneath the turquoise water. The final stop is the village of **Kale** (Turkish for castle), named after the Byzantine fort whose crenellated walls crown the hilltop, enclosing a tiny ancient theater with seats cut into the rock. A few simple fish restaurants have grown up on the waterfront, overlooking more submerged ruins.

The round-trip journey to Kaş takes about two-and-a-half hours.

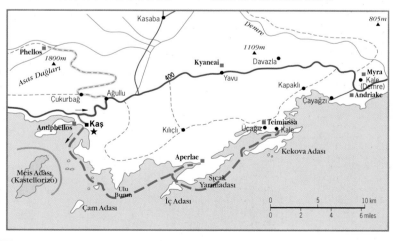

Local leather goods on sale at Kaş

A near-deserted beach at Karayellari, near Kaş

▶ Kaş

134A1

Like Kalkan (see page 156), Kaş is an excellent base for exploring the Lycian sites, but while Kalkan still feels like a village, Kaş is definitely a town, offering a good choice of shops and restaurants and a range of hotels and small family *pansiyons* (inns). Set in a striking bay encircled by high mountains all around, it still has a very traditional feel, with an attractive harbor frequented by fishermen and yachting enthusiasts alike. Much development has taken place on the snakelike headland to the west; the rocky beaches are not so good for children, however.

A few fragments of the ancient site of **Antiphellos** remain, including the small theater above the town and a number of huge sarcophagi strewn about the streets and harborfront. The whitewashed mosque is recognizable as a former Greek church, a relic of the days before 1923, when Kaş had a thriving Greek community.

ENVIRONS OF KAŞ Kekova Adası (Kekova Island)▶▶ See page 157.

Letoon▶▶ (*Open* daily 8–sunset. *Admission charge*) Try to visit this site at sunset, when it is at its best. The remains of this ancient Lycian sanctuary to Leto and her two children, Artemis and Apollo (see panel), consist of three temples and a *nymphaeum* (monumental fountain). The other major building is a theater, reflecting Letoon's other role as a central meeting place for the Lycian League (see page 162). Leto, Artemis, and Apollo were the patron deities of Lycia, and festivals were held here, with ceremonies conducted by the chief priests of the league.

The greater part of the site is underwater, which lends it a particular charm—especially at sunset, when the frogs in the sacred pools croak for all they're worth.

Patara►► (*Open* daily 8–sunset. *Admission charge*) This ancient site, with its natural harbor, once served as the port for Xanthos. Now the river disappears into marshland, and an immense sandbank has accumulated over the centuries to silt up the harbor, but also to give Patara its superb 14-mile-long sandy beach. No development is allowed on the beach because of the proximity of the historical site, but a small cluster of hotels has grown up half a mile inland. The ancient city itself has never been excavated, and the theater, half-buried in sand, makes a strangely attractive sight. The distances involved in exploring the ruins are considerable, and the terrain is tricky, with sand and occasional marshy areas. From the top of the theater you can assess the effort required to reach each part. A small temple buried in sand and undergrowth is probably the closest monument, remarkably well preserved and with a beautifully decorated lintel. The indefatigable may not be able to resist a trek across the silted-up harbor to **Hadrian's Granary**, a colossal building that serves as an evocative reminder of how these outlying parts of the empire served as breadbaskets to feed the citizens of Rome.

Phellos► See pages 160–161.

Üçağiz (Teimiussa)► The drive to this village at the end of the Kekova peninsula is an interesting one, through rural, sparsely populated countryside. The remains of a number of ancient cities lie on these wild, remote hillsides, but it would take many days and much stamina to explore them all.

The road ends here, in Üçağiz, a surprisingly sophisticated little place, more frequently visited from the sea than from the land. Right on the water's edge, not far from the soccer field, lie the remains of ancient Teimiussa (*Open* daily. *Admission free*), with a little fortress on a low summit and many sarcophagi scattered about, some of them with very fine carvings.

The harbor at Kaş attracts fishing boats and yachts alike

THE LEGACY OF LETO
In ancient times, the cult of Leto was widespread in this part of Turkey. According to Greek mythology, she was loved by Zeus, who fathered her twins, Artemis and Apollo. Persecuted by Hera, the jealous wife of Zeus, she was forced to flee while still pregnant. Many cities refused her entry, fearing the gods' wrath, and she finally arrived in a land known as Termilis, where she gave birth to her twins. As she was bathing them in a spring near where Letoon now stands, she was driven away by local shepherds; Leto turned them into frogs in punishment, and it is their descendants that we hear today (see page 158). Wolves then guided her to the River Xanthos, where she bathed her children and drank. In gratitude, she dedicated the river to Apollo and renamed the land Lycia (from *lykos*, the Greek word for wolf).

Walk

See map on page 157.

Mountain ridge from Kaş

The starting point for this walk is reached by a short drive inland to the village of Çukurbağ. From here there is a wonderful ridge-top walk with superb sea views, ending in the rarely visited Lycian ruined town of **Phellos**. Allow three hours altogether.

Drive out of Kaş inland on the Finike road for 6 miles until you reach the village of Ağullu, then take the easy dirt road that forks back to the west (refer to the map on page 157). On reaching the village of Çukurbağ, pass the village spring to the left and continue on a broad track that sweeps up the hillside in a loop. It then winds in and out of thick forested patches, giving superb

A typically fine Lycian landscape

views down over Kaş, Kastellorizo, and the coast. After 3 miles the road ends at a forest lookout post at the crest of the ridge. The total distance from Kaş is no more than 12 miles and the drive takes approximately half an hour.

The Turkish name for Phellos is Felandağ (the name of the mountain). If anyone is on duty in the forest ranger station, you can ask for directions, or simply head west along the ridge top to a little path, usually clearly visible, but sometimes prickly and boulder-strewn.

A delightful half-hour walk brings you to the first signs of the ruined town, with fine sarcophagi bearing reliefs and carvings. The finest of all lies down the hillside to the south, raised up on a solid base and with reliefs on three sides. The long south-facing side shows the deceased reclining on a couch drinking from a cup and being waited upon by servants.

Most exciting of all is the area at the far end of the ridge, set down in a hollow that is surrounded by what were clearly the fortified city walls. Here, heavily overgrown with scrub, are two enormous house tombs,

carved from huge freestanding boulders at least 12 feet high.

In a corner nearby there seems to have been a small sanctuary, with a low, semicircular wall recalling the apse of a church. On a large, flat rock face beside it is a carved bull, twice life-size: this is one of the few pieces of evidence to support the existence of a bull cult in ancient Lycia.

The position of Phellos, which has commanding views in all directions, conveys the feeling of a fortification rather than a settlement. Extensive sections of the beautifully crafted wall remain. There are also two wells, still in use, with cool, clear drinking water: this is the only ancient hilltop town in Lycia still with an abundant water supply. In the far southeastern corner stands a small watchtower, and there are more sarcophagi scattered down the north-facing side of the valley.

An ancient rock tomb along the route of this walk

A crescent-shaped bay on the coast south of Kemer

THE LYCIAN LEAGUE
The Lycians always had an instinct for unity, an unusual phenomenon in an age of constant warfare between city-states. To defend their region, the Lycians formed themselves into a league of 23 cities in the 2nd century BC. They even introduced a system of proportional representation: at their meetings, which rotated from city to city, the chief cities had three votes, middle-sized ones two votes, small-sized ones a single vote. Taxes were levied in the same proportions. Peace meant that the country prospered and huge fortunes were amassed by private citizens, many of whom lavished money on public building works.

▶ **Kemer**   *134B2*

This resort for Antalya (see page 146) is the most easterly town in Lycia and also probably the most developed, with a wide range of hotels, vacation villages, restaurants, and shops. Its setting is very attractive, backed by wooded mountains tumbling into the sea, and its sand and gravel beaches are immaculately maintained. There is a busy yachting marina, and the atmosphere is of a popular yet sophisticated family resort. The **Moonlight Beach** complex offers excellent sports facilities and water sports for a small fee. In the **Yürük (Nomad) Theme Park** you can watch traditional crafts demonstrations. Kemer is also well placed for excursions to nearby Lycian sites and to places near Antalya, such as **Aspendos** and **Termessos** (see pages 146–147).

▶▶ **Olympos**   *134B1*

Open: daily 8–5. Admission charge
Set in its own national park, Olympos probably enjoys the loveliest site in all Lycia. Allow at least three hours for a visit to this remote spot, or spend the day, picnic, and allow plenty of time to enjoy the ancient ruins, the beach, and the wonderful scenery.

The approach to the site follows the river valley lined with flowering oleander bushes. The ruins—many of them covered in dense undergrowth, or partly submerged—are difficult to explore, but if you persist you'll discover the collapsed remains of a theater, baths, a basilica, and a fine temple doorway from the 2nd century AD.

A short drive or long walk from the Olympos beach brings you to the **Chimera** (see pages 164–165).

▶ Phaselis 134B1

Open: daily sunrise–sunset. Admission charge

Just 20 miles from Antalya (see page 146), Phaselis is a popular destination for school trips and picnics. The site has been extensively excavated and visitors are well provided for—a complex of buildings by the entrance includes a souvenir shop and teahouse. There are three natural harbors where you can swim, with pine-clad mountains tumbling down to the sea.

The path leads to a Roman aqueduct among the trees. Foundations of shops line the paved main street, and there are extensive baths, complete with underground central-heating systems. A stairway leads off the main street to the pleasantly overgrown and shady theater. The street then continues across the headland to the far harbor and a large gateway erected in honor of a visit by Emperor Hadrian in about AD 130.

▶ Rhodiapolis 134A1

Open: daily. Admission free

Allow a full day and take a picnic when you visit the ruins of this ancient city, high in the hills above Kumluca. You'll need a guide to find the site, an hour's walk up through the forest from the nearest drivable road. The walk itself is so enjoyable and the ruins themselves so charmingly buried in the forest, that the exertion is well worth it.

The city's claim to fame is its funeral monument to Opromoas. A citizen of Rhodiapolis, Opromoas amassed a great fortune, and on his death bequeathed large sums of money for the construction of public monuments here and elsewhere in Lycia. The walls of his funeral monument are covered with inscriptions narrating the honors poured upon him, amounting to the longest single inscription in Lycia, and perhaps even in Asia Minor. The tomb is now in ruins, its carved blocks scattered about the forest floor by treasure-seekers convinced that a mighty hoard must lie within.

PHASELIAN TRICKS

Demosthenes described the Phaselians thus: "They are clever at borrowing money in the market, then as soon as they have it they forget it was a loan, and when called on for repayment think up all sorts of excuses and pretexts, and if they do repay it they feel that they have been done out of their own property; and in general they are the most scoundrelly and unscrupulous of men."

163

One of the three harbors at the Lycian site of Phaselis at sunset: a wonderfully romantic setting for swimming

Walk

The Chimera

This short but dramatic walk leads up through forest, inland from Olympos, to the extraordinary flames that burn eternally on the hillside above Olympos, the home of the mythical fire-breathing Chimera.

The starting point for the walk, which takes about an hour each way, is the site of Olympos, on the eastern Lycian coast between Kemer and Finike (see page 162). Boat trips run daily from Kemer in season. Bring a picnic if you intend to be here during lunchtime. The pebbly beach offers excellent swimming against the lush backdrop of the mountains and constantly flowering oleander bushes; the river estuary is a good place for children. If you swim around the bay you can examine the castle crenellations up on the cliffs, part of the defenses erected by the den of pirates who made this their base in ancient times. As early as the 5th century BC pirates plagued the whole southern Turkish coast, preying on trading ships from Syria and the Aegean, and selling their captives into slavery in wealthy Roman households. In the 1st century BC Olympos became the headquarters of the pirate chief Zeniketes.

Begin the walk by heading northward along the beach toward some huts, then follow a dirt road through a small village. Continue

A curl of flame licks up as it has for centuries on this site

north through the village, asking for ateş (which literally means "fire") if in doubt.

Beyond the village the track comes to a dead end in a cleft between two hillsides. Red paint on rocks and tree trunks now indicates the path, which climbs gently from this point to reach the Chimera—walking this section takes less than 30 minutes.

Suddenly the character of the hillside undergoes a curious change, becoming strangely bare. Issuing from it in at least a dozen places are flames the size of campfires. These were the natural eternal flames that inspired the ancient pirates of Olympos to hold secret rites to Mithras, the Zoroastrian god of light whose cult they must have encountered in their Eastern exploits. Visible far out to sea, the flames also served to guide sailors around the cape, which was notorious for its violent storms and shipwrecks.

In antiquity this was believed to be the home of the Chimera, a mythical beast described in the Iliad: "in front

a lion, and behind a serpent, and in the midst a goat, and she breathed dread fierceness of blazing fire." Homer describes how the King of Lycia set Bellerophon, the youthful suitor for his daughter's hand, the task of slaying the Chimera.

Over the ages the flames have fluctuated greatly in their intensity, from a huge fire that the ancients claimed could not be extinguished, to a few feeble flames easily put out with handfuls of earth. In the 19th century travelers used to come here to wallow in the waters of a nearby sulfurous pit, supposedly good for skin diseases, while their servants boiled tea and cooked food on the flames of the Chimera.

At the lowest part of the bare mountainside stand the remains of the pirates' temple, where the citizens of Olympos later came to worship Hephaestus (Vulcan to the Romans), god of fire and forging.

165

The ruins of the shrine to Hephaestus, god of fire and metalworking

From the vast 2nd-century theater at Side you can take in magnificent views over the ancient site and to the sea beyond

The Manavgat falls, a cooling alternative to the seashore with a refreshing breeze

▶▶ Side

134B2

Open: daily 9–12 and 1:30–3. Admission charge

Side, where the ruins of the ancient city mingle with the new, is the most charming resort on Turkey's southern coast. It offers an ever-increasing number of hotels, motels, *pansiyons* (inns), and campgrounds, most lining the excellent long, sandy beaches. Despite this development, Side succeeds in holding onto its special identity and unique atmosphere. It also serves as an excellent base for visitors wishing to combine a beach vacation with excursions to inland sites—and it is less than an hour's drive from Antalya Airport.

Side lies on a promontory; a fine Roman aqueduct, which used to carry water over 20 miles from the mountains, heralds the town. You must leave your car in the parking area beside the site museum.

Side is the only ancient city on Turkey's southern shore to have been excavated systematically. It flourished under the Roman Empire, and most of the extant monuments date from this period. In the 10th century it was abandoned after a fire, and the present town on the site dates only from the beginning of the 20th century, when it was founded by a group of Greek-speaking Muslim exiles from Crete. After the earlier abandonment of the town, sand drifted in to block the old harbor and cover many of the ruins. Somewhere under this sand there probably lies buried Side's stadium, of which no trace has yet been found.

A tour of the site can take anywhere from two to four hours. The museum is housed in the 5th-century Roman baths, still with their original room plan. It now makes an effective display area for all the significant sculpture found on site. Many of the statues are headless, having been decapitated by overzealous Christians soon after their conversion by Saint Paul.

Directly opposite the museum is the *agora* (marketplace), from which you can climb into the theater, built in the 2nd century and one of the largest in Asia Minor, seating about 17,000. From here there are fine views over the rest of the site and its Hellenistic defense walls, and on toward the sea.

The restaurant at Manavgat makes an unusual lunch stop

167

ENVIRONS OF SIDE Manavgat►

Lunch at Manavgat makes a very pleasant change, and it is only a 20-minute drive from Side. There is a nominal admission fee to the waterfall area, which is laid out with crass souvenir shops. Beyond this is an unusual restaurant, with tables scattered beneath the trees or perched on individual platforms built on the edge of the rushing river. Even in the height of summer there is always a cooling breeze here, and the staple fare is the river trout, accompanied by refreshing white Turkish wine.

Seleukeia (Seleuceia)► A half-day outing from Side to the ruined city of Seleukeia is a good opportunity to see the landscapes inland and do a little walking. The site is rarely visited—surprisingly, given its closeness to Side and its good state of preservation. It is reached from the village of Şıhlar, from which you can either drive on the rough track or walk for about an hour to reach the hill on which the ruins stand. At the entrance is a narrow hollow with a cave on the left that shelters a very welcome spring. Just above this are the baths, the city gate, flanked by rectangular towers, and the *agora* (marketplace) beyond. Beside the *agora* is the market hall, Seleukeia's most impressive monument (*Open* daily. *Admission free*).

Selge►► See pages 168–169.

COMMUNAL LATRINES
In the western corner of Side's *agora* (marketplace), against the theater, are the ancient public latrines, consisting of a semicircular arched passage, lined with marble and originally containing 24 seats above a water channel. In classical times one's daily achievements were not, as now, private affairs to be performed in solitary confinement, but rather an excuse for social gatherings and a chat.

Walk

Selge Canyon

If you're based in Side or Antalya, make time for an inland trip to the magnificent Köprülü Kanyon National Park and the ancient town of Selge. Because this is one of the most exciting excursions on Turkey's Mediterranean coast, it merits a whole day. Though there is a simple restaurant at the bottom of the canyon, you should take your own provisions if you plan to venture all the way to Selge.

The breathtaking mountain scenery of Selge Canyon makes an unforgettable day's excursion

Turn off the main Antalya-to-Side road and drive inland 23 miles to Beşkonak, also signposted Köprülü Kanyon Milli-parkı. From Side the drive takes one-and-a-quarter hours, winding through forest with glimpses down over the wide Eurymedon river. At Beşkonak the paved road stops and an easy dirt track continues north for 4 miles to the Roman stone bridge that spans the canyon over the river. Just before this is the attractive **Kanyon Restaurant**, on the river's edge.

Follow the signs to Altınkaya ("Golden Rock" in Turkish), the new name for the small settlements 9 miles away on the plateau, where ancient Selge and the modern village of Zerk lie.

Cross the Roman bridge. If you want to shorten your walk to the canyon and river area, take the left fork for half a mile or so to reach a second Roman bridge beside a picnic area.

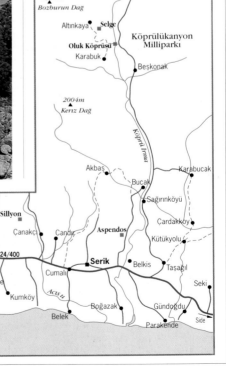

The fork right to Altınkaya is pretty rough in some places, but recent improvements mean that most cars can now make the trip. From the bridge to Selge is 8 miles, so you can stop the car at any point and walk if you prefer. The scenery along the way is very dramatic, with weird rock formations called "fairy chimneys" in the higher parts, and in all directions the deep gullies and precipices that successfully defended ancient Selge against the strategies of successive conquering armies.

The plateau at the end of the road is 2,800 feet high, and the temperature here is noticeably cooler than on the coast. The cultivated fields of Zerk are quickly followed by the first sight of Selge's ancient theater, standing in the middle of the village against the backdrop of the impressive snow-covered peaks of the **Kuyucuk** range (approximately 8,000 feet).

In the designated area there are usually children who escort you around for a small tip. When you walk up through the village, you'll pass the remains of a *stoa* (colonnade of shops) on your right and a stadium (for horse races) on your left, then emerge at the back of the well-preserved theater.

From the top of the theater a small path leads off to the hill where the temples of Artemis and Zeus, now just heaps of rubble, have been

The wildness of the surrounding terrain acted as an impregnable defense for the ancient town of Selge

identified. Following the course of the main street (with traces of the drainage system still visible), the path eventually reaches the fine paved courtyard of what was once the *agora* (marketplace), littered about with fragments of carved marble blocks. Climb the short route up the second hill to the scant remains of a Christian church, and from here scramble down the hillside for good views of the extensive walls that encircled the city in its heyday, when 20,000 fiercely independent citizens lived here.

Making bread in Selge Canyon

Cappadocia

A map of the Cappadocia region showing towns, mountains, rivers and roads.

Grid 4 (top row):
- Kirşehir, 1554m Kızıl Dağ, İmran, Büyüköz, Kurşunlu Dağı
- Mucur, Topaklı, Kızılırmak

Grid 3:
- Kesikköprü Hanı, Hacıbektaş, 1769m, Himmetdede, Kızılırmak, Erkilet
- Gümüşkent, 1670m, Kızılırmak, Özkonak, Mamattatar, Boğazköprü
- Ortaköy, Tuzla, Göreme Milliparkı, Sarıhan, 1754m, Kayseri
- Balcı, Gülşehir, Avanos Zelve, Hacılar
- 2133m, Çavuşin Üçhisar, Ürgüp, Hisarcık
- 1562m Karadağ, Nevşehir, Göreme, Ortahisar Mustafapaşa, İncesu, Kayak Evi
- Acıgöl, Cardak, 1937m, Dörtyol, 3916m Erciyes Dağı

Grid 2:
- Alay Hanı, Mamasın Barajı, 1982m Erdas Dağı, Kaymaklı Yeraltı Şehir, Çöl Gölü, Develi
- Aksaray, Derinkuyu, Derinkuyu Yeraltı Şehir, Soğanlı, Yeşilhisar, Yay-Gölü
- Sultanhanı, Yüksek Kilise, Güzelyurt, Göllü Dağı 2143m, Sultansazlığı Milliparkı
- Belisırma Ihlara, Kizil Kilise, Bağlama, Gölcük, Araplı, Ovaçiftlik
- Kemerli Kilise, Kara Kilise, Çiftlik, Melendiz Suyu, Huyük, Yahyalı
- 3268m Hasan Dağı, Melendiz Dağı, 2963m, 2140m

Grid 1:
- Altınhisar, Niğde, Gümüşler, Kavlaktepe
- 1332m, Bor, Eski Gümüş
- Çukurkuyu, Emen, Kemerhisar, 2689m, Çamardı

Scale: 0   10   20   30 km / 0   10   20 miles

Columns A, B, C

Above right and far right: troglodyte dwellings hollowed out of the soft tufa

A scene typical of the Göreme Valley

CAPPADOCIA This extraordinary region of Central Anatolia (Anadolu) has now become justly famous for its weird volcanic landscapes and painted churches, unique in the world. It was largely unknown in the West until a French priest, Guillaume de Jerphanion, decided to devote his life to the study of its churches, publishing the results of his vast research in the 1930s and 1940s.

LANDSCAPE The natural agent responsible for the famous Cappadocian landscapes was the (now extinct) volcano **Mount Erciyes**, which rises behind the town of **Kayseri**. Thirty million years ago, the volcanic ash it spewed forth consolidated into a layer of the soft, porous rock known as tufa, covering an area of about 1,560 square miles. Over the millennia, the soft tufa was eroded by wind, snow, and rain, but where it was protected above by a deposit of harder stone, the result was the curiously shaped rock cones that we see today, often still capped by the protective blocks of hard stone, which gives them a toadstool shape. The fanciful epithet "fairy chimneys" derives partly from local folktales of men being carried off by *peris*, or fairies, after venturing into old churches in the rocks. Whereas the usual colors in volcanic landscapes are harsh grays and blacks, the rocks

▶▶▶ REGION HIGHLIGHTS

Derinkuyu *page 175*
Göreme *pages 176–177*
Ihlara *pages 182–183*
Kaymakli *page 180*
Niğde *page 180*
Soğanı *page 186*
Zelve *page 187*

The "fairy chimneys" of Cappadocia

FAIRY CHIMNEYS
These extraordinary rock formations, which have become the symbol of Cappadocia, can be found in greatest numbers in two valleys close to Ürgüp. Nearly 3 miles north of Ürgüp is the amazing Devrent Valley, where you can park and walk down among the pink fairy chimneys, and a mile west of the town is the Çatalkaya Valley with its mushroom-shaped formations.

here are in soft shades of pale gray, yellow, mauve, pink, and umber, the color variation reflecting the variety of metal ores and minerals emitted over the millennia during different eruptions.

CHANGING SEASONS Cappadocia lies in the triangle formed by the three main towns of **Nevşehir**, **Kayseri**, and **Niğde**. The best place to base yourself is probably the attractive rural town of **Ürgüp**, which has a good selection of hotels. The tourist season begins in earnest in April and continues until the end of November; in peak season, the area is subject to a major invasion of tourists from all parts of Europe, almost all of them in organized bus tours. The **Göreme heartlands** have been particularly hit by tourist development, with forests of signs and billboards advertising hotels and restaurants. For an independent traveler, however, it is possible to get off the tour bus routes and visit some of the less well-known places, such as **Soğanlı** and **Mustafapaşa**, where you can still enjoy some relatively untouched Cappadocian landscapes and a variety of churches.

A winter visit is in many ways the best: the whole region is frequently lightly covered in snow, and all the sites stay open, but there are few, if any, bus tours. Even in spring the region remains remarkably cold, and snow is not unlikely as late as early May. Most hotel swimming pools do not open until June, when the really hot weather starts. Fall is probably the most colorful season, when the leaves of the apricot and poplar trees turn to lovely yellows, reds, and oranges under clear blue skies.

Houses hollowed out of rock near Yaprakhisar

ITINERARIES Cappadocia covers a large area, and the sheer number and variety of places to visit can be bewildering at first. To help plan your stay, here are some detailed day trips that can all be done from Ürgüp (or from **Nevşehir** or **Avanos**).

1 Ortahisar, Üchişar (lunch), Göreme Valley.
2 Çavuşin, Zelve (lunch), Avanos, Sarıhan, Özkonak, Peribacalar Valley.
3 Ürgüp, Mustafapaşa, Soğanlı (lunch), Derinkuyu, Kaymaklı, Nevşehir.
4 Ürgüp, Avanos (lunch), Hacıbektaş, Gülşehir, Nevşehir.
5 Nevşehir, Ihlara (lunch), Güzelyurt (Sultanhanı, if you are going on to Konya, see pages 204–205).
6 Ürgüp, Mustafapaşa, Soğanlı (lunch), Eski Gümüş, Niğde (you can continue on to Adana the same day if you wish, see pages 138–139).

CAVE PAINTINGS

The beautiful and moving wall paintings in the rock churches and monasteries of Cappadocia constitute an essentially provincial art form, described by the art historian Steven Runciman as "expressions of an intense but unsophisticated piety." Dating from the Iconoclastic period (8th and 9th centuries) to the 11th century, the paintings are characterized by crudely drawn figures, strongly outlined to produce an immediately powerful effect. Some of them reflect the artistic traditions of Egypt, Syria, and Palestine, while others show the influence of the Byzantine capital, Constantinople. As so few works of art from this period survive outside Istanbul, these cave paintings are an exceptionally important record of Byzantine cultural history.

173

Typical Cappadocian villages combine cave dwellings with surface-built houses

▶ Avanos
170B3

North of Göreme on the road to Özkonak, Avanos is a pretty little town on the banks of the **Kızılırmak**, the Red River, the longest river in Anatolia. The distinctive deep red soil that tinges the water also colors the clay used to make the famous local pottery, which was exported even in earliest times to Greece and Rome.

On the southern outskirts of the town, a yellow sign points to **Sarıhan** (*Open* daily 9–1 and 2–6. *Admission charge*), the Yellow Caravansary. The inn is remarkable for the soft color of the stone exterior and for its very small proportions. It was restored in the early 1990s.

▶ Çavuşin
170B3

As the landscape flattens out between Avanos and Göreme, you reach Çavuşin Church (*Admission charge*), slightly set back to the right of the road. The front section of the church has been eroded away, exposing frescoes of the archangels Gabriel and Michael guarding the entrance. The frescoes inside, in clashing orange and yellow, are different from those at Göreme (see pages 176–177), and some experts believe they are the work of Armenians. Outside, steps lead up to the monastery next door, with four carved tombs inside. In the village of Çavuşin itself (some 400 yards before this church) is the **Church of Saint John the Baptist**, dating back in part to the 8th century and generally regarded as the oldest in Cappadocia. Its façade has collapsed and the exterior is heavily damaged, but the interior still has fine paintings.

Avanos, famous for its pottery since classical times

174

▶▶ Derinkuyu   170B2

Open: daily 8–6. Admission charge

A yellow sign in a muddy parking lot in the grubby little village of Derinkuyu announces this underground city, offering no clue from the outside to its scale and extent. Discovered by accident in 1963, this is one of the most extensive of Cappadocia's 37 known underground cities, and was home to at least 20,000 people (see panel). The full number of stories is still not known, but is thought to be as many as 18 or 20, of which only the top eight are open to the public.

No one is sure who the original builders were, but the current belief is that the first level was built by the Hittites in about 1400 BC as a store area: Hittite seals have been found by locals digging foundations for their houses, and certainly the Hittites built a surface city 12 miles southwest of Derinkuyu at Göllü Dağı. It is thought that the air chimneys, 200 to 250 feet deep, were dug first until water was reached, and then horizontal passages cut between them. The volcanic tufa (porous rock) was very soft to cut, as it hardens only on contact with air, and the tufa chambers make surprisingly pleasant living areas, with good air circulation, constant temperatures and humidity, and, very importantly, no insects.

The first two stories consist of communal kitchens, areas for eating, sleeping, storage, wine cellars, stables, and toilets, while the lower levels contain hiding places with wells (Derinkuyu means "Deep Well"), chapels, armories, dungeons, burial places, and a meeting hall. The villagers at Derinkuyu still depend on these wells for their water. Several of the tunnels have cartwheel-shaped stones to seal them off, and some of them were intended to serve as escape routes—one tunnel, leading to the underground city of Kaymaklı, is an astonishing 5½ miles long.

Part of the network of subterranean corridors in the underground city of Derinkuyu

UNDERGROUND CONGESTION
Throughout history the people of Cappadocia have used their underground cities as refuges from the invading hordes that regularly poured across the Anatolian plain. As recently as 1839, the locals hid here from the invading Egyptian army, led by Ibrahim Paşa. Today, they are invaded by the tourist hordes who pour underground by the busload. Derinkuyu has eight stories open to the public, with only one single-file stairway to the bottom. If you encounter a tour group on the second story, your chances of reaching the eighth story within the hour are slim. If two tour groups going in opposite directions pass each other on the stairs, there will be a major traffic jam.

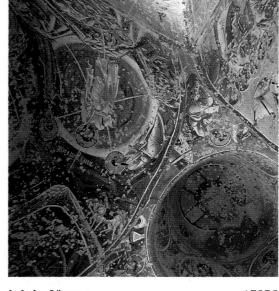

*Frescoes inside the
Çarıklı Kilise, or Shoe
Church*

176

*Some farmers use old
rock dwellings as
pigeon cotes*

▶▶▶ Göreme   170B2

The churches of the Göreme Valley contain unquestionably the most spectacular paintings of the region; as a
result, this area has been designated the Göreme National
Park, a huge open-air museum (*Open* daily 8:30–5:30.
Admission charge). The inevitable corollary is heavy
tourist development, with steep admission and parking
fees, a bank and shops at the entrance, and a definite
sense of being "processed" around, as you follow the
arrows in a one-way system. Try to visit off season or
very early in the day to avoid the worst of the
crowds. Alternatively, choose the less well-known
sites such as **Soğanlı** (see page 186) and **Ihlara** (see
pages 182–183).

The tour begins with the **Elmalı Kilise** (Apple
Church), named after either the dwarf apple trees
growing near the entrance, or a round object held
by Jesus in one of the frescoes, thought to resemble
an apple, though it is probably the Earth. After a
narrow, arcaded tunnel entrance, the church
opens up into the usual dome over four pillars.
The 11th-century frescoes depict the Baptism of
Christ, his Entry into Jerusalem, the Last Supper,
the Crucifixion, and the Betrayal of Judas.

Next is the **Church of Saint Barbara**, cut into the
back of the same rock as the Apple Church and decorated with the unexciting geometric red lines of the
Iconoclastic period (AD 726–842), when the use of
images was forbidden. These churches are curiously
small, a feature in direct compliance with the views
of Saint Basil, the founder of Eastern monasticism,
on the importance of keeping monastic communities small.

After this you reach the **Yılanlı Kilise** (Snake
Church), one of the most interesting, with a vaulted

ceiling with frescoes on its sides. The name derives from one of these, showing Saint George on horseback fighting the dragon, which is depicted as a serpent with the damned trapped in its coils.

Passing through a series of rooms and refectories, part of a monastic complex cut in the rock, you next reach the **Karanlık Kilise** (Dark Church). This originally had only one window, making it very gloomy inside, but the façade has now fallen away to expose the interior. The 11th-century frescoes here—depicting the Last Supper, the Adoration of the Magi, and the Betrayal of Judas— have retained their colors because they've been out of the light for so long.

Next is the **Çarıklı Kilise** (Shoe Church), reached by an iron staircase. *Çarık* means a kind of moccasin, referring to the shoe prints at the bottom of one of the frescoes of Christ. Finally you reach the **Kızlar Kilise** or convent, thought to have housed some 300 nuns.

The most beautiful church, the **Tokalı Kilise** (Buckle Church), lies opposite the parking lot. The guardian comes with you to turn on the lights, revealing a magnificent interior still in excellent condition. The frescoes depict the Miracles of Christ and other scenes, such as the Last Supper, the Flight into Egypt, the Nativity, and the Entry into Jerusalem, all against a superb, deep blue background. This is the largest of the Göreme churches, and its paintings are the most sophisticated. Nearby is a scattering of other churches with frescoes; these are generally kept unlocked.

MIRACULOUS BREW

Much of the damage to the frescoes in the Göreme Valley was inflicted by the Greek Christians themselves, who apparently believed in the medicinal powers of a brew made by adding fragments of broken frescoes to water. The perpetrator would then carve his name and the date beside the chunk he had chiseled out, just to make sure that God had registered who he was.

DATING PROBLEMS

The precise dating of the churches and monasteries in Cappadocia is frequently very difficult. Most were built before the 11th century, and only a few after the 13th. The architecture tends to conform to standard Byzantine arrangements of dome, arches, and pillars, the latter being purely decorative. As a general rule, the paintings within the churches are considered to be of greater significance than their architecture.

177

MODES OF TRANSPORTATION

Cappadocia's landscape is well suited to horseback riding and bicycling, and local travel agencies can arrange trips into the countryside, sometimes involving camping. Hot-air ballooning has also become popular; the best time is in the early morning, when the air is still clear enough for superb aerial views.

Its beautiful frescoes make the Tokalı Kilise, or Buckle Church, the loveliest church in the Göreme Valley

Turkey was one of the first countries to which Christianity spread from the Holy Land, with Saint Peter the Apostle founding the first Christian community in Antioch between AD 47 and 54. It was here that the followers of Jesus first became known as Christians.

CONFLICTING DOCTRINES

Early Christianity fought numerous battles against heresy. Three Church Councils were held in Asia Minor to resolve critical issues. In AD 381 the Council of Constantinople confirmed the Nicene Creed of AD 325, which had rejected the Arian heresy concerning the precise nature of Christ's relationship to God the Father. The Nestorian heresy, which stressed Christ's human nature, and so questioned his divinity, was denounced at Ephesus in AD 431. Lastly, the Monophysite doctrine, in which God the Father and God the Son share a single nature, was rejected in AD 451 at the Council of Chalcedon.

THE JEWISH INFLUENCE

An important feature of the area in Asia Minor where Christianity emerged was its Jewish communities, founded by the Seleucids. When Saint Paul arrived in the cities of Asia Minor, he began his preaching among these communities. The Jews enjoyed many privileges and their religion was tolerated on the whole, despite the Roman requirement of universal allegiance to the imperial cult. Sardis had a large Jewish community, hence the famous synagogue.

Ephesus became the chief center of Christianity in Asia Minor, principally because Saint John is said to have lived there from AD 37 to 48, accompanied by the Virgin Mary, who had been entrusted to his care by Christ when on the cross. When Saint Paul arrived there in AD 53, he thus found a small group of converts already in existence. The success of his preaching gave rise to a riot against the Christians by local people, who claimed that the new teachings were challenging the greatness of Artemis. After this Paul left Ephesus, later writing his celebrated letters to the Ephesians.

The Seven Churches of Asia As Christianity gradually became established, the "Seven Churches of Asia Minor" referred to in the Revelation of Saint John were founded at Smyrna, Ephesus, Pergamum, Thyatira, Sardis, Philadelphia, and Laodiceia. Over the next two centuries the Christians were routinely persecuted by the Roman authorities for their staunch refusal to comply with the imperial cult.

Then in the 4th century the Roman Emperor Constantine the Great converted to Christianity, and at the Council of Nicaea (Iznik), Christianity was proclaimed the official religion. When Constantine founded his new Eastern Empire in Constantinople, five years later, he set out to make it a Christian city, the first time Christianity had ever been actively embraced, rather than merely tolerated, by a Roman emperor.

The grotto of Saint Peter at Antakya (Antioch), perhaps the world's first Christian church

Christianity in Cappadocia Monasticism began to develop in Cappadocia in the 4th century, when followers of the order of Saint Basil (AD 329–379) built hermitages in the rocks. In the 7th century, when the area became an important frontier province with the onset of Arab raids on the Byzantine Empire, Christians may well have resorted to these caves in order to avoid persecution. The soft tufa had by then been tunneled into the chambers and passages of underground cities, in which life could continue during difficult times.

When the Byzantines re-established secure control, between the 7th and 11th centuries, this troglydyte population resurfaced to carve their churches into the rock faces and cliffs of the **Göreme** and **Soğanlı** areas, now so celebrated. Their churches and monasteries were many and small: the landscape was well suited to recluses in quest of spirituality, and the region was far distant from the contending doctrines of orthodox Constantinople and Monophysite Syria. Saint Basil, a 4th-century monk from **Kayseri** (see page 180) held that small, intimate, and disciplined communities were the most conducive to religious feeling, and such communities flourished here. Icons continued to be painted after the Seljuk conquest of the province in the 11th century, and even under the Ottomans, Christian practices were tolerated in Cappadocia, where the population was largely Greek, with some Armenians. Decline eventually set in, however, and Göreme, Ihlara, and Soğanlı lost their early influence. The Greeks finally ended their long history here with the mass exchange of populations between Greece and Turkey in 1923 (see page 283).

One of the exceptional mosaics in Istanbul's Kariye Camii, dating to the 14th century

CHRISTIAN SYMBOLISM
When images based on the human form were forbidden during the Iconoclastic period, they were replaced by other images with secret symbolic meanings, including the following:
fish*: pious followers
vine*: Jesus
palm*: heaven and eternal life
deer*: eternal being and healing
rabbit*: sexuality, the devil, and magic
lion*: victory and salvation
peacock*: the resurrection and transfiguration of the body after death
pigeon or dove*: love, peace, and innocence

CAVEAT EMPTOR
The traders of Kayseri are notoriously shrewd: one story tells of a merchant who sold a neighbor a white donkey, then stole it from him in the night and painted it black. The next morning the neighbor told his tale to the merchant, who sympathized with him and promptly sold the donkey to him once more.
Tourists should be wary of Kayseri silk, which is known as rayon in most people's vocabulary.

► Hacıbektaş 170B3
Open: Tue–Sun 8:30–12:30 and 1:30–5. Admission charge
The Hacı Bektaş Monastery was opened as a museum in 1964. Beyond the main courtyard lie a mosque and two *türbe* (tomb) shrines: one to Hacı Bektaş himself, and the other to Balim Sultan, the secondary founder. Shoes must be removed inside all buildings of the Bektashi Dervish order (see panel), and visiting Turks speak in awed whispers and kiss every tomb in sight. The abundant local onyx, used by the disciples to make everyday implements, is now used to make souvenirs.

►► Ihlara 170A2
See pages 182–183.

►► Kaymaklı 170B2
Open: daily 8–5. Admission charge
Kaymaklı, discovered in 1964, has a pretty entrance with steps leading up to a honeycombed mound. It has only four underground stories open to the public, compared with Derinkuyu's eight, but they are arranged in a more interesting fashion. There are bedrooms, food warehouses, wine cellars, ventilation chimneys, water depots, and a church with a double apse and stone doors that could be rolled shut from the inside.

► Kayseri 170C3
The approach to Kayseri improves as you reach the main square, with its inevitable equestrian statue of Atatürk and the black walls of the citadel looming to the left. The monuments that have managed to survive the town's changing fortunes are the 13th- and 14th-century Islamic buildings of the Seljuks and the Turcoman emirs, now in uninspiring settings surrounded by ugly modern buildings. The **Sahibiye Madrasa**, off the main square, was built by the famous Seljuk architect Sahip Ata in 1267; the citadel, with its 19 black basalt towers, has been renovated and turned into a shopping center. Opposite the citadel and near the tourist office stands the **Huant Foundation** (*Open* daily 8–5. *Admission charge*), the first mosque complex to be built by the Seljuks in Anatolia. Consisting of a mosque, a *türbe* (tomb), a bath, and a *çeşme* (fountain), it is now a museum of local ethnography and crafts. See also the drive on page 184.

►► Niğde 170B1
Do not miss the unique 10th-century rock-cut monastery of **Eski Gümüş** (*Open* daily 9–12 and 1:30–5:30. *Admission charge*), discovered in 1963, on a site a mile north of Niğde. The condition of the frescoes here is almost perfect, far better than those at Göreme (see pages 176–177).
The monastery church with its tall pillars and vaulted roof, is particularly beautiful. In the monks' bedrooms look for the wall paintings of deer, ostriches, and men hunting with bows and arrows. You can reach the rooms by a metal staircase.
In Niğde itself, with its 11th-century citadel rising up in the center, are a handful of interesting Seljuk and Mongolian monuments, the most notable of which is the superb 16-sided Mongolian conical *türbe* (tomb) of Hudabend Hatun (1312).

▶ Ortahisar

170B2

The main attraction here is the huge honey-combed cone fortress. In the village are the Harin Church, with its huge columns, and the Sarica Church, with a good fresco of the Annunciation.

T.C. NEVŞEHIR VALILIĞI

308450

BIRD-RICH MARSHES

To the south of Kayseri lie the Sultan Marshes (Turkish Sultan Sazlığı Milliparkı), much frequented by bird-watchers, especially in April and May. If you arrive early in the day at the village of Ovaçiftlik, the villagers will take you through the marshes by boat to watch the bird life.

181

Ortahisar is remarkable for its colossal tufa cone, which has been honey-combed into a maze of tunnels, stairways, and refuges

THE BEKTASHI DERVISHES

The Bektashi Dervish order, founded by Hacı Bektaş in the 13th century and closely connected with the Janissaries, was extremely popular because of its sceptical and irreverent attitude to religion. With a reputation for free-thinking and loose ways, including permitting women to participate unveiled in their ceremonies, it enjoyed its major following among the rural poor of the villages. Centuries ahead of his time, Hacı Bektaş declared that a nation which did not educate its women could not progress. The order survived the abolition of the Janissaries in 1825 and was dissolved only in 1926, along with the Mevlevis and other Dervish orders.

Walk

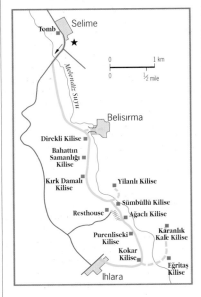

The Ihlara Gorge

This walk, removed from the crowds in Cappadocia, combines magnificent scenery with a chance to explore some early rock-cut churches in the gorge. The whole valley is estimated

A Cappadocian shepherd silhouetted against the setting sun

to have 4,500 man-made caves and 105 churches or shrines. Most of the painted churches are thought to date back to the 8th and 9th centuries, constituting rare examples from this period that escaped the wrath of the Iconoclasts.

If you have the whole day free, begin your walk at Selime, the village at the head of the gorge; from here you can walk all the way along the river, through the exceptionally pretty village of **Belisırma**, to reach Ihlara village, a total distance of some 6 miles, taking three–four hours. At Ihlara you can easily get a taxi to take you back to Selime. If you have less time, drive to the cliff-top resthouse just before Ihlara village and descend the steep concrete steps 600 feet into the gorge to explore the main churches in around two hours. Though shorter, this is the more energetic option, which also takes you to the busier part of the gorge.

If you are using **Nevşehir** as your base, set off on the Aksaray road, then turn off for 19 miles along a narrow paved road dominated by the **Hasan Dağ** volcano (10,000 feet). Melted snow from the volcano formed the Melendiz river, which in turn eroded a passage through the soft volcanic tufa to create the deep Ihlara Gorge.

Setting off from Selime along the southwest riverbank, you immediately enter a different world, a hidden valley with no sound except the wind in the poplar and willow trees and the rushing, shallow water. Wildlife is abundant, with birds, frogs, and lizards at every turn, and more butterflies than anywhere east of Ankara. The contrast with the bleak and featureless Anatolian plateau is complete.

The first church of note, just beyond Belisırma, is the 11th-century **Direkli Kilise** (Church with the Columns), with fine frescoes. Next come the small **Bahattin Samanlığı Kilise** (Church with a Granary) and the **Kırk Damalı Kilise** (Church with Forty Roofs), the latter set 150 feet up the hillside. Inside, a fresco shows Saint George with the 13th-century benefactor and his wife.

One of the frescoes in the Yilanlı Kilise, or Church of the Snake

The next landmark is a pretty wooden bridge; cross this and follow the path up to the **Yilanlı Kilise** (Church of the Snake), perhaps the most interesting of the churches, shaped like a long cross. One of its frescoes depicts the Archangel Michael consigning sinners to a grizzly end in the coils of the snake.

Now cross back over the bridge to visit the **Sümbüllü Kilise** (Church of the Hyacinth), with blind arches and an elaborate rock-cut façade that give it one of the most attractive exteriors of any of the churches. A little farther on, concrete steps descend from the cliff-top restaurant. Up a few steps is the curious **Ağaçlı Kilise** (Church under a Tree), cross-shaped with a central dome and frescoes depicting biblical scenes.

Next along the path toward Ihlara is the **Purenliseki Kilise** (Church with a Terrace) with fragmentary frescoes, followed by the **Kokar Kilise** (Fragrant Church), which contains scenes of the Annunciation, the Nativity, the Flight into Egypt, and the Last Supper. If you have the courage to ford the river at this point, you can seek out the **Karanlık Kale Kilise** (Dark Castle Church), with fragmentary paintings, and **Eğritaş Kilise** (Church with a Crooked Stone), a set of large, interlinked chambers with extensive but eroded frescoes; both are set high above the river.

183

The contrast with the emptiness of the Anatolian plateau is clear

Drive

Kayseri to Mount Erciyes

A short drive (16 miles) from Kayseri brings you part of the way up Mount Erciyes, and from the point where the road ends you can take a magnificent walk up the mountainside and have a picnic. Allow half a day for this drive.

Kayseri itself lies on the eastern fringes of Cappadocia, dominated by Mount Erciyes (12,139 feet), snowcapped for most of the year. It was this now extinct volcano, known in antiquity as Mount Argaeus, which in an eruption aeons ago spewed out the volcanic tufa (soft, porous rock) that was to be molded over the centuries into the fantastical shapes for which Cappadocia is famous.

Armed with supplies of the local specialty, *pastırma* (thinly sliced beef dried in the sun and rolled in garlic and herbs, with a slight flavor of aniseed), head out of town on the road due south from the black basalt citadel, passing Kayseri's most famous tomb, the *Döner Kumbet* ("Revolving Kumbet"), on the right about half a mile from the center. This tomb of a Seljuk princess dates from 1276; its external walls are decorated with Tree of Life symbols, a pair of winged leopards, a griffin, and a two-headed eagle, the Seljuk sign of royalty, and it now looks a bit lost in its suburban setting.

After 9 miles you reach the village of Hisarcık, from where a road continues to **Kayak Evi**, where there is a municipally run mountain hut with 100 beds. Climbers come here in summer to enjoy the fabulous volcanic scenery, with numerous small cinder cones. The altitude at Kayak Evi is 6,665 feet, and the temperature is cooler than in the town. There is skiing here from December to May, with a chairlift operating from Kayak Evi up to the slopes. In summer bring plenty of fluids; if you feel inspired to climb to the top, you will also need a guide, ice ax, and crampons, all of which you can rent from Kayak Evi.

Kayseri's Döner Kumbet

Names such as "nightingale's nest," "lady's navel," and "lips of the beautiful beloved" sum up the Turkish attitude to desserts. The abundance of pastahanes *(pastry shops) bursting with every conceivable gooey concoction betrays the Turkish sweet tooth. Milk, nuts, honey, eggs, and pastry are the basic ingredients of Turkish desserts, of which the best-known are sticky pastry such as* baklava *and* kadayıf.

185

Pastries *Kadayıf* are long, finely shredded strands of dough with a mixture of ground hazelnuts and honey inside. *Baklava* is generally bought from a *pastahane*, as it takes an expert pastry chef to prepare these sticky, syrup-sodden triangles of flaky pastry filled with ground walnuts. *Dilber dudağı* ("a beautiful woman's lips") are little oval-shaped pastries soaked in oil, with fresh cream and crushed pistachio nuts tumbling from a small slit down the middle.

NOAH'S FEAST
Aşure is the food that the Bektashi Dervishes use to break their 10-day fast on the 10th day of the Islamic month of Muharram. Apparently it contains 40 ingredients, in honor of the traditional belief that after the Ark had sailed its 40 days and 40 nights, Noah ordered a stew made of the remaining supplies in celebration of the end of the Flood. These days you can buy ready-made *aşure* mix in Turkish supermarkets, but this usually has only 20 ingredients.

Milk and gelatin desserts The classic Turkish milk desserts are *muhallabi*, a type of rice pudding with cinnamon, sometimes flavored with rosewater, and *keşkül*, a smooth mixture of milk, ground almonds and pistachios, garnished with dried coconut and pistachio. *Aşure* (see panel) is a Jello-type dessert, a rosewater gel full of chickpeas and dry beans and decorated with dried figs and apricots, raisins, walnuts, pine nuts, and pistachios. When using fresh fruit in their desserts, the Turks favor delights such as black cherry bread and peach bread, pumpkin with nuts, and banana rice pudding.

Of all Turkish candy, the best known is undoubtedly Turkish delight (*lokum*), made from solidified sugar and pectin flavored with rosewater, lemon, or pistachio and dusted with powdered sugar.

Baklava, halva, and Turkish delight are just a few of the temptations awaiting the visitor with a sweet tooth

THE SULTAN'S CARAVANSARY

Sultanhanı, the largest and best-preserved caravansary in Turkey, lies on the western edge of Cappadocia on the road to Aksaray. Built between 1229 and 1236 by the great Seljuk Sultan Alaeddin Keykubad I, it dominates the cluster of village houses that have grown up around it. Here traveling merchants would receive lodging, food, and stabling, all free of charge; trade and commerce flourished under the Seljuks as a result of this.

A precarious rock dwelling in the Soğanli Valley

A single cone might once have sheltered an entire community in a picturesque hodgepodge of superimposed chambers and tunnels

▶ Özkonak   170B3

Open: daily 8–5:30. Admission charge

To the north of Avanos (see page 174) a small road forks west to Özkonak, one of Cappadocia's underground cities, once housing 60,000 inhabitants. Lying slightly off the beaten track, it receives fewer visitors than Cappadocia's other underground cities and therefore makes for a more relaxed sightseeing experience.

▶▶ Soğanlı   170B2

Open: daily 8:30–5:30. Admission charge

Soğanlı Valley, 20 miles away from Ürgüp (see below) to the south, makes a pleasant, quiet excursion for a day or longer. The drive is a delightful one, through wooded valleys and colorful villages. The pretty troglydyte village of Soğanlı is set in a huge table-topped mountain; either side of this lie the valley's churches, some 60 of them in all, though many have been filled up with earth or turned into pigeon cotes by the villagers. The most interesting ones are along the right-hand side of the valley, especially **Yılanlı Kilise** (Snake Church), **Saklı Kilise** (Hidden Church), and the amazing three-story **Kubbeli Kilise** (Domed Church) in its own curious domed rock formation.

▶ Üçhisar   170B3

This scruffy village is dominated by a tall cone fortress similar to the one at Ortahisar (see page 181). From the top there is an impressive view over the whole Göreme Valley, and at night the cone is illuminated, making it look like a colossal, hollowed-out Halloween pumpkin.

▶ Ürgüp   170B3

The best base for a few days in Cappadocia, Ürgüp is an attractive rural town set at the heart of the main valleys. The cobbled streets that wind up and down its hills are lined by many grand old Greek houses, with fine loggias and carved decoration around the doors and windows. Many of the houses are set partly into the cave-riddled cliff faces, and the locals use the caves as garages, store-rooms, and stables. Unique to the Ürgüp region is the traveling library, carried on the back of a donkey, which brings books to eager borrowers in the far-flung areas of the town.

Ürgüp's cobbled main street, by the museum, has a number of good souvenir shops, offering silver jewelry set with semiprecious stones such as amethyst, lapis lazuli, jade, and garnet, along with good carpets, elaborate woodwork, and stunning metalwork and boxes. Colorful knitted woolen socks and gloves are also for sale, at government-regulated prices.

▶▶ Zelve   170B3

Open: daily 8:30–5:30. Admission charge

Just north of Çavuşin (see page 174), a fork in the road leads to Zelve, a pretty series of three valleys peppered with troglydyte dwellings. There is no longer a village here: the Greeks left in 1923, and the Turks who moved in after them had to leave in the 1950s because of landslides and erosion. The hour-long walk and scramble around Zelve will likely be one of your most enjoyable in Cappadocia.

187

Head first into the main right-hand valley, going past a little mosque to reach the monastery complex, a huge bowl cut out of the rock. A gallery runs around it halfway up, from which a tunnel leads up steep steps to the very ceiling of the dome. You need a flashlight to explore the deeper recesses of the monastery rooms. Scattered about in the second and third valleys are more churches, and even a rock-cut mill with grinding stone. A host of little footpaths run up and down the hillsides to aid your explorations.

Evening light at Üçhisar

Central Anatolia

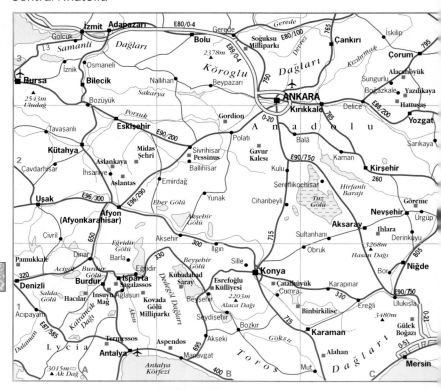

ITINERARIES

One week:
Day 1 Ankara
Days 2–3 Afyon
Days 4–5 Konya
Days 6–7 Ürgüp
Day 8 Ankara

Two weeks:
Days 1–2 Ankara
Day 3 Boğazkale
Day 4 Amasya
Day 5 Sivas, Divriği
Day 6 Elazığ
Day 7 Diyarbakır
Day 8 Şanlıurfa
Day 9 Nemrut Dağı
Day 10 Antakya
Day 11 Adana
Day 12 Göreme
Day 13 Ürgüp
Day 14 Ankara

A detail of the intricately carved portal of the mosque at Divriği

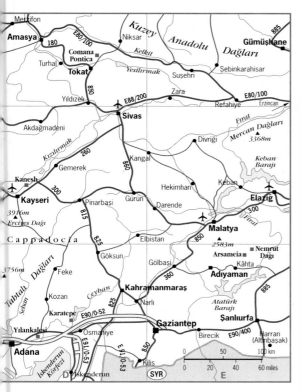

TURKISH HEARTLAND Central Anatolia (or Anadolu), once dismissed by foreign visitors as a bleak, featureless plateau, is now appreciated as the cradle of the extraordinary Hittite civilization (1500–1200 BC), contemporary with the river cultures of Egypt and Mesopotamia. Turkish civilization originated in these central step-pelands, where the Seljuks also chose to base themselves, in their capital Konya.

LANDSCAPE The prospect of inhospitable steppeland stretching to the horizon is a forbidding one, and many balk at this entryway to a different Turkey, far removed from the semi-European resorts of the Mediterranean. Once you have overcome any resistance, however, you're in for some curious surprises on this 3,000-foot-high plateau, some manmade, others natural. After adjusting your eyes to the barrenness of the landscapes, you'll notice details of a different kind: the sparse villages clinging to the edges of the hills; soil changes and weird rock color-ings, reflecting the mineral deposits in which Turkey is so rich; and above all the abundant bird life. A number of large rivers cross the plateau, such as the **Kızılırmak** and the **Yeşilırmak**. The mountains encircling it isolate the plateau geographically and climatically from all maritime influence, and the small amount of rainfall is concentrated in a very short period in the spring. The central depression around **Tuz Gölü** (the Great Salt Lake)—"shining waters of saline deposit," as 19th-century English explorer

Central Anatolia

Characteristic riverside houses at Amasya

HOW TO TRAVEL
Car and bus are the best ways to travel. A train runs from Eskişehir to Ankara, then continues southeastward to Kayseri on the edge of Cappadocia; if you don't have a car, this train route is exciting as it follows the many dramatic river gorges of the plateau, notably between Divriği and Erzincan.

FORBIDDING PLAIN
Reflecting on her first experience of the Central Anatolian plateau, Gertrude Bell wrote in *A Thousand and One Churches* (1904): "It is Asia, with all its vastness, with all its brutal disregard for life and comfort and the amenities of existence; it is the Ancient East, returned after so many millenniums of human endeavor to its natural desolation."

Typical Afyon streets

Gertrude Bell described it—is virtually uninhabited, the most barren place in Turkey.

TOWNS Ankara is the most likely base for any stay in Central Anatolia, not least because of its airport, the only international one in the region. For a capital city Ankara has a remarkable lack of signs telling you how to get around, but it is nevertheless relatively easy to find your way. It has little charm, and most visitors stay only long enough to visit the museum before setting off into Central Anatolia.

The two most attractive cities of the region are **Amasya** and **Afyon**, by virtue of their settings: Amasya lies on a

Central Anatolia

▶ ▶ ▶ REGION HIGHLIGHTS

Afyon page 208
Alahan page 207
Amaysa page 198
Boğazkale page 199
Divriği page 202
Konya pages 204–205
Museum of Anatolian Civilizations page 193
Sivas pages 210–211

One of the mosaics in the Kariye Camii (Saint Savior in Chora)

riverbank with a cliff face behind, and Afyon lies below a rocky citadel. They both make good bases for an exploration of the surrounding area, and Afyon in particular is a far better choice than the somewhat dull and faceless Eskişehir or Kütahya. There is no obvious base for a visit to the Hittite heartlands around **Boğazkale**, so the best bet is to stay in one of the simple accommodations in Sungurlu.

Distances between major towns in Central Anatolia can be great, and as gas stations are scarce, remember to fill up before you are down to a quarter tank. The dearth of good accommodations also makes it imperative to plan an itinerary.

ITINERARIES The longest you'll want to stay in Central Anatolia is two weeks; you'll probably also have time for Cappadocia, or perhaps the Black Sea coast or the inland lakes of Eğridir and Beyşehir. To reach parts of eastern Turkey from Ankara, you'll need three weeks. (See page 188 for more information on itineraries.)

Hittite relief from Yazılıkaya, near Boğazkale

Central Anatolia

ORIGINS AND ANGORA
Although we tend to think of Ankara as a new city, its origins go back to the 2nd millennium BC, when it was a Hittite settlement called Ankuwash on the royal road from Hattuşaş to Sardis. The prefix *ank* meant gorge or ravine in early Indo-European languages, an obvious reference to the town's setting. In the 11th century Ankara was in the hands of the Seljuks, who brought with them the longhaired angora goats that gave the city its modern name.

One of the traditional buildings of old Ankara

Parts of Ankara remain deceptively like simple rural communities

▶ **Ankara** *188B3*

As the capital of modern Turkey, Ankara has many new roles to play, and it is the conflicts between these roles that make the city so intriguing today. When Atatürk declared it the capital of the new republic in 1923, he was making a calculated move away from the Byzantine and Ottoman associations of Istanbul and its past, and back to the Anatolian heartlands where Turkish civilization originated.

Role dilemma When Atatürk first moved his headquarters to Ankara in 1919, at the beginning of the War of Independence, the town had a mere 30,000 inhabitants. The city's present population is close to the four million mark. The striking contrast between the old town and the new city center contributes to Ankara's strange character and points to its split identity, which is more marked than that in any other city in Turkey. The main boulevard is lined with luxury highrise hotels and impressive new embassies and government buildings, while in the old streets around the citadel and the Ulus Meydanı (the People's Square) you could easily be forgiven for thinking you were back in a simple and traditional Anatolian town. It is a split that symbolizes the curious dilemma of Turkey as a whole: part modern, part traditional.

Sights It is fitting that Ankara's two major sights should reflect both its ancient and modern ties: the **Museum of Anatolian Civilizations**, and Atatürk's mausoleum, known as **Anıtkabir**.

One day should be sufficient to visit Ankara's attractions; even an energetic half-day is enough for you to spend two hours in the museum, take a brief stroll around the citadel (*Hisar*) and visit Anıtkabir, then leave for the Hittite heartlands after lunch.

For most people the Arkeoloji Müzesi **(Museum of Anatolian Civilizations)**▶▶▶ (*Open* Tue–Sun 8:45–5:15. *Admission charge*), with the most spectacular and comprehensive display of Hittite and Urartian finds in the world, is the main reason for visiting Ankara. Set in a renovated 15th-century Ottoman *bedesten* (covered market hall with courtyard), the museum, although small, is beautifully laid out. The most notable exhibits are the 8,000-year-old murals of the Çatalhüyük cave sanctuary; the Alacahüyük royal tomb jewelry and bronze sun disks; the huge Hittite sculptures; the Urartian gold and silver work; and the world's oldest coin, from Sardis, dating from 615 BC.

Medieval and Roman Ankara▶ See pages 194–195 for more information.

Anıtkabir (Atatürk's Mausoleum)▶▶ (*Open* Tue–Sun 9–12:30 and 1:30–5. *Admission free*). The precincts of this extraordinary monument occupy an entire hill over a half-mile square in the center of Ankara.

Four evenings a week during the summer months the site also hosts *son et lumière* dramas, which, by means of narration, sound effects and music, relate the compelling story of Turkey's transformation into a modern state. A visit to the mausoleum cannot fail to impress on you the extent of the personality cult built around the memory of Atatürk, who died over half a century ago.

Parking is available at the summit of the hill, from where a colossal avenue, 300 yards long and flanked by mock Hittite lions, leads to a vast, open courtyard. The monumental limestone mausoleum itself, completed in 1960, stands at the highest point. The marble interior is stark and empty. Armed guards stand everywhere, and an atmosphere of reverence pervades the place.

A fine display in Ankara's spice market

193

FAT IS BEAUTIFUL
The Museum of Anatolian Civilizations in Ankara houses one of the earliest known examples of the Anatolian earth mother figure, grotesquely fat by modern standards, with colossal arms, legs, breasts, and belly. Female corpulence was much admired in Turkey until relatively recently. An Ottoman saying observes: "She is so beautiful she has to go through the door sideways."

Hittite sculptures in the Museum of Anatolian Civilizations

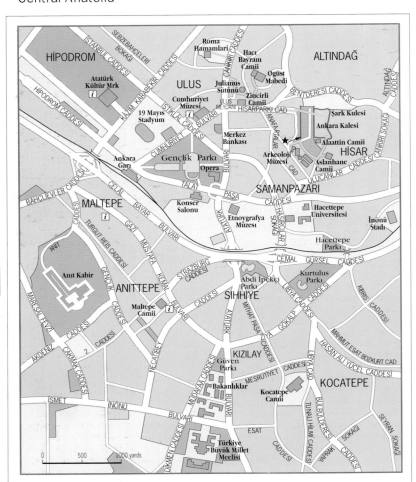

Walk

Ankara

Starting from the Arkeoloji Müzesi (Museum of Anatolian Civilizations), this 2½-mile walk of about two-and-a-half hours takes you through the poor quarters of the medieval citadel, then to the remnants of Roman Ankara. Refer to the Ankara city map above for directions.

From the museum, walk up the hill to the right to find the **Aslanhane Camii**, the only mosque that is really worth visiting in Ankara. Tucked into a little side street in the old bazaar quarter, this 13th-century Seljuk mosque is particularly memorable for its 24 wooden columns supporting a beautifully carved wooden ceiling.

Doubling back to the museum road, continue uphill to reach the **citadel** (see Hisar on the city map) to catch a glimpse of the contrast between Turkey old and new. As you climb through the powerful gateway you will find that you step back into medieval times. Cars can barely navigate here, and children play barefoot in the dusty, narrow streets between the decaying houses.

The citadel walls as they stand today are of mainly Byzantine construction, with much subsequent Turkish addition. Ankara's long, eventful history is reflected in the fabric of the citadel walls and the houses within it, a hodgepodge of reused stones and fragments from different eras.

Head over to the eastern walls and to the ruined tower of **Şark Kulesi**, from which there is a good view over the city and the *gecekondu* (literally "night lodgings"), squatter settlements of rural migrants. These have been responsible for an astonishing surge in population in the last 25 years. A legacy of the Ottoman law decreeing that anyone who could build a house on unused land in a single night had legal ownership, today they are colorful, established neighborhoods with their own schools and utilities.

Leave the citadel by the western side and descend the steps through the terraced gardens below, to enter **Hisarparkı Caddesi**, a lively cobbled street that brings you down into the city once more. Turn up a side street to the right, just before the Zincirli Camii; take the right-hand fork to reach the unmistakable **Temple of Augustus** (Oğüst Mabedi), the most prominent of Ankara's Roman monuments. The mosque beside it is dedicated to Ankara's favorite saint, Hacı Bayram, whose adjacent *türbe*

The remarkable Museum of Anatolian Civilizations, set in a 15th-century bedesten

(tomb) is still a popular place of pilgrimage.

Return now to the fork and go left to the **Column of Julian** (Julianus Sütunu), erected in AD 362 in honor of the Emperor Julian's visit to Ankara. Head along the side street behind the column to the main Atatürk Bulvarı, then follow this north a short way to reach the **Roman Baths** (Roma Hamamları) to the left of the road. The site, discovered by chance in 1926, contains central-heating pipes, marble paving, and fragmentary statues.

Ankara's extensive Roman remains reflect a significant period in the city's long history

While all nations have their great men, the cult of Atatürk in modern Turkey is unique. His monolithic tomb in Ankara (see page 193) is a kind of secular Mecca, signifying the virtually divine status he has achieved—for many, a virtual substitute for religion.

UNDYING RESPECT
Each year on the anniversary of Atatürk's death, at 9:05 AM on November 10, 1938, a minute's silence is observed and all traffic comes to a standstill.

196

Childhood and background Atatürk—born Mustafa Kemal in Salonica in 1881—had a humble background. He inherited his determined and domineering nature from his mother Zubeida, a profoundly religious woman. His father, Ali Reza, was a former customs official who had a small business dealing in wood, and had liberal ideas. In his autobiography their only son recalled the battle that took place between his parents over whether to send him at seven years old to a religious school or a new science establishment. Eventually a compromise was reached: Mustafa spent six months at Islamic school before going on to the more liberal alternative. When Mustafa was just nine Ali Reza died, and the boy had to leave school and go with his mother to live on her brother's farm near Salonica. Here he soon adapted to his new country life, cleaning out stables and looking after the animals. He also gained two qualities that would be essential to his later development: robust health and an abiding love of the peasantry, among whom he would afterward find his most ardent supporters in the fight for independence.

Military matters When he was 12, Mustafa got Zubeida's permission to continue his studies and to pursue a career in the army. He passed his exams at cadet school with distinction and progressed quickly through the ranks. In 1911, at 30 years old, he accompanied an army general to Paris, where he followed the diplomatic maneuverings of the French with great fascination. After the outbreak of war he acquired some practical battle experience in Tripoli against the Italians, and in 1915 he was presented with his great opportunity. As Lieutenant Colonel controlling the zones where the Allies landed *en masse* to take the Dardanelles, he employed strong tactics and paralyzed their offensive. His role in the Dardanelles campaign earned him the admiration even of his enemies.

Atatürk depicted as military hero

Political involvement At military college Atatürk had met many like-minded young men who also regarded with fierce impatience the clumsy machinery of the decaying Ottoman Empire that they were being trained to serve. It was at this time that Atatürk was introduced to the writings of Voltaire, who denounced the mingling of the secular with the religious—the very factor that Atatürk believed was responsible for drawing the allegiance of the uneducated masses to the sultan.

Throughout his military training he had been politically active, even setting up a secret society and being arrested by police spies. His frequent quarrels with Enver Paşa, Commander-in-Chief of the Turkish forces, and his vociferous criticism of his masters in general saw him consigned to several peripheral commands in Libya and Syria. Thus by 37 years old, Kemal proved to be an efficient and energetic military commander but no more, while his military college contemporaries such as Enver Paşa had already risen to much higher positions.

It was not until May 1919, when the Greeks were landing in Izmir (Smyrna) and Kemal was appointed as Inspector-General in the interior, that his position changed. He landed at Samsun to begin this appointment on May 19, 1919—the date generally considered the start of the four-year-long War of Independence. This was the moment when Atatürk turned his back on Istanbul and the decadent Ottoman authorities, and instead sought to build the foundations of the new Turkey in the Anatolian heartlands, making direct appeals to the Anatolian soldiers and peasantry to rise up and defend their nation (see pages 42–43 for what happened next).

An equestrian statue in Ankara: every town has its effigy

ATATÜRK'S WORDS
"There are two Mustafa Kemals. One is that sitting before you, the Mustafa Kemal of flesh and blood, who will pass away. There is another whom I cannot call 'Me.' It is not I whom this Mustafa Kemal personifies, it is you—all you present here, who go into the furthermost parts of the country to inculcate and defend a new ideal, a new mode of thought. I stand for these dreams of yours. My life's work is to make them come true."

THE FACE OF MODERN TURKEY
The face that hangs in every office and house in Turkey tells of the character of the man: determined, capable, and without illusions; energetic; an originator and a force for change, not an administrator; a man who inspires devotion and whose leadership created modern Turkey.

THE PONTIC KINGDOM
Amasya, the capital of the Pontic kingdom, was founded in the 3rd century BC by the adventurer Mithridates. The kingdom survived more than two centuries of turbulence before being crushed by the Romans, under Julius Caesar, in 47 BC. The tombs of the Pontic kings, cut into the rock above the town, are Amasya's most memorable relic today.

Amasya's setting beneath a rocky outcrop on the banks of the Yeşilırmak river is exceptionally picturesque

►► Amasya   *189D3*

Set under a dramatic rock outcrop beside the Yeşilırmak river, Amasya is a pretty town that makes an excellent stopover between the Hittite heartlands of Boğazkale and the Black Sea. To explore the town, walk from the main square to the bridge across the river, admiring the picturesque timbered Ottoman houses overhanging the water: one of them, the **Hazaranlar Konağı** (Museum House), has been converted into an ethnographic museum (closed Mondays). Yellow signs point the way to **Kralkaya** (King's Rock), a steep, 10-minute climb up steps between houses, passing the **Kızlar Sarayı** (Maidens' Palace or Harem; *open* daily 8:30–6. *Admission charge*), all that remains of the Pontic kings' palace. A remarkable tunnel with steps cut into the rock leads the way around to the two largest royal tombs.

In the town, the Islamic buildings worth looking at are the **Seljuk Gök Madrasa** on the main street; the **Fethiye Camii**, originally a 7th-century Byzantine church; and the remarkable lunatic asylum built on the riverbank by the Mongols in 1308, only the elaborate façade of which remains today.

A short way outside the town on the Samsun road, a somewhat rough road leads the way a mile or so up to the **citadel**; the surprisingly large and dramatic ruined castle makes a good picnic spot. Some of the towers date back to Pontic times, but the walls are thought to be of Byzantine or Turkish construction. During the sacred month of Ramadan, an old Russian cannon is fired here at sunset.

►► Boğazkale (Hattuşaş)   *188C3*

If you have come from Ankara to visit these ancient Hittite heartlands, the contrast between city and village lifestyles will strike you forcibly. Here geese meander across the dirt street, and heaps of circular dung cakes lie drying in the sun to be used as fuel.

The huge, fenced-in site of the Hittite capital is open daily except Mondays until dusk, sometimes as late as 7:30 or 8 PM. A car tour of the site takes about one-and-a-half hours; on foot it would take more like three–four hours, as distances are considerable, and they involve steep climbs. The remains consist largely of foundations and low walls, but the scale of the site's conception cannot fail to impress. The earliest surviving example of a walled city, Hattuşaş covered an enormous area: the defense walls were 4 miles long, with nearly 200 towers. At the highest point are the three city gates—the **Lion Gate**, the **Sphinx Gate**, and the **King's Gate**—all set about 500 yards from each other. At the Sphinx Gate you can still walk through the extraordinary 220-foot-long postern tunnel that runs through the hillside, then climb the monumental stairways used in peacetime for access to the city, and in wartime for attacking the enemy.

Continue downhill to the signposted **Büyükkale** (Great Fortress), the palace of the Hittite kings. At the bottom is the **Great Temple of the Weather God**, the largest and best-preserved of the Hittite temples on the site. The admission charge covers Yazılıkaya (see below), too.

ENVIRONS OF BOGAKZALE Alacahöyük►

This small fortified Hittite city about 20 miles northeast of Boğazkale is the source of many of the stupendous finds displayed in the Museum of Anatolian Civilizations in Ankara and in the **site museum** here (*Open* Tue–Sun 8–12 and 1:30–5:30. *Admission charge*). Do not miss the wonderful postern tunnel.

Yazılıkaya►► Just 2 miles beyond Boğazkale lies this 13th-century BC rock-cut sanctuary formed from two natural rock galleries, the only open-air Hittite temple to have survived. The inner walls are carved with reliefs of the gods and goddesses of the Hittite pantheon.

The two stone lions of the Lion Gate have been guarding the Hittite fortress at Hattuşaş for over 3,000 years

DEFENSIVE MENTALITY
The most remarkable feature of Boğazkale is the clever manner in which the natural contours of the land have been incorporated into the city's fortifications. The modern name Boğazkale, meaning "fortress of the narrow mountain pass," reflects this unusual topography.

COMIC ART
The figures on the rock-cut façade at Alacahöyük could have been taken straight from a circus: while one entertainer is doing a sword-swallowing act, an acrobat climbs a freestanding ladder, and another stands ready to catch him. The stumpy little figures are endearingly like comic-strip characters.

Turkish is a fiendishly difficult language in which the average Westerner will recognize nothing. It does not have regional dialects, but there is a difference in pronunciation between the soft tones of Istanbul and the harsher Anatolian diction, which becomes more guttural as you move farther east.

OTTOMAN TO MODERN

Where the modern Turkish civil servant might write: "I have been thinking about your suggestion," his Ottoman predecessor would have been more likely to declare: "Your slave has been engaged in the exercise of cogitation in respect of the proposals vouchsafed by your exalted person."

200

POSTERIOR DOMES

The architectural term *kümbet,* applied to the distinctive conical mausoleums found throughout eastern Turkey, literally means "dome." Not inappropriately, it is also slang for the human posterior.

Calligraphy is a highly valued skill

Nomadic origins Turkish derives from a Turco-Tartar language group called Altaic, a distinction it shares with Mongol, Tunguz, and possibly Korean. The migrations of the Turkish peoples from the central steppelands, and their consequent intermingling with other peoples of different languages over the course of history, have created a linguistic structure of great complexity, which is still the subject of academic research. The original language of the nomadic tribesmen had a wealth of vocabulary for describing livestock and weather conditions, but was obviously inadequate to cope with the complexities of the urban life that the Turks discovered in the countries they conquered. They therefore borrowed the majority of their words for abstract and intellectual concepts from Arabic (amounting to some 40 percent of the language, similar to the proportion of French words in medieval English), and they borrowed from Persian most of their words to do with crafts, trades, and associated matters. With the conversion of the Turks to Islam and their adoption of the Arabic script, their language became increasingly artificial and removed from its linguistic roots. The Arabic alphabet, in which vowels are not written and all words are based on three root consonants, was never suited to the Turkish language, in which vowels and vowel harmony are of critical importance.

Atatürk's reforms When Atatürk came to power in the early 1920s, he set about removing foreign influences from the Turkish language, trying instead to find Turkish substitutes for Arabic and Persian words. The academic body he set up to oversee this process informed him that it would take at least six years to reform the language and adopt the Roman alphabet—he gave them six months. Not surprisingly, this led to many problems of adjustment, not least between the generations, as grand-parents who had grown up with Arabic and Persian words struggled to communicate with their grandchildren, who were taught a whole new vocabulary at school.

A mosque bookstall selling books in both Roman and Arabic scripts

The Turkish press in all its variety

The ultimate negative One of the most infuriating characteristics of Turks, as any traveler to Turkey soon discovers, is their way of saying "no." The famous Turkish negative, *yok*, accompanied by an upward movement of the head with eyes half closed, is the negative to end all negatives, as it also manages to convey an attitude of complete indifference. When the hotel is full, or there is no orange juice, no fish, no fruit, no whatever, this upward nod of the head and weary closing of the eyes conveys: "No, there isn't any (and who cares anyway)." Freya Stark described it as "that eloquent gesture which is the Turkish equivalent of a blank wall."

GOATS IN BRAS
The Anatolian plateau was not always as barren as it is now; centuries of deforestation by goats and man have transformed the landscape. The government tries to encourage people to breed cattle instead of the destructive goat, but old habits die hard. In some rural areas you can even still see goats wearing bras—not an expression of modesty or Islamic fundamentalism, but a practical way of stopping kids from suckling too long.

202

The wild mountain landscape that surrounds the remote Divriği mosque means that few visitors manage to reach this remarkable site

►► Çavdarhisar (Aizanoi)   188A2

Near the village of Çavdarhisar is one of the largest and best-preserved temples in Turkey. Though accessible from Afyon or Kütahya, it is rarely visited because of its remote and difficult position. Built in the Ionian style in the 2nd century AD, the magnificent Temple of Zeus stands virtually intact on this barren plateau. Inside, you are surprised to discover a subterranean sanctuary dedicated to the worship of the Phrygian goddess Cybele, predecessor of Artemis. Notice especially the animal figures and hunting scenes on the stone blocks of the walls, which are thought to have been drawn by Turkish nomadic clans many centuries ago.

►► Divriği   189E2

The famous Divriği mosque and *madrasa* (theological college) complex has been declared by UNESCO to be one of the most important centers of cultural heritage in the world. Its exceptional remoteness—two hours' drive from Sivas, with no real accommodations in the town—means that any visit involves such a detour that it takes on the nature of a pilgrimage. Originally a Byzantine stronghold, Divriği was taken by the Seljuks and beautified with this lovely and unusual building. It was commissioned in 1228 by the local emir, and has lavishly carved portals with floral and geometric motifs and the occasional bird or animal concealed among the garlands and fronds.

ARTISTIC MIX
Craftsmen from Tiflis in Georgia and Ahlat in Armenia are known to have been brought in to work on the extraordinary façades of the Divriği mosque; the huge floral and geometric motifs seem also to owe much to Mogul influences.

ESCAPE FROM ANKARA
To the north of Çankırı and northeast of Ankara lies the attractive Ilgaz National Park, very popu-lar with Ankara residents on weekends. In winter it has a well-equipped ski center and chairlifts.

203

The beautifully carved 13th-century portal of the mosque at Divriği

Near Çavdarhisar is the magnificent Temple of Zeus

► **Eskişehir**   *188A2*

A largely modern town in spite of its name ("Old Town"), Eskişehir has become prosperous due to its position at the fork of the railroad track that arrives here from Haydarpaşa, Istanbul's Asian Station; here the line splits, going east toward Ankara and south toward Kütahya and Konya. The town is famed today for its meerschaum (a white, claylike material), which comes from quarries 15 miles away on the Ankara road. The meerschaum keeps a large part of the population working, and the famous pipes, walking sticks, and other objects can be obtained more cheaply here than anywhere else in Turkey. In the old quarter of town, to the northwest, stands a Seljuk cas-tle. The 16th-century **Kurşunlu Mosque** is attributed to the architect Sinan (see page 65).

► **Kırşehir**   *188C2*

One of Turkey's holy cities, Kırşehir became the center of the influential Ahi Muslim brotherhood in the 14th century. In the town are several Seljuk buildings of inter-est, notably the **Cacabey Mosque** (1272), a former astro-nomical observatory, and the **Ahi Evran Mosque**, beside which stands the *türbe* (tomb) of the founder of the Ahi sect. On the road toward Kayseri, notice the attractive Mongol *türbe* of Asık Paşa, dated 1333.

"Turkish pizzas" are a local specialty

RAMADAN
Konya is Turkey's most religious city, and during Ramadan, the Muslim month of fasting, it is one of the few places in Turkey where you'll have a hard time finding restaurants and cafés open during the day. The restaurants of the top hotels are probably the only places where food and drink are available before nightfall.

MEVLANA THE MYSTIC
Mevlana, the founder of the Whirling Dervishes, was a 13th-century poet and philosopher who believed that an ecstatic state of universal love could be induced by the practice of whirling around and around. This religious rite can be seen in Konya each December, the dervishes dressed in their white robes and tall, conical hats and dancing with abandon to the accompaniment of haunting music played on a reed flute called a *ney*.

▶▶▶ Konya   188B1

The very name of Konya—home to Sufism, a mystical sect of Islam, and to the famous Whirling Dervishes—conjures up for many visitors magic and mystery. The city has a number of exceptionally beautiful Seljuk buildings in varying states of preservation, all dating from the 12th and 13th centuries, the period when Konya was the Seljuks' capital and a veritable haven for Muslim art and culture, attracting a great many learned people.

Apart from these buildings, Konya is not very prepossessing; in fact, many visitors are disappointed. Essentially a city of the steppe, it is a small oasis of relative greenery surrounded on all sides by vast, bleak horizons. In the summer it is hot and dusty, like all cities of the plateau, and in winter it is perishingly cold. The major sights are concentrated within a square half-mile of the city center; as it takes the best part of a day to see them, two nights is generally the minimum time to spend here.

Mevlana Tekke (Mevlana Monastery)▶▶▶ (*Open* daily 9–5. *Admission charge*) The highlight of any visit to Konya, this *tekke* (dervish monastery), with its unforgettable blue-green dome, lies in the heart of the city. It is this building that endows Konya with its special status as a religious city, for Mevlana himself is buried here, and it was here that the dervishes were based for more than six centuries until the Mevlevi Order was dissolved by Atatürk in 1925. In 1927 the *tekke* was opened as a museum, for it is crammed with precious works of art and opulent furnishings, even housing what is said to be a remnant of the Prophet Muhammad's beard.

The entrance leads to a courtyard containing the ablution fountain around which the dervishes used to perform their whirling dance. The heavily decorated tombs of Mevlana (died 1273), his father, his son, and other distinguished dervishes lie in the main building, draped in richly embroidered cloth with the distinctive turban on top. Mevlana's tomb is an exquisitely carved sarcophagus inscribed with verses from his poetry, placed centrally beneath the dome, covered on the inside with stars. The treasures on display were all gifts to the Mevlevi order from wealthy patrons and converts. Next door to the

ESCAPE TO CAVES
Some 5 miles northwest of Konya is the little village of Şille. Set in a valley with an interesting series of hermit caves in the cliffs and some Byzantine church ruins, it is a pleasant place in which to escape the bustle of the city.

Souvenirs on sale in Konya

The unusually ribbed dome of the Mevlana dervish monastery

205

tombs is the **Semahane**, the vaulted hall with fine carpets and chandeliers where the *sema* dance is still performed every December (see pages 24–25).

Alaeddin Camii (Alaeddin Mosque)▶ This 13th-century Seljuk mosque, the largest in Konya, took 70 years to build. It has an irregular ground plan, and the actual sequence of construction is uncertain. Eight sultans are buried here.

Karatay Madrasa▶▶ (*Open Tue–Sun 9–12 and 1–5. Admission charge*) This theological college, built in 1251, is now a museum of Turkish tiles from the Seljuk and Ottoman periods. The most beautiful of the tiles are from the Seljuk palace on Lake Beyşehir (see pages 148–149).

Alaeddin Park▶ Laid out on the former acropolis in the heart of the ancient city, this park has a network of pathways and cafés, making it a delightful place to stroll and linger. On the far side of the park from the Karatay Madrasa you can also visit the **Ince Minare** (Slender Minaret) and **Madrasa**, the **Sırçalı (Glazed) Madrasa**, and the **Sahip Ata** complex of Seljuk mosque, *türbe* (tomb or shrine), and oratory.

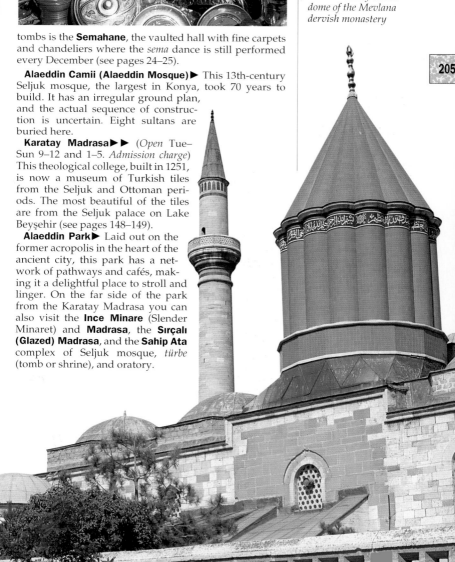

Drive

Konya to Çatalhüyük, Karaman, and Alahan

This fascinating day's drive from Konya gives you a glimpse of Turkey's extraordinary variety, incorporating visits to the oldest known city in the world, a Seljuk oasis, and a unique Byzantine monastery. The round trip is 210 miles and takes a whole day, so bring a picnic lunch.

Leave Konya on the Silifke road to the south to reach the first stop at **Çatalhüyük**, 37 miles away across the bleak Anatolian plateau. After Konya fork left to Çumra, a small town 7½ miles off the main road; turn left in the center of town in front of a modern

The remote and beautiful Byzantine monastery at Alahan

Landscapes in this region combine savage grandeur with colors of luminous clarity

mosque, then right ¼ mile later, then immediately left to cross the railroad track. From here the road is signposted. Discovered in 1961 by James Mellaart, Çatalhüyük is Turkey's most important neolithic and Bronze Age site, and the earliest known city in the world. The sophisticated tools, jewelry, and sculpture found here, and above all the wall paintings decorating the shrines, all dating from 6800 BC, indicate a remarkably advanced civilization in Anatolia at this time. These objects are now in the Ankara Museum of Anatolian Civilizations, but the site is nevertheless impressive for its size. The complex houses, all crammed together without streets to separate them, were entered through holes in the roof via ladders.

The next port of call, again across the Anatolian bleakness, is **Karaman**, a surprisingly green oasis that was the capital of a powerful emirate from 1277 until 1467, when it was incorporated into the Ottoman Empire. There are two monuments in the town center that merit a brief look: the Ak Tekke (1371), formerly a monastery of Mevlevi mystic dervishes, and the Yunus Emre Mosque (1349).

For a long time, the Karaman region was inhabited by Turkish-speaking Orthodox Greeks who even wrote Turkish in Greek script. As a result there are many monasteries here. The most important monastic complex is **Binbir Kilise** ("A Thousand and One Churches"), dating from the 9th to the 11th centuries and the subject of a study in 1905 by Scottish archaeologist Sir William Ramsay and

206

Gertrude Bell, an explorer. The churches are not easy to visit: 5 miles of dirt road leads to the most impressive cluster of churches and monasteries, near the hamlet of **Değler**. The nearest town is **Maden Şehir**.

South of Karaman, the Silifke road leaves the plain and crosses a pass; beyond, a fork leads to **Alahan**, the site of a remote Byzantine monastery complex of great beauty. The scenery here is stunning, and the monastery itself stands on a terrace overlooking the lovely **Göksu Gorge**, with wild mountains all around. It has two churches, and you arrive at the great western one, built at the end of the 5th century. Elaborate reliefs on its doorway depict the four Evangelists and the Archangels Gabriel and Michael trampling a bull and a priest

The wild scenery in and around the Göksu Gorge is typical of the arid mountains of Central Anatolia

of Isis underfoot, representing the triumph of Christianity over paganism. The eastern church, with its elegant, well-preserved façade and its graceful, slender columns, was built some 50 years later. Hollowed out of the cliff behind are the refectory, kitchen, bakery, and guest rooms, as well as an intriguing series of caves that served as the monks' cells.

On the return journey to Konya, you can vary the route by taking a left fork (close to the Çumra/Çatalhüyük fork) towards **Alaca Dağı** (6,830 feet). Here there is superb mountain scenery and pretty **May Baraji dam** and its lake.

Kütahya is famous for its ceramic ware

208

OPIUM IN ABUNDANCE
Afyon is Turkish for "opium," and this region actually does produce 35 percent of the world's legal opiates. In the 1960s, there was illegal drug trafficking, with lax controls on the harvest and who picked it. Now the poppy fields are patrolled, and although locals continue to sprinkle seeds liberally on bread, and the leaves are used in salads, most of the harvest ends up in processed capsules destined for pharmaceutical factories. The other local specialty is *kaymak*, a thick cream made from buffalo milk.

THE GOLDEN TOUCH
Stories of King Midas and the phenomenal wealth of his kingdom of Phrygia abounded in ancient times. Legends of the king's power to turn everything he touched into gold were in fact inspired by a river rich in gold particles that ran through the kingdom.

Afyon boasts some unusually fine Ottoman houses

Kütahya is dominated by its Ottoman citadel and its ceramics factory. The city is now Turkey's leading tile-producing center, having taken over from Iznik (see page 61), its rival since the 16th century. Almost every street has shops selling tiles, china, and porcelain, and even the *otogar* (bus station) is covered in tiles, while the main square has a huge ceramic vase as its centerpiece. You can drive to the citadel for fine views over the town.

ENVIRONS OF KÜTAHYA Afyon► Afyonkarahisar (the name means "Black Castle of Opium") makes the best stopover place in the Kütahya area, being interesting in itself and having reasonably priced accommodations. The town's skyline is dominated by a 700-foot-tall black rock with a ruined citadel on its summit, fortified by the Hittites, Phrygians, Romans, and Byzantines in turn. A flight of 700 steps on the southern rock face leads up to the crenellated remains on top of the rock, at the foot of which sits the old town, a warren of narrow streets with many old Ottoman houses. Some still have the traditional wooden latticework on the overhanging upper stories, which enabled the women to look out while remaining unseen.

The **Ulu Cami**, Afyon's oldest mosque (1272), stands directly opposite the steps up the rock and still retains its original wooden capitals with stalactite carving. Afyon was the second most important Mevlevi center after Konya, and the **Mevlevi Camii**, usually locked except at prayer times, served as the dervish meeting center. The church-like building dates from 1908.

Aslankaya and Aslantaş▶ These two Phrygian monuments (both names mean "Lion Rock") are similar to Midas Şehri (see below) and easily reached from Afyon. Both consist of two lions cut from a rock face and guarding the entrance to a niche containing a statue of Cybele. Aslankaya is the more impressive because of its enormous lions; it is found near Lake Emre in the small town of Döğer.

Midas Şehri (City of Midas)▶ Though it is the most impressive site west of Ankara, this monument is rarely visited because of its remoteness. Although the name implies the remains of a whole town, there is in fact just one monument to be found here, a colossal, gabled, rock-cut building with an ornamented façade.

The first Western travelers to see it thought it was the tomb of the legendary King Midas, who ruled Phrygia during the prosperous 8th century; the mistake is understandable since the façade was inscribed with the word "Midai." It is now known that the monument is a temple to Cybele, the early Anatolian fertility goddess. Her statue once stood in the niche, flanked by attendant lions. Nearby in the hills are additional rock tombs and a monumental rock stairway leading up onto the acropolis.

The old town of Afyon is a picturesque maze of narrow streets lined with old houses

Local traditions and crafts survive in these remote provinces

Central Anatolia is an important carpet-making region, as can be seen from the goods on sale in the bazaar at Sivas

The Gök Madrasa at Tokat, now an ethnographical museum

▶▶ Sivas   189D2

As one of the principal cities of the Seljuk sultanate, Sivas was adorned with an abundance of beautiful Seljuk buildings. The jewel of the city is the **Çifte Minare (Twin Minaret) Madrasa**, built in 1271 and now set among the pretty gardens of the small municipal park. All that remains is the spectacular façade, giving a hint of what it would once have looked like. Close by is the restored **Şifaiye Madrasa**, a combined hospital and medical school and the largest and most elaborate medical institution ever built by the Seljuks. Inside, note the beautiful tiles on

the *türbe* (tomb or shrine) of Keykavuş, some with lions marching in relief, showing Hittite influence.

Another Seljuk masterpiece in the town is the **Gök Madrasa**, also of 1271, built by Sahip Ata, whose work is also prominent in Konya (see pages 204–205) and Kayseri (see page 180). It is considered the most beautiful *madrasa* (theological college) ever built by the Seljuks. Nearby stands the **Ulu Cami** (Great Mosque), the oldest Turkish monument in Sivas, with its leaning minaret and forest of pillars inside. It is still in use.

► **Tokat**   *189D3*

Open (both museums): Tue–Sun 9–12:30 and 1:30–5. Admission charge

In Tokat the major monument is the **Gök (Turquoise) Madrasa**, named after its blue tiles, most of them missing today. Blue is a holy color in Turkey (the English word turquoise derives from "Turkey"). The *madrasa* is now used as a museum to display a hodgepodge of Seljuk, Roman, and ethnographic exhibits. A 19th-century house in the town, the **Latifoğlu Mansion,** has recently been restored as a museum of Ottoman life.

► **Yassıhüyük (Gordion)**   *188B2*

Open: daily 8–5. Admission charge

Lying 60 miles west of Ankara, the site of the ancient capital of Phrygia is difficult to incorporate into an itinerary, and thus remains little visited, despite its importance. The site, which stands on a great mound nearly 500 yards long and 350 yards wide, includes foundations of the Phrygian royal palace, paved with pebble mosaics in geometric patterns of dark red, white, and deep blue—the oldest mosaics ever discovered (8th century BC). Bordering the palace square are buildings called *megarons* (large vestibules opening onto an inner room with a round hearth near the center). These *megarons* are known to have had gabled roofs, a feature first seen in Urartian buildings much farther to the east, which spread from there via Gordion westward to Greece and the rest of Europe.

THE BEE GODDESS
Some 30 miles southwest of Gordion stand the remains of Pessinus, the religious center of Phrygia, with its temple to Cybele, the Anatolian fertility goddess later adopted by the Greeks as Artemis. In Phrygia Cybele was worshipped as a bee, which explains the Turkish name for the site Ballıhisar, meaning "Honey Castle."

The twin minarets of the Çifte Minare Madrasa, the only façade left

211

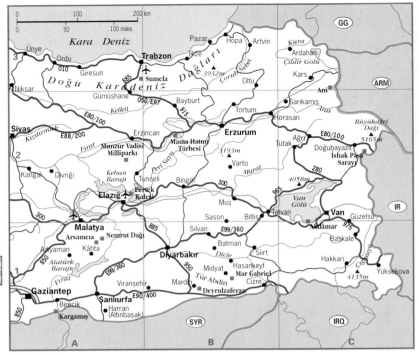

Shepherdesses near Kars

▶▶▶ REGION HIGHLIGHTS

Ani *page 227*
Diyarbakır *page 220*
Georgian valleys
pages 218–219
Hoşap *page 233*
Ishak Paşa Sarayı
page 224
Lake Van
pages 234–235
Mardin *page 221*
Nemrut Dağı *page 230*
Şanlıurfa *page 231*
Tûr Abdin *page 221*

Far right: The pleasure palace of Ishak Paşa Sarayı, set incongruously in the near wilderness at Doğubayazıt

Eastern Turkey

EASTERN TURKEY For most people this region remains unknown, and indeed much of it is currently out of bounds. Until the Kurdish dissident problem, which escalated in 1993, is under full control again, you should exercize caution in the extreme southeast (that is, from Diyarbakır and Tunceli eastward) by keeping to the main roads. The Nemrut Dağı site is reachable, and Lake Van, Malatya, Erzincan, Erzurum, Kars, and all points northward to the Black Sea coast remain relatively safe.

Eastern Turkey

ITINERARIES
One week:
Day 1 Adana
Days 2–3 Adıyaman
   (Nemrut Dağı)
Day 4 Urfa
Day 5 Diyarbakır
Days 6–7 Antakya
Day 8 Adana

Two weeks:
Day 1 Ankara
Day 2 Boğazkale
Day 3 Amasya
Day 4 Ünye
Days 5–6 Trabzon
Day 7 Artvin
Day 8 Erzurum
Day 9 Doğubeyazıt
Days 10–11 Van
Day 12 Diyarbakır
Day 13 Adana
Day 14 Fly to Istanbul

Three weeks:
Day 1 Adana
Day 2 Adıyaman (Nemrut
   Dağı)
Day 3 Urfa
Day 4 Diyarbakır
Day 5 Mardin
Days 6–7 Tatvan
Day 8 Van
Day 9 Hakkari
Day 10 Van
Day 11 Doğubeyazıt
Day 12 Kars
Day 13 Sarıkamış
Day 14 Erzurum
Day 15 Hopa
Days 16–17 Trabzon
Day 18 Samsun
Day 19 Boat to Istanbul

214

EARTHQUAKE ZONE
Earthquakes measuring
five and over on the
Richter scale occur in
this part of the world
every few years. The main
belt runs northeast
between Malatya and
Varto, but Erzincan and
Erzurum are also regular
seismic targets.

*Traditional transporta-
tion near Nemrut Dağı*

LANDSCAPE The east of Turkey is very different geographically from the western and southern coastal regions. There are vast tracts of bleak wilderness, the climate is subject to harsh extremes of heat and cold, and facilities for eating and accommodations are generally meager. Despite all this, the sheer scale and wildness of the country exert their own powerful fascination. Most surreal of all is the vast and eerie **Lake Van**, its thin, piercing blueness encircled by snow-covered peaks.

The **Tigris** and **Euphrates** both have their sources here, and these majestic rivers rolling across the flat mudlands of Mesopotamia are certainly an awe-inspiring sight. South of the new Lake Atatürk, these mudplains are difficult to reconcile with the image of Mesopotamia as described by Robert Byron: "...once so rich, so fertile of art and invention, so hospitable to the Sumerians, the Seleucids and the Sassanids." He goes on: "The prime fact of Mesopotamian history is that in the 13th century Hulagu destroyed the irrigation system; and from that day to this, Mesopotamia has remained a land of mud deprived of mud's only possible advantage, vegetable fertility." The great hope is that the irrigation schemes now possible as a result of Lake Atatürk will, by 2005, restore the area's former fertility and prosperity.

TOWNS AND SITES The high point of any visit to eastern Turkey is Van and its extraordinary lake. The towns of most beauty and note are **Diyarbakır** and **Mardin**. Otherwise, the major sites of eastern Turkey lie in remote spots such as the **Nemrut Dağ** mountaintop sanctuary near Adıyaman, and the **Ishak Paşa Palace** near Doğubeyazıt. Many of the other towns, such as **Kars** and **Erzurum**, give a poor first impression, but improve after you have had

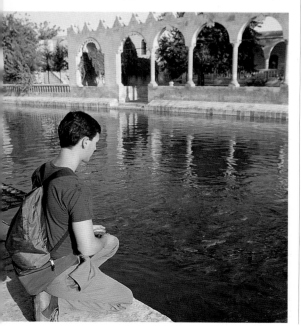

the chance to seek out their more interesting monuments. Because of the great distances involved, many Turks choose to travel by air, and all the main towns are connected by regular THY flights to Ankara and Istanbul. There are rental-car outlets at Adana, Erzurum, Diyarbakır, Malatya, and Van, as well as at Samsun and Trabzon on the Black Sea.

A shoe shine at work in Erzurum

POTHOLES
Owing to the extremes of temperature, maintenance of tarmac roads is very difficult, and potholes are a near-permanent feature of the roads. It is therefore infinitely preferable to travel by bus or rental car than to take your own car.

KURDISH PROBLEMS
Since early 1993 there has been an intensification of activity by the PKK Kurdish guerrillas, but this time hostile to tourists, part of a deliberate attempt to affect tourist revenues. In recent years there have been several violent incidents involving Westerners, even occasional killings. The PKK has declared that anyone entering the area known as "Kurdistan" without authorization risks being kidnapped.

The Pool of Abraham at Şanlıurfa

The valley of the Kinalicam river near Artvin

GEORGIAN MOUNT ATHOS
The eastern valley opposite Artvin once contained such a wealth of monasteries that it became known as the Georgian Mount Athos. Some of these buildings are still relatively well preserved and can be visited on drivable roads. The most commonly visited is the 10th-century church of Dolişhane, now in use as the village mosque of Hamamlıköy.

FREE WOMEN FOR SALE
In the 19th century a tribe was discovered in the remote village of Sason, to the east of Bitlis, whose members were neither Christians nor Muslims, and who spoke a mixture of Arabic, Kurdish, and Armenian. They had no churches or mosques, and the institution of marriage did not exist. Women went free and unveiled, but could be bought and sold.

A farmer in the mountains of the Georgian heartlands around Artvin

▶▶ **Artvin**   *212B3*

As you approach from a dramatic gorge in the Georgian valleys, the first glimpse of Artvin is unforgettable. As the gorge widens out you suddenly look up to see the houses of the town lying in a magnificent setting on the upper slopes of the valley. At its foot, on a jagged cliff with a sheer drop to the river below, there looms an impressive 15th-century castle. Described as the point where "Turkey and the Caucasus meet," Artvin makes an excellent base for exploring these Georgian heartlands.

▶ **Bitlis**   *212B2*

Set on the outer fringes of the former Byzantine Empire, Bitlis is the gateway to another world. As you enter the steep black gorge with its curious houses set up on the cliff sides, you feel you are on the brink of the unknown. Above loom the walls of an impressive citadel, and below rush the waters of the Bitlis Suyu, a tributary of the Tigris. On the main street of Bitlis is the fine **Şerefiye Camii** with a pointed *türbe* (tomb or shrine) attached, built in 1528 by a local Kurdish emir. Farther up the main street is the 12th-century Ulu Camii, with its detached minaret. The population today is largely Kurdish, but up to the 1920s about half the inhabitants were Armenian. Bitlis is famous for its light-colored honey and its Virginia-type tobacco.

Nemrut Dağı Volcano

A most unusual outing that ventures up a volcano and then descends into the crater, this exhilarating trip combines superb scenery, with tremendous views over Lake Van and its ring of mountains. The total distance from Tatvan is only 12 miles, but because nine of these are on a poor, unpaved road, a full hour should be allowed each way for the trip. July and August are the best times for the ascent, as there is a high chance of snow making the track impassable at other times of the year.

Set out from Tatvan on the Bitlis road. At the edge of town is the small harbor with the large ships that ferry train passengers across the lake to Van, where the railroad track resumes. Just by the harbor a road marked by a yellow sign labeled "Nemrut" heads off to the right around the lake's northern shore.

After 2½ miles on this road you come to a second yellow sign, this time pointing to the left up a dirt road. This is the road that slowly bumps its way right up to the crater rim, at 9,455 feet. *Yürük* (nomad) shepherds and small children can be a bit unfriendly, and stone-throwing is a common pastime, but just ignore it and drive on.

From the rim the view is stupendous, over the bleak cone itself and down into the lush vegetation within. The track continues for 2 miles right down inside the crater: it last erupted in 1441, so it is relatively safe to consider it dormant now. With a 4¼-mile diameter, it is one of the largest complete craters in the world. The western half holds—some 2,200 feet below the rim—a huge lake beside which are hot springs in which you can take a dip. The whole area is uninhabited but for occasional nomad camps. There is talk of Nemrut Dağı becoming the center of a national park. (Do not confuse this spot with the Nemrut Dağı described on pages 230–231!)

Nemrut Dağı looms large above Lake Van, itself at an altitude of roughly 5,500 feet

217

Set in Turkey's extreme northeastern corner, between Erzurum and Artvin, is this pocket of stunning mountains and valleys, still inhabited by the descendants of the Georgians.

THE RED-HEADED LEAGUE
Racially quite distinct from the inhabitants of surrounding towns such as Erzurum and Kars, many Georgians still have red hair and freckles. They are different in manner, too, being somewhat more formal. In these valleys you are treated as a guest who has taken considerable trouble to visit the remoter parts of the country.

218

Origins of the Georgians The Georgians have had little influence on the history of Turkey. They speak a non-Indo-European language that belongs, like Laz (the language spoken on the Black Sea), to the Caucasian group, and they have always had close links with the Byzantine Greeks. Byzantine emperors endowed churches here, even sending architects, masons, and craftsmen to build and decorate them. The Georgians provided little architectural inspiration of their own, though they may well have been the channel through which the Byzantine influence passed into Russia. The churches all have the Armenian drum and conical dome, and the stone carvings on the external walls, with

ARMENIAN LINKS
Although ethnically distinct, the Armenians and Georgians shared a similar history of invasions and counterinvasions, and through frequent intermarriage they also became somewhat mixed. Thus the Bagratid family were rulers of both Armenian and Georgian territories; their rule was punctuated by squabbles and rivalries, generally resolved by matchmaking.

Monasteries of the Georgian valleys

animals and rich garlands, are reminiscent of Armenian styles. There are some 50,000 Georgians in Turkey, and the Georgian language is still spoken in the remoter valleys and mountains of the extreme northeast.

From Queen Tamara to the Ottomans In the 12th century Georgia entered a period of relative peace, which reached a high point under the leadership of Queen Tamara, a gentle and humane leader as well as a shrewd administrator and diplomat. By the time of her death in 1212 she had extended her kingdom, with its capital at Tiflis, to include Armenians, Kipchaks, Kurds, and Azerbaijanis, Muslims and Christians alike. In the 13th and 14th centuries Georgia suffered heavily from Mongol attacks under Ghenghis Khan and Tamerlane, whose armies left its towns and villages in ruins. Thus weakened, Georgia was unable to withstand the increasing power of the Ottomans, and in 1552 a detachment of Janissaries was stationed in the ancient Bagratid fortress of Ardanuç. By the 17th century most Georgians had converted to Islam, though actually the Ottoman Empire exercized only a loose control over it, content to let its princes and barons squabble among themselves in their endless family feuding.

Georgian churches The best of the Georgian churches, relics of the Christianity that died out under the Ottomans, are to be found between **Tortum** and **Artvin**. Some are still in use as village mosques and are well maintained, while others are severely dilapidated. Some 15 miles north of Tortum, a sign points over a bridge to **Bağbası**, the Turkish name of the village in which the 10th-century church of **Haho** lies. This interesting church, with its conical dome in the local soft yellow sandstone, was originally part of a monastic complex, and has now been carefully restored by the villagers and converted to a mosque. The walls bear highly comic reliefs of biblical scenes, such as Jonah and the Whale. Look for the strange mythical beasts that appear in some of the scenes.

Nine miles farther north along the main road, a road forks off left to reach the colossal monastery church of **Vank**, a derelict shell standing in the heart of the village. Inside there still remain some 11th-century frescoes showing the faces of angels and Mary and Jesus, and on the gable outside are reliefs of the archangels Michael and Gabriel. Like Haho, Vank was originally part of a 10th-century monastery. Some 22 miles north of the Vank turn-off is a fork right to Olur, after which a dirt road winds up to the 11th-century bishop's church of **Işhan**. Set in the middle of the village beside some small ponds, the church sits on a terrace overlooking the mountains. The windows are richly decorated with stone carvings, and inside there are still some murals of flying angels.

219

The conical dome of the 10th-century church of Haho, now restored and converted by the villagers to become their mosque

Eastern Turkey

KURDISH MAJORITY

With its predominantly Kurdish population, Diyarbakır is a natural center of Kurdish dissident groups. After the 1980 coup, thousands of dissidents were locked up in its prison, the most notorious in Turkey. More recently, some young dissidents have been turning to Sufism (mystic Islam) as a channel for their energies, much to the relief of the authorities. In the words of one Kurdish student: "Who needs the Kurdish Workers' Party when you've got God?"

MAGNIFICENT WALLS

The magnificent black basalt city walls of Diyarbakır have a rampart walk, of which the best stretch is from the Urfa Gate to the Mardin Gate, where a wide, grassy path allows two or three people to walk abreast. Sunset is the best time, with unforgettable views toward the Tigris Valley.

Diyarbakır viewed from the town walls with one of the city's rare green spaces

▶▶ Diyarbakır   212B1

Positioned at the highest navigable point on the Tigris and backed by the eastern Taurus mountains, Diyarbakır dominates the expanse of the northern Mesopotamian plain. Inside its walls, the city exudes the confidence that comes from having been a key city with its own special identity for centuries, and it hums with vitality. It is divided into distinct quarters—Armenian, Christian, Kurdish, and Arab—each with its own churches or mosques and community buildings, and behind the large carved wooden doors on the narrow winding streets there are hidden courtyards. Diyarbakır has more historic mosques, churches, and other notable buildings than any other Turkish city except Istanbul.

Visiting the various quarters takes several hours of dusty and strenuous walking. Aside from the 3-mile-long walls, the monuments to seek out are the **Nebi Camii** (the Mosque of the Prophet), near the Harput Gate, with its striped minaret, built in 1524 by the White Sheep clan; the **Saray Kapı** (Palace Gate), the most beautiful of the gates and the entrance to the citadel; and the dour black basalt **Süleymaniye citadel mosque**, built by the Artukids in 1160. Do not miss, either, the **Ulu Cami** (the Great Mosque), modeled on the great Umayyad Mosque at Damascus and built by Malik Shah in 1091–1092, making it the very first of the great Seljuk mosques of Anatolia. Other major monuments are the elegant **Safa Mosque**, Persian in feel with its graceful white minaret; the **Syrian Orthodox Church**, set in its own lovely courtyard and still used by the 25 or so Syrian Orthodox families here; and the Armenian **Surp Giragos Kilesesi**, the only other Christian church still in use in the city.

ENVIRONS OF DIYARBAKIR Hasankeyf▶ Originally founded by the Romans as a frontier outpost, this ruined capital city of the 12th-century Artukid (Kurdish) dynasty stands on a spectacular cliff overlooking the Tigris. The bridge, whose crumbling supports can still be seen in the river, was another skillful Artukid construction, described by early travelers as the grandest in all Anatolia. The cliff-top city, covering an area of about 1 square mile,

is reached via a narrow gully behind the modern town of Hasankeyf, which will be flooded by 2005.

Mardin►► This important Syrian Christian center, 60 miles southeast of Diyarbakır, covers a craggy hillside with the striking Syrian-influenced architecture that inspired the English historian Arnold Toynbee to call it "the most beautiful town in the world." It faces south over the Syrian desert. Many of the decorated Arab-style buildings are now decaying, but enough remains to hint at their past splendor. The town's masterpiece is the **Sultan Isa Madrasa**, a 14th-century Artukid (Kurdish) monument, recognizable by its two white ribbed domes. A rough path leads up from it to the ruined citadel on the hill summit, inside which are the ruins of a vast palace and mosque dating from the 15th century.

Tûr Abdin►► Literally "The Servants' Plateau," this highland region (between Mardin and Cizre, with Midyat at the center) is the Mount Athos of the Syrian Orthodox Church. During the Middle Ages there were four bishoprics and 80 monasteries here, and the population grew prosperous through trade and farming. Tragically, of the 200,000 Syrian Christians who remained just 80 years ago, there are now only 2,000, caught up in the crossfire of the PKK Kurdish rebels and the Turkish government forces. The metropolitan (bishop) at Mar Gabriel is waging a one-man battle to try to keep his people together: one of the incentives he offers is free education for 40 boys a year. Only four of the monasteries are still functioning, served by a handful of monks. The two to visit today are **Deyrulzaferan** near Mardin, and **Mar Gabriel**.

BLACK AND WHITE
In contrast to the black Diyarbakır, Mardin is sometimes called the White City, because of the distinctive pale limestone used in its buildings. Some of the mosques in Diyarbakır also feature a black- and- white striped effect created by alternating layers of basalt and limestone. One theory maintains that the stripes also represent the black and white sheep of the two Turcoman tribes, the Akkoyunlu (White Sheep) and the Karakoyunlu (Black Sheep), both of which set up important states in this part of Turkey.

221

The minarets (below and left) both exhibit the black and white stripes typical of Diyarbakır mosques (see panel above)

Ancient and traditional enemies of the Armenians, the Kurds are a distinct racial group indigenous to the region known as Kurdistan, which today straddles the modern borders of Turkey, Iran, Iraq, Georgia, Armenia, and Syria.

222

DEVIL IN A CABBAGE

Some 50,000 Kurds are still said to be Yazidis, or peacock-god worshippers, often referred to in the West as devil-worshippers. They worship the sun, and water is also sacred to them. Their Manichaean creed views the universe as a struggle between light and dark, good and evil, but they never refer to Satan by name. They abhor the color blue and never eat cabbage, believing that the devil inhabits the leaves.

Minority status There are 25 million Kurds spread across six countries, making them the world's largest stateless people. By far the greatest number—between 8 and 10 million—are in Turkey. Traditionally, the Kurds have been a nomadic mountain people, and in Turkey today they are known officially as "mountain Turks," the existence of a separate Kurdish race being studiously ignored by the authorities. Had the 1920 Treaty of Sèvres been implemented, Kurdistan would have become an autonomous state, but the Turks, rallied by Atatürk, rejected the treaty. Ironically, the Kurds joined Atatürk in warding off the Greek Christians and Persians. When Atatürk declared the Turkish Republic and abandoned the sultanate for a secular state, they felt betrayed. In the Kurdish revolts that followed, in the 1920s and 1930s, hundreds of thousands of Kurds were killed or deported by the Turks. It should be emphasized that not all Kurds today are nomads or guerillas. The majority are integrated throughout the country and many own businesses and participate in government, despite some discrimination.

Language problems The Kurdish language—Indo-European in origin, like Persian, Armenian, and most western European languages—has several dialects, all of which are mutually unintelligible, a fact that has not helped the Kurds in their attempts to unite: there are no fewer than seven rival Kurdish national movements. Within Turkey, the language used to be banned; Kurdish children must still go to Turkish schools and speak Turkish there, reverting to Kurdish when they are at home with their families.

A Kurdish mother and child traveling with carpets and bedding

Current aspirations After the Gulf War of 1991 the "safe haven" dubbed Kurdistan was set up in Iraq's northwestern corner to protect some three million Kurds from Saddam Hussein's forces. Amid high hopes of achieving an autonomous unified Kurdistan, the two main parties, the KDP (Kurdish Democratic Party) led by Barzani, and the PUK (Patriotic Union of Kurdistan) led by Talabani formed a 50:50 coalition government. Tragically, the personality clash between the straightforward Barzani and the mercurial Talabani and the increasing rivalry of the two ruling parties erupted in open fighting in May 1994 and there have been

THE KURDISH CHARACTER

Although historically the Kurds have practiced a policy of evasion in the face of invading armies, they have been ready to fight in other people's wars away from their home ground. The great Saladin, hero of the Crusades, was a Kurd, and the Kurds are naturally proud to have produced one of the greatest heroes of Islam. Ethnically distinct, the men have long, bony faces with aquiline noses, and the women are forthright and unveiled. Traditional ceremonies, such as weddings and Now Rouz (Kurdish New Year), continue to be practiced, to the accompaniment of Kurdish music, despite attempts to discourage them.

A Kurdish family in the doorway of their beehive hut

clashes ever since. The quarrels have been over customs revenue on the Turkish border, the use of government funds, and the extensive rival patronage networks. The whole setup is complicated by further alliances in which the PKK (the Turkish Kurds) are fighting against Barzani's KDP with Syrian help. Turkey has retaliated by supporting Barzani, and Talabani's PUK is receiving help from Iran. Kurdish leaders are deeply embarassed by the fighting, which has understandably led to a perception that the Kurds are incapable of self-rule.

Since 1984 more than 30,000 have been killed in the fighting between the PKK rebels and the Turkish government security forces. Tourists have occasionally been targeted with the intent to damage tourism revenue. In early 1999 Turkey succeeded in capturing PKK leader Abdullah Ocalan, dealing a major blow to PKK aspirations.

KURDISH ARCHITECTURAL GEM

Standing isolated in the midst of ploughed fields near Hasankeyf is one of the best-preserved and loveliest of all Kurdish monuments, the *türbe* (tomb) of the Ayyubid king Zeyn El-Abdin, descendant of Saladin. Built of red brick with an onion dome, it is covered on the outside with exquisite turquoise glazed tiles.

Kurds remain close to their nomadic roots and so tend to furnish their houses sparsely, but no Kurdish home is without its carpet

HODGEPODGE DESIGN

The architecture of the Ishak Paşa Palace is mixed, with elements of the Seljuk, Persian, Georgian, Armenian, and baroque Ottoman styles. It is said to have been built by a Kurdish chieftain, who asked the Armenian architect to design him the most beautiful residence in the world, then cut off his hands when it was finished to ensure that no rival chieftain could build a similar one. The Kurdish pasha met his just desserts, dying from a snakebite.

224

Ishak Paşa's indulgent palace—intended as the most beautiful dwelling in the world—sits above a dusty plain close to the Iranian border

▶ Doğubayazıt
212C2

A drab frontier town, Doğubayazıt is of interest only as a base for the ascent of Mount Ararat (see pages 228–229), or (more commonly) for a visit to the ultimate "Turkish château," the pleasure palace *extraordinaire* of Ishak Paşa, which is located 4 miles away.

Ishak Paşa Sarayı▶▶ (*Open* daily 8–4. *Admission charge*) The ticket office is tucked just inside the palace's vast courtyard. Built in about 1800 by Ishak Paşa—the feudal overlord of this area that was nominally under Ottoman control—this remarkable palace dominated the lucrative silk caravan routes from its vantage point on the hillside.

The palace has a sybaritic air, and it was certainly conceived more as a pleasure dome than as a defensive castle. The largest section is given over to the harem, with its mazelike series of rooms, large blackened kitchen and dining area, bathrooms, and 14 long, thin harem bedrooms. The superb colonnaded feast room originally had mirrors in the blind arches, so that the harem women could partake of the feast without being seen by the pasha's guests. The *selamlik* (reception) and mosque areas are also very fine, though a little more modest. In the late 19th century, during preparations for the war against Russia, the palace was used as a barracks: the stained-glass windows, bought at great expense, all disappeared, to be replaced by sheets of newspaper; the marble pillars and alabaster carvings were chipped and hacked; and around 400 soldiers slept in the bedrooms intended for the pasha's concubines.

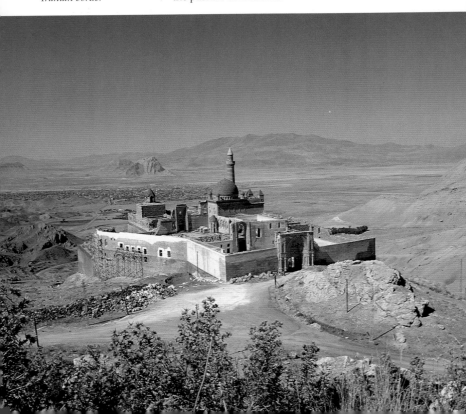

225

One of the pleasures of a stop in Elazığ is sampling the excellent local Buzbağ wine

► Elazığ   212A2

A modern, unremarkable town possessed of a good hotel, Elazığ makes a comfortable place to stay on the way to points farther east. Some 3 miles north, on a hill overlooking the lake, stands the old fortress city of **Harput**, now almost derelict. Just 100 years ago Harput had 800 shops, 10 mosques, 10 religious schools, 8 churches, 8 libraries, 12 *hans* (inns), and 90 baths, but its population moved down to Elazığ when the new town was built, prompted partly by earthquakes in the region. By following the yellow signs to the *kale* (castle) you pass the 12th-century Ulu Cami, with its severely leaning minaret, before reaching the castle itself, set on its rocky outcrop. It is also worth looking at the 14th-century castle of Eski Pertek, once the proud guardian of the Euphrates Valley, now an indignant rocky island cut off in the middle of the lake and accessible only by boat.

A decorative detail from the Ishak Paşa Sarayı

► Erzincan   212A2

Erzincan was rebuilt after the terrible earthquake of 1939; its very name means "life-crusher." The destruction wrought here was especially sad, as 19th-century Erzincan was considered to be one of the most beautiful cities in Asia, with over 79 mosques. Twelve miles east of Erzincan is the important Urartian site of **Altıntepe** (Golden Hill), where Turkish archeologists have discovered a wealth of jewelry, bronze, and pottery in tombs built into the hillside.

BLEAK ENOUGH FOR WOLVES

Set in a great bowl at an altitude of nearly 6,000 feet, Erzurum is Turkey's highest provincial capital, ringed by broad, eroded mountains. The landscape is harsh, and the dull gray stone of the buildings is in perfect harmony with it. In 1958, Erzurum was chosen (in preference to Van) as the site for eastern Turkey's main university. Unless they are dedicated archaeologists or agriculturalists (the two strongest faculties at the university), teachers from Ankara and Istanbul are unwilling to face Erzurum's severe climate and limited entertainment. In winter wolves have been spotted roaming the campus.

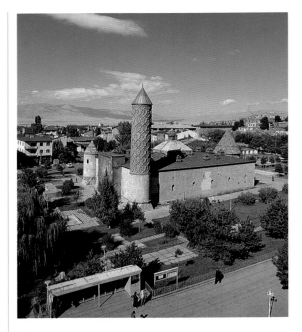

The Yakutiye Madrasa in Erzurum, built in 1310 by the Mongol rulers of Persia

A shoe shine in Erzurum: seasoned travelers rate Turkish shoe shines as the best in the world

► Erzurum 212B2

Erzurum, remotely set high on its plateau, can be mercilessly cold in winter. But with its shop-lined streets that are lit up at night, Erzurum can still seem like a haven of urbanity and modernity in comparison with the other cities of eastern Turkey. The local specialty is *oltutaş*, or black jet, made into necklaces, worry-beads, ornaments, and just about everything else. Aside from the walls of the citadel there is nothing left in Erzurum from before the Seljuk conquest in the 11th century. Severe earthquakes and years of wars have taken their toll, but there are still some fine buildings to see near the center of town, notably the **Yakutiye Madrasa** and the **Çifte Minare** (Twin-Minaretted) **Madrasa**.

The Yakutiye, built in 1310 by the Mongol rulers of Persia, is the most attractive building in Erzurum, with pretty turquoise tiling on the minaret and traces of green and yellow in the portal. Flanked by two lions and an eagle, this portal shows a markedly Persian influence, displaying a more feminine quality than that found in Arab or Turkish architecture.

The Çifte Minare Madrasa (*Open* daily 8:30–6. *Admission charge*) is Erzurum's most famous building, built in 1253 by Sultan Alaeddin Keykubad II, grandson of the builder of the great fortress at Alanya (see page 142). Used for years as a military store, it has now been restored, though its two fluted brick minarets have far fewer turquoise tiles than that of the Yakutiye Madrasa. Behind the *madrasa* are three conical stone Seljuk *kümbets* or tombs. Take a stroll into the old citadel area (*Open* daily 8–12 and 1:30–7:30. *Admission charge*), enclosed by crumbling walls and still with a few rusting cannons lying around. It has an unusual clock tower, originally an 11th-century Seljuk minaret.

► Kars   212C3

In wet weather—and it is frequently wet here—Kars is about the most dismal spot in eastern Turkey. *Kar* means "snow," and Kars can get up to 40 feet of it. Today the town has little to offer besides its Russian buildings from the turn of the century and its Armenian **Church of the Apostles**, set in a clearing near the river and Ottoman bridge. Built in 932 in coarse black basalt by the Armenian Bagratids, the church is not overly pretty. The carvings of the 12 Apostles on the outside of the dome are so crude as to be faintly grotesque.

ENVIRONS OF KARS Ani►► (*Open* daily 8:30–5. *Admission charge*) The real reason anyone comes to Kars is to visit Ani, the ruined Armenian city of a hundred gates and a thousand churches. Because of its proximity to the Armenian border, a permit is required, a formality that takes half an hour at the Kars tourist office. The military escort that used to accompany visitors has now been abandoned, and you are free to wander around the ruins of this extraordinary city at your leisure. No city in Europe in the mid-10th century could rival the size and magnificence of Ani, and in the East only Constantinople, Baghdad, and Cairo could match it. In the superb architecture you can see the inspiration for much that we now know as the Seljuk style, including the powerfully built walls and graceful *türbe* (tomb or shrine) shapes that were to become the standard form for mausoleums for centuries. The Armenians were celebrated stonemasons, and the quality of the workmanship that is on view here testifies to their technical virtuosity, the best in the world at that time. The Mongol raids, a severe earthquake in 1319, and the advent of Tamerlane—the *coup de grâce*—destroyed forever this city whose population at its height was said to number 200,000, four times the current population of Kars.

SWASTIKA ORIGINS
The swastika motif has been used for thousands of years—as a symbol of the sun, infinity, and continuing fertility—in Sumeria, China, India, Egypt, Scandinavia, Greece, and the Americas. It is found in Rome's catacombs, on Inca textiles, and on relics unearthed at Troy. It is also one of the sacred signs of Buddhism. The word comes from the Sanskrit *svastika*, which means prosperity; the sign was thought to bring good luck.

MUD? WHO CARES?
A 19th-century traveler in Kars asked an aged Turk who had just waded across the muddy street to visit his friend's house, "Why do you not clean the street?" Looking surprised, the old man answered: "The mud will dry up in the summer. Why worry about it now?"

227

The spectacular Girvelik Selalesi falls near Erzincan (see page 225)

Eastern Turkey offers a tremendous range of climbing for the mountaineer, from the near-tropical landscapes of the Pontic mountains along the Black Sea to icy peaks permanently covered in snow, such as Mount Ararat and the Hakkâri range in the extreme southeast.

NOAH'S ARK
According to Armenian tradition, Mount Ararat is the center of the universe, and the Armenians themselves came down from its slopes. It is also cited in Genesis as the final resting place of Noah's Ark after the Flood. In recent years the search for the Ark has gained momentum, with the convinced and ever-hopeful climbing the mountain from Doğubayazıt. Some claim to have found pieces of the biblical vessel.

Behind the nomad encampment rises the snowy peak of Mount Ararat, dominating the Anatolian plateau for a radius of over 30 miles

Volcanoes The flat countryside of the Anatolian plateau is naturally dominated by many major mountain peaks, especially volcanoes such as **Nemrut Dağı** (see page 217: not to be confused with the other Nemrut Dağı described on pages 230–231), **Erciyes Dağı** (near Kayseri, see page 184), and above all **Ararat** (**Büyükağri Dağı**). At 16,000 feet, this is Turkey's highest mountain, dominating the landscape for well over 30 miles in every direction. In summer the snow line retreats up the mountain to cover the top third, while in winter it comes down to the base, itself at 5,600 feet above sea level. From afar, Ararat looks deceptively easy to climb, but in practice the jagged lava fields are very tricky; climbers regularly lose their lives in attempting the ascent, often because of the changeable weather, the mountain's specialty. It was first climbed in 1829 by a Professor Parrot; nowadays, when safe, weekly expeditions are organized by a few agencies from Doğubayazıt, usually taking three days to go up and two down. Attacks by PKK terrorists can mean that the route is closed; when open, the requisite permit must be applied for at least three months in advance, or longer for Ark-hunters' expeditions (see page 265). The Turks have long been convinced that the CIA has a listening post on the summit of Ararat, and that the Ark-hunting groups are really CIA agents up to no good.

The Hakkâri and Munzur mountain ranges near Tunceli are out of bounds for the forseeable future because of Kurdish guerrilla activity. All climbing in these areas is banned at present.

BOILING BATH
In the simple hotels at Ayder, hot springs take the place of baths. Men and women have set bathing times, and the scalding-hot water reaches 140°F.

UNIQUE FREEDOM
The beauty of climbing in these remote mountains is well summed up by the English climber Sidney Nowill, who described it as the sensation of living "for a time completely free of every worldly link, self-reliant and untrammeled by any human agency or service, something which is healthful and cleansing to achieve, if only once in a lifetime."

229

The Kaçkar mountain range is becoming increasingly popular with climbers

Women from a remote Anatolian village near Mount Ararat

The Arabs traditionally believed that Ararat was the roof of the world and the source of the two great rivers, the Tigris and the Euphrates. The Kurds, too, regard Ararat as their mountain; one of the main Kurdish rebellions in Atatürk's day actually made its headquarters on the peak.

Ala Dağları Since the loss to climbers of the Hakkâri area, the Ala Dağ range, southeast of Niğde, offers the best substitute, with the great advantage of easy access. The base point is **Çamardı**, a small town reachable on a paved road, from where guides and mules can be arranged. No permits are required.

Kaçkar Dağları This range, which lies inland from the eastern end of the Black Sea between Trabzon (see page 246–247) and Hopa (see page 241), is becoming increasingly popular because of its accessibility and the fact that it lies outside Kurdish territory. The favorite starting point is **Ayder**, reached along the attractive valleys of **Hemsin** and **Çamlihemşin**. Ayder has about half a dozen simple hotels to accommodate trekkers, one of which boldly calls itself the Hilton. From this base you can attempt anything from a one-day, eight-hour trek to 9,000 feet, to a week's full-scale climbing. Mountain guides are available, and permits are not necessary.

Eastern Turkey

Antiochus, deluded creator of this grandiose folly, saw himself as a god among equals

LESS AND LESS REMOTE
In the 1960s, the only way to the summit of Nemrut Daği was by donkey and on foot, taking at least two days. Now the whole way has a paved surface, and the ascent takes less than two hours. Snow makes the road impassable between the beginning of October and the beginning of May, and the site is sometimes closed due to PKK guerilla activities.

BIRD SANCTUARY
Birecik, near Urfa, is one of the world's two remaining nesting places for the bald ibis, now nearly extinct. It leaves Birecik in July to fly to its winter home in Morocco. Its return in mid-February, regarded as heralding the coming of spring, is celebrated each year by the villagers in a remarkable festival.

▶▶▶ **Nemrut Daği** *212A1*

Along with Cappadocia and the Sumela Monastery (see page 245), Nemrut Daği, with its colossal stone heads on the mountaintop, is one of the best-known and most visited sites east of Ankara.

Historically Nemrut Daği is of no significance, being no more than a vast funeral monument to King Antiochus, ruler of a small local dynasty who suffered delusions of grandeur. The kingdom, called Commagene, was established in the 1st century BC by Antiochus' father, Mithridates, and remained independent until AD 72, when the Roman Emperor Vespasian incorporated it into the Roman province of Syria.

On the drive up from Kahta, the nearest town (there are minibuses if you do not have your own transportation), you pass a fine Roman bridge. Higher up, near Eski Kahta, a fork in the track leads up to **Arsameia** (*Admission charge*), the Commagene capital, with a superb relief of Mithridates shaking hands with Hercules, a cave cistern, and the scattered column bases of ancient Arsameia on the hilltop. It also makes an excellent picnic spot away from the crowds

Continuing up to the summit of Nemrut Daği (which at 6,665 feet is very impressive), the road ends near a building where souvenirs and simple refreshments are sold. It is always chilly at the summit because of the altitude, and it is best to arrive there after the morning mists have cleared. Walk 10 minutes up the path, past the tumulus that is the burial place of King Antiochus, to the eastern terrace behind the tumulus. The deluded Antiochus claimed descent on his father's side from Darius the Great of Persia, and on his mother's from Alexander the Great, and the statues on this and the western terrace reflect this

Persian and Macedonian ancestry. Antiochus himself (the one with the beard and mustache) makes his appearance among the great kings and gods as their equal. The statues reflect the Oriental and Hittite practice of enthroning images of gods on mountaintops. On the western terrace, where the five deities sit facing the sunset as opposed to the dawn, do not miss the dramatic lion relief. This is, in fact, a complex astronomical chart showing the conjunction of the planets Mars, Jupiter, and Mercury, complete with stars and a crescent moon.

ENVIRONS OF NEMRUT DAGI Harran▶ Close to the Syrian border below Nemrut Daği, Harran, like Urfa, is visited for its biblical associations (it is said that Abraham lived here) and also for its beehive houses, a form of architecture that has not changed since biblical times. Their extraordinary shape is dictated by the only material at hand in abundance—the mud of Mesopotamia. Nearby is the vast and ruinous **Ulu Cami**, founded in the 8th century as part of the earliest university complex.

Malatya▶ A 19th-century new town, like Elazığ, Malatya is a local center of commerce with a fast-growing population. With its hotels and sophisticated shopping, it makes a good base. Nearby are the ruins of **Eski Malatya**, a Roman/Byzantine walled town, and the scant remains of **Aslantepe** (Lion Hill), the capital of a neo-Hittite kingdom (ca1000–700 BC).

Şanlıurfa (Urfa)▶ *Şanlı*, meaning "glorious," commemorates the fight Urfa put up against the invading French armies in 1920, but it is a town of no great beauty aside from two monuments: the 12th-century Seljuk **Ulu Cami**, modeled on the great mosque at Aleppo; and the **Pool of Abraham**, full of sacred carp. According to legend, the pool was created by God to extinguish the funeral pyre on which the angry Assyrian king Nimrod was preparing to burn Abraham.

Carried away by his delusions of grandeur, Antiochus followed the Oriental and Hittite practice of enthroning images of gods on mountaintops

231

The Pool of Abraham at Şanlıurfa

MILITARY ESCORT
On the Syrian border, south of Adıyaman, is the famous site of Carchemish, capital of the most powerful of the neo-Hittite kingdoms, which prospered after the collapse of the Hittite Empire at Hattuşaş (ca1200 BC). Because of its closeness to the border a permit is needed, and a soldier escorts all visitors. Such luminaries as T.E. Lawrence, D.G. Hogarth, and Gertrude Bell dug here, and some of the first clues to the identity of the Hittites were found on the site. Little remains today.

SPLENDID LAKE WATERS
Van, Turkey's largest lake (six times as big as Great Salt Lake), changes constantly with the seasons and the weather. There is almost no pollution, and the water's high alkalinity is so cleansing that fishermen simply trail their dirty clothes behind their boats to get a whiter-than-white wash. Locals also insist that the lake water clears dandruff.

A sheep market in north-eastern Turkey

VAN CATS
The curious cats of Lake Van—fluffy white creatures with one blue eye and one green eye—love swimming, and will gaily dive into the water for the sheer pleasure of it. The strain is now dying out as their peculiar characteristics are weakened by crossbreeding.

A Kurdish grandmother and child near Lake Van

► **Van** *212C2*

One of the high points of any visit to eastern Turkey, this region was formerly one of legendary fertility. Just a century ago the lakeshore was thickly wooded—"Van in this world, Paradise in the next," ran the old Armenian proverb. The town itself is nothing special, having none of the sophistication of Diyarbakır (see pages 220–221), none of the beautiful architecture of Mardin (see pages 221), and none of the atmosphere and fascination of Bitlis (see page 216). What it does have is proximity to Lake Van (see pages 234–235), 2½ miles away, as well as two of the best hotels in eastern Turkey in which to base yourself for exploring the region. Van's small museum (*Open daily 8–12 and 1–5. Admission charge*) is worth a visit for its stunning collection of Urartian artifacts.

Van Kalesi (Van Castle)►► (*Open daily. Admission free*) A visit to this freakish Urartian citadel, capital of the Urartian Empire for 300 years, is best made at sunset to witness the changing moods of the lake. Also called the Rock of Van, this narrow rock outcrop is about a mile long and 300 feet high, with sheer sides dropping to the south. Climb and follow all the little paths that weave around the citadel to discover the foundations of a Urartian temple, the tombs of four Urartian kings cut into huge chambers, and the crumbling Ottoman castle resting on large Urartian masonry blocks. In Ottoman times, 3,000 Janissaries were based here. Down below are the rubblelike mounds of Old Van, a city once enclosed by 16th-century walls and with one of the largest populations in Anatolia, two-thirds of it Armenian. Today it is a vivid example of a town that has been literally razed to the ground, with only the shells of a few mosques left. How and why this total destruction was wrought by the Turks after World War I remains a matter of controversy.

ENVIRONS OF VAN **Akdamar**►► See pages 234–235.

   Çavuştepe► (*Open daily 8:30–sunset. Admission charge*) This royal Urartian citadel, 14 miles from Van on the Hakkâri road, is the second largest after Van Kalesi. The buildings on the summit were used by the royal family only, while ordinary Urartian citizens lived on the plain below. In addition to the temple buildings, palace, and sacrificial altar, notice the extraordinarily advanced water system, with its series of large cisterns hollowed out of the rock.

   Güzelsu (Hoşap Castle)►► (*Open daily 8:30–12 and 1:30–5. Admission charge*) Like a hallucination from a fairy tale, with its crenellations and battlements, Hoşap is the best-preserved Kurdish castle in Turkey. Built by a local Kurdish despot in 1643, when Ottoman power was slipping, it lies 30 miles from Van on the Hakkâri road. Its colossal and impressive entrance gate leads into a surprisingly open and grassy interior. The best-preserved part is the keep, at the highest point.

   Hakkâri► Backed by the 12,820-foot-high massif of Çilo Daği, Hakkâri looks from a distance almost like an Alpine ski resort in summer. Its population of 18,000 is almost entirely Kurdish: the town is highly traditional and Ramadan is strictly observed, with no alcohol being served all month. The women are veiled and wear black from head to toe. There are no monuments of interest to the tourist here; in times of less Kurdish unrest, it is the mountains and the scenery that attract visitors.

LITTLE-KNOWN URARTIANS
The Urartians were distinguished builders who always chose long, thin spurs for their fortress sites. Van Kalesi and Çavuştepe are the two largest of the 30 fortress cities that are scattered over eastern Turkey. The Urartians were similar in looks and language to the Hittites, and their particular specialty was metalwork, using gold, silver, and bronze. Their fine work was exported westward, and there is mounting evidence that the ancient Greeks and Etruscans copied heavily from Urartian originals.

233

Hoşap Castle is the most picturesque of all Turkey's Kurdish fortresses

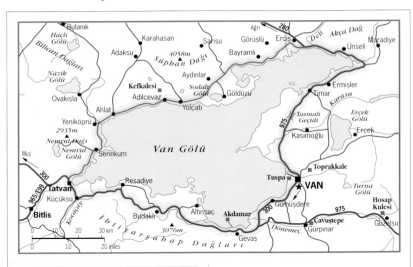

Drive

Circuit of Lake Van

Covering a total distance of 206 miles, this day trip would make one of the most memorable experiences of any visit to Turkey. It incorporates a short boat ride to an Armenian cathedral set on its own island, and visits a volcano, a Seljuk cemetery, and superb fortresses, all set against the eerie beauty of Lake Van, encircled by haunting mountains. The roads are all

Lake Van at sunrise

paved (though possibly a little potholed) and traffic-free: you may have whole sections of the lakeshore to yourself. It is best to take your own provisions.

After 29 miles en route from Van toward Gevas, you come to a yellow sign to **Akdamar**, beside a landing stage. In the morning you will find boats here waiting to ferry you (for a fee) the mile across to the tiny island. There, in solitary splendor, stands the Armenian cathedral. Off-season (from October to May) you will have to rent a boat: this is straightforward, but a bit more expensive.

Steps climb up to the cathedral, built in 915 by King Gagik I of the independent Armenian kingdom of Vaspurakan (Armenia was the first country to adopt Christianity as its national religion, in AD 303). The reliefs that cover the outside have never been restored, yet survive in remarkable condition despite the harshness of the climate. Depicting Old Testament stories, they are a masterpiece of early Armenian art. The series telling the story of Jonah and the Whale is one of the most hilarious, with a whale (the Armenians had never seen one) resembling an elongated pig with ears and teeth. Also recognizable are Abraham and Isaac, David and Goliath, and on the back wall Adam and Eve, heavily defaced.

The grassy island is a popular picnic spot for Turkish families, especially on weekends and holidays. There is also a

pebbly beach from which, in the summer months, the hardy can slip into the clear, silky waters of the lake. The alkaline sodas leave a wonderfully smooth feeling on the skin, and a level of salinity six times higher than that of the sea means that even the most leaden of swimmers can float.

Continuing the circuit westward toward Tatvan, the road leaves the lake for a time and zigzags up a high mountain pass with beautiful bubbling streams and flower-filled meadows. From Tatvan, follow the yellow sign to **Nemrut** (see page 217), the volcano whose eruptions aeons ago formed Lake Van by creating a huge dam of lava, thereby blocking the outflow. The level now remains constant, as the melted snow that flows into it each winter evaporates during the hot summer months. The shore views here are constantly changing—sometimes treeless and gaunt, sometimes lush and almost alpine—but they are all bathed in Lake Van's strange and timeless pale blue light. The breathtaking beauty and serenity this imparts to them will long continue to haunt you.

The next stop is **Ahlat**, where an atmospheric Seljuk cemetery sprawls over about 1 square mile, its lichen-covered headstones leaning at drunken angles. Also here—ripe for exploration—is a splendidly overgrown 16th-century fortress on the shore. Scattered around are distinctive

At an altitude of 5,740 feet, Lake Van is a high point of any trip to Turkey

conical *kümbets* (dome-tombs), dating from the 13th to 15th centuries. The Armenian stonemasons here were famous for their work, and only the town of Kayseri (see page 180) has tombs in such number and variety.

Some 15 miles beyond Ahlat you reach **Adilcevaz**, with its attractive, chocolate-colored mosque on the shore. On the hill above is a fine Seljuk fortress, from which there are wonderful lake views.

On the final stretch of the circuit, look for **Arin Gölü**, a freshwater lake whose shores are alive with a noticeably rich bird population, unlike the still and silent shores of Lake Van.

Jonah and the Whale at Akdamar

A mosque looks out over the blue waters of the Black Sea

236

ITINERARIES
One week:
Days 1–3 Trabzon
  (Sumela)
Days 4–5 Artvin
Day 6 Erzurum
Day 7 Trabzon

Two weeks:
Days 1–3 Trabzon
  (Sumela)
Day 4 Samsun
Day 5 Amasya
Day 6 Boğazkale
Day 7 Sivas
Day 8 Erzincan (Divriği)
Day 9 Erzurum
Days 10–11 Kars
Days 12–13 Artvin
Day 14 Rize
  (Çamlıhemşin)
Day 15 Trabzon

Two weeks:
Days 1–3 Trabzon
  (Sumela)
Day 4 Artvin
Days 5–6 Kars (Ani)
Day 7 Doğubeyazıt
Days 8–9 Van
Day 10 Tatvan
Day 11 Ağrı
Day 12 Erzurum
Day 13 Artvin
Day 14 Hopa
Day 15 Trabzon

Far right: an elegant bridge at Çamlıhemşin, near Rize

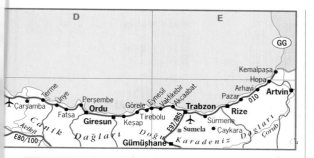

THE BLACK SEA There are two surprises in store for the first-time visitor to the Black Sea coast. The first is the lush green vegetation, and the second is its high concentration of buildings and population. Since the introduction of tea cultivation (see panel on page 239), the region has prospered and attracted more and more people, hence the quantity of newly built houses strung along the coast.

The best time to visit is late spring, when all is in bloom. Summer temperatures rarely exceed 85°F.

LANDSCAPE The name Black Sea is misleading to those who don't know that the landscape is green and fertile. The tea plantations deck the extensive lower slopes of the Pontic mountain range, dropping down in terraces like a gently descending staircase to touch the very edge of the coast road. The mountain ranges along the coast have served to keep the region fairly isolated from the Anatolian hinterland, with the result that a host of remote valleys are still home to ethnic subgroups such as the Laz.

►►► REGION HIGHLIGHTS

Kastamonu *page 241*
Konuralp *page 241*
Safranbolu *page 242*
Sinop *page 245*
Sumela Monastery
page 245
Trabzon *pages 246–247*

The Black Sea

The Fırtına river, near Çamlıhemşin, surges down from the mountains through a beautiful but precipitous valley, where getting from place to place and across the river requires some ingenuity

This also explains the strength of tradition here: Black Sea dances, for instance, have remained virtually unchanged for centuries.

FRINGE HISTORY Historically the region has lacked the dynamism of Turkey's Aegean and Mediterranean coasts, and the major events of history seem largely to have passed it by. The earliest-known settlements were founded here in the 7th and 8th centuries BC by enterprising colonists from Miletos, the greatest of the ancient Greek Ionian cities. The Milesians founded nearly 100 colonies along the shores of the Hellespont, the Sea of Marmara,

Fishing boats brighten the rocky shoreline

A traditional rural house

and the Black Sea, including **Sinop**, **Samsun**, **Ordu**, **Giresun**, and **Trabzon**. None of these colonies ever attained any real status, and the only significant kingdom to be established here was that of the Pontic kings, which sprang up after the death of Alexander the Great in the 4th century BC.

TOWNS AND SITES The main resorts of the Black Sea lie not far from Istanbul, at **Kilyos** to the west, **Şile** to the east, and **Akçakoca** and **Amasra**, though the most attractive part of the coastline begins east of Samsun. **Samsun** itself, though easily the largest city, is also the least interesting. **Trabzon** and **Sinop** are the most worthwhile places to stay for a few nights. The only real tourist attraction is the **Sumela Monastery**, inland from Trabzon. The general absence of ancient ruins in this area is due partly to the fact that the Romans penetrated only to the western parts of the coast, and partly to the heavy rainfall, which has washed away all but the strongest ruins.

PERFECT FOR TEA
The rain-saturated hillsides east of Trabzon are perfect for the cultivation of tea, and the bushes are planted up the steep hillsides to a height of 1,800 feet. Tea was introduced to the Black Sea only in the 1930s, but it quickly became the mainstay of the local economy. In 1986 the crop was condemned because of the nuclear disaster at Chernobyl, but even so production levels have increased to the point where some is now exported. Women dressed in colorful clothes and white headscarves do the work, clipping the bushes and collecting the tea in bags, which they empty in turn into huge baskets. You see them carrying these baskets on their backs along the road.

Crossing a suspension bridge inland from Pazar, near the eastern Black Sea coast

The Black Sea

BLOSSOMING HILLS
West of Giresun the coastline becomes very pretty. The towns are resort-like—cleaner, less sprawling. The trees covering the hillside right down to the edge of the road are spectacular. They are all either hazels (*fındık*), providing an important Turkish export, or cherries. In late spring the hills are smothered with blossoms.

SCALY STAPLE
Food along the Black Sea coast is generally good, far better than in eastern Turkey. The fish available vary with the season. In April there is turbot (*kalkan*), and from May onward there are red mullet (*barbunya*), tuna (*palamut*), and anchovies (*hamsi*). The latter, the most abundant and the cheapest fish, are the staple diet of the fishing villages.

A stretch of sandy beach near Tirebolu

▶ **Amasra**   236B2

Founded originally by the Milesian colonists, Amasra is now an attractive resort, beautifully set on its own wooded peninsula, with a Genoese castle on its citadel. It is a relaxing, sleepy place, divided into two sheltered bays by the peninsula. The castle is heavily fortified, and the walls and gateways are still largely intact. Notice the Genoese coat-of-arms scattered about liberally on the walls. There are also two Byzantine churches in the town's maze of alleyways, one now a ruin and the other still in use as a mosque. For swimming, head out of town to the beaches to the east.

▶ **Bolu**   236B1

Known to the Romans as Polis, this town lies in the mountains that separate Ankara from the sea, and is the center of the region's most popular mountain recreation area. The hills here are not as steep as farther east along the Black Sea, but are heavily forested. The woodland includes many deciduous trees such as oaks, rarely seen in Turkey today, making a welcome change from the heavy and somewhat monotonous dark green of the conifers of the Pontic Alps. **Lake Abant** to the south is especially beautiful and is full of trout for fishing. There is skiing at **Kartalkaya**, southwest of Bolu.

▶ **Giresun**   237D1

A bustling town some two hours' drive from Trabzon (see pages 246–247), Giresun is an attractive place dominated by its castle, Giresun Kalesi, which crowns the acropolis of the ancient Milesian colony of **Cerasus**. It was from here that the Roman general Lucullus, who captured the town in the Pontic Wars in 69 BC, brought back the first cherry trees to Europe. The name Cerasus is the origin of the words cherry and cerise. Just offshore is a small island with a second castle: Jason and the

Argonauts are said to have put in here on their quest for the Golden Fleece, and to have been attacked by birds dropping feathered darts. Today it is called **Büyük Ada** and is inhabited by fishermen. The island can easily be visited by boat.

▶ Hopa
237E1

A small and simple town, Hopa seems like a haven of sophistication if you arrive here after a spell in the interior of eastern Turkey. A number of charming small hotels overlook the pebbly beaches.

▶ Kastamonu
236C1

Inland from Inebolu, this sleepy town has some fine old Ottoman houses. Overlooking them is a castle built by Tamerlane, now a ruin but still with impressive walls and main gateway. Kastamonu is a good place to stop on the way to the **Ilgaz Milliparkı** (national park), which has skiing facilities.

▶ Konuralp
236B1

The village of Konuralp, near Düzce between Bolu and Akçakoca, is interesting for its traditional wooden houses, as well as the remains of ancient **Prousias** and **Aypium**. The theater, lying among the houses and gardens, still has most of its rows of seats. The school playground serves as an open-air museum for carved fragments and sarcophagi found in this ancient Bithynian town.

241

AMAZONIAN HABITS
The land around the Black Sea was associated in ancient times with the Amazons, remarkably independent women described by the ancient Greek geographer Strabo as spending 10 months of the year "off by themselves, performing their individual tasks such as ploughing, planting, pasturing cattle, and particularly training horses, though the bravest engage in hunting on horseback and practice warlike exercises. The right breasts of all are seared when they are infants, so that they can easily use their right hands for any purpose, and especially that of throwing the javelin... They have two months in the spring when they go up into the neighboring mountain which separates them from the Gagarians, who also go thither to sacrifice with the Amazons and also to have intercourse with them for the sake of begetting children, doing this in secrecy and darkness, any Gagarian at random with any Amazon." Any girls born as a result of this yearly encounter were kept by the Amazons; boys were taken to the Gagarians.

Drive

Amasra to Safranbolu

From Amasra, one of the prettier resorts on the Black Sea (see page 240), you can make a half-day trip inland through pine-clad hills to the towns of Bartin and Safranbolu, famous for their profusion of splendid old Ottoman wooden houses.

Set off inland from Amasra, following signs to Ankara. The small road winds its way up the pine-forested Pontic mountains, with terrific views over Amasra and the coast. After some 10 miles you reach **Bartin**, with its many timbered houses, especially around the bazaar.

Another breathtaking drive through the mountains, climbing up to a pass, brings you after 50 miles to the spectacular town of **Safranbolu**, set in a steep-sided gorge. All around are Ottoman houses and mansions with their half-timbered gables, whitewashed walls, and red-tiled roofs. Having as it does the largest concentration of these houses anywhere in Turkey, Safranbolu is relatively well established on the tourist route, but in a pleasantly low-key sort of way.

As you stroll the narrow streets, look for the restored Ottoman baths and the large, ramshackle caravansary (called **Cincihanı**) that dominates the town center. There are plans to turn this into a hotel. The **Arasta bazaar** has been restored and is well stocked with souvenirs and antique stalls. Also restored is **Kaymakamlar Evi**, the Governors' House, open to the public as an example of a typical Ottoman mansion. Stroll up to the castle above the town to enjoy more stirring views.

The harbor at Amasra, an attractive resort on a wooded peninsula

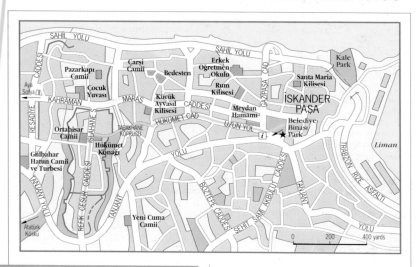

Walk

Trabzon Towers

This walk takes you from Trabzon's main square and along its major shopping street to the famous old walled citadel and its churches, before climbing to the citadel summit and the remains of the romantic royal palace of Trebizond's exiled Byzantine dynasty. The distance is about 2 miles one way, and it takes one-and-a-quarter hours.

Head west from the main square along **Uzun Yol** (Long Street), which becomes Hükümet Caddesi. On a small side street to the right, as the road begins to go downhill, stands Trabzon's oldest church, **Saint Anna** (Küçük Ayvasil Kilisesi), dating to the 7th century. It is always locked. Continue on to the walled citadel and **Ortahisar Camii**, built in the 10th century as the Byzantine church of Panayia Chrysocephalus (Golden-Topped Virgin), so called because of its copper dome. Now follow the long, steep hill to the summit and its *kale* (castle keep). Little children will guide you through a few backyards, from which you emerge onto a magnificent stretch of crenellated battlements, above a vertical drop of 300 feet or so down into the gully

below. This is all that remains of the palace of the exiled Comnene emperors and their lovely princesses, and it is from this vantage point that you can best imagine the fabled *Towers of Trebizond* (Rose Macaulay, 1956) in their 15th-century heyday. Of this spot Miss Macaulay wrote: "All the centuries of lively Byzantine chatter, they had left whispering echoes in that place where the hot sun beat down..."

243

Aya Sofya's 13th-century frescoes

The Black Sea

The harbor and Genoese castle at Şile

▶ Rize   237E1

The tea capital of the Black Sea, Rize is the largest town on the coast east of Trabzon. Its prosperity has been built entirely on tea, introduced to Turkey in the 1930s from Georgia (in the former Soviet Union), where it was planted at the end of the last century.

Inland 15 miles west of Rize is **Çaykara▶**, which has a remarkable old wooden roofed bridge, unique in Turkey.

The magnificent mansion of **Kestel Kale▶** (sometimes called Memisağa Konağı) lies hidden behind a high hedge some 2½ miles east of Surmene. Built in about 1800 by the local lord of the valley, this remarkable brick and timber building has a wonderful overhanging roof that makes it look like a gigantic mushroom.

▶ Samsun   236C1

Founded as the ancient town of Amisos by the Greeks from Miletos in the 7th century BC, Samsun is today the largest and busiest port on the Black Sea and is the center of Turkey's tobacco industry. Nothing of historical interest remains to be seen here because the Genoese, who were given trading privileges here by the Seljuks, burned the city down when it fell to the Ottomans in the 15th century.

INLAND EXCURSIONS
It is worth making the detour inland from Pazar (between Rize and Hopa) to the beautiful Hemsin valleys and to the attractive village of Çamlıhemşin, with its neat wooden houses. To the south is the impressive castle of Zil Kale, perching on a heavily forested hill and with trees growing out of its turrets.

▶ Şile   236A1

Just 45 miles from Istanbul, Şile has a pleasant beach, which becomes very crowded during vacation times. It also has a Genoese castle.

The coastline to the north of Sinop

► Sinop
236C2

The only natural harbor along the Black Sea, Sinop is known to have served as the port for the Hittite capital Hattuşaş, due south of here (see page 199), and in the 8th century BC was the largest of the Milesian colonies.

Of its illustrious past, little remains beyond the ruined Genoese castle, the 13th-century Alaeddin Mosque, and the Alaiye Madrasa, which now houses a museum. Have lunch at one of the variety of quayside restaurants serving fish and seafood.

►►► Sumela
237E1

The 30-mile excursion inland from Trabzon to the stunning mountain monastery of Sumela takes a good half day. The unforgettable monastery, set into the sheer rock face, hangs as if by levitation above the heavily wooded slopes and mountain mists, looking more Tibetan than Turkish.

The road ends at a forest clearing with an attractive restaurant, from which a path zigzags up to the monastery. The ascent takes about 30 minutes, depending on your level of fitness, and some may perhaps feel the effects of altitude (it is 3,875 feet above sea level). Behind the imposing 18th-century façade only a few crumbling monks' cells remain. The original monastery was founded in the 6th century to house a portrait of the Virgin Mary painted by Saint Luke, and it was inhabited continuously thereafter until 1923, when the Greeks were expelled from the country in the "exchange of populations" (see page 283) and all the monks were forced to leave. A fire soon afterward was responsible for much of its present ruined state.

The surviving frescoes on the inner façade and on the ceiling of the cave church are outstanding. On the façade, notice especially the top row, a fascinating series telling the story of Adam and Eve. The most striking fresco in the cave church depicts the Madonna and Child seated on a golden throne.

GOOD TIMING
If at all possible, time your arrival at Sumela for 1 PM or later; before this, bus tours flock here in continuous streams. Remember, too, that in wet weather the path up to the monastery gateway gets very muddy, so take appropriate shoes. Do not forget your money, either, as a fee is charged at the top. The site stays open until 5 PM.

245

VANDALISM
Nowhere in Turkey, except perhaps in the Göreme churches of Cappadocia, is there anything to equal the degree of defacement found at Sumela. Great chunks of fresco have been gouged out over the years and the surfaces covered in graffiti. As in Cappadocia, the names are mainly Turkish and Greek, with the occasional German or French addition.

The spectacularly sited monastery at Sumela, clinging perilously to the sheer cliff face

FABLED TREBIZOND
"Still the Towers of Trebizond, the fabled city, shimmer on a far horizon, gated and walled and held in a luminous enchantment."Rose Macaulay, *The Towers of Trebizond*, 1956

CLIMATIC CONTRAST
The reason why Turks (and Arabs) call this the Black Sea and the Mediterranean the White Sea is thought to be that the sun glinting on the Mediterranean gives it a white sheen, whereas the rain of the north makes the water here seem blacker. This climatic difference is the reason why the Black Sea will never be a major tourist destination. Even in the height of summer it can rain heavily any day, and the temperature can fluctuate from a pleasant 88°F to a cool 64°F.

The Georgian market in Trabzon

►► Trabzon (Trebizond) 237E1

As long as you adjust your expectations of Trabzon downward from the fabled city you may have read about, the city does have some interesting sights to offer and can even grow on you after a few days. **Aya Sofya**, 2 miles west of the main square, is justly the most famous site, outshining all Trabzon's other architectural monuments; these include 10 churches (a number of which were converted to mosques by the Ottomans), a convent, and an Armenian monastery. All these are relics of the Comnene dynasty founded by Alexius Comnenus, 22-year-old son of the Byzantine Emperor Manuel I, who fled Constantinople just before its fall to the Fourth Crusade in 1204.

Trebizond's Greek roots went back to the 7th century BC, when it was founded by the great sea-trading Milesian colonists. It grew in prosperity through trade with Persia, with camel caravans coming from Erzurum and Tabriz laden with silk and spices. Through its role as the last flickering flame of Byzantium, a distant outpost defiant against Islam after the fall of Constantinople, Trebizond acquired a certain romantic mystique in Europe.

Aya Sofya (Cathedral of Haghia Sophia)►► (*Open Tue–Sun 8:30–5. Admission charge*) is best visited by car or taxi, as it is a good hour's walk from the center. Built as a monastery church in the mid-13th century, in the heyday of the Comnene Empire, it was converted to a mosque in 1461, after the Ottoman conquest. As was usual, the walls were whitewashed and covered with hard plaster, which inadvertently preserved them for posterity. In 1950 a six-year project began to uncover the murals that lay beneath.

The magnificent frescoes for which the cathedral is famous adorn the walls and ceiling of the narthex (vestibule). Among the most beautiful are the Marriage Feast at Cana, the Feeding of the Five Thousand, and Christ Walking on the Water, all from the late 13th century and in the Byzantine tradition, with some Cappadocian influence. They are thought to have all been the work of a single artist. On the northern façade, looking out to the Black Sea, the external porch has a heart-rending fresco depicting Job plagued by boils.

If possible, make the short excursion to **Atatürk Köskü▶** (*Open* daily 9–5. *Admission charge*), Atatürk's summer residence, high up in heavily wooded hills 2½ miles behind the city. An attractive white stucco villa set in beautifully manicured gardens, it serves today as a museum of Atatürk memorabilia. Atatürk himself graced it with his presence just once, for three days back in 1921.

For other Trabzon sights see page 243.

▶ Ünye 237D1

Along the rocky shore near Ünye are caves inhabited by seals. Just east of Ünye, a road leads inland to **Niksar** (source of one of Turkey's main mineral waters), then 4 miles farther to the striking castle of **Çaleoğlu** set up on a volcanic hill. Inside, it still has a tunnel with 400 steps leading down to water. Ünye itself is a resort with good-quality motels and *pansiyons* (inns) along the beach.

▶ Zonguldak 236B1

A coal-mining center and industrial port, Zonguldak is the second-largest city in the Black Sea region after Samsun, but it has little to offer the tourist.

SKILLED MANIPULATORS
The Comnene dynasty and its capital, Trebizond, flourished because of Trebizond's position, the skill of its traders, and a string of beautiful and marriageable princesses, who helped to cement useful alliances with potentially troublesome neighbors. Though only the size of a province, it posed as an empire—Byzantium in exile. It sustained its pretentions with a court of pomp and ceremony and acquired a reputation beyond its achievements through diplomatic maneuvering, palace revolutions, and civil wars—truly Byzantine in the popular sense of the word.

247

Although Ünye itself is not exceptional, it enjoys a lovely setting, and there are delightful bays and fishing villages along the coast

The Laz, a seafaring race of obscure Caucasian origins, inhabit the region between Rize and Hopa. They are remote cousins of the Georgians, but with the important difference that they converted to Islam early and have remained staunch Muslims.

UNLAZY LAZ

A Caucasian minority concentrated in the valleys between Rize and Trabzon, the Laz are a hardworking people with a good deal of business acumen. Much of Turkey's shipping is owned and operated by Laz, using men from their own villages, while the women work on the tea plantations. Envied because of their relative prosperity, they have become the butt of Turkish humor, with many jokes referring to their supposed stupidity and slowness.

The coloring of this Laz herb seller hints at the distant relationship with the Georgians

248

The Laz were loyal to the Turks in the wars against Russia, while the Christian Georgians and Armenians were viewed as suspect. Their language, too, is related to Georgian; it is still spoken in the villages, though it is not written. There are thought to be about 100,000 Laz still living in and around Pazar, Ardeşen, Fındıklı, Arhavi, and Hopa, as well as some inland enclaves.

Laz business enterprises have brought them a certain affluence. They are relatively progressive in outlook and in their dress, which is colorful and fashionable. Often outgoing by nature, they traditionally enjoy dancing and playing the bagpipes. Their houses, well-made of wood and stone and always set in large yards, are unlike others in Turkey. They are never clustered together in rows instead they are spread out along the tops of ridges to ensure breathing space.

The ancient Greeks described the Laz as savage tribesmen, and they have a reputation for being fiercely aggressive as enemies but generous as friends. Like most Turks, they are generally patient and good-natured until pushed beyond a certain point. "The Laz talks with a pistol," runs a rather derogatory local saying.

Travel Facts

Arriving

Taxis are reasonably priced in Istanbul

By air—Istanbul Most international flights arrive at Atatürk Airport in the suburb of Yeşilköy, 12 miles west of the center. Taxis to the center take 30 minutes and are reasonably priced. Turkish Airlines runs buses every hour to Şişhane in the center, which are cheaper but do not stop en route. Flights to North Cyprus (Ercan) depart from the international airport, but transit flights to cities within Turkey depart from the near-by domestic terminal, linked by a shuttle bus.

By air—other cities International flights also arrive at Ankara, Izmir, Antalya, Adana, Trabzon, Bodrum, and Dalaman airports. Ankara airport (Esenboğa) lies 19 miles north of the center, a half-hour by taxi, while Izmir airport (Adnan Menderes) is 12 miles south of the center, a half-hour by taxi.

By sea There are three ways to arrive in Turkey by boat. Turkish Maritime Lines (TML) operates car ferries from Venice to Izmir, once a week from April to October. Daily services operate from North Cyprus all year round from Girne (Kyrenia) to Taşucu (near Adana) and Alanya, and from Mağosa (Famagusta) to Mersin. There are also ferries from the Greek islands of Lesbos, Chios, Samos, Cos, Symi, and Rhodes (see pages 110–111).

By train Rail travel via Europe is severely disrupted by the war in Bosnia. The Istanbul Express runs erratically from Munich, Vienna, and Athens, with connecting services from Sofia in Bulgaria. Each week, services to Istanbul leave from Moscow, Budapest, and Bucharest.

By bus Regular bus services run to Turkey from Austria, France, Germany, Holland, Italy, Switzerland, and Greece, and, from the other direction, Iraq, Iran, Jordan, Syria, Saudi Arabia, and Kuwait.

By private car No special documents are required for visits of less than three months; the car is entered on the driver's passport as imported goods. For stays of over three

İÇ HATLAR, YOLCU - OTO BİLETİ

DENİZYOLLARI

№ 222472

months, you must obtain a *carnet de passage* from the **Turkish Touring and Automobile Club**, 1. Oto Sanayi Sitesi Yani, 4. Levent, Istanbul (tel: 0212/282-8140), or from your own national automobile association.

Customs regulations
The importation of all narcotics is strictly forbidden and carries stiff prison sentences. On leaving, you need to show proof of purchase for a new carpet, or a certificate from a museum directorate for an old one.

Travelers with disabilities
Istanbul International Airport has adapted elevators and restrooms, and the arrival hall, baggage collection point, and customs are on the first floor, so carts and wheelchairs can easily be maneuvered straight to the taxi line. Ramps have been installed in many museums, state theaters, and opera and concert halls. Turkish State Railways (TCDD) offers a reduction of 70 percent for travelers with disabilities, and 30 percent for those accompanying them. For more information contact: **Ortopedik Özürlüler Federasyonu**, Gürabba Huseyinama Caddesi, Bostan Sokak, Mermer Iş Hanı, Aksaray, Istanbul (tel: 0212/534-5980).

Passports
U.S. citizens need a passport to enter Turkey for stays of up to three months. You may renew your passport in person or by mail. First-time applicants must apply in person at least five weeks before departure; applications are accepted at the 13 U.S. Passport Agency offices and at local county courthouses, many state and probate courts, and some post offices. You'll need a completed passport application; proof of citizenship; proof of identity (e.g. a valid driver's license); two recent, identical, 2-inch-square photographs; and $65 in check, money order, or cash for a 10-year passport ($40 for a five-year passport, issued to those under 18). Passports are mailed 10–15 business days from receipt of application. Contact the Department of State Office of Passport Services (tel: 202/647-0518) for specifics.

Foreign currency
There is no limit on the amount of foreign currency you can take into Turkey. Keep exchange slips, as you may be asked for them when converting Turkish lira into foreign currency or to prove that goods have been purchased with legally exchanged foreign currency. There is no departure tax, so change all Turkish lira back into foreign currency at the airport, where the rate is likely to be better than it is in the U.S.

A ferry on Istanbul's Golden Horn

251

Essential facts

Following the arrest of P.K.K. leader Abdullah Ocalan in 1999, tensions in Turkey increased. Visitors are advised to take sensible precautions when visiting certain parts Turkey. Contact the tourist office for further information.

When to go
Istanbul, Aegean, and Mediterranean coasts The tourist season runs from April 1 to October 31. May, June, and September are the best months; July and August can be too hot for sightseeing in the midday sun. The swimming season in the Sea of Marmara and northern Aegean is from June to September, while in the southern Aegean and Mediterranean you can swim from April to November. Istanbul is at its best from April to June, and in September and October.
   Central Anatolia The skiing season is from December to April. Summer visits are best from June to September.
   Eastern Turkey Skiing is from November to June, and summer visits are best from June to September.
   Black Sea coast June to September is the swimming season. Summer temperatures rarely exceed 85°F. Winters are mild, with high rainfall.

What to take
Loose, light, cotton clothing is best, with a pullover for the cooler

Dancers at the Silifke Music and Folklore Festival

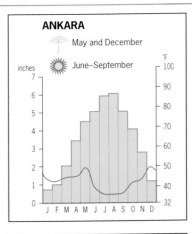

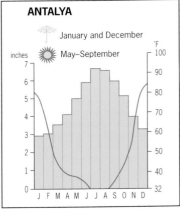

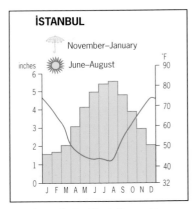

evenings. At the Black Sea and in Central and Eastern Anatolia, much warmer clothing is needed, even in summer. Comfortable shoes are essential for sightseeing, and sun hats, sunglasses, and high-protection factor sunscreen are recommended. A head scarf is useful for women when visiting mosques, and a flashlight can be handy when visiting castles and caves. If you like instant coffee at breakfast, bring your own and just ask for hot water, as the standard breakfast drink in nontourist places is black tea. Color print film is widely available, though expensive; color slide film is virtually unobtainable. Spare rolls of toilet paper are always useful.

National holidays
Government offices and businesses shut on these days, but shops and tourist sites remain open.
January 1: New Year's Day
April 23: National Independence and Children's Day
May 19: Atatürk Commemoration and Youth and Sports Day
August 30: Victory Day (end of War of Independence)
October 29: Republic Day

Religious holidays
The **Feast of Ramadan** (*Şeker Bayramı*) is a three-day national holiday at the end of the month of fasting. The **Feast of the Sacrifice** (*Kurban Bayramı*) is a four-day holiday commemorating Abraham's willingness to sacrifice his son Isaac.

Shops (except food shops, which are open from the third day), bazaars, offices, and banks are shut during these festivals, the dates for which follow the lunar calendar and therefore change each year. Museums and tourist sites are open as usual.

Time differences
Turkish time is GMT + 2 hours in winter and GMT + 3 hours in summer.

❏ **Statistics**
Area: 305,000 sq. miles
Population: 65 million, 41 percent of whom live in rural areas.
Major cities: Istanbul 12 million, Ankara 4 million, Izmir 3 million, Adana 2 million, Bursa 1.5 million, Antalya 1 million. ❏

Australia +8, Canada –7, England –2, Ireland –2, New Zealand +8, USA (East Coast) –7, (West Coast) –10

Money matters
The monetary unit is the Turkish **lira** (TL). Exchange rates are published daily in the newspapers. Most banks exchange foreign currency, as do most hotels of three stars and upward. There are also numerous exchange offices in major cities, which tend to offer better rates and are open longer hours than banks.

Visa cards can be used to obtain local currency from automated teller machines (ATMs) at **İş Bank** and **Yapı-Kredi Bank** (the latter bank also accepts MasterCard). Traveler's checks can be cashed at banks and hotels. Credit cards are now widely accepted throughout the country.

❏ **Opening times**
• **Government offices**
8:30–12:30, 1:30–5:30, closed Saturdays and Sundays
• **Banks** 8:30–12 or 12:30, 1 or 1:30–5, closed Saturdays and Sundays
• **Shops** 9:30–1, 2–7, closed Sundays
• **Grand Bazaar**, Istanbul 8–7, closed Sundays
• **Museums** 8:30–12:30, 1:30–5:30, closed Mondays
• **Archaeological sites** 8:30–dusk, daily

Opening times are subject to change. Readers are advised to check locally before planning visits to avoid any possible disappointment. ❏

Public transportation

A bus—Izmir transportation

Domestic air travel Internal flights are operated by **Turkish Airlines** (THY) between Ankara, Istanbul, Izmir, Adana, Antalya, Bodrum, Dalaman, Diyarbakır, Elazığ, Erzurum, Gaziantep, Kars, Kayseri, Konya, Samsun, Şanlıurfa, Trabzon, Malatya, and Van. All major cities have THY offices where you can buy tickets. Fares are reasonable and flights are frequent. There is a 90 percent discount for children under two traveling on your lap, 50 percent for children from two to 12, and 10 percent for a family or married couple traveling together. THY buses run from all city airports to the THY office in the city center. The main THY offices are in **Istanbul** (tel: 0212/663-6300, fax: 0212/663-4744) and **Ankara** (tel: 0312/398-0100, fax: 0312/398-0336).

Intercity buses Many private companies offer frequent day and night services between all Turkish cities. The buses—comfortable, air-conditioned, reliable, and inexpensive—depart from the bus station (*otogar*). Reserve your seats a day or two in advance, either at the *otogar* or with a travel agent.

Train Turkish State Railways has connections between many major cities, offering *couchettes,* sleeping cars, and restaurants, with first- and second-class seating, but trains are both more expensive and less efficient than the

bus network. On the European side, trains from Edirne and Greece arrive at **Sirkeci Station** near Eminönü Square in Istanbul; on the Asian side, trains from Ankara and all points east terminate at **Haydarpaşa Station** (20 minutes across the Bosphorus by ferry). The **Mavi Tren** (Blue Train) is a fast intercity service, leaving Haydarpaşa twice daily.

Ferries Turkish Maritime Lines (TML) operates coastal services from Istanbul's Karaköy, Sirkeci, and Eminönü, and car ferries from Istanbul to Izmir, Marmaris, and

Ferries are frequent and very cheap

İSTANBUL BÜYÜKŞEHİR BELEDİYESİ İSTANBUL DENİZ OTOBÜSLERİ

1993 YAZ TARİFESİ

254

Mersin three times a week. From May to September, TML operates a line from Istanbul to Trabzon leaving on Mondays, stopping at Sinop, Samsun, Ordu, and Giresun. Contact **TML Central Office** (tel: 0212/249-9222, fax: 0212/251-9025). Ferries across the Bosphorus are frequent and cheap. Main departure points are the quays beside the Galata Bridge at Eminönü and Karaköy; Beşiktaş and Kadataş on the European side; Üsküdar and Kadiköy on the Asian shore.

*Typically
Turkish yellow taxis*

❏ The favorite means of public transportation outside the cities in Turkey is the bus, being efficient, punctual, comfortable, and inexpensive. If you are traveling light, the bus system is excellent, but if you are traveling with children and you have luggage, then car rental is much more convenient. It also enables you to drive straight to the more remote sites. Within the cities, taxis are the most popular and are a very good deal. ❏

Taxis and _dolmuş_ Yellow taxis are the best way to get around in Turkish cities. They are metered, with a day rate (one light on the meter) and a night rate (two lights on the meter). The night rate operates between midnight and 6 AM and costs 50 percent extra. Tipping is not common. The _dolmuş_, recognizable by its yellow band, is a shared taxi that follows

specific routes. Passengers pay according to the distance traveled and may get out at any convenient place. Fares—cheaper than a taxi—are fixed by the municipality.

Trams Within Istanbul, high-speed trams run from Aksaray to Ferhatpaşa and Topkapı to Sirkeci. This line runs to the airport and terminates at Atakoy on the Sea of Marmara. An old-fashioned tram has been reinstated along Istiklal Caddesi, between Tünel Square and Taksim.

Student and youth travel Turkish Airlines, Turkish Maritime Lines, and Turkish State Railways offer reductions to holders of most internationally recognized student cards. Students are also entitled to accommodations at Turkish Youth Hostels: the main office is in Istanbul at the Gençtur Turizm ve Seyahat Acentasi, Yerebatan Cad. 15/3, Sultanahmet (tel: 0212/520-5274).

*An old-fashioned tram runs along
Istiklal Caddesi in Istanbul*

255

Driving

Car rental desks, Istanbul Airport

Car rental This is expensive, though you can usually get a discount by making advance reservations. Drivers must be over 21 and have a valid driver's license from their own country. Third-party insurance is compulsory, and it is advisable to take out additional collision damage waiver (CDW) and personal accident insurance, which give you comprehensive coverage. Cars commonly available are Murat (a locally made Fiat) and Renault, with Suzuki Jeeps for those who want four-wheel drive.

Seat belts are compulsory in front seats only, so specify if you want them in the back. It is also worth asking what the rental agency will do if the car breaks down.

Car breakdown If your own car breaks down, call the **Turkish Touring and Automobile Club** (Istanbul head office tel: 0212/282-8140). There are also numerous car mechanics in towns, usually grouped together, and spare parts are readily available. Turkish mechanics are surprisingly resourceful when it comes to fixing foreign makes of car.

Driving tips
Traffic regulations Traffic drives on the right in Turkey. Speed limits are 30 mph (50 kph) in towns, 55 mph (90 kph) on state highways, and 55 mph (120 kph) on expressways. Traffic police often carry out spot checks, especially at the approaches to towns, where the limit changes from 75 mph (90 kph) to 30 mph (50 kph). On-the-spot fines are imposed according to how much over the speed limit you're going. Turkish road signs conform to international protocol. The road network is extremely good and generally well maintained. The Istanbul-to-Ankara highway, which

> ❏ Night-driving outside the cities can be an unnerving experience in Turkey, as oncoming vehicles frequently have no lights; their drivers switch them on at the last minute, when they are nearly on top of you, dazzling you completely. Agricultural vehicles often drive on the road with no lights at all, and broken-down trucks often display no warning triangle. Road reflectors are rare, so it is important to make sure that your own lights are strong and properly adjusted to give maximum visibility. ❏

continues as the E23, the E5, and the E24 transit routes to Iran, Syria, and Iraq respectively, is the only really busy road. These three routes should be avoided if possible. All other roads are clear of traffic, and driving in most parts of Turkey is a pleasure.

Gas Gas stations selling super (premium equivalent), normal (regular equivalent), and diesel are abundant in western Turkey, though less so in central and eastern regions. Unleaded gas is found only in the biggest cities and the tourist areas. Gas stations on the main highways often have service stations and are open around the clock.

> ❏ **Road signs**
> **Dur**: stop
> **Dikkat**: watch out, e.g. because of roadwork ahead
> **Şehir merkezi**: town center
> **Yellow signs** indicate archaeological sites ❏

Speed traps are common on the edge of towns; offenders may be fined

Communications

The media

There are numerous Turkish newspapers, many of them printed in color. Foreign newspapers and magazines, mainly English, American, and German, are available in the big cities and tourist centers one day late. The *Turkish Daily News*, the only English-language daily, is informative but dry. The *Voice of Turkey* radio broadcasts daily in English on general subjects and current events, 7:30–12:45 and 6:30–10 local time, on the following FM frequencies: 100.6 MHz, 97.4 MHz, 101.6 MHz, 100.5 MHz, 101.9 MHz, and 103 MHz. For further information contact: **T.R.T. External Services**, P.O. Box 333 Yenişehir, Ankara 06443 (tel: 0312/490-9817, fax: 490-9840).

❏ **Useful telephone numbers**
110 fire
112 emergency ambulance
115 international operator
118 information operator
131 operator
155 city police
156 rural police
(gendarmerie) ❏

Post offices The main post offices (P.T.T.) in Ankara and Istanbul are open 8–midnight Monday–Saturday, 9–7 Sundays; the smaller ones throughout the country are open 8:30–12:30 and 1:30–5:30, closed Saturdays and Sundays. General delivery letters should be addressed "*postrestant*" to the central post office (*Merkez Postanesi*) in the relevant town. Identification is required. Most post offices also offer fax and "valuable dispatch" services, and will exchange foreign currency, international postal orders, and traveler's

A Turkish post office sign

checks. An express postal service (**Acele Posta Servisi** or A.P.S.) is available for sending letters, documents, and small packages abroad.

Telephones The cheapest way to make a phone call is from a P.T.T. telephone booth, though most decent hotels have direct-dial national and international lines in guest rooms. P.T.T. offices sell phone cards and three sizes of *jeton* (token), for local, intercity, and international calls. Cheap rates within Turkey apply between 6 PM and 8 AM. International calls are cheap between 12 midnight

Phone cards are widely available

and 8 AM and on Sundays. To call abroad from Turkey, dial 0, then dial 0 again for an international line, followed by the country code and the number. U.S. country code is 1, Ireland 353, U.K. 44, Australia 61, Canada 1, and New Zealand 64.

Language guide
Pronunciation
c = j, as in cami (mosque) = **jami**
ç = ch, as in Foça = **Focha**
ğ = soft g, unpronounced, but used to extend the preceding vowel, as in dağ (mountain) = **daa**
ı (dotless i) = the initial "a" in away, as in Topkapı = **Topkapeu**
ö = oe, as in Göreme = **Goereme**
ş = sh, as in Kuşadası = **Kushadaseu**
ü - as in French *tu*, e.g. **Ürgüp**

Numbers

1 bir	8 sekiz
2 iki	9 dokuz
3 üç	10 on
4 dört	20 yirmi
5 beş	50 elli
6 altı	100 yuz
7 yedi	1,000 bin

Greetings and polite expressions

hello merhaba
goodbye (said by the person staying behind) güle güle
goodbye (said by the person leaving) allaha ısmarladık
good morning günaydın
good evening iyi akşamlar
good night iyi geceler
please lütfen
thank you mersi or teşekkür ederim
how are you? Nasılsınız?
I am well, thank you iyiyim, teşekkür ederim

Everyday expressions

yes evet
no hayır or yok
there is var
there is not yok
I want istiyorum
I would like coffee, please kahve istiyorum, lütfen
how much is this? Bu ne kadar?
expensive pahalı
cheap ucuz
money para
very beautiful çok güzel
restroom tuvalet
men's restroom baylar
ladies' restroom bayanlar

Time

today bugün
yesterday dün
tomorrow yarın
what is the time? şaat kaç?

Travel

airport hava alanı
port liman
is it far? uzak mı?
where is...? nerede...?
bus station otogar
gasoline benzin
oil (engine) yağı

tire lastik
brakes frenler
it does not work çalışmıyor

Food

bread ekmek
water su
mineral water maden suyu
fruit juice meyva suyu
wine şarap
sweet wine tatlı şarap
dry wine sek şarap
red wine kırmızı şarap
white wine beyaz şarap
beer bira
ice buz
breakfast kahvaltı
tea çay
coffee kahve
milk süt
sugar şeker
jam reçel
cheese peynir
soup çorba
salad salata
fish balık
eggs yumurta
french fries patates
ice cream dondurma

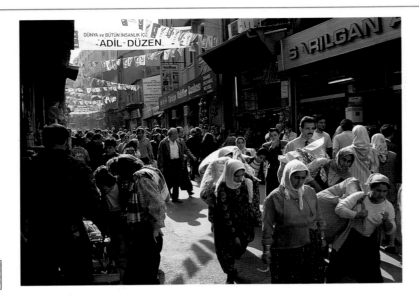

Emergencies

Crime and police

Rates of petty crimes such as theft have always been low, as in all Islamic societies, but with rising unemployment they are increasing in the cities. Pickpockets are also becoming more common in the bazaar areas. Violent crime is much rarer than in Western countries.

In the event of a crime, report it to the **tourist police**, recognizable by their beige uniforms and maroon berets. They have offices in all towns (Istanbul tel: 0212/527-4503/528-5369; Ankara tel: 0312/384-0606; Izmir tel: 0232/445-9376). **Traffic police** wear navy uniforms and white caps; report any traffic accident to them. **Market police**, in blue uniforms, patrol the markets and bazaars to check commercial practice. The **Jandarmas** (*gendarmerie*) are soldiers dressed in green army uniforms with a red armband. Their duties include keeping the peace, preventing smuggling, and the like.

> ❏ **Emergency phone numbers**
> • **Ambulance** 112
> • **Police** 155
> • **Fire** 110 ❏

Crowded areas such as this in Istanbul are fertile ground for pickpockets

Embassies and consulates

United States of America
Ankara: Kavaklıdere, Atatürk Bulvarı No. 110 (tel: 0312/468-6110); Istanbul: Tepebaşı, Meşrutiyet Caddesi No. 104/108 (tel: 0212/251-3602) Izmir: Amerikan Kültür Derneği 2. Kat (tel: 0232/421-3643).

Australia Ankara: Gaziosmanpaşa, Nenehatun Caddesi No. 83 (tel: 0312/4461-1180/87); Istanbul: Etiler, Tepecik Yolu Uzeri No. 58 (tel: 0212/257-7050).

Canada Ankara: Gaziosmanpaşa, Nenehatun Caddesi No. 75 (tel: 0312/436-1275/79); Istanbul: Gayret-tepe, Büyükdere Caddeso No. 107, Begün Han, Kat 3 (tel: 0212/272-5174).

Republic of Ireland Istanbul (Honorary Consul), Harbiye (tel: 0212/246-6025).

United Kingdom Ankara: Çankaya, Şehit Ersan Caddesi No. 46/A (tel: 0312/468-6230); Istanbul: Beyoğlu/Tepebaşı, Meşrutiyet Caddesi No. 34 (tel: 0212/293-7540); Izmir: 1442 Sokak No. 49, Alsancak (tel: 0232/463-5151); Antalya: Kazim Özalp Caddesi No. 149/A (tel: 0242/247-7000).

❏ Preventive measures

Drink bottled water, as the tap water, though chlorinated, can become contaminated in the water tanks. Avoid eating raw salad, or if you do, keep the quantities small and squeeze lots of lemon juice on it. Eat plenty of yogurt and bread to counterbalance the olive oil in meat and vegetable dishes. Use a high-protection sunscreen, and from June to August stay out of the sun from 11 AM until 3 PM. ❏

Health and vaccinations

There are no mandatory vaccination requirements, although immunization against typhoid, tetanus, polio, and hepatitis A is recommended.

There is no risk of malaria in the Mediterranean coastal regions, but east of Ankara antimalarial tablets are recommended between March and November.

Avoid swimming in fresh water near the Syrian border because of bilharzia. AIDS is present in Turkey, as in all parts of the world.

For minor problems, go to the pharmacy (*eczane*). Most medicines, including antibiotics, are available over the counter. In cities there is always a 24-hour drugstore; normal opening hours are Monday to Saturday 9–7. If necessary your hotel will call a doctor, and you will be charged. In Istanbul the three best hospitals are the **American Hospital** in Nişantaşı (tel: 0212/231-4050); the **International Hospital** at Yesilköy (tel: 0212/663-3000); and the **German Hospital** in Taksim (tel: 0212/293-2150). All treatment must be paid for, so make sure that your travel insurance includes medical coverage.

Dangers

In the sea, watch out for the black sea urchins that lurk on rocks in shallow water. Their spines are poisonous and very painful if stepped on.

On land, poisonous snakes and scorpions are sometimes found in remote areas. Watch your step and make sure you wear sturdy protective footwear.

Seek medical attention if you are stung by the Mediterranean scorpion

Hitchhiking

Hitchhiking is not illegal, but neither is it widespread—and hitchhikers are an unusual sight. Since public transportation is so cheap, most people simply use the bus.

Maps

Turkish tourist offices provide a free road map, which is adequate for most purposes. If you want a more detailed map, Kümmerley and Frey and Roger Lascelles both produce larger-scale maps.

Organized tours

All resorts and tourist centers have travel agencies, which operate organized tours and excursions. One of the principal ____ s in Istanbul __

Turkish resorts now offer a wide variety of water sports

Places of worship

There are mosques for Muslim worship on most street corners throughout Turkey. Istanbul, with its large Christian and Jewish communities, also has the Catholic **San Antonio di Padova** on Istiklal Caddesi, Beyoğlu; the Anglican **Christ Church (Crimean Memorial)**, Serdar Ekrem Sok. 82, Beyoğlu; and the **Neve Shalom Synagogue** on Büyük Hendek Caddesi, Şişhane.

Restrooms

On the whole, Turkish plumbing is surprisingly good. In hotels and *pansiyons* (inns) restrooms are gener-

---

❑ **White-water rafting**
Though still in its infancy, this sport is now practiced in Turkey, especially on the Çoruh river, between Bayburt and Artvin in eastern Turkey. Sobek Expeditions, P.O. Box 1089, Angels Camp, CA 95222, (tel: 209/736-4524) offers two-week trips. ❑

ally clean and of the conventional sitting-down variety. Toilet paper is something of a rarity in public places, as most Turks prefer to use the water pipe by the cistern. The worst public restrooms are on the old ferry steamers that ply up and down the Bosphorus and to the Princes' Islands.

Stamps

You can buy stamps at all candy/cigarette stands in resorts and at some souvenir shops. In cities, you can get them from hotels and post offices.

Tipping

When a 10 or 15 percent service charge is added to your restaurant bill, you should still leave a 5 percent tip for the waiter. In smaller restaurants, where a charge is not included, leave 10 percent. Taxi drivers do not expect tips, but it is normal to round the fare up. In a Turkish bath the masseurs/masseuses will be delighted with a tip. Mosque attendants should be given a reasonable tip if they have opened a mosque or *madrasa* for you; shoe attendants expect small change.

Water sports and sports

Water sports are on the increase on the Aegean and Mediterranean coasts, with most larger resorts such as Fethiye, Alanya, Kuşadası, Bodrum, and Marmaris offering windsurfing, waterskiing, parasailing, and pedal boats. Scuba diving is also popular, with professional diving centers at Fethiye and Turunç Bay running five-day courses leading to internationally recognized qualifications. There are also fully equipped marinas at Istanbul, Çanakkale, Çeşme, Sığacık, Kuşadası, Bodrum, Datça, Marmaris, Göçek, Fethiye, Kalkan, Kaş, Finike, Kemer, and Antalya. For more yachting information, get in touch with the **Yacht Enterprises Association**, Bodrum (tel: 0252/316-6283, fax: 0252/316-8499).

Tennis courts are available at all major Aegean and Mediterranean resorts. Ballooning, bicycling, and horseback riding are alternative means of viewing the extraordinary landscapes of Cappadocia. Skiing is now popular with tourists, notably at Uludağ, near Bursa, Turkey's premier ski resort.

Permits for climbing Mount Ararat (if safe to do so) should be obtained three months before the ascent either from the Turkish embassy or from Trek Travel, Aydede Caddesi 10, 80090 Taksim, Istanbul (tel: 0212/254-6707; fax: 0212 253-1509).

Women travelers

As long as women are careful about body language and etiquette, they should encounter few problems. You are less likely to receive unwelcome attention if you are accompanied by a man; if this is not possible, it may be best to travel with Turkish women. Avoid a lot of eye contact with male strangers. This is frequently misread as encouragement. Images of women in Western films and magazines have fostered the misapprehension that Western women are "available," so counteract this through careful dress and behavior.

Women walking alone at night, or in pairs, are regarded as inviting attention. If you receive any uninvited attention, the best response is to shout *ayip!* (shame on you!) loudly enough for passersby to hear—the culprit should be shamed into retreat.

Tourist offices

There are Turkish Information Offices in the United States at 821 United Nations Plaza, New York, NY 10017 (tel: 212/687-2194/5/6, fax: 212/599-7568) and at 1717 Massachusetts Avenue NW, Suite 306, Washington D.C. 20036 (tel: 202/429-9844; fax: 202/429-5649)

Within Turkey each town has its own tourist office, open the same hours as government offices (see page 253). The airports at Istanbul, Ankara, Izmir, Adana, Trabzon, and Dalaman also house tourist offices.

Istanbul Central Office, Beyoğlu Mesrutiyet Caddesi No. 57/5 (tel: 0212/243-3731, fax: 252-4346
Entrance to the Hilton Hotel, Taksim (tel: 0212/233-0592)
Karaköy Maritime Station (tel: 0212/249-5776)
Sultanahmet Square (tel: 0212/518-8754)

Izmir Adnan Menderes Airport (tel: 0232/274-2110, fax: 274–2214)
Alsancak Harbor (tel: 0232/422-1022, fax: 421–9257)

Ankara Central Office, Gazi Mustafa Kemal Bulvarı No. 121, Tandoğan (tel: 0312/229-2631, fax: 229-3661)

Adana Central Office, Atatürk Caddesi, No. 13 (tel: 0322/363-1287, fax: 363-1346)

Antalya Central Office, Selçuk Mah, Mermerli Sokak, Ahiyusuf Cami Yanı, Kaleiçi (tel: 0242/247-5042, fax: 247-6298)

Bodrum Bariş Meydanı (tel: 0252/316-1091, fax: 316-7694)

Bursa Central Office, Fevzi Çakmak Caddesi, Fomara Han Kat 6 (tel: 0224/223-8307, fax: 223-8309)

Diyarbakır Central Office, Kültür Sarayı, Kat 6 (tel: 0412/221-7840, fax: 223-1580)

Konya Central Office, Mevlana Caddesi No. 21 (tel: 0332/351-1074, fax: 350-6461)

Marmaris Iskele Meydanı No. 2 (tel: 0252/412-1035, fax: 412-7277)

Side Side Yolu Uzeri (tel: 0242/753-1265, fax: 753-2657)

Trabzon Central Office, Vilayet Binası Kat 4 (tel: 0462/230-1910, fax: 230-1911)

Ürgüp Park Içi (tel: 0384/341-4059, fax: 341-4059)

Van Cumhuriyet Caddesi No. 19 (tel: 0432/216-2018, fax: 216-3675)

Ballooning in the Göreme Valley, Cappadocia

Accommodations & Restaurants

ACCOMMODATIONS

Accommodations in Turkey range from Hiltons and Sheratons in the big cities to simple family *pansiyons* (inns) in the towns and villages. Even in these, a private shower and toilet in each room is the norm. Most visitors find the standards high and the service helpful and friendly. In the following listings, accommodations are grouped in three price categories:

$$$ is expensive, at $150–$360 for a double room with breakfast; $$ is moderate, at $80–$150; and $ is inexpensive, at $40–$80. Rates in Istanbul tend to be at the high end of each category.

ISTANBUL

Grand hotels

These are Istanbul's top luxury hotels, located throughout the city.

Çırağan Palace Hotel Kempinski ($$$)
Çırağan tel: 0212/258-3377 fax: 259-6687
An elaborately restored Ottoman palace in a superb setting on the lower Bosphorus, with 294 spacious rooms, fine cuisine in its restaurants, and a fabulous outdoor swimming pool on the edge of the Bosphorus. This is probably Istanbul's top hotel.

Conrad Istanbul ($$$)
Beşiktaş tel: 0212/227-3000 fax: 259-6667
This stylish hotel, run by Hilton Hotels, set up on a hill in the commercial quarter, has wonderful views of the Bosphorus and the Yıldız Gardens. Inside, there's a health club and swimming pool; outside there's another pool and floodlit tennis courts. The restaurants serve excellent international cuisine. There is a total of 627 rooms.

Four Seasons ($$$)
Tevkifhane Sokak No. 1, 34490 Sultanahmet tel: 0212/638-8200 fax: 638-8210
This popular hotel lies in the heart of the city by the Aya Sofya, an exquisitely renovated neo-classic bastille. The 65 spacious rooms are set around a courtyard; the rooftop restaurant serves excellent food and provides stunning views. There is also a health club.

Swissôtel The Bosphorus ($$$)
Maçka tel: 0212/259-0101 fax: 259-0105
Set on the hill above Dolmabahçe Palace, this enormous, splendid hotel has 600 rooms with fine views, several restaurants and bars, indoor and outdoor pools, shopping arcade, fitness club, tennis courts, and Turkish bath.

The older grand hotels, such as the Hilton, Sheraton, Mövenpick, and Divan, are much less glamorous and comfortable.

Stamboul: the Old City

The hotels given are all within walking distance of the main tourist sites. Many are in renovated Ottoman houses.

Avicenna Hotel ($$)
Amiral Tafdil Sokak 31–33
tel: 0212/517-0550 fax: 516-6555
Just 400m from Aya Sofya and the Blue Mosque, this converted Ottoman house provides a quiet base. Of the 49 small rooms, those in the attic are the best, with private balconies and excellent sea views. Restaurant, bar, and satellite TV.

Ayasofya Pansiyonlar ($$)
Sultanahmet tel: 0212/516-9446
fax: 518-0700
This charming group of brightly painted old wooden houses, furnished in Ottoman style, are between the Topkapı and Aya Sofya. The facilities include 57 rooms, in addition to restaurants, cafés, bars, and a Turkish bath.

Citadel Hotel ($$)
Kennedy Caddesi 32 tel: 0212/516-2313
fax: 516-1384
On the coast road overlooking the Sea of Marmara, below Aya Sofya, this excellent hotel has 31 rooms with traditional atmosphere. Superb Turkish cuisine is served in indoor and outdoor settings, the latter incorporating parts of the original city wall.

Empress Zoe Hotel ($)
Adliye Sokak 10 tel: 0212/518-2504
fax: 518-5699
This 19-room hotel, peacefully set in a Byzantine cistern beside an Ottoman bathhouse, has a tiny garden and rooftop terrace bar. The rooms are small but decorated in an interesting way. It is run by an American woman and is a good choice for women traveling alone.

Halı ($)
Klodfarer Caddesi 20, Çemberlitaş
tel: 0212/516-2170 fax: 516-2172
Set close by the Covered Bazaar, this beautifully restored old building has 35 rooms, all with their own bathroom.

Hippodrome ($)
Mımar Mehmetağa Cad. 17
tel: 0212/517-6889 fax: 516-0268
The attractive 17-room Ottoman house has a pleasant terrace and is close to the Blue Mosque. There is no restaurant and only showers.

Kariye ($$)
Edirnekapı tel: 0212/534-8414
fax: 521-6631
This attractive, 27-room hotel, in a converted Ottoman house, stands just inside the city walls, beside the Kariye Museum and a taxi ride from the Aya Sofya area. It has an excellent restaurant set in a peaceful garden.

Kalyon ($$)
Sarayburnu tel: 0212/517-4400
fax: 638-1111
The refurbished 1960s motel on the coast road below the Blue Mosque overlooks the Sea of Marmara. There are 110 rooms, a terrace, and a restaurant serving international cuisine.

Küçük Ayasofya ($)
Şehit Mehmetpaşa Sokak 25, Sultanahmet
tel: 0212/516-1988 fax: 516-8356
A rebuilt Ottoman house, not far from the Blue Mosque and near the Sokullu Mehmet Paşa mosque, with 14 simply decorated rooms, each with a bath.

Merit Antique ($$$)
Laleli tel: 0212/513-9300 fax: 512-6390
Formerly known as the Ramada, this is the only
five-star hotel in the old city. The building is a
restored early 19th century apartment building
close to the Grand Bazaar, with 275 rooms, an
indoor heated pool, health club, and excellent
Turkish and Chinese cuisine.

Obelisk Hotel ($$)
Amiral Tafdil Sokak 17/19
tel: 0212/517-7173 fax: 517-6861
This converted Ottoman house, within sight of the
Blue Mosque, has a roof terrace restaurant with
views of the Sea of Marmara. Some rooms have
fine brass bedsteads.

Pierre Loti Hotel ($)
Çemberlitaş tel: 0212/518-5700
fax: 516-1886
A 36-room establishment close to the Grand
Bazaar, the hotel has an attractive terrace garden
facing the main road. There is also a pleasant
restaurant and Turkish bath.

Poem ($$)
Akbıyık Caddesi, Terbıyık Sokak 12,
Sultanahmet
tel: 0212/517-6836 fax: 529-3807
This pretty restored Ottoman wooden house with
18 rooms, some with sea views, is within walking
distance of all the main sights in the old city.

President ($$$)
Beyazıt tel: 0212/516-6980 fax: 516-6999
This popular hotel is close to the Covered Bazaar,
with 204 rooms and a popular English-style pub.

Sokullu Paşa ($$)
Şehit Mehmetpaşa Sokak 5/7, Sultanahmet
tel: 0212/518-1790 fax: 518-1793
Sokullu Paşa, in an elegant 18th-century mansion
below the Blue Mosque, has 37 rooms. The
garden has a fountain, the restaurant is in a
Byzantine wine cellar, and there is also a Turkish
bath.

Sümengen ($$)
Mimar Mehmetağa Caddesi, Amiral Tafdil
Sokak 21, Sultanahmet tel: 0212/517-6875
fax: 516-8282
Close to the Blue Mosque with good views to the
rear over the Sea of Marmara, this elegant
19th-century house has 30 rooms, each with its
own bath.

Turcoman Hotel ($)
Asmali Çeşme Sokak 2 tel: 0212/516-2956
fax: 516-2957
Next to the Museum of Turkish and Islamic Art
(Ibrahim Paşa Sarayı), this 12-room hotel has
some good views over the Hippodrome.

Turkuaz Mansion Hotel ($$)
Kumkapı tel: 0212/518-1897 fax: 517-3380
Only a five-minute walk from the Blue Mosque
area, this very attractive 1870s pink and gray
mansion has 14 rooms, garden, terrace bar, and
Turkish bath.

Yeşil Ev ($$)
Sultanahmet tel: 0212/517-6785
fax: 517-6780
In a marvelous location between the Blue Mosque
and Aya Sofya, this 20-room hotel in a restored
Ottoman house has a large rear garden with an
outdoor restaurant and a fountain. It is the most
popular of the hotels in renovated Ottoman mansions and is right at the top of its price category.

BEYOĞLU AND THE BOSPHORUS

These hotels are located either in the
European business quarter, a 15-minute taxi
ride away from the old city, or on the
Bosphorus itself.

Bebek Hotel ($$)
Bebek tel: 0212/263-3000 fax: 263-2636
The hotel enjoys a perfect waterside location and
stylish terrace bar, but is a bit like a sleepy guest-
house.

Büyük Londra Hotel ($)
Tepebaşı tel: 0212/293-1619
fax: 245-0671
This 1850s building with a beautiful façade has an
air of faded grandeur. Some of its 54 rooms have
fine views of the Golden Horn. It is close to (but
much better value than) the famous Pera Palace.

Fuat Paşa Hotel ($$)
Büyükdere tel: 0212/242-9860
fax: 242-9589
The pretty house on the Bosphorus front at
Büyükdere, 30 minutes by taxi from the old city,
has 51 rooms, indoor and outdoor restaurants,
and a Turkish bath.

269

Golden Age I ($$$)
Topçu Caddesi 22, Taksim
tel: 0212/254-4906 fax: 255-1368
This 112-room hotel, in the heart of the commercial district, has modern facilities, including a
rooftop pool, health club, and Jacuzzi.

Hidiv Kasrı ($$)
Çubuklu tel: 0216/331-2651 fax: 322-3434
On the Asian shore overlooking the Bosphorus,
this former Khedive's palace sits in splendid
isolation, 7 miles outside the city center, in its
own rose garden and woodland. It has 14 rooms
with sumptuous art nouveau decor, and a
charming restaurant.

Pera Palace ($$)
Tepebaşı tel: 0212/251-4560
fax: 251-4089
The famously grand 19th-century terminal for the
Orient Express, the Pera Palace is now overpriced
and overrated. This said, rooms are decorated
with period furniture, and guests can enjoy the
elegant *patisserie* and bar.

Richmond Hotel ($$)
İstiklal Caddesi 445 tel: 0212/252-5460
fax: 252-9707
Next door to the Russian Consulate, this
109-room hotel is the only one on Istiklal, the
heart of the shopping district. Behind the 19th-
century façade lies a modern interior. The hotel
has an attractive French-style café and a Turkish
restaurant which puts on dancing displays.

ISTANBUL ENVIRONS

Bursa
Çelik Palace ($$$)
Çekirge tel: 0224/233-3800 fax: 236-1910
A sumptuous 173-room hotel, the best in Bursa,

Çelik Palace has its own hot thermal springs, indoor pool, two Turkish baths, and shopping center.

Termal Hotel Gönlüferah ($$)

Çekirge tel: 0224/233-9210 fax: 233-9218
This modern hotel with 62 rooms has a Turkish thermal bath and good restaurant.

Büyükada
Splendid Palas Hotel ($$)

Büyükada tel: 0216/382-6950
fax: 382-6775
Less than 100 yards from the ferry terminal pier, this slightly run-down but very atmospheric 19th-century mansion sits right on the waterfront, with superb views over to the other islands from its terrace. It has 74 rooms and an outdoor pool. The twin domes conceal water tanks, essential on an island with no springs or streams.

Çanakkale
Anzac Hotel ($)

Saat Kulesi Meydanı
tel: 0286/217-7777 fax: 217-2018
This 27-room hotel, with roof bar and restaurant, provides clean, simple accommodations in the center of Çanakkale.

Tusan Hotel ($$)

Güzelyalı tel: 0286/232-8210 fax: 232-8226
In a wonderful woodland setting with a private beach, 9 miles outside Çanakkale, this 64-room hotel provides a choice of both indoor and outdoor restaurants. Guests can enjoy a variety of watersports.

Edirne
Rüstempaşa Caravanserai Hotel ($)

Iki Kapili Han Caddesi 57
tel: 0284/225-2195 fax: 212-0462
This authentically converted Ottoman caravansary (inn with a courtyard) lies in the center of Edirne. It has 74 rooms which can seem cell-like.

THE AEGEAN

Altınkum
Göçtur Hotel ($$)

This 51-room modern hotel is a mile from the resort center and just 50 yards from Altınkum's famous sandy beach. It has a pleasant swimming pool, terrace, and Turkish bath.

Ayvalık
Cunda Hotel ($)

tel: 0266/327-1598 fax: 327-1943
This small hotel stands on the sandy beach of Alibey Island, connected to Ayvalık by a narrow spit and small bridge. The owner has his own jetty and boat for exploring the islands. There is also a simple restaurant.

Hotel Florium ($)

Alibey Island tel: 0266/312-9628
fax: 322-9631
At the end of the causeway linking Alibey Island to Ayvalik, this comfortable hotel makes a good base for visiting Troy and Pergamum.

Behramkale
Assos Behram Hotel ($)

Iskele tel: 0286/721-7017 fax: 721-7049
An attractive 36-room, stone-built hotel, the Assos Behram stands right on the harborfront. It has an indoor and outdoor restaurant, and watersports are available.

Assos Eden Beach

Kadirga Koyu tel: 0286/752-7039
fax: 757-2054
A 68-room hotel right on the beach, with watersports, children's playground, restaurants, and cafeteria.

Bodrum
Baraz Hotel ($)

Cumhuriyet 70 tel: 0252/316-1857
fax: 316-4430
This 24-room, air-conditioned family hotel lies on Bodrum's eastern bay. It has a good restaurant, with tables on the beach on balmy evenings.

Eldorador T.M.T. Holiday Village ($$)

tel: 0252/316-1232 fax: 316-2647
The well-designed vacation complex has 239 rooms and 32 villas on its private beach. It is a mile from Bodrum center, with two pools, watersports, and good children's facilities.

Manastir Hotel ($$)

Kumbahçe tel: 0252/316-2854
fax: 316-2772
Built on a hillside on the site of an old monastery, the hotel overlooks the harbor and castle. Its facilities include two restaurants, a pool with a children's section, a fitness center, and sauna.

Mandarin Pension ($)

Gümüşlük.
A *pansiyon* (inn) with 20 village-style rooms, the Mandarin is set in mandarin groves 12 miles west of Bodrum, just 30 miles from the sea. A simple beach bar serves light snacks, and the renowned Gümüşlük fish restaurants are nearby.

Myndos Hotel ($$)

tel: 0252/316-3080 fax: 316-5252
This 72-room hotel a mile from the center of Bodrum is attractively arranged around a pool with children's section. There are both indoor and outdoor restaurants, and tennis is available.

Çeşme
Marinisa Hotel ($)

Set on one of Çeşme's most beautiful sandy bays, a mile from the resort center, this simple hotel provides welcoming accommodations, a pool, restaurant, and bar.

Dalyan
Göl Hotel ($)

tel: 0252/284-2096
This pretty lakeside hotel, two minutes from Dalyan marina, has basic accommodations, a pool, restaurant, and bar. The Istuzu beach is 35 minutes away by water taxi.

Sultan Palace ($$)

Some 10 minutes upriver from Dalyan, this exceptional and traditional Turkish hotel is isolated on its own hillside, set in gardens by a large pool. It serves good food, and turtle beach is 40 minutes away by courtesy water taxi.

Efes—see Kuşadası

Foça
Club Méditerranée Foça Holiday Village
($$$)
tel: 0232/812-3691 fax: 812-2175
A 376-room vacation complex with superb
water-sports facilities, scuba diving, pool, and
Turkish bath.
Villa Dedem ($)
*Sahil Caddesi 66 tel: 0232/812-2838
fax: 812-1700*
A 20-room hotel set on the seafront, with a
restaurant on its top floor.

Izmir
Balçova Thermal Hotel ($$)
tel: 0232/259-0102 fax: 259-0829
This 196-room hotel 3 miles outside Izmir has two
thermal swimming pools and a fully equipped
medical rehabilitation center for rheumatic
disorders.
Büyük Efes Hotel ($$$)
tel: 0232/484-4300 fax: 441-5695
This luxury hotel, Izmir's oldest, stands in the city
center in its own gardens. It has two outdoor
pools and one indoor, five restaurants, and a
fitness center.
Kaya Hotel ($)
Çankaya tel: 0232/483-9771 fax: 483-9773
A modest 55-room hotel, with restaurant and
lobby bar, providing city-center accommodations.

Kuşadası
Club Kervanseray ($$)
tel: 0256/614-4115 fax: 614-2423
This converted Ottoman inn in the center of
Kuşadası has 40 rooms set around the lush
central courtyard where the restaurant is
situated. Rooms are decorated traditionally. It's
attractive, but noisy in season.
Kısmet Hotel ($$)
tel: 0256/614-2005 fax: 614-4914
Standing on its own small peninsula a mile from
the town, this exclusive hotel is set in subtropical
gardens. Many heads of state, attracted by its
secluded position, have stayed here. Excellent
international cuisine is served.
Nero Hotel ($)
*Güzelçamlı koyu tel: 0256/646-1795
fax: 646-1794*
This well-designed 53-room hotel has two
restaurants, a pool with children's section, and an
attractive poolside terrace.

Marmaris
Doğan Hotel ($)
Set on the Bay of Orhaniye, on the west coast of
the Bozburun peninsula, this secluded family-run
hotel sits on the beach with pretty gardens,
attractive restaurant, and Turkish bar. Boat trips
are available for those eager to explore the coastline.
Gökçe Hotel ($)
Lying off the beaten track on its own farmland,
this family-run hotel is a five-minute walk from
Turunç and its beach. It has an excellent
restaurant and a pool.

Grand Azur and Laguna Azur ($$$)
*tel: 0252/412-8201 fax: 412-3530 and
tel: 0252/455-3710 fax: 455-3622*
The Grand Azur is the most prestigious hotel in
Marmaris, overlooking a marina and beautiful
sandy beach, with lush tropical gardens and a
host of restaurants, bars, and shops. The Laguna
Azur, on a quiet beach with palm trees in Içmeler,
is its much smaller sister hotel, with just 64
rooms that are decorated in art-deco style.

Muğla
Hotel Grand Brothers ($)
tel: 0252/212-2700 fax: 212-2610
Muğla's best—with a pool, Turkish bath, and
sauna. It makes a good base for inland
exploration.

Pamukkale
The hotels that used to sit among the ruins have
been closed and knocked down to protect the
pools' environment.
Club Polat's Hotel ($$$)
tel: 0258/271-4111 fax: 271-4092
In the village of Karahayıt below Pamukkale, this
225-room hotel has thermal pools, indoor and
outdoor restaurants, and a tennis court.
Colossae Hotel Thermal ($$)
tel: 0258/271-4156 fax: 271-4251
The luxurious 230-room hotel sits in the center of
town. It has indoor/outdoor pools, 6 restaurants,
Turkish bath, sauna, and Jacuzzi.

Pergamum
Berksoy Hotel ($$)
tel: 0232/633-2595 fax: 633-5346
A pleasant 57-room hotel a mile from the center
of town, with one indoor and two outdoor restaurants, a swimming pool and children's pool, and a
playground.
Tusan Motel ($)
tel: 0232/633-1173 fax: 633-1938).
A 42-room hotel 5 miles from the archaeological
site, at the intersection with the main Çanakkale–
Izmir road, with a small but amusing Roman spa
pool for wallowing. There is a simple restaurant.

THE MEDITERRANEAN

Adana
Büyük Surmeli Hotel ($$$)
*Özler Caddesi tel: 0322/351-7321
fax: 351-8973*
This is probably the best hotel in Adana, ½ mile
from the city center, with a total of 166 rooms, a
pool, nightclub, and casino.
Raşit Ener Motel ($)
Yüregir tel: 0322/321-2758 fax: 321-2775
A fairly modest motel running to only 16 rooms,
with a simple restaurant, swimming pool with
children's section, and playground, in addition to
a campground and trailer park.

Alanya
Bedesten Hotel ($$)
tel: 0242/512-1234 fax: 513-7934
Set between the walls of Alanya's hilltop castle is

this converted Ottoman market with 20 rooms around a courtyard. Large pool.

Blue Sky Hotel ($)
tel: 0242/513-6487 fax: 512-4320
A pleasant 54-room establishment in the town center, the Bly Sky has a good-size pool and children's playground. Basic restaurant.

Club Alantur ($$$)
tel: 0242/518-1740 fax: 518-1756
Excellent for sporty types, Club Alantur is set on the beach 3 miles outside Alanya. Its facilities include one indoor and three outdoor pools, a gym, four tennis courts, miniature golf, and a very wide range of water sports, including scuba diving. It has a total of 365 rooms and 12 apartments, with four restaurants.

Anamur
Hermes Hotel ($$)
tel: 0324/814-3950 fax: 814-3995
On the beach, with 70 rooms, a pool and children's section, windsurfing, and two restaurants.

Antakya
Büyük Antakya Hotel ($$$)
Atatürk Caddesi tel: 0326/213-5860 fax: 213-5869
In a modern building in the city center with 72 rooms, nightclub, casino, and indoor and outdoor restaurants, this is Antakya's best. No pool.

272

Antalya
Argos Hotel ($$)
Kaleiçi tel: 0242/247-2012 fax: 241-7557
This attractively converted Ottoman house in the old quarter above the marina has 15 rooms, a pool, live music, and a restaurant.

Lara Hotel ($$)
Lara Yolu tel: 0242/323-1460 fax: 323-1449
Set on the cliff 5 miles outside Antalya, with an attractive pool terrace. There are two restaurants, and water sports from the beach below.

Marina ($$)
Kaleiçi tel: 0242/247-5490 fax: 241-1765
Set in private gardens of date palms and banana trees, this luxurious small establishment provides comfortable spacious rooms on split level and a restaurant with an excellent menu.

Tütav Türkevleri Hotels ($$)
Kaleiçi tel: 0242/248-6591 fax: 241-9419
Standing 300 yards from the old harbor within the walls of the old fort, this group of converted Ottoman wooden houses has 20 rooms, babysitting, a pool, indoor and outdoor restaurants, a sauna, and a choice of three cafeterias.

Villa Perla ($)
Kaleiçi tel: 0242/248-9793 fax: 241-2917
This charming family-run hotel in a converted Ottoman house has 16 rooms, private courtyard garden for outdoor eating, and small pool.

Eğridir
Eğridir Hotel ($$)
tel: 0246/311-4992 fax: 311-4219
The Eğridir provides modern facilities in the center of town. Some of the 51 rooms have balconies overlooking the lake. Restaurant terrace, but no pool.

Fethiye
Doruk Hotel ($)
Near Fethiye harbor tel: 0252/614-9860
This hotel is an attractive older-style building with 24 small, clean rooms, and a pool, disco, and restaurant.

Letoonia Holiday Village ($$)
tel: 0252/614-4966 fax: 614-4422
Set on its own peninsula 2 miles from the center of Fethiye, this 680-room, 110-villa complex is considered one of the loveliest vacation villages in the area. There are three sandy beaches, two swimming pools, three restaurants, three snack bars, and the full range of water sports, including scuba diving.

Mutlu Han Hotel ($)
Çalış Bay, 100 yards from the beach tel: 0252/622-1180
This 45-room hotel, set in open fields, provides simple, comfortable accommodations. Facilities include a pool and outdoor covered restaurant.

Hisarönü
Montana Hotel ($$)
tel: 0252/616-6366
The Montana, set on a hillside just a mile from Hisarönü and 1½ miles from Ölüdeniz, has stunning views. There are traditional-style, landscaped gardens, a pool, a restaurant, and air-conditioned rooms.

Kale
Kale Pansiyon ($)
A delightful family-run inn with 7 rooms (some with shower), opposite the island of Kekova. Shady terrace and veranda. Good cuisine. Speedboat and rowboat for rent. Very simple.

Kalkan
Club Xanthos ($$)
tel: 0242/844-2388 fax: 844-2355
An elegant and stylish place, Club Xanthos has 70 grand rooms, a Turkish bath and sauna, and seawater pool. Follow path to a beach for diving and sunbathing 160 yards.

Dionysia Diva Hotel ($)
Cumhuriyet Caddesi tel: 0242/844-3681 fax: 844-3139
Two attractive small hotels, both with stunning sea views and excellent roof terraces for bars and breakfast. Kalkan center is just a five-minute walk away.

Patara Prince Hotel ($$)
P.K. 10 tel: 0242/844-3338 fax: 844-3337
An immaculately designed establishment with 54 rooms standing within the Club Patara, an ambitious re-creation of a Roman town, complete with triumphal arch, forum, and fountains. There is a magnificent balustraded terrace with large pool. Excellent cuisine in four restaurants. A free water taxi takes you across to Kalkan marina, 10 minutes away.

Pension Patara ($)
tel: 0242/844-3076
Close to the town's shingle beach and tea garden, this pretty inn has 10 rooms overlooking the harbor, and an attractive roof terrace on which guests are served breakfast by the family.

Kaş

Aqua-Park Hotel ($$$)
tel: 0242/836-1901 fax: 836-1906
This luxurious and exclusive complex of villas and chalet-style rooms spread over the Kaş peninsula is very well equipped for water sports, with scuba diving, three swimming pools, and two water slides. It has 116 rooms and 24 apartments. There is a free bus link to Kaş town center, 3 miles away.

Club Antiphellos ($$)
Çukurbağ Peninsula tel: 0242/836-2651 fax: 836-2654
An attractive hotel with 16 rooms and a pretty pool and terrace, set on an isolated peninsula with access to a rocky beach. It offers water sports and a volleyball court and has indoor and outdoor restaurants.

Me & Di Hotel ($$)
tel: 0242/836-1914 fax: 836-1426
Set up on a hillside above the Kaş–Kalkan road, this exclusive 17-room establishment has villa-style rooms each with its own terrace, a lovely pool in a private courtyard, pretty gardens, and good restaurant. Service is excellent.

Melisa Pension ($)
A family inn on a quiet street near Kaş harbor, with 16 good-size rooms and breakfast on the rooftop terrace. No pool or restaurant.

Kemer

Antalya Renaissance ($$$)
tel: 0242/824-8431 fax: 824-8430
A modern hotel in a delightful setting in the resort of Beldibi, between Kemer and Antalya, the Antalya has an excellent range of facilities including a private beach, large outdoor and indoor pools, tennis courts, fitness center, Turkish bath and sauna. A range of restaurants and shops make it virtually a self-contained resort.

Beltaş Hotel ($$)
Beldibi tel: 0242/824-8192 fax: 824-8344
A well-designed 75-room hotel set in lush gardens with private beach, water sports, pool with children's section, playground, and tennis court. Indoor and outdoor restaurants.

Princess Orange ($$)
Tekirova tel: 0242/821-4059 fax: 821-4069
A pretty 48-room hotel set around a pool in Tekirova center, with a cafeteria and outdoor restaurant.

Kızkalesi

Club Hotel Barbarossa ($$)
tel: 0324/523-2364 fax: 523-2090
This comfortable, pleasantly designed hotel with 103 rooms is set on a private beach 15 miles from Silifke, with views across to Kızkalesi. There is a good pool, water sports, disco, indoor and outdoor restaurants.

Mersin

Mersin Hilton ($$$)
A. Menderes Bulvarı tel: 0324/326-5000 fax: 326-5050
Modern five-star building on the waterfront by the docks, with 188 rooms, pool, health bar, tennis courts, gym, disco, casino, and two restaurants.

Ölüdeniz

Meri Motel ($$)
tel: 0252/616-6060 fax: 616-6456
The best-placed hotel in Ölüdeniz, right on the lagoon, with 75 rooms climbing up a steep hillside. A private beach ensures total tranquility, and an elevator is provided from beach to rooms. The Meri has a lovely terrace restaurant with live music, a pool, windsurfing, and playground.

Patara

Xanthos Hotel ($$)
tel: 0242/843-5015
Set in beautiful sprawling gardens arranged around a large pool, this attractive hotel has 18 rooms, a lovely terrace and bar area, a tennis court, and a simple restaurant.

Side

Bella Sun Hotel ($$)
½ mile from center. tel: 0242/753-5108 fax: 753-5105
Just 100 yards from beach, this well-positioned place has 31 good-size rooms, two restaurants—one indoors, one outdoors—and a pool.

Kleopatra Hotel ($)
tel: 0242/753-1033 fax: 753-3738
Pleasant accommodations in a town-center hotel with its own private beach and a pretty garden. There are 42 rooms with shower and a restaurant.

Turquoise Hotel ($$$)
tel: 0242/756-9330 fax: 756-9345
A luxury complex 2 miles from the resort center, in a peaceful beach and forest setting. Facilities include a huge pool, gym, water sports, tennis courts, children's pool, and nursery.

Silifke

Altınorfoz Hotel ($$)
Susanoğlu tel: 0324/722-4211 fax: 722-4215
This beach complex, 10½ miles from Silifke, provides water sports, a pool with a children's section, Turkish bath, nightclub and casino, indoor and outdoor restaurants.

Lades Motel ($)
Taşucu, 6 miles from Silifke tel: 0324/741-4008 fax: 741-4258
A 21-room hotel set on a private beach, with a pool and an attractive restaurant and bar.

CAPPADOCIA

Avanos

Altınyazı ($$)
Zelve–Göreme road tel: 0384/511-2010 fax: 511-4960
The Altınyazı's accommodations are plush, with 84 elegant, traditionally decorated rooms. Turkish bath, disco, restaurant, and babysitting. No pool.

Sofa Hotel ($)
Avanos center tel: 0384/511-5186 fax: 511-4489
A well-restored group of old stone houses, with 34 rooms partly built into the rock, like troglodyte dwellings. Facilities include a garden and indoor and outdoor restaurants.

273

Accommodations & Restaurants

Göreme
Ataman Hotel ($$)
tel: 0384/271-2310 fax: 271-2313
A well-renovated, traditional stone house in the town center, with 33 rooms, three indoor restaurants and a terrace restaurant, indoor and outdoor pools, Turkish bath, gym, and tennis.

Güzelyart/Aksaray
Karballa Hotel
tel: 0382/451-2103 fax: 451-2107
This elegantly restored convent has 20 centrally heated rooms—a necessity in the Cappadocian winter. It has an indoor/outdoor restaurant, garden, and pool. Horseback riding is available nearby.

Ortahisar
Burcu Hotel ($$)
tel: 0384/343-3800 fax: 343-3500
A converted caravansary surrounded by 49 rooms, indoor and outdoor restaurants. Swimming pool.

Üçhisar
Kaya Club Méditerranée Hotel ($$)
tel: 0384/219-2007 fax: 219-2363
This spectacular 70-room hotel set up on the rock has superb views. Facilities include a pool terrace, restaurant, nightclub, and children's pool.

Ürgüp
Alfina Hotel ($)
Istiklal Caddesi tel: 0384/341-4822 fax: 341-2424
An imaginatively designed place, cut into the rock in terraces, with 32 rooms (each with terrace), disco, indoor and outdoor restaurant, and occasional Turkish show.

Esbelli House ($$)
tel: 0384/341-3395 fax: 341-8848
An exclusive 6-room hotel set in a converted fortified caravansary. The original rooms are cut out of the rock and are simply furnished in traditional style. Breakfast only.

Perissia Hotel ($$)
Kayseri Caddesi tel: 0384/341-2930 fax: 341-2524
A modern hotel with 230 rooms, large pool with children's section, three indoor restaurants and one outdoor, disco, nightclub, and tennis courts.

CENTRAL ANATOLIA

Amasya
Ilk House ($$)
tel: 0378/218-1689 fax: 218-6277
Set right in the center of Amasya in a 200-year-old Ottoman house with authentic decor, complete with dowry chests and carved wood ceilings. Basement dining room and courtyard garden for breakfast. Views across the river. 5 rooms.

Boğazkale
Hitit Motel ($)
Sungurlu tel: 0364/311-1042
An unpretentious overnight stop. Buses touring the Hittite sites often stop for quick meals in its excellent restaurant.

Ankara
King Hotel ($)
tel: 0312/418-9099 fax: 417-0382
An attractive smaller hotel in the city center, with 36 rooms. Facilities include two restaurants, a pool, garden, and sauna.

Mega Residence Hotel ($$)
tel: 0312/468-5400 fax: 468-5415
This old-style, well-located city-center establishment has been converted from an Ottoman house (and as such is one of Ankara's few special-category hotels). The 29 rooms are air-conditioned and well furnished.

Sheraton Ankara Hotel and Towers ($$$)
Kavaklıdere tel: 0312/468-5454 fax: 467-1136
This is Ankara's best hotel, in the city center; 311 rooms, pool, health club and Jacuzzi, plus three indoor restaurants and one outdoors.

Konya
Başak Palas ($)
Hükümet Meydanı tel: 0332/351-1338 fax: 351-1339
Basic accommodations in the city center. The Başak has 39 rooms; breakfast hall and snack bar only.

Dergah Hotel ($$)
Mevlana Caddesi tel: 0332/351-1197 fax: 351-0116
This is a central 82-room hotel. Facilities include a restaurant, bar, and sauna.

Hüma Hotel ($$)
Aladdin Bulvarı tel: 0332/350-6618 fax: 351-0244
Centrally located traditional-style building with 30 rooms, restaurant, and disco.

Kütahya
Erbaylar Hotel ($$)
Afyon Caddesi tel: 0274/223-6960 fax: 216-1046
This modern hotel has 42 rooms, a restaurant and bar.

Tokat
Büyük Tokat Hotel ($$)
tel: 0356/228-1661 fax: 228-1660
A 60-room hotel in a central location, with a swimming pool, sports facilities, restaurant, and bar. It's quite a surprise to find a place like this in a place like Tokat.

EASTERN TURKEY

Artvin
Karahan Hotel ($)
tel: 0446/212-1802 fax: 212-2420
This 57-room hotel has neat rooms and a good restaurant with fine views from its terrace.

Diyarbakır
Demir Hotel ($$)
Izzet Pasa Caddesi tel: 0412/221-2315 fax: 222-4300
With 58 rooms, a pool, and a good restaurant and bar, the Demir is the best place to stay in Diyarbakır.

Kervansaray Hotel ($$)
tel: 0412/228-9606 fax: 223-7731
A renovated 17th-century Deliller Hanı, with court-yard garden and restaurant.

Doğubeyazıt
Hotel Nuh ($)
tel: 0472/312-7232 fax: 312-6910
There are views of Mount Ararat and Ishak Pasa Sarayi from the terrace. Private parking.

Elazığ
Büyük Elazığ Hotel ($)
tel: 0424/212-2001 fax: 238-1899
This modern 100-room hotel in the center is used by business people and has a functional restaurant and bar.

Erzurum
Diluver Hotel ($$)
tel: 0442/235-0068 fax: 218-1148
Providing luxurious accommodations for this part of Turkey. There are also excellent views from top-floor restaurant.
Oral Hotel ($$)
tel: 0442/218-9740 fax: 218-9749
A 90-room modern hotel, with busy dining room and bar used by tour groups.

Kars
Karabağ Hotel ($)
tel: 0474/212-2585 fax: 223-3089
Best in the area, this town center establishment is rivaled only by the out-of-town Anihan Motel.

Malatya
Büyük Malatya Hotel ($)
Yeni Cami Karşişi tel: 0422/321-4000 fax: 321-5367
A simple 52-room hotel providing bed and breakfast only.

Mardin
Denktaş Turistik Tesisleri ($$)
Derik tel: 0482/212-1508
This 44-room hotel with a swimming pool, restaurant, and bar provides the best accommodations in the area.

Nemrut Dağı
Bozdğan Hotel ($$)
Adıyaman tel: 0416/216-3999 fax: 216-3630
This modern 74-room hotel in the center of Adıyaman has a pool with children's section, restaurant, and two bars.
Euphrat Hotel ($)
tel: 0416/737-2175 fax: 737-2179
A 30-room establishment providing simple lodgings, 6 miles from the summit of Nemrut Dağı. Dinner is included.

Şanlıurfa
Harran Hotel ($$)
Atatürk Bulvarı tel: 0414/313-4743
A modern faceless building in the city center with 63 rooms, the best in Urfa, with indoor and outdoor restaurants, pool, and Turkish bath.

Van
Akdamar Hotel ($$)
tel: 0432/216-8100 fax: 212-0868
An older 69-room hotel with an attractive top-floor restaurant and good service.
Büyük Urartu ($$)
Cumhuriyet Caddesi tel: 0432/212-0660 fax: 212-1610
The newest hotel in Van, three-star, 75 rooms, two restaurants, two bars, and a disco.

THE BLACK SEA

Bolu
Abant Palace Hotel ($$$)
tel: 0374/224-5012 fax: 224-5011
Set on the shores of Lake Abant, this hotel is much used by Ankara residents on weekends. It has an indoor pool, restaurant with lake view, nightclub, bars, tennis, and children's playground.

Düzce
Çobantur Hotel ($$)
tel: 0374/514-1132
A comfortable 43-room hotel with restaurant and bar.

Kilyos
Kilyos Kale Hotel ($)
Kale Caddesi tel: 0212/201-1818 fax: 201-1823
This 36-room hotel, set on cliff top, has a pretty terrace restaurant.

Ordu
Belde Hotel ($$)
tel: 0452/214-3987 fax: 214-9398
Set on its own spit of land half a mile outside Ordu, Belde has a large pool, Turkish bath, sauna, gym, nightclub, disco, and restaurants.

Safranbolu
Havuzlu Konak ($$)
tel: 0372/712-2883 fax: 712-3824
This immaculately restored Ottoman mansion in the city center has 11 rooms, two indoor restaurants and one outdoors.

Samsun
Yafeya Hotel ($$)
Cumhuriyet Meydanı tel: 0362/435-1131 fax: 435-1135
A 96-room modern hotel in the city center with two restaurants and a café.

Şile
Değirmen Hotel ($)
Plaj Yolu tel: 0216/711-5048 fax: 711-5248
A beach hotel in the resort center, with 76 rooms, disco, restaurant, and a jazz bar.

Sinop
Diyojen Hotel ($)
tel: 0368/261-8822 fax: 260-1425
An attractive modern hotel, about a mile from Sinop with 33 rooms, a pool, and simple indoor/outdoor restaurant.

275

Trabzon

Usta Hotel ($$)
Iskele Caddesi *tel: 0462/321-2195*
fax: 322-3793
Central 76-room hotel with a restaurant and bar.

Zorlu Grand Hotel ($$)
tel: 0462/326-8400 fax: 326-8458
Exceptionally stylish for this part of Turkey, this 160-room hotel has an indoor pool, Turkish bath, sauna, Jacuzzi, and two restaurants.

RESTAURANTS

Prices are per person without alcohol:
$$$ = over $10
$$ = $5–$10
$ = under $5

ISTANBUL

Grand hotels

All the grand hotels have superb, if very expensive, restaurants offering a range of international and Turkish cuisine. Those worth singling out are the **Çırağan Restaurant** for seafood, the **Dynasty** in the Merit Antique for Chinese food, **Miyako** in the Swissôtel for Japanese food, **Monteverdi** in the Conrad for classy Italian food, and the restaurants of the new **Four Seasons Hotel**.

The Old City

Asitane ($$)
Kariye Hotel, Edirnekapı tel: 0212/534-8414
Unusual Ottoman cuisine beautifully presented in a tranquil courtyard garden accompanied by classical Turkish music.

Borsa ($$)
Sirkeci, opposite the train station
tel: 0212/511-8079
Rated now as one of the best Turkish restaurants in Istanbul, though it is nothing to look at from the outside, Borsa serves many rare Turkish dishes. Open lunchtime only. Very popular with business people.

Darüzziyafe ($$)
in the Süleymaniye mosque complex
tel: 0212/511-8414
In the courtyard of the original *imaret* (soup kitchen), this unusual restaurant serves authentic Ottoman cuisine. No alcohol is served. This is a popular choice with tour groups.

Hamdi Et Lokantası ($)
Kalçın Sokak, Eminönü tel: 0212/528-0390
An unpretentious lunchtime-only restaurant that is good for simple grilled meat dishes. No alcohol is served. Closed Sundays.

Havuzlu Lokanta ($$)
Grand Bazaar tel: 0212/527-3346
The snazziest place in the bazaar, this is a safe bet for a lunch or coffee break. Food is simple Turkish fare.

Hünkar ($$)
Perçin Sokak, Fatih tel: 0212/523-7561
A friendly place serving an excellent selection of classic Turkish dishes. No credit cards.

Kathisma ($)
Yeni Akbıyık Caddesi, Sultanahmet
tel: 0212/518-9710
Turkish and international cuisine served in a traditionally decorated dining room, with tables on three floors and a terrace.

Konyalı ($$)
Topkapı Palace tel: 0212/513-9696
In the fourth court of the Topkapı itself, this restaurant serves good Turkish food and provides excellent views over the Bosphorus. Arrive early for lunch to beat the tour groups.

Pandeli ($$)
Spice Bazaar, Eminönü tel: 0212/527-3909
This splendid traditional restaurant, above the entrance to the Spice Bazaar, is decorated from floor to ceiling in Turkish tiles. It serves excellent Turkish cuisine, but is open for lunch only, and is closed Sundays.

Rami ($$)
Utangaç Sokak, Sultanahmet
tel: 0212/517-6593
Next to the Blue Mosque in a restored Ottoman building, with good Turkish cuisine, candlelight, and classical music.

Sarnıç ($$$)
Soğukçeşme Sokak, Sultanahmet
tel: 0212/512-4291
A converted Roman cistern, between the Topkapı and Aya Sofya, remarkable for its architecture rather than its cuisine. Closed Mondays.

Sedir ($$)
Telliodalar Sokak, Kumkapı
tel: 0212/517-0264
A good choice for seafood in this quarter bursting with fish restaurants.

Subası ($)
Nuruosmaniye Caddesi, Cağaloğlu
A simple informal restaurant near the Nuruosmaniye gate of the Grand Bazaar, with only 10 tables, where delicious home-cooked Turkish food is served.

Sultanahmet Köftecisi ($)
Divanyolu Caddesi, Sultanahmet
tel: 0212/526-2782
On the corner of Aya Sofya square near the Yerebatan Saray, this place is famous for its meatballs and is always busy. No alcohol is served. Also does takeout.

Sultan Pub ($$)
Divanyolu Caddesi, Sultanahmet
tel: 0212/526-6347
One of the classier places around Aya Sofya the Sultan has European and Turkish food on the menu.

Ümit Restaurant ($)
Nuruosmaniye tel: 0212/512-9094
This clean attractive *lokanta*, set in the cellar of an antique inn beside the Grand Bazaar, opens lunchtime only. It serves traditional Turkish food. No credit cards. No alcohol.

Yeşil Ev ($$$)
Sultanahmet tel: 0212/517-6786
Between Aya Sofya and the Blue Mosque, Yeşil Ev has a lovely courtyard setting away from the bustle of the streets. Good quality, though slightly overpriced, European and Turkish food is served here.

Beyoğlu and the Bosphorus

Ali Baba ($$)
Kireçburnu Caddesi, Kireçburnu
tel: 0212/262-0889
This simple *lokanta* serving good fish and *meze* (appetizers) in a garden beside the Bosphorus is a popular place for Sunday brunch.

Anadolu Kavağı ($)
This northernmost village on the Asian side of the Bosphorus is full of simple and colorful fish *lokantas.*

Asır ($$)
Beyoğlu next to the police station
tel: 0212/250-0557
A popular Greek restaurant serving an excellent selection of *meze* (appetizers) and fish dishes. Beware—it can get very smoky.

Baca ($$$)
Emirğan Yolu, Boyacıköy tel: 0212/277-0808
A fashionable restaurant with international cuisine, live music, disco, and a terrace with a spectacular view of the Fatih Sultan Mehmet bridge. Reached via a long steep flight of steps.

Café de Paris ($$)
Min Kemal Öke Caddesi 19/1, Nişantaşı
tel: 0212/225-0700
A fixed menu of steak, french fries, and salad is on offer in this crowded Parisian-style café. Closed Sunday lunch.

Café de Pera ($$)
Fuat Uzkınay Sokak 17/2, Beyoğlu
tel: 0212/249-9598
Open 11:30 AM to midnight, this café is a popular eating place after the movies. Try the excellent crêpes.

Çamlıca Café ($$)
Şefa Tepesi, Çamlıca tel: 0212/329-8191
Typical Turkish dishes and classical Turkish music served up in restored Ottoman pavilions set on Istanbul's highest hill with superb skyline views.

Çiçek Pasajı ($)
Istiklal Caddesi, Beyoğlu.
A collection of noisy and atmospheric small restaurants serving *meze* (appetizers) and meat dishes in the old flower market. No credit cards. A bit overpriced.

Çiftnal ($$)
Yenimahalle, Ihlamur Yolu 6, Beşiktaş
tel: 0212/261-3129
Set in a 19th-century police station, this restaurant offers grilled Turkish dishes and is open from noon to midnight.

Deniz Park Gazinosu ($$)
Daire Sokak 9, Yeniköy tel: 0212/262-0415
With a wonderful terrace offering Bosphorus views, this long-established fish restaurant is owned by a Greek family.

Ece ($$$)
Kamacı Sokak 10, Arnavutköy
tel: 0212/265-9600
Open from 6 PM until dawn, this old Greek house offers *meze* on the first floor, a pop music bar on the second floor, and an excellent à la carte restaurant on the top floor.

Façyo ($$)
Kireçburnu Caddesi, Tarabya
tel: 0212/262-0024
This is the best fish restaurant in Tarabya, the Bosphorus suburb famous for its nightlife and seashore restaurants.

Four Seasons ($$)
Istiklal Caddesi, Tünel tel: 0212/293-3941
Handy for the movie theaters, this smallish restaurant has cultivated a European atmosphere and serves good food.

Galata Tower ($$$)
Kuledibi tel: 0212/245-1160
Indifferent food accompanied by Turkish music and belly-dancing, but the location is superb and so are the views. Reservations are required.

Hacı Abdullah ($)
Istiklal Caddesi tel: 0212/293-8561
This simple, tasteful hotel has been established for over a century. It serves excellent Turkish and Ottoman cuisine (no alcohol).

Hacıbaba ($$)
Istiklal Caddesi, Beyoğlu
tel: 0212/244-1886
A pleasant *lokanta* with a balcony overlooking the courtyard of a Greek church.

Han ($$$)
Rumeli Hisarı tel: 0212/265-2968
A good fish restaurant with a terrace overlooking the Bosphorus.

Hidiv Kasrı (the Khedive's Summer Palace) ($$)
Çubuklu tel: 0216/331-2651
Splendid restored palace in art deco style overlooking the Bosphorus from the Asian side. Turkish cuisine with live music.

Huzur (Arabin Yeri) ($$)
Üsküdar tel: 0216/333-3157
This long-established, unpretentious fish restaurant has amazing sunset views of the Asian side of the Istanbul skyline.

Kadife Chalet ($$)
Kadife Sokak 29, Bahariye, Kadıköy
tel: 0212/437-8596
Open 10 AM till 10 PM, this pretty restaurant with period decor is set in an Ottoman house and offers Ottoman and international dishes.

Kamil ($)
Gümüşsuyu Yolu 9/1, Beykoz
tel: 0216/331-0594
A good, small fish restaurant with a unique atmosphere on the Asian side of the Bosphorus, selling interesting *meze* (appetizers).

Kız Kulesi Deniz Restaurant ($$)
Salacak Sakil Yolu, Üsküdar
tel: 0216/341-0403
Excellent views toward the old city from Üsküdar across the Bosphorus, with delicious seafood.

Körfez ($$$)
Kanlıca tel: 0216/413-4314
The clientele of this chic fish restaurant on the Bosphorus are picked up by the restaurant's private boat from Rumeli Hisarı.

Liman Lokantası ($$)
Karaköy tel: 0212/244-1033
Located above the Turkish Maritime Lines' waiting room, this old classic has good views and excellent food. Lunch only, Monday to Friday.

Rejans ($$)
Beyoğlu tel: 0212/244-1610
Istanbul's classic Russian restaurant, now a bit shabby, stands opposite San Antonio's church.

277

Accommodations & Restaurants

Süreyya ($$$)
Istinye Caddesi, Istinye tel: 0212/277-5886
This is one of Istanbul's gastronomic landmarks, serving superb Russian, Turkish, and European cuisine. Reservations required. Closed Sundays.

Ziya ($$$)
Ortaköy tel: 0212/261-6005
Under the Bosphorus Bridge, this restaurant serves Turkish and international cuisine with a fabulous view and tables outdoors in the summer.

ISTANBUL ENVIRONS

Bursa
Hünkar Doner Kebab House ($)
The best of the well-located group of restaurants looking out over the quiet cobbled square of the Yeşil Cami.

Büyükada
Büyükada ($)
A simple café on the summit of the hill by the Monastery of Saint George, offering a lunch of cheese, olives, and red wine. A long steep path leads up to it from the middle of town.

Edirne
Many fish restaurants line the promenade, with simple kabob houses in the little town square.
Balta Restaurant ($$)
tel: 0284/225-5210
The best restaurant in town, in the Balta Hotel.

THE AEGEAN

Afrodisias
Near the village of Dandalaz, 2 miles before the site, is a cluster of riverside restaurants offering fresh trout.

Ayvalık
The best restaurants in this region are on Ali Bey island just opposite Ayvalık, notably **Artur Restaurant** ($$) (tel: 0266/327-1014) and **Günay Restaurant** ($$) (tel: 0266/663-71048) On the road west of Ayvalık, beyond Çanlık, the **Şeytan Sofrası (Devil's Dining Table) Restaurant** ($) has unremarkable food but a spectacular setting overlooking the Gulf of Edremit. Farther afield, near Altınoluk on the north of the Gulf of Edremit, the remarkable **Chalet Chopin** (Değirmen) ($$) (tel: 0266/396-1313 fax: 396-1370) has delicious Turkish food with live music in a beautiful garden.

Bodrum
Alp Kaptan ($$)
Dr. Mümtaz Ataman Caddesi tel: 0252/316-8686
Traditional European and Turkish favorites and the occasional sophisticated special dish are available here.
Kocadon Restaurant ($$)
Neyzen Terfik Caddesi tel: 0252/316-3705
This popular place, set in a romantic courtyard enclosed by stone houses, serves good Turkish cuisine. Reservations required.

Çeşme
Sahil Restaurant ($$)
Cumhuriyet Meydanı tel: 0232/712-6646
Long-established and typical of Çeşme, the Sahil Restaurant faces the sea. Relax at its outdoor tables and enjoy some of the best fish dishes in town.

Dalyan
Beyazgül ($$)
tel: 0252/284-2304
Freshwater fish is the specialty in Dalyan, and Beyazgül is notable among the many restaurants along the riverbank.
Denizatı ($)
tel: 0252/284-2634
A riverside establishment, a little out of town, serving fresh fish and seafood and an excellent selection of *meze*.

Efes (Ephesus)
Beside the Isa Bey Mosque and again by the Cave of the Seven Sleepers are simple traditional restaurants serving snacks like *gözleme* (filled pancakes) and *ayran* (chilled yogurt drink). **Bahçesaray Restaurant** ($) at Meryemana Kavsağı (tel: 0232/892-3486) is a good choice.

Foça
Ali Baba ($$)
Büyükdeniz Sahil Caddesi tel: 0232/812-1173
A popular choice among the many fish restaurants along Foça's harborfront. The **Bedesten** ($) (tel: 0232/812-2517) and the **Palmiye** ($$) are also worth investigating.

Izmir
Altınkapı Restoran ($$)
1444 Sokak, Alsancak tel: 0232/422-2709
A favorite in arty circles, the Altınkapı serves good food.
Deniz Restoran ($$)
Atatürk Caddesi, Kordon tel: 0232/422-0601
The best place in town to eat fish, the Deniz is popular with Izmir's business community. The menu includes imaginative *meze* (appetizers) and unbeatable squid. The outdoor tables are in demand—reservations are essential.
1888 Restaurant ($$$)
Cumhuriyet Bulvarı, Alsancak tel: 0232/421-6690
Delicious Mediterranean specialties, notably some fine Jewish dishes. Live music on weekends.
Kemal' Usta ($$)
1453 Sokak, Alsancak tel: 0232/422-3190
This is a good choice for moderately priced seafood. Enjoy a relaxed meal and friendly service at one of the outdoor tables.
Liman Restoran ($$)
Atatürk Caddesi, Kordon tel: 0232/422-1876
Good seafood restaurant on the waterfront.
Mask ($$$)
1453 Sokak, Alsancak tel: 0232/463-0425
An expensive restaurant with elegant decor, dancing, and international cuisine.
Palet Restoran ($$$)
Atatürk Caddesi, Kordon tel: 0232/425-0440
A popular, floating restaurant serving fish.

Park Restoran ($$$)
Kültürpark İçi tel: 0232/489-3590
Another plush, expensive restaurant, this one is also floating. It offers good international cuisine with French leanings.

Vejetaryen Lokantası ($)
1375 Sokak, Alsancak tel: 0232/421-7558
Simple vegetarian dishes are served in this small place—the only vegetarian restaurant in Izmir.

Kuşadası
Sultan Han Restoran ($$)
Bahar Sokak 8 tel: 0256/614-6380 or 614-3849
Set in a large renovated caravansary in the old part of town, the Sultan Han has a traditional feel. Turkish dishes are the best choice on the wide-ranging menu: the *meze* are excellent. Belly dancers occasionaly provide live entertainment.

Marmaris
Alba ($$$)
Kaleici 30, Sokak 10 tel: 0252/412-4299
A relatively small, exclusive restaurant on a hill-top, which has gained a good reputation for its European-style cuisine.

Begonia ($$)
Haci Mustaf Sokak 101 tel: 0252/412-4095
A small new hotel on 'Bar Street' serving Turkish and international specialties.

Mona Titti ($$)
Atatürk Caddesi tel:0252/412-8799
The brightly colored exterior is easy to spot on the waterfront. The menu is imaginative and the curries are some of the best you are likely to enjoy on the coast.

Pamukkale
Kervansaray Hotel ($$)
İnönu Caddesi, Pamukkale Köyü
tel: 0258/272-2209 fax: 272-2143
The rooftop restaurant of the hotel serves good food. The **Gürsöy** (tel: 0258/272-2218) and **Mustafa** (tel: 0258/272-2240) restaurants are also worth a try.

Pergamum
Asklepieion Restaurant ($)
Izmir Caddesi 54 tel: 0232/633-1050
This is one of the best places to eat in the town of Bergama.

Berksoy Restaurant ($$)
Izmir Yolu tel: 0232/633-2595
Good food from the restaurant of the hotel of the same name.

THE MEDITERRANEAN

Adana
Ağacpınar Tesisleri ($)
Ceyhan-Adana Eski Karayolu. Ağacpınar Koyu
tel: 0322/321-9166
Good restaurant sited 6 miles outside town on the Ceyhan road.

Gözde Restaurant ($$)
Çifte Minare Camii Yanı tel: 0322/453-5501
Pleasant food by the Çifte Minare mosque.

Alanya
From the huge range and selection all along the main road and the seafront, the **Canus** ($) (tel: 0242/513-2694), the **Halimağa Konağı** ($$) (tel: 0242/512-1362), the **Mola** ($) (tel: 0242/513 3021), and the **Yakamoz** ($$) (tel: 0242/512-2303 are among the best.

Antakya
Didem Turistik Tesisleri ($)
Reyhanli Yolu Uzeri
tel: 0326/212-1928
A good range of Turkish dishes is on offer here.

Saray Restaurant ($$)
Atatürk Bulvarı 57
tel: 0326/617-1383
The best place in the city center, with Turkish specialties.

Antalya
The best restaurants tend to be found in the old quarter situated around the renovated marina area. Among the most notable here are **A La Turca** ($$), **Hisar** ($$), **Kral Sofrası** ($), **Orkinos** ($), and **Yat Restaurant** ($$).

La Trattoria ($$)
Fevzi Gakmak Caddesi 3/C
tel: 0242/243-3931
La Trattoria, run by a Turkish man and his English wife, serves very good European food in a bistro-style setting.

Burdur
Akçeşme Dinlenme Tesisleri—Salda Gölü ($) *tel: 0248/631-3488*
On the Burdur–Denizli road by Lake Salda, 2½ miles from Yeşilova, this is a good place to stop for lunch.

Eğridir
Derya Restaurant ($)
Sahil Yotu 2
Opposite Hotel Eğridir with tables on the lakeshore, the Derya serves fish dishes and a good selection of *meze*.

Fethiye
Rafet Restaurant ($$)
Kordon Boyu tel: 0252/614-1106
This long-established fish restaurant on Fethiye's harbor promenade is one of the best places to eat in town. It is a great place to spend warm evenings in summer.

Finike
Petek Restaurant ($)
Mahmut Nedim Kunt tel: 0242/855-1782
This is an attractive, friendly place in the village center, which serves good traditional Turkish food, and has views over the harbor.

Kale/Demre
Güneyhan Restaurant ($)
Saint Nicolas Kilisesi Yani
tel: 0242/871-3810
A pleasant place with an outdoor terrace that serves simple food. It is well placed beside Saint Nicholas' church.

279

Accommodations & Restaurants

Kalkan

Korsan ($$)
Yaliboyu Mah tel: 0242/844-3622
This pleasant harborfront establishment serves
excellent kabobs, salads, and seafood.

Kalkan Han ($$)
Kalkan tel: 0242/844-3151
The modestly priced food is served on a pleasant
outdoor terrace.

Kaş

Mercan Restaurant ($$)
Çarşı İçi, Liman Başı tel: 0242/836-1209
On a prime harborfront site and with a large outdoor terrace, Mercan is a popular choice. The food
is good, but be prepared to pay a little extra for
the location.

Kemer

Most of the best of the many restaurants in
Kemer are found around the yachting marina,
notably the **Arsemia** ($$) (tel: 0242/814-3376),
the **Ayısığı Tesisleri** ($) (tel: 0242/814-3250),
the **Duppont** ($$) (tel: 0242/814-1902), and the
Yörük Parkı Restaurant ($$) (tel: 0242/814-
1777).

Kızkalesi

Most of the best restaurants in this and the
Silifke area are in Narlıkuyu, the village by the
caves known as Cennet Cehennem (Heaven and
Hell).
Look in particular for the **Deniz** ($), the **Çınaraltı**
($$), and the **Lagos** ($).

Mersin

Ali Baba 1 Restaurant ($$)
Uluçarşı Otopark Girişi Karşisi
tel: 0324/223-3088
This ia a convenient place to eat after shopping by
the main parking lot entrance.

Ali Baba-Kordon Restaurant ($$)
The best place to eat in Mersin, near the Hilton
Hotel.

Ölüdeniz

Beyaz Yunus Restaurant ($$$)
Belcekiz, near Padirali tel: 0252/616-6036
Of the places to eat on the lagoon and beach, this
is the best. Turkish and international food is
served in cool surroundings, with excellent sea
views.

Side

Toros Restaurant ($$)
Liman Caddesi tel: 0242/753-2005
In a good position in front of the old harbor, the
Toros serves good Turkish food .

CAPPADOCIA

Avanos

Tuvanna ($$)
Kenan Evren Caddesi tel: 0384/511-2300
One of the most popular of the many restaurants
along the riverbank, the Tuvanna serves a
selection of traditional Turkish dishes.

Göreme

Mehmet Paşa ($$)
Konak Türk Evi tel: 0384/271-2463
A splendid place to eat, the Mehmet is housed in
a converted Ottoman mansion and has a pleasant
outdoor terrace. Turkish and international dishes
are served.

Ataman ($$)
Orta Mah Mevkii tel: 0384/271-2310
fax: 271-2313
The Ataman, built in a traditional style, provides
good food and service in pleasant surroundings.

Kaymaklı

Erciyes Restaurant ($)
no phone
A new restaurant beside the underground city,
offering simple Turkish food.

Kayseri

The town has a handful of acceptable restaurants:
the **Beyaz Saray** ($$) on Millet Caddesi (tel:
0352/336-9106), the **Ekol Turistik Tesisleri** ($)
on Sival Caddesi (tel: 0352/233-3131), and the
Yıldız ($$) on Kumarlı Mevkii (tel: 0352/231-
1531) are the best.

Ortahisar

Kaya Restaurant ($$)
Ulus Meydanı tel: 0384/343-3100)
The Kaya serves traditional Turkish cuisine.

Üçhisar

Bindallı Restaurant ($$)
tel: 0384/219-2690
Hollowed out of the tufa rock, and the crockery is
traditional Cappadocian pottery.

Ürgüp

There are several good restaurants here, all
selling traditional Turkish and Cappadocian
specialties. Try the **Şömine** ($), a well-
established, bustling place with good kabobs, the
Han Çırağan ($$), and the **Hanedan** ($$).

CENTRAL ANATOLIA

Ankara

Chez Le Belge ($$)
Gölbaşı tel: 0312/484-1478
This popular lakeside restaurant, 12 miles south
of the city, serves sophisticated French and
Belgian cuisine. Fresh crayfish is a specialty.

Iskele ($$)
Tuna Caddesi, Kızılay tel: 0312/433-3813
Sample some of the freshest fish in Ankara at this
informal restaurant.

La Bohème ($$)
Gaziosmanpaşa tel: 0312/436-3101
French cuisine, Ankara-style.

Mangal 2 ($$)
Çankaya tel: 0312/440-0959
Turkish cuisine in a restored Ankara house.

Merkez Lokantası ($$)
Çiftlik Caddesi tel: 0312/213-1750
This *lokantasi* specializes in roast lamb, stuffed
lamb, and lamb kabobs.

Poupée Dönen ($$$)
Atakule tel: 0312/440-7412
There are fabulous views from the top of Atakule Tower; international cuisine.

Rıhtım ($$)
Kavaklıdere tel: 0312/427-2432
The Rıhtım, which is a popular meeting place for the young, serves a good range of Turkish dishes.

Yunus's ($$$)
Çankaya tel: 0312/438-5856
At Yunus's, Italian and Turkish dishes are available and there is a special vegetarian menu. Dinner is accompanied by live music.

Zenger Paşa Konağı ($)
In the old citadel, Dogram Sokak 13 tel: 0311/7070
Enjoy authentic Ottoman cuisine in an atmospheric old house. There are excellent views from the top-floor dining room.

Konya
The best of Konya's not very impressive selection of restaurants are **Damla** ($) on Hükümet Alanı, **Hanedan** ($) Mevlana Caddesi, and **Metin** ($$), Cumhuriyet Alani (tel: 0332/351-1707).

EASTERN TURKEY

Diyarbakır
Food in Diyarbakır is good, always fresh, and the local specialty is lamb. The best of the restaurants in town are the **Selim Amca Sofra Salonu** ($) on Ali Emir Caddesi 22 (tel: 0412/221-7378), the **Beyzade Restaurant** ($) on Lise Caddesi (tel: 0412/221-1221), and the restaurants of the **Demir Hotel** on Izzetpasa Caddesi (tel: 0412/221- 2315) and **Büyük Hotel** on Inonu Caddesi 4 (tel: 0412/221-15832).

Doğubeyazıt
Isfehan Hotel ($$)
Emniyet Caddesi 26
The restaurant of the Isfehan is the best bet for eating out in town.

Erzurum
The **Güzelyurt** ($$) on Cumhuriyet Caddesi 54 (tel: 0442/218-9222) and the **Tufan** ($), also on Cumhuriyet Caddesi (tel; 0442/218-3107), are the best choices here.

Gaziantep
Kervansaray
Kervanbey Passage on Hurriyet Caddesi tel: 0322/231-2651
Gaziantep is noted for its good food with strong Arab influences, and the Kervansaray, with its pleasant outdoor terrace, is the best place in town to sample the local dishes.

Malatya
Melita Restaurant ($$)
Atatürk Caddesi tel: 0422/322-4300
The Melita, around the corner from the Sinan Hotel, has a regular clientele. The menu features beautifully presented Turkish specialties, with everything swathed in rose petals.

Mardin
The restaurants here are worth trying for their excellent *meze* (appetizers), heavily Arab-influenced, with *hummus* and *tahine* among their specialties. Try **Nezirhan Restaurant** (tel: 0482/415-1425).

Nemrut Dağı
The farther up the mountain you go, the worse and more expensive the food gets, so your best bet is the hotel restaurants in Kahta, where the turnover is highest. None is especially recommended.

Sanlıurfa
Harran Hotel($$)
Atatürk Bulvarı tel: 0414/313-4743 fax: 313-4918
The hotel restaurant is the best choice for eating out in Sanlıurfa.

Van
The restaurants belonging to the **Akdamar** and the **Büyük Urartu** hotels are the best bets (*see page 275*), though it is also worth trying the **Kösk Restaurant** ($) near the museum in case they have the local *otlu peynir*, or herb cheese.

281

THE BLACK SEA

Bolu
Restaurants worth trying here include the **Filiz** ($) Geçit (tel: 0374/215-1026), the **Idris** ($) on Belediye Sarayi Alti (tel: 0374/215-1202), and the **Ulusoy** ($) on Karayolu (tel: 0374/225-2084).

Fatsa
Dolunay Restaurant ($$)
This is part of the motel of the same name, which stands in an attractive position on its own spit of land. It also has its own private beach.

Giresun
The restaurants to sample here are the **Kale** ($) (tel: 0454/216-1739) and the **Kerasus** ($$) on Ayvasil Caddesi (tel: 0454/314-4263).

Ordu
Try some of the good fish restaurants on the seafront, such as the **Midi** ($$) on Sahil Caddesi (tel: 0452/214-0340), the **Gülistan** ($$), and the **Sahil Balık** ($$).

Samsun
Nothing very exciting here, but you can try the **Çanlı Balık** on Kücük Ev ($$) and the **Altınbalık** ($) for fish.

Trabzon
Kösk Restaurant ($$)
Akçaabat tel: 0462/228-3223
This is the best restaurant on the coast. The best in the town itself are the **Trabzon** ($) on the main square opposite the Özgür hotel, and the **Zindan** (tel: 0462/322-3259)in a bastion of the city walls.

Chronology

7500 BC First Stone Age settlements in existence at Çatalhüyük—the earliest known urban society, with religious shrines and frescoes.

1900–1300 BC The Hittite Empire, with Hattuşaş (Boğazkale) as its capital, and roughly contemporary with ancient Egypt and Babylon, thrives as a mountain culture with storm and weather gods.

1259 BC The Treaty of Kadesh between the Hittites and the Egyptians—the earliest recorded peace treaty.

1250 BC The Trojan War between the Greeks and the Trojans, culminating after 10 years' fighting in the famous ploy of the Trojan horse and the subsequent Fall of Troy (Truva). At the time, Troy was the foremost trading city of the northwest Aegean.

1200–700 BC The migration of Greeks to Aegean coastal regions. The kingdoms of Phrygia, Ionia, Lycia, Lydia, Caria, and Pamphylia grow up in the western Aegean and Mediterranean regions. The Urartian civilization flourishes in eastern Anatolia.

700 BC The birth of Homer in Smyrna (Izmir) coincides with the beginnings of Hellenistic culture in Aegean Turkey.

546 BC Cyrus the Great of Persia invades. Anatolia is under Persian rule, with local Persian governors (satraps) ruling specific areas.

334 BC Alexander the Great conquers Anatolia, freeing it from the Persians. Hellenistic culture takes hold.

130 BC Anatolia becomes the Roman province of Asia with its capital at Ephesus (Efes); a long period of peace and prosperity.

40 BC Antony and Cleopatra marry at Antioch (Antakya).

AD 47–57 Missionary journeys of St Paul; his first missionary activity being at Antioch among gentile converts.

AD 313 Christianity is accepted as the official religion by the Roman Emperor, Constantine the Great.

330 Byzantium is renamed Constantinople by Emperor Constantine and becomes the new capital of the Byzantine Empire, the eastern half of the Roman Empire; Rome remains the capital of the western part.

527–565 The reign of Emperor Justinian and the height of Byzantine power; an enormous building program goes on throughout the Byzantine Empire.

636–718 Muslim Arabs (in the Holy War of their young faith, Islam) defeat Byzantines and besiege Constantinople.

1054 The schism between the Greek and the Roman churches.

1071–1243 Seljuk Turks from Central Asia conquer Anatolia; Konya becomes their capital. They establish the Sultanate of Rum, convert the population to Islam, and establish Turkish as the dominant language of Anatolia.

1096–1204 The Crusades; Latin armies enter Anatolia for the first time. Constantinople is sacked in the Fourth Crusade of 1204. The Byzantine Empire is effectively dismembered.

1288 The birth of the Ottoman Empire, founded by the Muslim Osmanli (Ottoman) tribe from eastern Anatolia. Its capital is Bursa.

1453 Sultan Mehmet II conquers Constantinople and renames it Istanbul as the new capital of the Ottoman Empire. Aya Sofya in Istanbul, like many other churches throughout Turkey, is converted to a mosque.

1520–1566 The reign of Süleyman the Magnificent and the Golden Age of the Ottoman Empire, which extended from the Danube to Aden and Eritrea, and from the Euphrates and the Crimea to Algiers. The Ottomans are the leading world power.

1682–1725 The reign of Peter the Great in Russia begins a new phase of Russo-Turkish rivalry.

1717–1730 The "Tulip Period," so-called because of Sultan Ahmet III's obsession with tulips, a century after Germany, France, and Holland conceived a passion for these Turkish bulbs.

1839–1876 The "Tanzimat Period," a program of reforms in the Ottoman Empire.

1854 The Crimean War: Ottomans are supported by the British and French against the common enemy, Russia.

1895–1896 The Armenian massacres, in which some 150,000 Armenians die.

1909 Abdul Hamid, the last Ottoman sultan, is deposed by the revolutionary group known as the Young Turks.

1914 Turkey enters World War I as an ally of Germany.

1915 The Gallipoli Campaign. Allied landings on Turkish soil are repulsed.

1918 The end of World War I. The Allies propose the division of the Ottoman Empire.

1919 Atatürk leads Turkish resistance in the fight for national sovereignty. The War of Independence, against both the Greeks and the British, begins.

1923 The Turkish state is proclaimed, with Atatürk as president. Minority populations are exchanged between Greece and Turkey in order to prevent future outbreaks of intercommunal conflict. Half a million Greek-speaking Muslims are sent from Greece to Turkey, and 1.3 million Turkish-speaking Christians from Turkey to Greece. Reforms to modernize and secularize the state are set in motion: the Islamic faith is disestablished, the Arabic script is replaced by the Roman alphabet, the Turkish language is revived, women's veils and the fez are banned.

1938 Atatürk, a national hero and the focus of a personality cult, dies unexpectedly at the age of 57.

1939–1945 Turkey decides to remain neutral throughout World War II.

1946 Turkey becomes a charter member of the United Nations.

1950 The first free nationwide elections, in which Adnan Menderes is elected prime minister, are held. A massive national debt builds up following many highly ambitious building programs.

1952 Turkey joins NATO in a new, pro-Western stance.

1960 An almost bloodless military coup is then followed by successive inefficient governments.

1964 Though geographically 97 percent in Asia, Turkey becomes an associate member of the E.E.C. (European Economic Community). The emigration of "guest-workers" to Germany begins.

1974 Turkey intervenes in (or invades, depending upon your point of view) Cyprus to protect the Turkish Cypriot community, seizing the northern third of the island. It is condemned by the international community, notably the E.E.C., but the island still remains divided, the border patrolled by soldiers from the United Nations.

1980 Another bloodless military coup under General Kenan Evren is followed by three years of military rule.

1983–1984 Turkey again returns to civilian rule with Türgüt Özal—founder of the Islamic, right of center Motherland Party (A.N.A.P.)—elected prime minister, moving to the presidency in 1984, the first civilian president of Turkey for 30 years.

1985–1998 Disputes with Greece over Cyprus and Aegean territorial waters damage Turkey's continuing attempts to join the European Union (E.U.), as does its human rights record in handling the P.K.K. (Kurdish Workers Party) insurrection in the southeast. The death toll since 1984 reaches 30,000. President Türgüt Özal dies in 1993. Veteran politician Suleyman Demirel succeeds him. Tansu Çiller is elected prime minister, but she is later discredited on corruption charges. Turkey accepts I.M.F. reforms and slowly embarks on privatizing state industries. Turkey enters the E.U. Customs Union in 1996 and signs a military cooperation accord with Israel the same year. The army forces the Islamist Welfare Party to step down in 1997, determined to keep Turkey's government secular in line with Atatürk's doctrines. The penalty for this has been a succession of weak coalitions.

283

Index

A

accommodations
268–276
The Aegean 270–271
The Black Sea 275–276
camping 262
Cappadocia 273-274
Central Anatolia
274–275
Eastern Turkey 276-275
Istanbul 88–89,
268–270
The Mediterranean
271–273
youth hostels 255
Ada Boğazi 109
Adana 138
Taş Köprü (Stone
Bridge) 138
Ulu Cami (Great
Mosque) 138
Adilcevaz 235
Adnan Menderes Inter-
national Airport 103
Adrianople 86
The Aegean 100–133
accommodations
270–271
boat trips 110–111
climate 103
drives 124–125, 129
highlights 101
itineraries 102
map 152
resorts 103
restaurants 278–279
sightseeing 104–105,
108–109, 112–119,
122–133
walks 116–117, 128
Afrodisias 104, 105
Afyon 190–191, 208–209
Mevlevi Museum
208–209
Ulu Cami (Great
Mosque) 208
Ahlat 235
airports and air services
250, 254
Aizanoi 202
Ak Han 131
Akçay 103
Akdamar 234–235
Akyarlar 109
Ala Dağlari 229
Alaca Daği 207
Alacahöyük 28, 199
Alahan 207
Alanya 137, 142, 143
grotto 142
Kızıl Kule 142
Seljuk dockyard 142
Alexander the Great 30,
144–145
Alibey 105
Alinda 116–117
Altınkaya 168
Altınkum 103
Altınoluk 103
Altıntepe 225
Amasra 240, 242
Amasya 190–191, 192
citadel 192
Fethiye Camii 192
Hazaranlar Konaği
(Museum House)
192
Kızlar Sarayı (Maiden's
Palace) 192
Kralkaya (King's Rock)
192

Seljuk Gök Madrasa
192
tombs of the Pontic
kings 192
Amazons 241
Anadolu Kavaği 81
Anamur 142–143
Anamurium 143
Anavarza 138
Andriake 153
Ani 227
Ankara 190, 193–195,
198
Anıtkabir (Atatürk's
Mausoleum) 198
Aslanhane Camii 194
citadel 194–195
Column of Julian 195
Hisarparkı Caddesi 195
medieval and Roman
Ankara 194–195
Museum of Anatolian
Civilizations 198
Roman Baths 195
Şark Kulesi 195
Temple of Augustus
195
türbe (tomb) of Hacı
Bayram 195
Ankuwash 193
Antakya 143
Hatay Museum 143
Mosque of Habib
Haccar 143
Antalya 137, 146
Karaalı Park 146
Yivli Minare (Fluted
Minaret) 146
Antioch 142, 143
Antiphellos 158
A.N.Z.A.C. memorial 87
Aperlae 157
Aphrodisias 104, 105
Ararat 19, 228–229
Arif 152
Arin Gölü 235
Aristotle 104
Armenia 34
Armenians 218
Arnavutköy 85
Arsameia 230
art and architecture
Byzantine 33
cave paintings 173
Ottoman 64–65
Seljuk 36–37
tile and ceramic art 61
Artemis Pergeia 147
Artvin 216
Arycanda 152
Aslankaya 209
Aslantaş 209
Aslantepe 231
Aspendos 146–147
Assos 104, 105
Atatürk Dam 26
Atatürk Köskü 247
Atatürk (Mustafa Kemal)
12, 14–15, 42–43,
44, 192, 196–197
Avanos 174
Avşa 87
Ayder 229
Aypium 241
Ayvalık 105
Ayvalık islands 110

B

Bağbasi 219
Bağla 109
banks 253

Bardakçi 109
Bartin 242
Bean, George 151
Bebek 85
Behramkale 105
Bektashi Dervishes 181
Belgrade Forest 84
Belisırma 182
Bell, Gertrude 191, 207
Bergama 132
Beyşehir 148
Eşrefoğlu mosque and
türbe (tomb) 148
Kızkalesi Island 148
Kubadabad Palace 148
Binbir Kilise 206–207
Bird Island 122
Bird Paradise 155
Birecik 155, 230
Bitez 109
Bitlis 216
Şerefiye Camii 216
Black Island 110
The Black Sea 236–248
accommodations
275–276
climate 238
drive 242
highlights 237
itineraries 236
the Laz 248
map 236–237
restaurants 281
sightseeing 240–247
tea crop 239
walk 243
boat trips 110–111, 157
Bodrum 108–9
beaches 109
Crusader castle 108
diving trips 109
Mausoleum 108
Museum of Underwater
Archaeology 108
shopping/nightlife 109
Boğazi 50
Boğazkale 28, 199
Büyükkale (Great
Fortress) 199
city gates 199
Great Temple of the
Weather God 199
Bolu 240
Bosphorus 51
Bosphorus University 85
Burdur 149
Bursa 82–3
Bedesten 82
Cekirge 82
Koza Hanı 82
Muradiye complex 82
Tophane Park 82
Ulu Cami (Great
Mosque) 82
Uludağ 82
Yeşil Cami 83
Yeşil Türbe 83
bus services
local 254–255
long-distance 250
Büyük Ada 241
Büyük Çamlıca 81
Büyükada 82, 83
Büyükadalar 83
Büyükağri Daği 19,
228–229
Byron, Robert 214

C

Çaleoğlu 247
Çamardı 229

camel-wrestling 24
Çamiçi 124
Çamlıhemşin 245
camping 262
Çanakkale 83
Çandarlı 103
Cappadocia 170–187,
179
accommodations 273-
274
cave paintings 173
churches and monaster-
ies 176–177,
182–183, 186
drive 184
fairy chimneys 170,
171
highlights 171
itineraries 173
map 170
restaurants 280
sightseeing 174–177,
180–184, 186–187
underground cities 175,
181
walk 182–183
car rental 256
caravansaries 36, 64,
174, 186
Carchemish 231
carpets 94–95
Castle of the Snakes 139
Çatalhüyük 206
Çatalkaya Valley 170
Caunus 112
Çavdarhisar 202
caves
cave paintings 173
Cennet and Cehennem
139
Insuyu caves 146
Karain cave 146
Çavuşin 174
Çavuşin Church 174
Church of Saint John
the Baptist 174
Çavuştepe 233
Cayağzi 153
Çaykara 244
Cedar Island 126
Cennet and Cehennem
139
Central Anatolia
188–211
accommodations
274–275
drive 206–207
highlights 191
itineraries 188, 191
public transportation
190
restaurants 280–281
sightseeing 192–195,
198–199, 202–211
Whirling Dervishes 37,
204
Cerasus 240
Çeşme 118
children 262–263
Chimaera 164, 165
Chios 103, 110
Cilicia 136
Çiller, Tansu 13, 21, 45,
223
City of Midas 209
climate 18, 252
Cnidos 129
Comana Pontica 210
Cos 110
Cotton Castle 130–131
Çukurbağ 160
Çumra 206
Customs regulations 251
Cyprus 10, 111

D

Dalaman International
Airport 103
Dalyan 112, 113, 154
Damlataş 142
dams 26, 207, 225
Daphne 143
Dardanelles 83
Dead Lagoon 136, 150
deforestation 18
Değler 207
Demosthenes 163
Derinkuyu 175
Devrent Valley 170
Deyrulzaferan 221
Didim 123
Temple of Apollo 123
Dilek Milliparkı 154
Dilekkaya 138
Diocaesarea 139
disabilities, travelers
with 251
diving 109
Divriği 202
Diyarbakır 220
Nebi Camii (Mosque of
the Prophet) 220
rampart walk 220
Safa Mosque 220
Saray Kapı (Palace
Gate) 220
Süleymaniye citadel
mosque 220
Surp Giragos Kilesesi
220
Syrian Orthodox Church
220
Ulu Cami (Great
Mosque) 220
Döğer 209
Doğubayazıt 224
Ishak Paşa Sarayı 224
Dolişhane 216
dolmuş (taxis) 255
driving
car breakdown 256
car rental 256
gas 257
nightdriving 256
potholes 215
road signs 257
to Turkey 250–251
traffic regulations
256–257
drugstores 261, 263
Düden Şelálsi 146

E

earthquakes 214
Eastern Turkey 212–235
accommodations 274-
275
drive 234–235
Georgian valleys
218–219
highlights 212
itineraries 214
map 212
restaurants 281
sightseeing 216–221,
224–227, 230–235
walk 217
Edirne 86
Muradiye Camii 86
Selimiye Camii 86
Üç Şerefeli Cami 86
Efes (Ephesus) 112,

113–115, 178
Arcadian Way 114–115
Artemision 113
Basilica of Saint John
114
Baths of Scholastica
115
Cave of the Seven
Sleepers 115
Church of the Virgin
Mary 115
Curetes Street 115
Harbor Baths 115
Isa Bey Mosque 114
Library of Celsus 115
Magnesian Gate 115
Marble Street 115
Roman gymnasium and
stadium 114
site museum 114
Temple of Serapis 115
theater 114
Eğridir 149
Elazığ 225
electricity 263
Elfatun Pınarı 148–9
embassies and
consulates 260
emergency telephone
numbers 260
entry regulations 251
Ephesus see Efes
Erdek 87
Erim, Kenan 104
Erzincan 225
Erzurum 226
Çifte Minare (Twin-
Minaretted) Madrasa
226
university 226
Yakutiye Madrasa 226
Eski Malatya 231
Eski Pertek 225
Eskişehir 203
Kurşunlu Mosque 203
etiquette 263
Euphrates 214
Euromos 126–127

F

Fatih Sultan Mehmet
bridge 50, 85
fauna and flora
bald ibis 155, 230
bird-watching 154–155,
181
Lake Van cats 232
loggerhead turtles 113,
154
national parks 154
pests and hazards 155,
261
pigeons 174
Felandağ 160–161
ferry services 250,
254–255
festivals 24–25
Fethiye 150, 151
Çaliş beach 150
Lycian sarcophagus
150
medieval castle 150
rock tombs 150
Finike 152
Foça 118
folk dance and costume
24
food and drink
desserts and pastries
185

drinking water 261
freshwater fish 149
restaurants 276–81
saltwater fish 240
foreign currency 251

G

Gallipoli (Gelibolu) 86–87
gasoline 257
geographical position 11
geology 19
Georgians 218–219
Gerga 148
Giresun 240–241
Göksu Gorge 207
Golden Horn 51
Gölköy 109
Gordian knot 145
Gordion 145, 211
Göreme 176–177
Çariklı Kilise (Shoe
Church) 177
Church of Saint Barbara
176
Elmalı Kilise (Apple
Church) 176
Karanlık Kilise (Dark
Church) 177
Kızlar Kilise (convent)
177
Tokalı Kilise (Buckle
Church) 177
Yılanlı Kilise (Snake
Church) 176–7
Great Salt Lake 189
Greek islands, boat trips
to 110
Greek and Roman
theaters 123
gülets (motor yachts)
111
Gulf of Edremit 103, 105
Gulf of Gökova 110
Gümbet 109
Gümüldür 103
Gümüşlük 109
Güney, Yılmaz 120, 121
Güzelsu 233

H

Hacıbektaş 180
Hacı Bektaş Monastery
180
Haho 219
Hakkâri 233
Hakkâri mountains 229
Haliç 51
Halicarnassus 108–109
hamams (public baths)
64, 74–75
hans (inns with court-
yard) 36, 64, 174,
186
Harput 225
Harran 231
Hasan Dağ 182
Hasankeyf 220–1
Hattuşaş 199
health 261
drinking water 261
hazards 261
medical treatment 261
drugstores 261, 263
preventive measures
261
vaccinations 261
Heaven and Hell (caves)
139

Hellespont 83
Hemsin 229
Hemsin valleys 245
Herakleia 124–125
defense walls 125
sanctuary 125
Temple of Athena 125
Herodotus 103
Heybeliada 82, 83
Hierapolis 131
necropolis 131
Plutonium Grotto 131
Roman baths
130–131
Temple of Apollo 131
theater 131
Hierapolis Castabala
138
history of Turkey 28–45
Alexander the Great 30,
144–145
Atatürk (Mustafa
Kemal) 12, 14–15,
42–43, 44, 192,
196–197
Byzantine Empire
32–35
Christian Church
Councils 178
chronology 282–283
Crusades 35
Greek and Roman rule
30–31
Hittites 28–29
Janissaries 39
Justinian the Great 32,
33
Lycians 150, 162
modernization 15, 41,
43
Ottoman Empire 38–40
The Reaction 44
Seljuk Turks 34, 36–37
Süleyman the
Magnificent 38–39,
40
Urartians 233
War of Independence
42, 244
World War I 41
Young Turks 41
hitchhiking 264
Hoca, Nasreddin
106–107
Hopa 241
horseback riding 172
Hoşap Castle 233
hot-air ballooning 172
hunting 154

I

Ihlara Gorge 182–183
Ağaçlı Kilise (Church
under a Tree) 183
Bahattin Samanlığı
Kilise (Church with a
Granary) 182
Direkli Kilise (Church
with the Columns)
182
Eğritas Kilise (Church
with a Crooked
Stone) 183
Kırk Damalı Kilise
(Church with Forty
Roofs) 182
Karanlık Kale Kilise
(Dark Castle Church)
183
Kokar Kilise (Fragrant
Church) 183

Index

Purenliseki Kilise
(Church with a
Terrace) 183
Sümbüllü Kilise (Church
of the Hyacinth) 183
Yilanlı Kilise (Church of
the Snake) 183
Ilgaz National Park 203,
241
Ilıca 112
Ingilizlimanı 126
Inönü, President 44
Insuyu caves 146
Ishak Paşa Sarayı 224
Ishan 219
Islam 14–15, 54–55
Istanbul 46–99
accommodations
88–89, 268–270
airport 250
Aqueduct of Valens
68–69
Archaeological Museum
70
Arkeoloji Müzesi 70
At Meydanı 51
Atik Valide Camii 62
Aya Irini Müzesi 58
Aya Sofya Meydanı 51
Aya Sofya Müzesi
52–53
Aynalı Kavak Kasrı 72
Beyazıt Camii 56
Beyazıt Meydani 56
Beyazıt Tower 56
Beylerbey Palace 72
Beylerbeyi Sarayı 72
Beyoğlu 50
Blue Mosque 67
Boğaziçi Köprü 50
Bosphorus 50
Bosphorus Bridge 50
bridges 50
Bulgar Kilisesi 58
Çadırcılar Caddesi 56
campgrounds 89
Çemberlitaş 57
Church of Saint George
59
Church of the
Theotokos
Pammakaristos 58
churches 58–59
Çinili Camii (Tiled
Mosque) 62
Çinili Hamam (Tiled
Baths) 69, 75
City Walls 78
Column of Constantine
57
cruise 81
Dolmabahçe Sarayı 72
drives from 81, 84–85
eating out 90–91,
276–278
Egyptian Spice Bazaar
67, 93
Eminönü Square 51
Emirgan Parkı 79
environs 81–87
Eski Imaret Camii 69
Eyüp Sultan Camii
62–63
Fatih Camii 62
Fatih Sultan Mehmet
Köprüsü 50, 85
Fesçiler Caddesi 56
Fethiye Camii 58
Galata Tower 50
Golden Horn 51, 79
Grand Bazaar 56–57
Gülhane Parkı 79
Haghia Eirene Museum
58

Haghia Sophia Basilica
52–53
Halı Müzesi 70
Halıcılar Çarşısı
Caddesi 57
hamams (public baths)
74–75
Hasan Baba Sokağı 69
highlights 46
Hippodrome 51
Iç Bedestan 57
Ihlamur Kasrı 73
Imrahor Camii 58–59
Istiklal Caddesi 50
Itfaiye Caddesi 69
itinerary 49
Ivaz Effendi Mosque 78
Kalpakçılar Caddesi 57
Kapali Çarşısı 57
Karaca Ahmet Mezarlığı
51, 81
Karikatür Müzesi 69
Kariye Camii 59
Küçük Aya Sofya 59
Küçük Mektep Sokağı
69
Küçüksü Kasrı 73
Linden Pavilion 73
Little Waters Pavilion
73
map 46–47
Mihrimah Sultan Camii
63
Mısır Çarşısı 67, 93
Mosaic Museum 70
Mosaik Müzesi 70
Mosque of the
Conqueror 63
mosques 62–63, 66–67
Museum of Turkish and
Islamic Art 70–71
museums 70–71
New Mosque 67
nightlife 96–97
Nişantaşı 51
orientation 50–51
Palace of the
Porphyrogenitus 73
palaces 72–73
parks 79
Pavilion of the Mirroring
Poplars 72
Pera Palas 50, 88
Pierre Loti Café 63
population 49
practical points 98–99
public transportation
98–99, 255
rampart walk 79
Rumeli Caddesi 51
Rüstem Paşa Camii 63
Sadberk Hanım Müzesi
70
Sahaflar Çarşısı 56
Saint John the Baptist,
of Studius 58–59
Saint Savior in Chora
59
Saint Stephen of the
Bulgars 58
Saints Sergius and
Bacchus 59
Sandal Bedestan 57
shopping 92–93
sightseeing 52–53,
56–59, 62–63,
66–73, 76–79
skyline 49
Sokullu Mehmet Paşa
Camii 66
Stamboul 50
Süleymaniye Camii
66–67
Sultanahmet 51

Sultanahmet Camii 67
Sweating Column of
Saint Gregory 53
Taksim Square 50
Tavukpazarı Sokağı 57
Tekfur Sarayı 73
Teşvikiye Caddesi 51
Topkapı Palace 76–77
tourist offices 266
Türk-Islam Eserleri
Müzesi 70–71
Turkish Carpet Museum
70
Underground Museum
71
University 56
Üsküdar 51
Vezir Hanı 57
walks 56–57, 68–69
Yedikule 78
Yeni Cami 67
Yerebatan Müzesi 71
Yıldız Parkı 79, 85
Yıldız Sarayı 73
Zeyrek 69
Istanköy 110
Izmir 118
Iznik 87
Aya Sofya Museum 87

J

Jewish communities 178

K

Kaçkar Dağları 229
Kale 153, 157
Çayağzı (harbor) 153
Hadrian's Granary 153
Kalkan 156
Kanlıca 81
Karaada 110
Karaca Ahmet Mezarlığı
51, 81
Karain cave 146
Karaincir 109
Karaman 206
Ak Tekke 206
Yunus Emre Mosque
206
Karatepe 138
Karpuzlu 116
Kars 227
Church of the Apostles
227
Kartalkaya 240
Kastamonu 241
Kaş 158
Kayaköy 150
Kayak Evi 184
Kaymaklı 175, 180
Kayseri 180, 184
Huant Foundation 180
Sahibiye Madrasa 180
Keban Baraji 225
Kekova 157
Kemer 162
Moonlight Beach 162
Yörük (Nomad) Amuse-
ment Park 162
Kestel Kale 244
Kilyos 87
Kınık 156
Kirksakallar 128
Kırmızı Yalı 81
Kırşehir 203
Ahi Evran Mosque 203
Cacabey Mosque 203
türbe (tomb) of Asık

Paşa 203
Kız Kalesi 138
Kızkalesi Island 148
Kızılırmak 174
Knidos 129
Lion Tomb 129
Sanctuary of Demeter
129
Temple of Aphrodite
129
theater 129
Konuralp 241
Konya 204–205
Alaeddin Mosque 205
Alaeddin Park 205
Ince Minare (Slender
Minaret) 205
Karatay Madrasa 205
Mevlana Monastery
204–205
Sahip Ata 205
Sırçalı (Glazed)
Madrasa 205
Köprülü Kanyon National
Park 168–9
Kovada Milliparkı 148,
154
Kovada National Park
148, 154
Küçükkuyu 103
Kudrak 151
Kurds 140–141, 215,
220, 222–223
Kurşunlu Şelâlesi 146
Kuş Cenneti 155
Kuşadasi 122, 124
Kütahya 208
Kuyucuk mountains 169

L

Labranda 126, 127
Lake Abant 240
Lake Bafa 124
Lake Beyşehir 148
Lake Burdur 149
Lake Eğridir 149
Lake Köyceğiz 112
Lake Salda 149
Lake Tortum 219
Lake Van 19, 232,
234–235
landscape 18–19
language 200–201,
258–259
Laodiceia 131
Lara 137
the Laz 248
Letoon 158
Limyra 152
Lycia 112, 140, 151, 153

M

Maden Şehir 207
madrasas 37
Maiden's Castle 138
Malatya 231
Manavgat 167
maps 264
see also Contents
Mar Gabriel 221
Mardin 221
Sultan Isa Madrasa
221
Marmara Denizi 87
Marmaris 126, 127, 129
Ottoman castle 126
May Baraji dam 207
media 258

medical treatment 261
Mediterranean 134–169
  accommodations 271–273
  boat trip 157
  highlights 134
  itineraries 136
  lakes 148–149
  Lycian tombs 153
  map 134
  resorts 136–137
  restaurants 279–280
  sightseeing 138–139, 142–143, 146–153, 156–169
  walks 160–161, 164–165, 168–169
meerschaum 203
Meryemana (Tomb of the Virgin Mary) 115
Mevlana 204
Mevlana Festival 25
Midas 208
Midas Şehri 209
Milas 126
  Firuz Bey mosque 126
  Gümüşkesen (Roman mausoleum) 126
  Peçin Kale (castle) 126
Milet 122–123
  Byzantine fortress 123
  Roman Baths of Faustina 123
Miletos 122–123
Misis 139
money 251, 253
  credit cards 253
  currency 253
  foreign currency 251
  traveler's checks 253
Morton, H. V. 112
mosques 14, 62, 63, 64, 263
movies 120–121
Mount Ararat 19, 228–229
Mount Erciyes 171, 184
Mount Latmos 124
mountains 228–229
Muğla 127
Munzur mountains 229
Mylasa 126
Myra 153
mythology
  Chimaera 165
  Cybele 211
  Endymion 125
  Leto 159
  Midas 208

N

national holidays 253
national parks
  Dilek Milliparkı 154
  Ilgaz Milliparkı 203, 241
  Köprülü Kanyon National Park 168–169
  Kovada Milliparkı 148, 154
  Olympos Milliparkı 154
  Sultan Sazliği Milliparkı 181
  Yedigöller Milliparkı 154
NATO membership 10–11
Nemrut Dağı (historic site) 230–231
Nemrut Dağı (volcano) 217, 235

Nevşehir 180, 182
newspapers and magazines 258
Nicaea 87
Niğde 180
  Eski Gümüş (monastery) 180
  türbe (tomb) of Hudabend Hatun 180
Niksar 247
Noah's Ark 228
nomads 140–141

O

Olive Riviera 103
Ölü Ata 150–151
Ölüdeniz 136, 150
Olympos 162
Olympos Milliparkı 154
opening times 253
Ören 103
Ortahisar 181
  Harın Church 181
  Sarıca Church 181
Ortakent Yalısı 109
Ortaköy 85
Ovaçiftlik 181
Özkonak 186

P

Pamphylia 136
Pamukkale 130–131
Paradise Beach 151
Patara 159
  Hadrian's Granary 159
Pazar 245
people and culture
  Armenians 218
  customs 16–17
  east–west divide 16–17
  economy 20–21
  ethnic minorities 17
  festivals 24–25
  folk dance and costume 24
  Georgians 218–219
  jokes and proverbs 106–107
  Kurds 140–141, 215, 220, 222–223
  language 200–201, 258–259
  marriage customs 16–17
  military service 23
  movies 120–121
  music 60
  nomads 140–141
  politics 13
  population 20–21
  religion 14–15
  Turkish character 22–23
  women 55
Pergamum 132–133
  ancient library 132
  Asklepieion 132–133
  Red Basilica 132
  Temple of Demeter 132
  Temple of Zeus 132
  theater 132
Perge 147
Pessinus 211
Phaselis 163
Phellos 160–161
photography 264
piracy 137

places of worship 264
Plutonium Grotto 131
police 260
politics 13
population 20–21
post offices 258
Priene 122
Princes' Islands 83
Prousias 241
public baths 64, 74–75
public transportation 254–255
  bus services 254, 255
  domestic air travel 254
  ferry services 254–255
  taxis and dolmuş 255
  train services 254
  trams 255
  travel discounts 254

R

radio 258
Ramadan 55, 204, 253
Ramsey, Sir William 206
religion
  Christian symbolism 179
  Christianity 178–179
  Islam 14–15, 54–55
  Seven Churches of Asia Minor 178
religious holidays 253
restaurants 276–281
  The Aegean 278–279
  Black Sea 281
  Cappadocia 280
  Central Anatolia 280–281
  Eastern Turkey 281
  Istanbul 276–278
  The Mediterranean 279–280
restrooms 265
Rhodes 110
Rhodiapolis 163
Rize 241
road signs 257
Roxelana 40, 66
Rumeli Hisarı 85

S

Sadberk Hanım Müzesi 70, 84
Safranbolu 242
  Arasta bazaar 242
  Cincihanı (inn with courtyard) 242
  Kaymakamlar Evi (Governors' House) 242
Sagalassos 149
Sakız 103, 110
Salda 149
Samos 103
Samsun 244
Şanlıurfa 231
  Pool of Abraham 231
  Ulu Cami (Great Mosque) 231
Sardis 119, 178
Sarıhan 174
Sarıyer 84
Şarköy 87
Sarmısaklı 105
Sart 119
  Roman ruins 119
  Temple of Artemis 119

Sason 216
Schliemann, Heinrich 133
Scutari 81
Sea of Marmara 87
Sedir Adası 126
Selçuk 113, 114
Seleuceia 167
Seleukeia 167
Selge Canyon 168–169
Selime 182
Side 137, 166–167
Sığacık 119
Şile 87, 244
Silifke 137, 138
  Haghia Thekla 138
Şille 205
Sillyon 147
Sinan 65
Sinop 245
Sisam 103
Sivas 210–211
  Şifaiye Madrasa 210–11
  Çifte Minare (Twin Minaret) Madrasa 210
  Gök Madrasa 211
  Ulu Cami (Great Mosque) 211
skiing 265
Smyrna 118
Soğanlı 186
  Kubbeli Kilise (Domed Church) 186
  Saklı Kilise (Hidden Church) 186
  Yılanlı Kilise (Snake Church) 186
Southern Anatolia Project (G.A.P.) 26
sports 265
Saint Basil 179
Saint Paul 104, 178
Saint Peter 142
Saint Philip 131
stamps 264–265
Stark, Freya 140, 151
student and youth travel 255
Sultan Marshes 181
Sultanhanı 186
Sumela 244, 245
swastika symbol 227

T

Tamerlane 106
Tarabya 84–5
taxis 255
tea crop 239
Teimiussa 159
telephones 258
Teos 119
Termessos 147
Thales, Sage of Miletos 123
thermal spa 130–131
Thrace 86
Tigris 214
tile and ceramic art 61
time 253
tipping 265
Tlos 151
  fortress 151
  rock tombs 151
  theater 151
Tokat 211
  Gök (Turquoise) Madrasa 211
  Latifoğlu Mansion 211
toplessness 263
Torba 109

Index

Tortum Gölü 219
tourist offices 266
tours, organized 264
Trabzon 243, 246–247
  Atatürk Köskü 247
  Aya Sofya 246
  Kücük Ayvasil Kilesesi
    (Saint Anna) 243
  Ortahisar Camii 243
  Panayia
    Chrysocephalus
    (Golden-topped Virgin
    church) 243
train travel 250, 254
trams 98, 255
travel
  to Turkey 250–251
  in Turkey 254–255
travelers' checks
  253
Trebizond 243, 246–247
Troy 133
Truva 133
Tür Abdin 221
Turgutreis 109
Türkbükü 109
Turkish Riviera 135
Turquoise Coast 135
Tuz Gölü 189

U

Üçağiz 159
Üçhisar 186–187
Ulu Cami 231
Uludağ 82
underground cities
  Derinkuyu 175
  Kaymaklı 175, 180
Ünye 247
Urfa 231
Ürgüp 172, 187
Üsküdar 81
  Mihrimah Camii 81
  Selimiye Barracks 81
Uzuncaburç 139
  Temple of Tyche 139
  Temple of Zeus Olbius
  139

V

vaccinations 260–261
Van 232–233
Van Kalesi (Van Castle)

232–233
Vank 219
visas 251
volcanoes 19, 217,
  228–229

W

water resources 26
waterfalls 146
water sports 264, 265
what to take 252–253
when to go 252
Whirling Dervishes 37,
  204
women travelers 265
wrestling 24

X

Xanthos 153, 156
  Byzantine basilica 156
  house tombs 156
  Lycian royal palace
    156

pillar tombs 156

Y

Yakapınar 139
Yalıkavak 109
Yassiada 83
Yassıhüyük 211
Yazidis (peacock-god
  worshippers) 222
Yazılıkaya 199
Yedigöller Milliparkı 154
Yeşilırmak 189
Yılankalesi 139
youth hostels 255
Yürük (Nomad) Amuse-
  ment Park 162

Z

Zelve 187
Zerk 169
Zil Kale 245
Zonguldak 247

288

Picture credits

The Automobile Association would like to thank the following photographers, libraries, and associations for their assistance in the preparation of this book.
M. ALEXANDER 229a Kaçkar Mountains, 246 Trabzon market
J. ALLAN CASH PHOTOLIBRARY 45 Galata bridge, 219 Haho church, 220 Diyarbakır, 221 Kasim Padishah mosque, 229b women and Mount Ararat
D. DARKE 128 Gerga, 160 inland Lycia, 161 Lycian walk, 235b Jonah and the whale, Akdamar
MARY EVANS PICTURE LIBRARY 34b capture of Constantinople, 35b siege of Istanbul, 40a revolution, Istanbul, 40b Yildiz-Kiosk 1909, 41a Greco–Turkish war, 43a Greek retreat, 74a Turkish bath, 75 Turkish bath, 144c Alexander the Great
THE RONALD GRANT ARCHIVE 121a The Herd, 121b Hope
ROBERT HARDING PICTURE LIBRARY 24a Whirling Dervishes, 60c flute player, 252 dancers
THE MANSELL COLLECTION 35a capture of Constantinople, 38b Suleyman II, 41b Abdul Hamid II
S. MORRIS 147a amphitheater at Aspendos, 147b ruined city of Perge
NATURE PHOTOGRAPHERS LTD 154a large whip snake (P. R. Sterry), 154b Cistus albidus (B. Burbidge), 155a loggerhead turtle (J. Sutherland), 155b short-toed eagle (K. Carlson), 261 scorpion (B. Burbidge)
PICTURES COLOUR LIBRARY 51a Istanbul, 54b prayer chain, 78b Dolmabahçe Palace
REX FEATURES LTD 44b Suleyman Demirel
SPECTRUM COLOUR LIBRARY 23a girls in traditional costume, 25a festival, Ephesus, 25b traditional costume, 29b Buyuk Mabet of Hittite Capital, 38a, 39a, 39b Ottoman costumes, 82 Bursa, 140b nomads, 149a Lake Egridir, 176b statue, "old man in shoe," 177 Tokalı Kilise, Göreme, 243 narthex, Trabzon, 245 Sumela monastery
ZEFA PICTURE LIBRARY (UK) LTD 11 Antalya, 24b Antalya dancers, 228b Mount Ararat

The remaining photographs are held in the Automobile Association's own photo library (AA PHOTO LIBRARY) and were taken by Paul Kenward with the exception of pages 3, 5b, 6a, 13a, 28b, 29a, 31a, 32a, 33, 50, 61a, 72, 73a, 74b, 79, 87, 88, 89b, 95, 96b, 97b, 98a, 104a, 104b, 113b, 115a, 116, 117, 118, 131, 132, 133b, 136, 137a, 143a, 143c, 145, 152, 156b, 170-171, 176a, 179, 183a, 183b, 189, 191a, 193b, 196a, 249, 255a, which were taken by Dario Mitideri, 8a taken by Jean-François Pin, 250 taken by Clive Sawyer and pages 2, 6b, 9b, 13b, 14a, 14b, 16b, 32b, 42a, 44a, 48a, 48b, 49, 51b, 52, 53, 54a, 54c, 56, 57a, 57b, 58a, 58b, 59, 60a, 60b, 61b, 61c, 62a, 62b, 64a, 64b, 65a, 65b, 66, 67, 69, 70, 71a, 71b, 73b, 76, 77a, 78a, 81a, 81b, 83b, 85a, 89a, 90a, 90b, 91a, 91b, 92a, 93a, 94b, 94c, 96a, 99a, 99b, 185a, 185b, 185c, 200a, 200b, 201a, 251, 260, 263, taken by Antony Souter.

Acknowledgments

The Automobile Association would also like to thank Zeynep Strömfelt and the Anglo-Turkish Society for their help in the production of this guide.

Contributors

Original designer: Tony Truscott
Original copy editors: Susi Bailey and Barbara Mellor
Indexer: Marie Lorimer   Revision copy editor: Alison Stern
Revision verifier: Diana Darke